No Ordinary Man

Arthur Guyon Purchas 1821-1906
PURCHAS FAMILY FILES

The extraordinary life and times of Arthur Purchas, the man described as probably the most gifted and versatile of all New Zealand's pioneers – a highly skilled surgeon and architect, artist, engineer, geologist, botanist, chemist, musician, diplomat, visionary, priest and inventor in earliest colonial times.

Also by John Steele

Smales' Trail (2012)
When Toawaka Met Cook (co-author, 2019)

No Ordinary Man

The extraordinary life and times of
Dr Arthur Purchas

John Steele

David Ling Publishing Limited
PO Box 401106 Mangawhai Heads
Mangawhai, Northland, New Zealand
www.davidling.co.nz

ISBN 978-1-927305-58-4

First Published 2019

Editor Michael Smith
Design by Express Communications Limited
Printed in Taiwan

Contents

Prologue

This is not so much a history book but more the story of an extraordinary, yet still largely unknown, pioneer who figured prominently in many different facets of early Auckland and New Zealand colonial history. Several writers and historians who have come across Arthur Purchas while documenting our early medical history, the Land Wars, architecture or science, geology or music, have argued that his story should have been written 100 years ago.

His exploits during those initial colonial days of the 19th century almost defy adequate retelling, such are their scope and diversity. His story also includes a fascinating personal relationship with Kīngitanga leaders in the crucial build-up to New Zealand's "great war". It covers years of dedicated public service involving surgery, engineering and architecture, the founding of significant cultural and educational institutions, and leadership in a multitude of social issues and events – all of which have helped shape Auckland and New Zealand over some 180 years of colonial and post-colonial history.

In particular, recent investigations into the background and events leading to the 1860s Waikato and Taranaki Land Wars – and the long reconciliation process – have also helped to focus more attention on Purchas's life because of his close connection with Waikato tribal leaders. In 2016 the then mayor of New Plymouth, Andrew Judd, stood up and was quickly pigeonholed on the origins of those wars, the subsequent confiscations and the whole matter of Māori redress, representation and inclusion. He led a hikoi to Parliament to encourage current generations to learn more about the subject, but was soundly abused in the process. Why, his critics argued, do Māori need greater representation? What is there still to understand? Prominent banker and politician Don Brash was one of many who stridently opposed what he called "special policies and advantage for Māori".

Judd explained that for much of his life, his views on Māori had also bordered on racism but were "natural" for a white Kiwi of those times. "Oh yeah, land stolen – move on," he had told himself. "Then I started to read what *actually* happened and how it happened. I wondered why I hadn't been taught this. I felt lied to."

Purchas was one who found himself caught up in the "preamble" to the Taranaki and Waikato wars. It was in researching his activities during that time – and those of another early pioneer for a different book some 10 years ago – that I also had a sense of a serious gap in our collective knowledge of this period of New Zealand history. After reading 60 or 70 different books about the people and events of the mid-19th century, I wondered why we had never been taught the real stories – especially those leading up to the most critical of events, the Land Wars.

Then Vincent O'Malley's immense work *The Great War for New Zealand* was published in 2016 – just when I began to write this book – and he, among others, raised the same question: why, in the 1940s, 50s and 60s, were we not taught all about the people and events of our Māori and colonial settler history? How could the school syllabus of those days teach us about Clive of India, the American Wild West, or Trafalgar, yet fail to teach us about our own Land Wars and the many male and female heroes of those days, both Māori and Pākehā? Why were Māori cast as "rebels" in their own country? Didn't the Treaty of Waitangi guarantee them undisturbed possession of their lands?

Of course, the 1860s Land Wars can only be covered superficially here as part of the wider Purchas story and readers should refer to the many excellent books listed in the bibliography for the detailed story of the conflicts. But possibly the initial signs of a large gap in the "national understanding" of those wars came when the first of the Waitangi Tribunal land claims was settled and many of us learned that over a million acres of prime Waikato land had been confiscated there alone, just to punish those "rebels" – despite guarantees enshrined in the Treaty.

Part 2 of the Purchas story, therefore, covering the slide into inevitable conflict, also aims to make another small contribution towards that greater "national understanding" of what actually happened. Purchas's role in the build up to war, his closeness to the Kīngitanga, and his strong and fearless promotion of Māori inclusion and representation, will hopefully provide additional context for many who continue to believe that more acknowledgement and understanding is needed if our claims to dual heritage are to be fully honoured today.

By far the greatest contribution towards advancing this generation's "national understanding", however, has been the enormous body of excellent research compiled for Waitangi Tribunal claims. In due time this will probably be seen as one of the greatest historical records of any indigenous people worldwide. The Northern and Taranaki-Waikato Land Wars, in particular, are arguably the most important and interesting historical events in our country's history. Their impact on Europeans and Māori ever since has been inescapable. Our history is no less exciting or fascinating than that of any other country, and the individuals from both sides who feature as part of it are no less extraordinary or heroic. And this is all part of the reason young people from a small country town in the Waikato sought to awaken new generations of New Zealanders to the stories by marking this significant time with a day of its own – equal in significance to the world war commemorations. Good on them.

Purchas's extraordinary life, however, including his involvement in the lead-up to the Waikato War, has only previously been chronicled in brief, isolated patches. As a result, the sheer breadth and depth of the whole – including his phenomenal accomplishments in abdominal surgery – has, until now, gone almost unnoticed. In fact, it was once said that his contribution to early New Zealand life and social development might never be fully recognised because his talents and achievements were so exceptional and widespread.

It is to be hoped that this biography will help to make up for such paucity of information. It might also help to explain, at least in part, why the early Māori-European relationship still needs more widespread understanding. Maybe in the process Purchas will finally acquire the recognition he deserves as one of Auckland's – if not New Zealand's – more prominent founding fathers.

John Steele
Cooks Beach
2019

PART 1

THE SELWYN YEARS

CHAPTER 1

Origins

At the same time Arthur Guyon Purchas was born in the peaceful little Monmouthshire town of St Arvans – just a few kilometres from Wordsworth's famous Tintern Abbey – on the other side of the world the curtain was about to go up on one of the most horrific events in New Zealand history.

It was September 1821. If Arthur's mother, Marianne, had known what was about to unfold on the Auckland isthmus that fateful month, she surely would have never expressed the wish, just seven years later on her deathbed, that one day Arthur might go and serve there.

Māori children playing on the shore of present-day Bucklands Beach that spring evening in 1821, during New Zealand's infamous Musket Wars, would have witnessed a fearful sight – something they probably would never forget.

Slipping quietly up the Tamaki River, past the area known today as Half Moon Bay, was a huge fleet of more than 50 war canoes, manned by over 2000 Ngā Puhi warriors under the great Māori chief Hongi Hika. He was on his way to settle a score and to wipe out his enemy, Te Hīnaki.

Hika's target above the Panmure Basin was Mokoia – the Ngāti Pāoa pā. More than half his men had guns. Their foe had virtually none. Hika's plan – if things went well – was to destroy them before moving on to attack Mauinaina – another of the Hauraki tribe's pā in nearby Panmure.

What followed were the biggest and bloodiest Māori tribal sieges and battles of the 19th century. Over the next three days, 2000 men, women and children were mercilessly slaughtered. The cannibal feasting went on for three more days. Another 1000 were captured and taken as slaves, while perhaps 1500 to 2000 more escaped south to their Hauraki and Waikato tribal friends. A short time later, a second attack yielded similar results at the Mauinaina pā. Hika returned home triumphantly to the north with his slaves and the heads of the chiefs his warriors had killed.

* * *

But just seven years later, in 1828, having been shot in the chest in another battle a year or so earlier and having lingered on since then, Hika himself was dead. At the same time, back in Wales the young Arthur Purchas watched on as his mother Marianne also faced imminent death. Rosy-cheeked and blue-lipped from consumption, feverish and struggling for breath, she talked gently to Arthur, who stared intently at her from the bedside.

For her husband Robert Purchas, from a solid West Country family, it was doubly tragic. His first spouse, Ann, had also died prematurely 10 years earlier, after having delivered him four children. Marianne Guyon, his second wife, came from a French aristocratic family[1] with a keen background in social justice. They had been married only eight years. In that time, Robert had also buried two of his first four children by Ann, while his new wife had borne him another four, all boys.

Arthur Guyon Purchas was the eldest son of this quartet. Taught at home by his mother before her illness took hold, he had been given a good start in languages such as Greek and French, together with reading, writing, spelling and arithmetic.

Both his parents would have known of Hongi Hika because his visit to England, before the Mokoia battles, had been widely reported in the British daily press. Back then, he and his companions were called "natives" from New Zealand. The collective name for the indigenous New Zealand race – "Māori" – did not exist. There was no written language for the New Zealand natives. Nor did they see themselves as a united people of one country.[2]

But unaware of the true extent of Hika's aggression and the scale of the killing and bloodshed which followed his return to New Zealand, Marianne had expressed a strong wish to her husband, before passing away, that one day their most promising son, Arthur, might go to New Zealand to serve.

The place was also well known to them via the many books and journals still being published about the famous voyages of Captain Cook. Perhaps, Marianne suggested, Arthur could help the brave missionaries already there – as a priest or doctor – which would make her very happy.

At just 33 years of age, Marianne died in her sleep a couple of days later. For the second time in 10 years, the shattered Robert Purchas stood numbly at his wife's graveside. Nearby, her head covered in a stylish, black tulle veil, stood his 51-year-old spinster sister, Ann.

---

1   Marianne's (also referred to as Marian) father Claude Guyon made his fortune from a substantial sugar estate on the island of St Domingo in the West Indies. Her grandfather had been France's Consul-General to Italy in the mid-1700s.

2   A Jones and K Jenkins, He Kōrero – Words Between Us. The word "maodi" appears in the Kendall Grammar of 1820, but as an adjective meaning "indigenous" or "native".

Her role, once again, was to be a mother to Robert's six remaining children … not only Arthur and his three younger brothers – Samuel (5), Albert (3) and Henry (2) – but also their 13-year-old half-brother Robert and half-sister Mary Anne, aged 11. The one positive thing was that Robert – a successful engineer whose family credit him with helping to design the biggest single-span iron bridge in Britain at the time – had the means to support them all in relative comfort.[3]

Robert told Arthur, when he was 12, about his mother's wish for him. It became a powerful motivating force for the boy. He made a promise there and then that he would indeed go to New Zealand and honour that wish and her memory. Neither he nor his father could imagine what a significant role he would later play in the early life of the city of Auckland – or how much colour and passion he would contribute to an absorbing colonial history.

Making a start

In the 15 years that followed the Hika massacres at Panmure in 1821 – while the young Arthur Purchas was growing up in Wales – the entire Auckland isthmus from today's St Heliers to Ponsonby, across to Onehunga and east to Howick remained a desolate, foreboding and unoccupied scrubby wasteland. By 1836 small numbers of Ngāti Whātua, who had first settled there 100 years earlier, plus assorted Māori from Ngāi Tai, Tainui, Ngāti Pāoa and other tribes, had begun to trickle back. They were the first to reappear since the initial European arrivals led by missionaries Samuel Marsden and John Butler, and lay reader William Fairburn, whose huge land purchase of 1836 was to cause so much difficulty only a short time later.

These men were followed by the early colonial leaders and traders like Hobson, Campbell, Selwyn, Williamson, Whitaker, Russell et al, who although completely unaware at the start of the awful background of Māori bloodshed and war, proceeded to write their own significant chapters of history in and around the isthmus wasteland which was soon to become the capital city of Auckland.

It would be difficult to imagine a more striking or graphic contrast between two worlds: Purchas's birthplace in a tranquil 19th century English village (as it was then) and the world of Hika and deadly cannibalistic assaults on peaceful native villages. Nevertheless, in honouring the promise to his mother, it would be the latter place – Tāmaki Makarau – where Arthur Purchas would settle

---

3   This was the Bigsweir Bridge, built around 1826-27 over the River Wye.

The Robert and Marianne Purchas home (Pilstone House) in Wales, where Arthur was born in 1821. His mother died only 7 years later.
TINA FRANTZEN

just a few years later and live out his extraordinary life.

By the time the Treaty of Waitangi (1840) had been signed around New Zealand and Hobson had completed his deal with Ngāti Whātua for land for his new capital, Arthur Purchas was moving ahead with his education. After his mother's death, his father organised private tutors who taught him much about science, biology and language. By the age of 15, Arthur had turned his attention to medicine – the subject which fascinated him most – and he was soon apprenticed to a local doctor, John Audland, with whom he worked for the next three years.

The nearby town of Tintern, and its surrounds, was also a significant iron manufacturing centre and when the pursuit of medical knowledge slowed occasionally, the young Purchas made the most of his opportunities to learn everything he could about metallurgy and iron processing – from both his father and other local experts and businesses.

At the age of 19, Purchas was recommended for further study at London's Guy's Hospital – in those days and ever since, one of the world's leading medical institutions and places of learning. He found a couple of rooms to rent nearby in Southwark where he lived with his younger brother Samuel. His two other brothers, Albert and Henry, remained at Pilstone House, the family home near Llandogo. Henry, then aged 14, was proving to be something of a teenage headache for his 'stepmother', Aunt Ann … and in letters home to her, Arthur was not afraid to offer occasional advice on how best to handle his troubled younger brother.

Purchas's dream of serving in New Zealand did not fade throughout this period. On an early spring day in 1841, he read of the consecration of Bishop George Augustus Selwyn at Lambeth and immediately made a note to contact him at the next opportunity. It was not long in coming. "A short time later," he wrote afterwards, "I had the privilege of meeting Bishop Selwyn for the first time in the vestry of Mr Dodsworth's church in London.[4]

"I told him I had been preparing for several years for work as a missionary in New Zealand and was a student at Guy's. I asked him whether he wished me to accompany him at once [back to New Zealand] or to complete my medical course and obtain my diplomas. He replied that he would much prefer the latter course and said if I would write to him when I had passed the necessary examinations, he would instruct me when and how to come to him."

Purchas went back to his studies. He was an able student who had the good fortune of studying under some of history's most well-known medical figures – men like Addison, Bright, and Benjamin Babington, and surgeons Alston Key and the great Sir Astley Cooper. Thomas Hodgkin (of lymphoma discovery fame) had just retired from Guy's where he had been curator of the museum. Joseph Towne, known as one of the fathers of anatomy, was in the process of pioneering the first anatomically correct human figures from wax – some of which are still on display today at the Guy's medical school museum.

These men wrote glowing testimonials about the young Purchas when he finally finished at Guy's. They praised his skill in obstetrics, anatomy and surgery, spoke of his "humanity, skill and great attention … one of the most active and intelligent students at Guy's".

In a letter to Purchas's father Robert, later in 1846, Sir Astley Cooper said: "… in addition to his excellent moral conduct, his studies have secured to him the respect and attachment of all who have had the opportunity of knowing his worth". Thomas Addison himself wrote: "Having had the benefit of Mr Purchas' assistance in the wards of Guy's Hospital, I have much pleasure in bearing testimony to his very superior attainment and to his extensive practical knowledge of the various departments of his profession."[5] One area of special interest to Purchas was chemicals and poisons, and he produced two papers in the summer of 1841 entitled *Symptoms of Poisoning* and *Medico-Legal Analyses of Oxalic Acid* – both of which clearly brought him to the attention of some

---

4   William Dodsworth was a well-known evangelical priest at St Pancras Church, London. Selwyn had preached there at an evening service and had spoken about his start-up work in New Zealand.

5   AML, MS 1701. Originals of all these testimonials are held here.

of the brightest medical minds of the day.

When not learning the rudiments of early medicine and surgery, he also became a friend and passionate student of one of England's great theologians and thinkers of the day, Professor John F D Maurice. Maurice was the chaplain at Guy's, before taking up the chairs of English literature and history at King's College, London ... later becoming professor of theology. This was a relationship which was to continue until Maurice's death in 1872, by which time he had been recognised as one of the great social thinkers of the 19th century.

Purchas gained his full medical qualifications – medical diplomas in those days – graduating as a Member of the Royal College of Surgeons (MRCS) and obtaining his general practice qualification, known as the LSA, or Licentiate of the Society of Apothecaries. He then wrote to Selwyn as instructed. But either his letter did not arrive or more likely Selwyn was too preoccupied at the time to respond. Purchas also wrote to the Church Missionary Society (CMS) of which Selwyn was now a director. The secretary advised him to be patient and to start learning "the natives' language". Selwyn's brother, meanwhile, heard of Purchas's interest and sent him some books including the first and newly published Māori dictionary.

Armed with his satchel full of testimonials, Purchas first sought out a new position, either as the house surgeon in the Glamorgan and Monmouth Hospital or in private practice in London. He chose the latter and spent a few months assisting in a private medical practice before accepting a bigger and more senior role in 1843 as resident surgeon at the large Southern and Toxteth Hospital in Liverpool.[6] Busy there no doubt, but Purchas still found time to pursue some social life – meeting and quickly becoming much enamoured of a very young lady called Olivia Challinor, the daughter of Charles, a Liverpool merchant, and his wife Eliza. A comfortable, prosperous and even distinguished life beckoned in Liverpool.

But Purchas had made that promise to his mother and would not break it easily. Impatient with the long delay in his plans to go to New Zealand and still not having received a reply from Selwyn, Purchas simply decided to take matters into his own hands. In October 1844, almost three years to the day since he had first met Selwyn, he resigned from his lucrative and sought-after surgeon's role in Liverpool and organised a free passage to New Zealand as ship's surgeon on the 600-ton barque *Slain's Castle* – sailing from Plymouth on October 24, 1844.[7]

The ship had made its first trip to New Zealand in 1841 and although it

---

6   Later to become the Royal Liverpool Hospital.
7   H Brett, White Wings, NZETC.

had already had several lucky escapes from shipwreck and collision, sailing on her was a risk Purchas was willing to take. His role as the ship's doctor would help to pay his way – at least as far as New Zealand. He was off to the other side of the world to fulfil his promise.

CHAPTER 2

Selwyn's World

The Anglican Church of England at the time was virtually a state institution with close political connections at all levels within the community, from local parish and town administration to the highest state and parliamentary offices. Aside from being a religious denomination, it was also what might be described as a "societal group leader".

Influential political leaders like William Gladstone and many of his colleagues were churchmen of England. Most key government ministers and senior bureaucrats of the day saw the church, whether Anglican or Wesleyan, as also having an important missionary role to perform – to bring light to the uncivilised savages of the world and to "teach them the way". It was a sacred responsibility and sincere, well-meaning clergy and politicians of all Protestant persuasions saw such a role not so much as the "conquering" of native races but about education and inevitable persuasion and inclusion into their own civilised world. Even Benjamin Disraeli, a Jew, conformed to the same great notions of the day – that British society had some responsibility to expand its expertise and influence throughout the so-called undeveloped world and to bring its peoples into Britain's supposedly more enlightened one.

In addition, clergy in those days had a status within English society which is almost impossible to comprehend today. If the British inventor and businessman had an obligation to produce machines and products to sell to the rest of the world for mutual benefit, then the clergyman had a responsibility to produce converted souls, particularly in 'foreign markets'. Conversion to Christianity in the "uncivilised" world was seen as the legitimate precursor to the introduction of trade and commerce. As men like Cook, Livingstone and other great 18th and 19th century British explorers had led the way to these new lands, so outward-looking, idealistic and evangelistic young clergymen of the early 1800s felt a keen obligation to follow up and help the great British Empire expand.

But by the 1830s, just before the signing of the Treaty of Waitangi, the

British Government had begun to come under pressure at home to not be quite so hasty about asserting itself in New Zealand, primarily because of growing concerns over the enormous costs involved in colonisation. Further, political reluctance then evolved into active official help for and support of any church institution which might still want to establish itself in the colonies. The presence of a small band of missionaries – working unofficially as a preliminary civilising force via the Anglican or Wesleyan "church armies" – was nevertheless a satisfactory next step while the politicians argued the merits and hazards of further expansion of the empire, with all the associated substantial costs and problems.

The Colonial Office was, however, finally forced to accept the need to implement some semblance of law and order in New Zealand for both the missionaries and the growing numbers of Europeans choosing to settle and work there … even though the office would not allocate funds with which to do a proper job, as its unfortunate representative, James Busby, soon discovered.

Inevitably, therefore, the legitimate British presence – as distinct from the decidedly illegitimate and largely ungovernable collection of whalers, sealers, seamen, timber traders and entrepreneurs – revolved around the sometimes fragile leadership of missionaries from the Anglican Church Missionary Society (CMS) and the Wesleyan Missionary Society. They had also been joined by a small Catholic presence under Bishop Pompallier, who made much of the ecclesiastical seniority denoted by his title – something which greatly irked the other denominations.

Edward Gibbon Wakefield's New Zealand Company had been vociferous in arguing for the appointment of its own Church of England bishop – to be based, naturally, in Port Nicholson (Wellington) to serve the company's first new settlement. Wakefield even promised financial assistance. The company then became a strong force in getting the required legislation covering a new Anglican bishopric for New Zealand through the British Parliament. The quid pro quo was to look to the bishop for his direct assistance in the company's own little battles with missionaries and government officials. Gibbon Wakefield, in a later letter to Canterbury's J R Godley, actually claimed credit for the appointment of the first New Zealand bishop, George Selwyn: "His See was *created* by us in spite of the many obstacles put in our way by the Church and Government," he wrote. Some time later, when Selwyn turned out to be very much his own man, Wakefield changed tack, writing that he did not consider Selwyn "to be a wise man … he turned round upon us and joined our foes, the anti-colonising Church Missionary Society".

So, the skirmishing which preceded George Selwyn's appointment within the Church of England in particular, was not without a certain edge. Selwyn was not even the first choice for the new bishopric, once its creation had been determined. It had been offered initially to his older brother William, who declined, much to his parents' and George's embarrassment.[8] When William made his decision known, George (to save the family's honour) immediately contacted his old Eton schoolmate, William Gladstone, and was confirmed within the week as the first bishop-elect of New Zealand.

So with the missionaries, north and south, receiving all the new settlers with mixed feelings, and believing Māori were nowhere near ready to receive them – and with CMS leader Henry Williams in Waimate at loggerheads with the New Zealand Company over who best to run church affairs in New Zealand – Bishop Selwyn's world on arrival was fraught with "divisions within and divisions without".

According to church historian William Morrell, following the appointment of the bishop, the big fear of Henry Williams and his senior missionaries was not only the arrival of some new form of "episcopal autocracy", but worse, the immediate loss of their influence as a voluntary society. Would Selwyn be a missionary bishop or a colonial government bishop? A fair question since at the time of his appointment, there was only one Anglican clergyman in New Zealand. The rest were all CMS missionaries.

In any event, with pressure from powerful Church of England members within the British Government, the CMS in London agreed to join forces with the state. On his consecration in the private chapel at Lambeth in 1841, Selwyn also became a director of the CMS with other England bishops. The British Government agreed to pay half his salary (£600) and the CMS the other half – an arrangement which was to continue until 1855.[9]

Selwyn, like Purchas, was no ordinary man. While Purchas was educated at Guy's, Selwyn was taught at Eton. There he met and befriended several of England's future leaders. He was a very good athlete and swimmer, and rowed in the first Oxford-Cambridge boat race in 1829. Strongly idealistic and imbued with values of loyalty, discipline and endurance, he was already a forceful advocate of a "cathedral" form of church government and education. That involved promoting the idea of self-governing bishoprics around the world, well-structured with a "disciplined governance"[10] – with all clergy, missionaries and lay readers or catechists, as they were known, coming under the Church of England's banner (not that of the CMS).

---

8   A K Davidson (ed), Living Legacy.
9   A K Davidson (ed), A Controversial Churchman.
10   Ibid., refer Warren Limbrick essay.

Selwyn was also sympathetic to many of the Tractarian principles[11], although he denied being Tractarian himself. But he liked the idea of reinstating some of the core Anglican Church practices and simple ceremonials which had been dismissed at the time of the break from the Catholic Church. At the same time, he was still fundamentally evangelistic and an enthusiastic supporter of the missionary cause.

Like Purchas, he also had a keen interest in architecture, particularly the Gothic Revival style. He enjoyed all church music and choirs, but hated the practice of private patronage for individual clergy, which had crept into the English church of the 18th and early 19th centuries.[12] He wanted church leaders to remove the "squire and parson" relationship which existed in so much of the United Kingdom with all the attendant risks of corruption, temptation and abuse of privilege. He stood for the simple life – hard work, self-denial and spiritual independence. His main defect, it was said, was an "impetuous temper which occasionally made him dictatorial and indiscreet".

Knowing in advance there would be no reliable government financial support in New Zealand, he went there nevertheless – confident in his own ability to establish a new system of stand-alone funding for the diocese he now headed, by seeking endowments, offertories, fees and charitable donations which would be administered via separate archdeaconry funds. His personal contacts in English society, parliamentary circles and among his own friends, he believed, would be invaluable in helping to fund his endeavours in the new colony. And he believed that, in New Zealand, his priest force – when he had one assembled – must combine common school teaching with parish duties as a way of ensuring the church's acceptance and longer-term success in the wider community.

Selwyn arrived in Auckland with his wife Sarah at the end of May 1842. Within days of regaining his land legs, he strode off on a tour around New Zealand. But instead of heading south towards the clamouring settlers of Port Nicholson and Canterbury – where the New Zealand Company's immigrants were keenly awaiting the arrival of their new bishop – he travelled north to the Bay of Islands and Waimate and the missionary heartland. Wakefield and company were not impressed.

In the north, Henry Williams and his CMS colleagues greeted the new bishop cautiously and invited him to take up residence among them at Waimate. This he did, before heading off to scout the rest of his new domain.

---

11   Tractarians were so called because they adhered mostly to beliefs in the Tracts, espousing more elaborate church ritual and ceremony.

12   W P Morrell, The Anglican Church in New Zealand.

While doing so, however, and right in the middle of setting up new contacts and relationships with Governor Hobson and his officials, he learned that Hobson's health was deteriorating rapidly. Just three months later the Governor was dead. Unfortunately for Selwyn, there was to be no serious hand on the government tiller until the arrival of Governor Robert FitzRoy in late 1843.

Missionary land problems

In that vacuum of colonial leadership, Selwyn's plans to build more permanently at Waimate came unstuck. The CMS man from England, a surveyor and some-time architect Samson Kempthorne, first initialled a seven-year agreement with Selwyn for him to lease land at Waimate and also Kerikeri – ostensibly on behalf of Henry Williams and his CMS northern committee. But when the society in England would not ratify Kempthorne's seven-year term, requiring instead a 12-month renewable lease, Selwyn simply took this as a good reason to shift entirely and start afresh with his college plans in Auckland, also by now the new capital. It proved a good call because, within a short time, the Bay of Islands would be engulfed in serious problems with Hōne Heke. Unhappy with the Treaty signing, Heke was even unhappier about the loss of so much land in the north being sold willingly and cheaply to ever more new European arrivals by Māori keen for European goods – and guns.

As Selwyn began the move to his new St John's College site at Purewa, or the Tamaki as it was known in those days, dark clouds were already gathering over the now very contentious issue of land ownership in the north, in particular missionary land. When newer settlers discovered details of some of the much earlier land purchases – while now suddenly facing new resistance to their own intended purchases of similar-sized holdings from Māori and their fellow missionary settlers – storm clouds began to gather.

Before 1840, CMS leader Henry Williams and others had purchased land from Māori (as willing sellers), primarily for the future benefit of their children. After the signing of the Treaty of Waitangi, all previous land sales required confirmation by the newly established Land Commission, with the maximum allowable purchase set at 2560 acres – the same figure used in New South Wales. Europeans needed authorisation from the Governor to confirm purchases above this figure.

Henry Williams – acting as a trustee for his children who were going to farm the land (although his deal did not legally state that intent) – had actually bought some 11,000 acres at about 3/4d an acre from Māori sellers, all fully satisfied with the purchase. His claim was first reduced to 2560 acres but upped again to 9000 acres in 1844 following a new review under Governor FitzRoy. When FitzRoy was recalled and Governor George Grey arrived on the scene in late 1845, he used Williams' land purchases to back his claims to his political masters in England that these very transactions were the main reason for the serious Māori "disaffection" over land and subsequent war with Hōne Heke in the north.

Grey then made continuing attempts to discredit all missionary land purchases, possibly anticipating future trouble from missionaries very protective of their growing Māori flock. The New Zealand Company settlers, although hungry themselves for land, together with many missionary supporters back in England, bought Grey's stories. Wakefield's colonists, also prompted by seething editorials in their newspapers, upped their hostility towards the missionary body, accusing its members of taking sides with Māori against their European colleagues' best interests.

It all culminated in Grey's famous letter[13] to Gladstone, in which he asserted that "these individuals' claims [the northern missionaries] are not based on substantial justice to the aborigines or to the large majority of British settlers … and that these individuals cannot be put in possession of these tracts of land without a large expenditure of blood and money". His intention was clearly to reduce substantially the power and influence he felt the missionaries had over Māori. He made a special point of highlighting that of 24 claims before the Land Claims Court for approval above the 2560-acre figure and after FitzRoy's "penny an acre" proclamation, eight of them were from missionaries including Henry Williams.

In spite of the fact that Grey's friend Tāmati Wāka Nene and other Māori chiefs loyally supported the missionaries' right to the land they had happily sold them, the ambitious and determined Grey – now backed by the soldiers and money denied previous governors – was not about to let go. He was also about to draw Bishop Selwyn into his arguments.

Purchas lands in New Zealand

Arthur Purchas naturally knew little of such significant issues brewing as he prepared to leave England and meet Selwyn in New Zealand – although he would learn about them soon enough. His ship, the *Slain's Castle*, made a very fast passage, an unprecedented 94 days port-to-port. It arrived in Nelson on Sunday morning, January 26, 1845. The locals turned out in force to welcome

---

13   The so-called "blood and treasure" document of August 1846 in which Grey virtually accused the northern missionaries of starting the war there.

the ship, having had no contact with the outside world for three months.

Purchas disembarked and with his usual vigour – no doubt intent on correcting the upset of inner balance that only 94 days at sea in a tilting, bucking sailing ship can induce – set out to walk from the wharf to the new church. Here his incredible intuition and foresight, bolstered by a not inconsiderable amount of sheer good luck, would help him strike gold.

"I found the people just coming out of the church," he wrote later. "To my great joy, I met Bishop Selwyn who just happened to be there in Nelson, on another journey south, this time to Wanganui and Wellington."[14] It can be imagined that the appearance of Purchas with outstretched hand, greeting a very surprised Selwyn that Sunday morning, would have also greatly pleased the senior man.[15] The Bishop had arrived two days earlier from Wanganui on the *Hazard*, Governor Grey's government sloop.

They adjourned to Mr Reay's local parsonage and, as Purchas described, in a discussion lasting just half an hour, "everything was satisfactorily arranged". The Bishop was delighted – and impressed – that the 24-year-old, highly qualified Dr Purchas was now ready and able to join his St John's College team and train there for the New Zealand priesthood. Selwyn also learned quickly that, apart from his considerable medical background, Purchas was also bringing solid musical and architectural skills and, of course, a new wife, who required Selwyn's approval in advance, but which was apparently gained with a nod.

Purchas noted matter-of-factly: "My object being attained, I was ready to return and bring out my wife". Olivia was not his wife yet, however, although it seems clear that before he sailed for New Zealand, he had secured her agreement and that of her parents to the union and her own new life in New Zealand.

When Purchas told Selwyn he would be returning to England immediately – next day if he could find a ship – Selwyn asked if he would relay some news and take some official papers back to his friend, William Gladstone. Gladstone was shortly to become British Colonial Secretary in Sir Robert Peel's new government. This agreed, Selwyn departed on the *Hazard* and Purchas on the *Slain's Castle*, via Wellington and New Plymouth, to Auckland, where he was hoping to find another ship returning to London.

After a two-week stopover in Wellington and a couple of days in New Plymouth, the *Slain's Castle* finally rounded North Cape and sailed on down past the Bay of Islands on March 10, 1845. Little did those on board know

---

14   G A Selwyn, *Journals & Letters* 1842-44.
15   At only 35, Selwyn was still comparatively young.

that the very next day the town of Kororareka (Russell) would be destroyed by Hōne Heke's men.

The news reached Auckland shortly after the *Slain's Castle* berthed there, followed by the arrival of a coaster loaded with terrified refugee settlers and their families, all fearing the worst from Hōne Heke and just happy to have escaped with their lives. Serious precautions, in preparation for an invasion of Auckland from the north, were being talked over. The town was very much on edge.

Purewa established

The new capital of Auckland was relatively well established by March 1845. In a mood of underlying tension between himself and the Williams brothers (Henry and William) over missionary land purchases and the unsatisfactory conclusion to the Waimate and Kerikeri lease issue, Selwyn was well advanced in his efforts to establish St John's College on a large block of land at Purewa, east of Auckland.

The uneasy relationship between the missionaries and their new bishop, initially over the land matters, quickly grew over the next few months to encompass several other irritations. For his part, Selwyn was always determined not to end up "beholden to the autocracy of mission secretaries and their committees"[16] in England or New Zealand – particularly to Henry Williams and his team who were committed to Māori first and foremost. For the missionaries' part, they were concerned over any possible "watering down" of their hard-won influence among Māori accrued in the previous 20 years. They had a real fear that this would be an inevitable consequence of a combined settler-missionary church under the influence of a somewhat dictatorial bishop like Selwyn.

A short while before he left Waimate, Selwyn called together a first synod[17] in an attempt to pour some oil on the troubled waters – even though he and Henry Williams knew big changes were inevitable. Selwyn had even made the Williams brothers archdeacons together with another CMS man, Alfred Brown, to help ease tensions.

Then he broke the news about shifting his headquarters to Auckland. While the CMS men were not entirely unhappy about that call, it was certainly not met with enthusiasm by northern Māori. They feared the loss of patronage of the "head man" (Selwyn) from England would deplete their mana (status)

---

16   A K Davidson (ed), *A Controversial Churchman*.
17   Basically a church administrative 'conference'.

and, together with the shift of the capital to Auckland, severely weaken their economic strength and future opportunities. For Henry Williams – although mollified a little by his appointment as New Zealand's first and most senior archdeacon in charge of the north – his new status was to mean nothing when it came to the real controversy about to emerge over the missionary land purchases and his own in particular.

Ignorant of all the background 'static', Purchas disembarked quickly from the *Slain's Castle* in Auckland on March 11, 1845. Although realising there was still very little set up at Purewa, he decided to walk out to the new site from his hotel in Princes St and take a look.

"The road to the Tamaki had been surveyed but not made and the bush from Mt Hobson onwards had been partly cut down along the road, and the lines of subdivision of a few of the allotments were cut," he wrote later. "Between Parnell and Newmarket at that time, it was almost wholly covered with fern, flax and tea-tree and there was a small wooden bridge called Hobson's Bridge across the gully which carried the overflow from the raupo swamp that filled up the whole space now occupied by the level road to the foot of Khyber Pass."

While still in its infancy, Auckland was nevertheless a busy and sociable place at this time, but its inhabitants remained decidedly nervous given the troubles up north. As historian R C J Stone famously noted: "It was founded as a capital city but was finding its permanent role as a city of capital."[18] Every day new businesses and houses were springing up around the edge of the Waitematā. Māori trade was in full flow with canoes and small ships arriving constantly, loaded with pigs, chickens and goats, potatoes, fruit and fish. The most important trade routes originated in the fertile Waikato regions – via the Awaroa River, Waiuku and Onehunga – and also from the Hauraki area into the Waitematā.

Governor FitzRoy continued to host a regular round of vice-regal meetings and "welcome" levees in his residence where he had been living since December 1843 ... but uncertainty remained about what Hōne Heke might be planning, given the various threats emanating from the north about possible attacks on Auckland. The people of Auckland remained on high alert, despite reassurances from Tāmati Wāka Nene and the powerful Waikato tribes to the south (led by the great rangatira Te Wherowhero) that they would protect them in the event of a clash.

When Purchas reached Purewa, he found a "large framed barn" and some of Selwyn's team from Waimate living in tents scattered about the property.

18   R C J Stone, *From Tamaki-Makau-Rau to Auckland*, Foreword.

"The Bishop's large church tent was also pitched on a small piece of level land near Purewa Creek and the college whale boat was in constant use to convey everything that had to be brought from Auckland and was manned by the young men who went by the name of students," Purchas wrote.

He had a good look around before walking back to his Auckland hotel to learn there, that Governor FitzRoy had finished his assessment of the situation and had just ordered new preparations be made to defend the town. The newly built St Paul's Church was loopholed – ready to provide a refuge for women and children. Down at the wharf, Purchas heard next that FitzRoy had chartered the *Slain's Castle* to take the panicked Bay of Islands refugees – and some Aucklanders – to Sydney, with orders to return as quickly as possible with as large a detachment of troops as could be spared.

Purchas immediately organised a bunk for himself in additional passenger quarters being built in the ship's hold, which carpenters fitted out over the three days of the Easter weekend before she sailed for Sydney. After an uneventful Tasman Sea crossing, he arrived safely in Australia … but it took him some three months to find another ship heading back to England.

Return and marriage

Undeterred and never one to remain idle, Purchas embarked on a couple of new projects in which his musical and architectural talents came to the fore. In his student days he had discovered – and then cultivated – a fine singing voice. He subsequently got to know the great choral works of Handel and Bach, the tunes of Mendelssohn and Liszt, and had begun to write original lyrics and tunes. He had also taken up the flute and during the long weeks spent at sea had become an accomplished player.

Just to round off his musical interest at that time, he wrote the draft of a small book entitled *First Lessons in Singing Classes*, explaining all the rudiments of how to sing, providing scales and tunes to practise with, and detailed information on how best to use and project the voice. He believed there had to be a quicker, more efficient way to teach novice singers how to read music and sing scored notes – perhaps, he reasoned, via a basic, numbered notation system. The extraordinary system he devised became the basis of his book, the draft of which he took back to London in his luggage.

In the evenings in Sydney, Purchas was invited to help set up a new choir being established at the church he had attended on arrival – Christ Church of St Lawrence, in the city centre. The rector, William Walsh, also happened to be a very keen singer and, recognising Purchas's excellent voice and musical abilities, enlisted his help to form a choir. Shortly after Walsh's new church was consecrated, the Purchas-Walsh choir was ready. Such was its success that within three or four weeks Purchas proposed that they establish a larger choral society for all Sydney. On April 18, 1845, with the support of Walsh and another enthusiastic member called Hatch, they called a meeting in the offices of the Church of England Lay Association in George St, "of people friendly to the formation of a choral society in Sydney".

Purchas had drawn up a set of 31 rules and made what the *Sydney Morning Herald* described as "a most apposite speech" endorsing the society's aims and objectives. His obvious musical gifts, engaging personality and determination profoundly influenced and energised the senior Mr Walsh. The rules were ratified and the meeting ended with a vote of thanks to Purchas and Hatch for their efforts.

A few days later in May, a second meeting led by Walsh and Purchas saw the formal establishment of their Sydney Choral Society with the objective of "performing both sacred and secular music". It included many of the members of the original church choir. Since its founding in 1845, the society has developed into what is described today as one of the finest liturgical choirs in Australia, touring the world extensively, singing and producing CDs. It has performed as resident choir in Westminster Abbey and continues to perform today in cathedrals and churches across Europe.

Knowing that when he returned to New Zealand, he would almost certainly have to help provide accommodation for himself in the new St John's College or elsewhere, Purchas next took himself off around Sydney to study the latest designs and ideas for houses, churches and ancillary buildings. The engineering and draughting insights and skills he had picked up as a young man from both his father and Dr Audland suddenly proved of great value.

By chance, Purchas came into contact with Edmund Blacket, the colonial architect given the job of designing St Andrew's, Sydney's first Anglican cathedral. Impressed with the young man's ideas and knowledge of major construction projects, Blacket invited Purchas to contribute some ideas of his own and he spent many hours conferring and collaborating with Blacket and his team on aspects of the Gothic Revival building.[19]

Purchas later wrote of his time in Australia, in his usual phlegmatic style: "I had to wait for three months in Sydney before I could get a passage to England and while there also had the pleasure of helping to found the Sydney Choral

---

19   Later media reports suggest his influence was significant, indicating an opportunity occurred which enabled "improved plans to be adopted" for the cathedral and Purchas then "induced" Blacket to stay in Sydney and carry out the scheme. *New Zealand Herald*, Jan 1896.

Society and to get up the music for the first cathedral choral service ever held in Australia." There is no doubt the young Purchas left a considerable mark in Sydney. When he and Olivia returned a year later, the Choral Society put on a special sold-out performance of the *Messiah* to honour Purchas.

He eventually found a ship to take him on to England, departing in midwinter on July 8, 1845. It was the *Parkfield* and was almost the death of him. In the days before the Plimsoll line, there were no regulations concerning the amount of cargo on such ships and the *Parkfield* – a 12-year-old East Indiaman barque and former convict ship – left Sydney heavily overloaded, much to the consternation of Purchas and many of his fellow passengers.

The weather on the day of departure from Sydney was bad and worsened considerably as the ship beat its way out past the heads. Purchas was extremely worried and he had good reason to be. Only hours after weighing anchor, the wallowing ship had her bulwarks stoved in and livestock, all supposedly well-secured on deck, washed overboard. A crewman trying to refix some of the cattle bindings was suddenly swept overboard and drowned. Purchas and his fellow passengers immediately bailed up Captain Whitechurch to tell him his ship was grossly overloaded and to demand he jettison cargo immediately or risk all being lost. Whitechurch backed down and two gangs were formed with Purchas heading one. As the gale thankfully abated, they spent the next three days off the Australian coast, heaving a large part of the cargo of rawhides over the side.

The ship sailed on through the South Pacific in gales and bitterly cold weather, around Cape Horn and into the Atlantic. Another gale then rolled the *Parkfield* so far that her foretopmast broke, crashing to the deck. An unfortunate crewman was crushed to death as the broken mast swung and hit him. Purchas climbed up to help him, narrowly escaping being crushed himself as the ship rolled in the heavy seas.

Despite a shortage of food and freezing weather, the *Parkfield* eventually reached England on October 27, 1845. Purchas and three others transferred to a fishing boat some 10 miles off the coast, so anxious were they to be off and away home. The other passengers were also so relieved when they finally berthed that they all gathered for a celebration dinner in a local hotel. But having been deprived of decent food for so long, most of them apparently found themselves unable to keep it down.[20]

Purchas's trip, to see Selwyn and arrange his future in New Zealand, had seen him away from England for almost a year to the day. Finally back

---

20   Purchas family papers – Ross Hamilton and Melville Brookfield.

in London at the onset of winter, he now had a lot on his mind. Before he could be reunited with his father, Aunt Ann and the rest of his family, he first had a visit to make to the Houses of Parliament where Robert Peel's Conservative Party was now in power and Selwyn's friend, Gladstone, was on the verge of his return to the cabinet as Colonial Secretary. Purchas met with Gladstone, handed over various papers from Selwyn and the Governor, and answered questions from a very interested politician.

While in London Purchas stayed with good friend Frederick Maurice, by now Professor of English literature and history at King's College, London, where they discussed the many pressing issues of social justice and reform, which interested both men. Then it was across the bustling city to Paternoster Row, the centre of British book publishing, where Purchas searched for a publisher

A very early photograph of Arthur Purchas thought to have been taken in the early 1850s when he was aged about 32, possibly at the time of his ordination. Purchas, like his friend John Kinder, was an enthusiastic pioneer of New Zealand photography.

for his singing book. He did a deal with one of them, J Van Voorst of No 3 Paternoster Row, before heading off to see his family briefly in Wales.[21] Finally, no doubt with some impatience, Purchas travelled back to Liverpool where Olivia and the Challinor family were waiting.

Undoubtedly, the Challinors would have been very relieved and happy to see him back safely after a year of little or no contact. Arrangements were quickly made for Arthur and Olivia's Christmas wedding, which duly took place in Liverpool on December 27, 1845.

The round of farewells then began again as Purchas organised return fares on the *Penyard Park*, a 377-ton barque due to sail for Sydney in a couple of months. Three days before their departure, he got word that Selwyn was advancing him £60 for their fares. The passenger list comprised just 18 people, with a crew of about 20 under the respected Captain James Weller. They sailed

21   A copy of this book is retained in Auckland Museum Library files.

on April 20, 1846 and arrived safely in Port Jackson (Sydney) in August. The two months they then had together in Sydney were crowned by the big night out at their *Messiah* concert, before the couple left for Auckland on the first ship they could find, the *Maukin*.

In company with just three other passengers, it was a routine crossing and Arthur and Olivia disembarked in Auckland on October 15, 1846 before immediately heading out to Purewa to start their new life at St John's. More important, the 21-year-old Olivia was now six months pregnant and heading into the usual hot and muggy Auckland summer. For her, the last 12 months since Arthur had returned to England – including her marriage, separation from family, a long and potentially dangerous sea voyage, and arriving in Sydney and Auckland – must have been an extraordinary time for one so young. The next 12 months would be even more eventful.

CHAPTER 3

Problems

If he didn't already know it when he first arrived at the CMS headquarters in the north, Selwyn certainly knew within months that the task he faced in establishing a new, self-supporting church in New Zealand was going to require all the energies and assistance that only a team of redoubtable men could provide.

His plans were to bring to New Zealand at least three fully ordained clergymen a year ... with one of them having had some medical training. So it can be imagined he would have awaited the arrival of Purchas with some enthusiasm.

The Selwyns shifted to the Purewa site – after moving first from Waimate to a temporary home in Parnell – arriving there in the first week of May 1846, just five months before Arthur and Olivia Purchas. They were housed at Purewa in a new two-storey stone building, solidly constructed of bluestone sourced from an area near Mt Wellington, only about a mile as the crow flies from the college.[22] The strict routines which Selwyn insisted on were already in place, with school classes between 12 and 2pm, and much of the rest of the day taken up with grinding the wheat, building, fencing, ploughing the fields, weeding, planting and preparing timber for the college carpenters' building programme.

Sarah Selwyn wrote of the meals: "We regularly ate hot pork three days a week and cold pork four days a week ... mutton was only available in the town."[23] The housekeeper and cook, Elizabeth Steel, was heavily pregnant with twins and somewhat restricted in what she could serve up. There was an English boys' school of about 34 pupils, a native boys' school about a mile away – which Selwyn himself conducted – and a small college for about eight young men undergoing their theological training. Five or six of these students were also expected to help with teaching in the younger boys' school. Two of the schools were housed downstairs in the stone building.

22   Roughly where today's suburb of Stonefields is situated.
23   AML, MS273 Vol 4, S Selwyn, *Reminiscences*.

The teachers in all three places were untrained and somewhat ineffective, and the parents were already starting to grizzle about too much time being spent doing manual labour and not enough time in the classroom. Selwyn not only had to build his college but he also had to feed and look after his staff and students. His idealistic plans for a self-supporting college of education were under threat from an early stage.

The building programme was always crucial to Selwyn's overall plan. He had specific views about aspects of Gothic Revival design, and realised he was mostly going to have to use timber, not stone. After quickly becoming disenchanted with Sampson Kempthorne's architectural ideas, Selwyn found someone far more amenable and practical to help with the design of the new buildings – architect Frederick Thatcher, a young emigrant widower from London, then working for Governor Grey. Purchas and Thatcher would soon become close working colleagues and friends.

Six months before Arthur and Olivia walked slowly up the hill from the Purewa Creek in October 1846 – with students lugging their few meagre possessions behind them – Selwyn and Thatcher had already finished their first "Selwyn" chapel. This was a small building for missionary Robert Maunsell's station at Maraetai, near Port Waikato. It was just 16 or 17 metres long and about 8 metres wide, which Maunsell described as a "little Gothic building which I hope will serve as a neat model for a New Zealand church".[24]

Purewa at this time had some 40 acres of wheat under cultivation and another 10 acres of potatoes, plus pigs and working oxen in the care of Mrs Steel's husband, who was also the college butcher. The whole site, including farm, school, chapel, hospital and staff cottages, was about 850 acres. Unfortunately, as many of today's residents of Meadowbank know full well, much of the land comprised poor clay soil. Consequently, cropping would never prove to be greatly successful in the years to follow.

Selwyn had given Purchas quite a 'build-up' among his staff and others at St John's. One of them, William Bambridge, a teacher and part of Selwyn's original New Zealand group, wrote later of the announcement: "… the new arrival which turned out to be Mr Purchas, the long-expected Mr Purchas, the much talked-of Mr Purchas".[25] The Bambridge house was not on the college site but close to the small Māori settlement of Purewa nearby and because rooms had not yet been readied, Selwyn asked Bambridge to accommodate the Purchases for a day or two in the absence of his wife Sophia, who was away with friends. Arthur and Olivia stayed in the Bambridge house for a

24   H Garrett, *Te Manihera*, p 148.
25   William Bambridge Journal, Oct 13, 1846 – Brookfield family papers.

week before moving to upstairs rooms in the new Thatcher-designed, wooden college hospital.

The night before moving there, Sarah Selwyn invited them to spend a relaxing evening with herself, George and his chaplain William Cotton. The sensitive, generous and kindly Sarah immediately struck up a friendship with the younger pregnant woman, called Livy by her husband. Sarah quickly discovered Olivia could play the piano and Cotton reported, "she played a number of good tunes … and when she had got to the end of her stock she said so. Mrs Selwyn asked her to begin again, which she did … and in a very nice manner".[26] Arthur also warmed to Sarah, although he probably would have detected a little strain in her husband's manner, unnoticeable when the two men had met in Nelson well over a year and a half earlier.

Purchas wasn't to know it just yet, but things between Selwyn and the CMS missionaries had not improved and it wasn't only due to irritation with the rules and ongoing paucity of school classes at St John's – or the poor teaching. When Selwyn had accepted the New Zealand bishopric, the CMS in London had also set 'guidelines' for him. He was not to control where its current missionaries – and those subsequently to be ordained by him at Purewa – were to live or work. Nor was he to require them to take services for Europeans unless the CMS first approved. Selwyn didn't appreciate these restrictions and took no notice.[27]

He also relied to some extent on the CMS body in New Zealand to identify or supply prospective ordinands, particularly from their own number of catechists and helpers. But trouble over his subsequent demands of them, couched in five "articles" which they had to sign – including his insistence that they go where he sent them – was another major irritant. Further, while his English boys' school was as much for the children of the missionaries as it was for local settlers, Selwyn could not provide teachers of sufficient quality to satisfy anyone.

The CMS in England had also made it known to Selwyn that if they were to surrender part of their prior autonomy to him, they still wanted him to continue with some of their own priorities … notably to build up the native church with as much, if not more, emphasis as the settler church and to ordain Māori deacons and priests.

So when Purchas first sat down with the CMS missionaries around the Purewa dining table in that summer of 1846-47, he quickly learned that things were "not quite right". He sensed the missionaries' annoyance over Selwyn's

---

26   U Platts, *The Lively Capital*, p 166.
27   K Newman, *Bible & Treaty*, p 182.

disregard for their ways and objectives – which was not only undermining their hard-won ground with Māori but was also having a marked impact on native attitudes towards the church and Christianity in general. In short, Māori were becoming confused by the actions of the two bodies and their respective leaders.

But it was the question of location for the missionaries which remained the biggest bone of contention. Their northern committee insisted – when they had met at Selwyn's first synod earlier in Waimate and then again at Purewa – that it was up to them to decide where their men served. The end result was that their leaders in England decided to stop sending Selwyn any more candidates from England for training. He would have to find them himself – and men like Purchas were not easy to find.

Trouble looms

Selwyn was also relying on the European settlers as a strong source of income to fund his longer-term plan for the church in New Zealand. But his dictatorial stance and sometimes abrupt manner – repeatedly requesting the missionary group to also minister to those European settlers whose support he needed, and their reluctance to do so – caused further friction. The missionaries saw it as effectively reducing further their own time and influence among Māori. Purchas sensed the trouble looming and before long was caught up in it himself.

Henry Williams' growing unhappiness over the various matters quickly came to a head when Selwyn made it very clear that he also opposed missionaries owning land or even leasing it from Māori and insisted that any land or buildings should only be owned by the Church itself.

Also irritating to the more evangelical missionaries, like the occasionally irascible Robert Maunsell, was Selwyn's predilection for even a small amount of ritual and ceremony, and his liking for robes, candles and chants, and some religious protocol. Purchas himself may have been mildly surprised on his arrival to see staff and students fully gowned and robed considering their small numbers … in obvious contrast with the clear informality among the missionary group and their Māori students. Selwyn had also said he would not ordain anyone who could not read the Greek Testament in its original version, something which greatly puzzled the missionary group who struggled to see what practical relevance this had for either themselves or their Māori audiences.

Further tension stemmed from the belief of many in the missionary and Māori communities, however incorrect, that Selwyn was still partly beholden to Wakefield's New Zealand Company. Its settlers wanted the new bishop to be training good clergymen and teachers to work in its churches, schools and

The hospital at Purewa where Arthur and Olivia lived for the first few years after arriving in Auckland as newlyweds in 1846. This was the first of the "Selwyn" style of buildings with familiar 60° roof angle.

AUCKLAND MUSEUM IMAGES PH NEG 6764

settlements – not among Māori.[28]

Nevertheless, it is clear that Purchas's cheerful and conciliatory manner, complemented by Olivia's sensible, bright and friendly personality, initially helped eased suspicions which may have formed as a result of him being seen by the missionaries on arrival as one of "Selwyn's men". By sheer force of character and presence, he got on well with them all – men like William Williams (Henry's brother and the new archdeacon in charge of the Hawkes Bay-East Coast area), his nephew Samuel (also training alongside Purchas for the priesthood), fellow doctor Christopher Davies, William Dudley, Benjamin Ashwell, Thomas Smith, Rota Waitoa (the first Māori ordinand), and later the troubled James Stack. Even the German Lutheran George Kissling and Selwyn's personal friends and confidants, William Martin and William Swainson, warmed to Purchas's disposition.

Although probably a little unsettled at first by the missionaries' dissatisfaction with the strict rules, the poor teaching and learning environment, disputes over discipline and personal disagreements with Selwyn, Arthur and

Olivia were happy upstairs in the Thatcher hospital, the roof of which had only gone on three weeks earlier. Thatcher was still acting as Grey's assistant private secretary, but also discussing with Selwyn new designs for chapels at both the college and on a site in Remuera.[29]

The wooden hospital was the next significant building to be completed after the stone house and kitchen, and was used initially for a variety of activities.[30] Thatcher's design, according to Selwyn's initial concept, used a basic H layout, incorporating the distinctive 60° gable, built on a substantial stone foundation with rooms upstairs in the roof space or lofts, where Arthur and Olivia lived, and seven rooms downstairs.[31]

Selwyn drew up his usual rules and regulations for the Brethren and Sisters of the Hospital of St John, the colony's first. He wanted it to be available for both Māori and Pākehā patients, not only residents of St John's but any settler or native. His original plan also involved female nurses on the staff but this quickly proved to be unrealistic. He insisted that no payments were to be taken for any medical services. Instead, the hospital's maintenance was to be covered by offerings at the nearby St Thomas Church which, according to Selwyn, were "given with the greatest goodwill by all our congregation, who know the purposes to which these offerings are applied".[32]

Yet another controversial and contradictory Selwyn policy covered the hospital activities. Those "suffering from contagious or infectious diseases were not to be admitted", although the hospital was built to "minister to all the wants of the sick of all classes, without respect of persons or reservation of service …"[33] The policy was soon to be severely tested and with deadly consequences.

Having approved the Thatcher designs for the Remuera church of St Mark's and also the St John's Chapel, Selwyn planned for the construction of both to begin in February 1847. Purchas watched on from the sidelines with great interest and it seems Thatcher was only too willing to share his ideas and design detail with him – recognising the younger man's obvious flair and sound knowledge of architectural and engineering principles. It was the start of significant collaboration between the two in the years that followed.

Just before the building of the St John's Chapel got under way, Olivia produced their first child on January 11, 1847. She was helped in delivery by Sarah Selwyn and the baby was named Arthur,[34] after his father. Sarah was

---

29   This was to be St Mark's, Remuera.
30   The building was finally demolished in 1920 – refer M H Alington, *An Excellent Recruit*.
31   ADA – Letters. The hospital was built by the college carpenters, Cochrane & Hunter.
32   G A Selwyn *Journal*, Part V, No XX, p 15.
33   J K Davis, *New Zealand Illustrated Magazine*, Vol VI, May 1, 1902.
34   Actually known in the family as 'Agape' – or Greek for love.

asked to be his godmother, an invitation she gladly accepted, and the child was baptised at St Thomas' on January 31. All seemed well in the cramped Purchas household in the top floor of the hospital.

Then calamity. Within weeks of the baby's birth and despite Selwyn's ruling that anyone with an enteric fever should not be admitted to the hospital because of the risk to the 70 or so people within the St John's community, an infected woman was admitted under Purchas's instruction. Perhaps her symptoms were not fully apparent at the time ... or her admission was deemed to have been in line with Selwyn's original premise for the hospital to "minister to all the wants of the sick".

But to Purchas's great dismay, this initial case turned out to be typhoid.[35] It spread rapidly and within days became a full-scale epidemic. In no time he had 40 people down, including the Selwyns' two small boys, Johnnie and Willie, and Sarah Selwyn's maid, Mary Crump, all suffering from varying degrees of fever. Then Olivia fell ill, followed soon after by Arthur himself. George Selwyn was away when it started but returned just before Easter to a dangerous situation.

"George took the lead in the hospital," Sarah wrote, "where we had eight patients. Our alarm was much excited on Johnnie's account for some days. Mrs Grey urged me to send Willie to her ..." With Olivia helpless, Sarah then took the Purchas baby into her own home. "The poor little dear at that busy time," she wrote ... "no-one had leisure to attend to it and we used to call it 'the French mark' which in a boarding school is parted with at the first opportunity. If anyone took it, the last holder ran off as quickly as might be!"[36]

As further residents among the St John's community succumbed to the fever, the dire situation now called for drastic and courageous action. Purchas decided to try something new and totally contrary to the prevailing international medical thinking and treatment of the day which was virtual starvation.[37] It was something he had first heard discussed and propounded while training at Guy's in London.

The innovative remedy, which he tried first on himself and then Olivia, involved a very careful selection of certain foods and liquids. By late April this diet, combined with his obsession for cleanliness, resulted not only in an immediate improvement in his own and Olivia's health, but also that of the baby and the two Selwyn children. Young Willie had been in the worst shape and for two weeks his life was in the balance. The others struck down also showed signs of rapid improvement. But Sydney, the 16-year-old son of

35   L K Gluckman, Tangiwai – *A Medical History of 19th Century New Zealand*, pp 94-98.
36   AML, MS273, Vol 4. Sarah Selwyn – *Reminiscences*.
37   E H Roche, *New Zealand Medical Journal*, Feb 1970.

William Williams, did not and the worst was feared. The lad finally shook hands with his Uncle Samuel two days before he died, telling him "he did not expect to recover, but was anticipating his removal".[38]

Despite this tragedy, the Selwyns in particular and everyone else at Purewa were now in Purchas's debt. Word quickly spread among other doctors in Auckland and he was asked to put his new treatment down in writing. It soon became standard practice in New Zealand and remained so for many years. It was the handling of this major crisis which first identified Purchas as a doctor of extraordinary medical skill, courage and innovation.

By the middle of June 1847, although there had been three deaths – Mrs Cooper, an initial "carrier", Sydney Williams and the unfortunate housekeeper/matron Elizabeth Steel[39] – general health was largely restored. The new St John's Chapel, although still unfinished inside, was used first for the funerals of Williams and Mrs Steel on June 12, 1847. George Selwyn, who never praised people for just doing their job, wrote in his journal: "The resources of the hospital are not large but we believe several lives have been prolonged by the care which our medical advisors have bestowed on them." He had two very good reasons to be grateful to Arthur Purchas. Johnnie Selwyn, one of his two sons struck down, would later also become a bishop and knight of the realm.

Other early historians have confirmed that the epidemic eventually proved far less deadly than would have been expected, due to Purchas's radical new treatment. But in hindsight, as noted by at least one church historian, it was probably a very unwise plan by Selwyn to build a hospital so close to a school on the same site. Fortunately, the opening soon after of the new Government hospital in Auckland removed much of the pressure which Purchas's small wards at Purewa had been under … as word spread about his skills and success, and his medical reputation began to grow.

Sound of music

Purchas always enjoyed being busy. There were never enough hours in the day for him. His keen interest in anything musical was evident immediately after they arrived at Purewa. The Bambridges had a musical box on their mantelpiece which Purchas noted did not work. Before Sophia Bambridge had returned from her holiday, he had fully dismantled it and restored it to full working order, much to everyone's delight. When Selwyn first heard him sing and play the flute, and learned of his music book and choral activities in Sydney, he

---

38   F Porter (ed), *The Turanga Journals*, p 437.
39   Her twins had just been delivered, one stillborn.

immediately made him precentor, in charge of all music at the college. Purchas took on this additional role with predictable enthusiasm. No sooner had he unpacked copies of his own singing book than he arranged singing classes two or three times a week for both Māori and European students – armed only with a silver tuning fork.

Sarah Selwyn later wrote: "Mr Purchas brought with him a knowledge of music which was a great gain ... he was an excellent teacher and ere long we had singing in the chapel which was popular and greatly enlivened the services ... the Maoris are excellent timists and soon learnt many catches and glees and used to sing *Bacon and Potatoes* as a dinner bell in default of a real bell or gong."

The system Purchas had invented, and was now teaching, enjoyed spectacular success. He had singing classes every Monday, Wednesday and Friday evening, attended by pupils of the senior and junior schools and their masters. They would learn and practise church music one week and popular secular songs the next, all sung a capella until a harmonium was available.

The system was based on a figure notation, in place of the standard minim, quaver and crotchet symbols, all sung to the Māori syllables for numerals one to eight.[40] The Selwyn circle of English friends – Sir William and Lady Martin, the Swainsons, Abrahams and others – were astonished at the results. Before long, both English and Māori children were very adept at some very difficult music. "The Maori boys are looked upon quite as a wonder in their singing," Sarah Selwyn wrote. "Many persons including Governor Grey and Mrs Grey have come out from Auckland on purpose to hear them."[41] In addition, Purchas began travelling into Auckland regularly to conduct community singing classes and to advise on and encourage the establishment of more choirs.

Lady Martin wrote: "The Maori boys and girls sang English glees and catches with great spirit ... no sooner were the young people in the school taught to read music by the figure system and trained by regular practices weekly, than we found out the gift of song that was in them. The girls used to sing some of Mendelssohn's chorales with great spirit and accuracy ..."

Missionary Benjamin Ashwell was also impressed: "The children sing and chant English tunes in parts. To hear the children of cannibals singing first and second tenor and bass to some of our beautiful tunes and hymns causes a thrill of joy which only a missionary can know ..."

James Stack's wife said she was more surprised "by their knowledge of

---

40   A more detailed explanation can be found in M McLean's Maori Music, pp 296-297. The Purchas "figure notation system" was later copied and used in Tonga in 1860 to teach students in Wesleyan churches, and is said to have started their fine tradition of choral singing.

41   AML, MS273, Vol 4, Sarah Selwyn, *Reminiscences*.

music than anything else yet witnessed. They sang correctly, in parts, difficult music by Mendelssohn and other composers – such as the *Hallelujah Chorus, Sleepers Awake* and *Dark Shades of Night.*"

But unfortunately for Selwyn and his great St John's collegial plan – even before the typhoid had taken hold and been beaten off – several of the English settler parents had begun quietly to withdraw their children from his schools. Although it initially seemed to be a great idea, many began to feel that Purewa was too far out of town. They also believed there was far too much discipline meted out, not enough teaching, too many rules and an excessive amount of manual labour – working in the fields, in the kitchen or on the new buildings. Some even thought there was too much insistence on racial equality.[42]

William Williams, who had been studying under Selwyn since the Waimate days in 1844 – and regularly visiting Purewa from his own station in Hawkes Bay – decided to send his other son, Leonard, back to England for schooling. He was quickly followed by another CMS missionary with his two boys. Money was also now very tight, despite Selwyn's apparent use of his wife's substantial financial resources to help complete the Purewa building programme.[43] But then he began blaming the college's problems and weaknesses on his staff. Despite Purchas's equable and obliging nature, even he became a little irritated at the state of affairs.

Missionary Robert Maunsell was one most inclined to criticise Selwyn, saying "he was more theorist than a practical man", and his fellow missionaries were all practical men. Besides, he argued, they had been here for 20 years or more before Selwyn arrived. Henry Williams, for instance, was now a very experienced and practical man in his fifties. By contrast, Selwyn was still relatively inexperienced, in his mid-thirties – although also intelligent and 'driven'. As church historian Allan Davidson put it: "Selwyn and the CMS represented two different liturgical and theological sub-cultures within the Anglican church."[44] Melding the two was always going to be difficult.

Purchas, already drawn deeply into the Selwyn plan, was only 26 at this stage, but physically and intellectually probably the equal of Selwyn. The Bishop would have quickly realised that Purchas was more gifted than he had first realised and that many of Purchas's talents would be vital to his own plans for St John's. Their mutual respect in those early days meant neither would have wanted to get offside with the other.

Although Selwyn's apparently ruthless and dictatorial manner would have

42   Garrett, p 181.
43   Ibid., p 106.
44   A K Davidson, *Selwyn's Legacy*.

irked someone like Purchas – trained in a far more collegial style at Guy's by Maurice, Bright, Addison and others – there were no overt signs of friction between the two of them at this stage. Olivia Purchas and Sarah Selwyn were firm friends from the beginning but things between their respective husbands would become increasingly fractious over the next couple of years.

Still, there were often exciting times at the college, such as the visit in July of 1847 by the Ngāti Toa chief Te Rauparaha, attended by several South Island chiefs. Te Rauparaha came to inspect St John's for his son Tamihana, who was soon to start training there. Ngāti Whātua chief, Āpihai Te Kawau, who had played the main role in gifting the land on which Auckland was now being built, was also a frequent visitor.

So for the moment, Purchas remained content to involve himself in music, architecture, his family and his theological studies, despite the inadequate teaching practices. In the background though, missionary frustration and upset continued over the Bishop's unrealistic objectives and short temper. The inevitable result, says Davidson, was that "Selwyn tried but failed to harness the support of the CMS and its missionaries and was unable to win the goodwill of the settler community … his visionary schemes and detailed planning outran his ability to bring them to reality."[45] William Williams, who was one of Purchas's occasional teachers, wrote of Selwyn at this time: "The more I see of the Bishop, the more I feel that he is unsound at bottom and I have no expectation of seeing a sound superstructure."[46]

Purchas, however, never seemed tarred by any perceived close, personal or clerical association with Selwyn's actions or approach. While there was an occasional raised eyebrow at some of the beautiful old chants and tunes he selected for the chapel services he conducted, his independence of thought, medical ability,[47] hard work and kindness quickly won him respect and friendship from everyone in the missionary and settler church communities.

Selwyn's difficult year

That year of 1847 – Purchas's first full year in New Zealand – turned into something of an 'annus horribilis' for Selwyn and a serious test of his resolve on many fronts. It began well enough in February with the pre-construction at St John's of the small Remuera church and the St John's Chapel, but deteriorated quickly from there.

---

45   A K Davidson (ed), *A Controversial Churchman*.
46   F Porter (ed), p 459.
47   Purchas was soon made the main medical officer for the CMS missionary body.

As St John's slowly righted itself after the dangerous typhoid episode, Selwyn and a still-weak Purchas officiated at the opening of St Mark's on May 30. It was a very small kauri building prefabricated by the Purewa carpenters. A team of students assembled it on its new site ... almost a replica of the St John's Chapel but with a straw thatch roof, later to be replaced by shingles.[48]

All this time, William Williams and other family members and colleagues were talking and writing regularly about their continuing unhappiness over things at St John's. His wife Jane wrote to a friend: "Our peep behind the scenes at school and college was anything but satisfactory to us. The Bishop's plans are very good but they are not followed up and the time appointed for instruction was sadly frittered away, particularly in the lower school, and the upper one was not much better ... the college discipline and course of instruction does not at all come to William's ideas and expectations."[49]

Once he had recovered, in between helping Olivia at home with the baby, Purchas was preoccupied with studying theology, the Māori language and Greek, and taking his various music classes. He was one of five being prepared in the somewhat haphazard classes for ordination as a deacon. The others were Thomas Hutton, a junior master in the English boys' school and one of those constantly criticised for poor teaching habits, Frederick Fisher, Thomas Tudor and Henry Butt, another with medical training who had come to New Zealand in Selwyn's original party.

Purchas was also spending as much of his spare time as he could with Frederick Thatcher on other new architectural projects. Selwyn was pressing for the completion of a new church for the settlement proposed at Howick. As well as the tight financial situation at the college, the market gardens were not producing particularly bountiful crops and, according to various accounts, Selwyn's sources of funds from friends in England were also drying up quickly.

Unknown to him at the time, however, were the contents of a serious letter already on its way from the CMS offices in London. Following Governor Grey's twisted despatches to the CMS and Gladstone about the missionaries' "large land purchases", the letter to Selwyn, dated March 1, contained the following bombshell: "It appears necessary to declare," it said, "that no missionary or catechist of the Society can be allowed to continue his connection with the Society who shall retain for his own use and benefit a greater amount of land than shall be determined as suitable by the Lieutenant Governor of New

---

48   C R Knight, The Selwyn Churches of Auckland, p 38. This building remained there until 1860 when it was shifted to the corner of Bassett Rd and used as a schoolroom.

49   F Porter (ed), p 424.

Zealand and the Bishop of New Zealand".[50]

The CMS now required that if any missionary (especially Henry Williams) wanted to keep land he had bought from Māori for his sons to live on and farm, he could no longer be a member of the CMS. When it arrived on Selwyn's desk, with a copy to Grey, the Governor immediately sent a strongly worded official communication to Selwyn making one thing quite clear about missionary land purchase. The CMS instruction was unequivocal and the job of laying down the law to the missionaries about prior land purchases and grants – and what was acceptable now – was quite clearly Selwyn's to deal with. Grey not only expected him to admonish Henry Williams and the others, but also left Selwyn in no doubt that he considered any grant over the 2560-acre limit – no matter who might have approved it earlier – to be illegal and unacceptable. Eight of the CMS missionaries, besides Henry Williams, held land via grants of more than 2560 acres.

Selwyn pondered the communication only briefly before grabbing the bull by the horns and writing in the same direct terms to his Archdeacon, Henry Williams, and the others. He demanded that Grey's terms be adhered to. Missionaries were not to keep land above the 2560-acre limit. They were to sell it, give it to their children or return it to the Native Trust. Furthermore, Williams' remaining land could be retained by the family but not the missionary himself.

Selwyn's official letter to the missionary group was handed to them on a Saturday in early September and they had only until the Monday – when their central committee was scheduled to meet – to agree or not. Williams did not agree. His children had already been farming the land in his name for years and were, by now, well established. He claimed to have never sought personally to benefit from it. For three or four days a furious argument raged between Selwyn and Williams – conducted from a distance via notes and letters each wrote to the other, which were carried back and forth by Henry's brother William.

But his fellow missionaries buckled and finally did agree to comply with Selwyn's demand. Henry Williams stood his ground for nearly two years before the sheer weight of settler criticism and condemnation, added to by Grey and other politicians, led to his unfortunate dismissal from the CMS in 1849. He remained one of Selwyn's archdeacons, however, but retired, shattered and upset, to the family land at Pakaraka near Waimate. There he would live out his life among his Māori people serving them first as he had always vowed.

His brother William, probably echoing the thoughts of most of the

---

50   CMS Archives, MC25.

missionary and church body, thought Selwyn had not only shown "much want of judgement" but had also further undermined his position in the minds of all the missionaries. Meanwhile the settlers and their main newspapers again began venting their anger about missionaries and their land. Their stance just confused and annoyed Māori even more since to them – already under mounting pressure from Europeans to sell land – it seemed a classic example of the settler pot calling the missionary kettle black.

Appointment as deacon

On September 19, 1847, amidst all the controversy, Purchas and three others travelled to St Paul's in Auckland for their ordination as deacons. In those days, this was a solemn but significant event which involved almost the entire community. Afterwards, the clergy were invited to refreshments at Government House with Grey.[51]

Then, on his 26th birthday a few days later, Purchas was pleasantly surprised to be told by Selwyn of his new appointment as priest-in-charge of a brand new parochial district. It included Onehunga, Epsom, Otahuhu, Waiuku and Mauku. He was to build a church first, on land in Onehunga organised for Selwyn by Grey, then a school and a home. Until the house was finished, he would have to use temporary accommodation if he stayed in Onehunga, but he and Olivia would remain based at Purewa. Purchas had no horse and would have to use Shanks's pony to get to his new district and conduct services and schooling – in settler houses or other buildings, mostly raupō huts – until his permanent premises could be built.

Despite having had only 10 months of somewhat sketchy training, Purchas found himself relieved at the news. He was anxious to take up this new assignment away from Purewa and "had found living with the dictatorial Selwyn much more difficult than he had imagined".[52] Over the previous three or four months, his relationship with Selwyn had started to come under the same strain experienced by the others living in the close confines of St John's College. More specifically in Purchas's case, much of the strain had been induced by the difficult matter of the very basic living expenses at the college.

It is still unlikely, however, that any tension between the two at this stage – at least as far as Selwyn was concerned – would have been the main factor behind Purchas's move. Selwyn had the more pressing priority of getting men into permanent appointments in the ring of chapelries he was establishing

51   F Porter (ed), p 444.
52   R Sweetman, *Spire on the Hill*, p 29.

John Kinder's beautiful watercolour of an early Onehunga street scene, showing the newly built St Peter's church in the centre background.
AUCKLAND LIBRARIES HERITAGE COLLECTIONS 4-1204

around Auckland. Despite an occasional terse remark, both men would still have been keen to keep the relationship on as co-operative a basis as possible, if only for the sake of their wives' close friendship. Up to now, Purchas had sacrificed much and had exercised considerable patience and fortitude in fulfilling the promise to his mother. For Selwyn, it would have been a very bad look to his supporters and backers in England to have men like Purchas possibly give up and leave the colony with the risk of exposing Selwyn's problems in more detail.

At least one historian has stated that Purchas was "firmly invited to go to Onehunga after a series of rows"[53], but it is more likely that Selwyn saw the

As an intellectual equal of Selwyn and extraordinarily gifted in so many areas, Purchas was still a very important cog in Selwyn's wheel. Each man was somewhat dependent on the other – Selwyn on Purchas's versatility and multiple skills, particularly in architecture and medicine; Purchas on Selwyn's leadership and influence in helping realise his hopes for a happy, fulfilling and productive life in New Zealand, from which there was really no turning back.

At least one historian has stated that Purchas was "firmly invited to go to Onehunga after a series of rows"[53], but it is more likely that Selwyn saw the

---

53   Sweetman, p 29.

appointment as a conciliatory gesture which Purchas found easy to accept. Although his appointment to Onehunga left him feeling very much on his own, he would have been happy not to be confronting Selwyn any more. Additionally, Selwyn did not have many options when it came to choosing clergymen. While Sarah Selwyn might eventually miss Olivia's pleasant company, all would have sensed that the timing for a move was now right. Purchas would not have wanted to get in the way of someone as single-minded and determined as George Selwyn. The Bishop no doubt accepted that Purchas might best serve his overall purposes now by being given his own 'patch' where, even as a 26-year-old, he could be completely trusted to take charge and become a respected leader within the new diocese.

Unfortunately Purchas could only start erecting the new home for his family after the church and schoolroom were built. It would take most of the following year before they could physically escape the confines of Purewa.

CHAPTER 4

Onehunga Beginnings

"A most desolate and wretched-looking place" was how a couple of Government surveyors described Onehunga only a year before Purchas arrived to have a look around in that early spring of 1847. However, it had been an important place for centuries before Samuel Marsden's original visit in 1820 – being a key Māori stop-off and staging point between the Tamaki isthmus portage from the Waitematā and access via the Manukau Harbour to Waiuku, the Waikato River and the rich lands further south.

The area had been reoccupied by Ngāti Whātua after more of Hongi Hika's merciless raids in the 1820s before an Australian, no less, bought thousands of acres from Ngāti Whātua for a sawmill in 1835. But the Australian died only a year later and the same land was then sold by his trustees to the agent for the newly established Waitematā and Manukau Land Company, Captain William Cornwallis Symonds. The Land Commission hearings, following the Treaty of Waitangi, eventually reduced the company's original holding to less than 2000 acres around what is now called Cornwallis. Then the kindly Symonds drowned in an unfortunate accident crossing the inner harbour to Awhitu on an errand of mercy – and the enterprise folded soon after.

After Auckland was founded by Hobson, Onehunga and Puketutu Island in particular – about four or five kilometres offshore – resumed their roles as important trading places for Māori and the early settlers. More land buyers began arriving in force soon after when a further parcel of about 163 acres (the site which today comprises the town's main business centre) was also sold by Māori to a John Jackson.[54] This 'mainland' site was onsold by him only two years later to three other settlers, only for them to be dispossessed by the Government, which simply took the land saying it was needed for military purposes. Grey's officials compensated the settlers to a degree (giving them back the same amount they had originally paid Māori) before undertaking a

---

54 Also named "Thomas" Jackson in some sources. He also bought Puketutu Island in 1845 before on-selling to Dr Henry Weekes in 1846.

survey of their new property.

The Government's interest in Onehunga followed the fallout and continuing unease arising from the northern war with Hōne Heke two years earlier. Apart from seeking to impose his version of British law and order on settlers and natives alike – particularly the British system of landownership and disposal – Grey was also wanting to secure his new capital against any further hostile action by Māori, from either north or south.

It wasn't only Heke and some of the other northern Māori tribes who were concerned at the extensive loss and permanent alienation of land. Various iwi and tribal chiefs in Hauraki, the lower Waikato and Taupō – many of whom had not signed the Treaty – were becoming increasingly angry with and suspicious of the growing numbers of European arrivals and their demands for the most fertile Māori land. And that despite the significant economic and trade benefits enjoyed by Māori following the settlers' arrival. The trade with Auckland was varied and considerable, with a wide range of fruit and vegetables (including potatoes and kumara), pork, fish and even flour, sold and bartered in return for tools, tobacco, clothes and gunpowder. Māori also profited from Europeans by providing their labour.

So Grey pushed ahead with plans for garrison outposts to be established on his newly acquired land at Onehunga and also at Panmure, Howick and Otahuhu. At Onehunga, Grey also made special grants of land to Selwyn (and the Roman Catholic bishop) on which to build a church and a school, and Selwyn agreed to supply a clergyman and teacher. Purchas's new church was to go on a one-acre corner block on what was soon to be named Church St.

Grey had also asked the British Government for a couple of thousand front-line soldiers to man his garrisons. Instead, he was sent army veterans, men under 48 years old who had already completed their term of service in the British Army and who had no desire to return to poverty in England. These were the Fencibles.[55] The soldiers were to be given a free house on an acre of land, which would be theirs after seven years' service, provided they gave 12 days of military service a year and attended church parades every Sunday. The soldiers were free to work their land and make whatever other income they could, in return for acting as a kind of home guard – on call for the growing town of Auckland, the capital and centre of commerce.

Purchas would therefore be guaranteed his congregation from day one since about 80% of the soldiers were of the Church of England. It would have also been his hope, and certainly Selwyn's, that these good folk would be able

---

55   The name was derived from Scottish "Defencibles" – the term given to soldiers enlisted for defence purposes only.

to contribute to the very basic deacon's stipend of only £90 per annum by their offerings every Sunday as soon as the new church opened. In this, they would quickly be bitterly disappointed.

The first Fencible ship, the *Ramillies*, had already arrived in Auckland in August, a few weeks before Purchas was ordained deacon. On board were 62 Fencible soldiers, their wives and children, all now having to wait patiently at the port for accommodation to be sorted out – even before they could walk out to Onehunga to begin their new lives. Two more ships, carrying another 150 Fencibles and their families ready to take up residence in Onehunga, were to follow. So by early August 1847 – well in advance of Purchas's appointment – Selwyn was under real pressure from Grey to get a church and school open for these new immigrants.

For the next few months after his ordination, Purchas left his wife behind at Purewa every Saturday to walk to Onehunga in order to take an early service for the mainly Fencible community at 7am on Sundays in one of the local buildings. Then he would walk to St Andrew's in Epsom[56] for a late morning service followed by a school session, before returning to Onehunga for the early evening service – and then sometimes back to Purewa! Whenever he could, before or after these Sunday duties, he would spend time on the Saturday or the Monday clearing the church land – a "wilderness of scrub and fern" – to make way for the new church and school, and his house a little further away in Selwyn St.

Not surprisingly, Purchas was a man described by family and friends as having "prodigious energy" and incredible physical strength. His grandson E H Roche, said two characteristics never deserted him – physical strength and a complete absence of fear. He described one particular incident when, as a young man in Wales, Purchas was watching a vet attend to a particularly high-spirited horse. The horse reared suddenly and struck out with its forelegs. A stablehand went to grab the horse, slipped and fell. Purchas immediately jumped under the horse as its front feet landed and, seizing it by the legs, "gave it such a heave that it toppled over backwards".[57]

After a hard day's labour preparing his site, Purchas would usually stay overnight in Onehunga with new Fencible acquaintances like Captain – later Colonel – Theodore Haultain, who would become a lifelong friend. At other times he would stay in a large converted whare down the road from the church site, the area's first licensed accommodation, owned by Robert and Margaret

---

56   This small single-room building, able to seat about 50, was opened in September 1846. Sweetman, p 26.

57   E Roche – lecture to Royal Australasian College of Physicians, Feb 1954.

Forbes. From there he would also regularly travel by canoe or boat to Waiuku on the southern shores of the Manukau, then by bush track to Mauku to conduct services in a settler's home or a Māori whare. Like other missionaries and clergy in those days, he thought nothing of walking 35 to 40 kilometres in a day – sometimes being away from his family for a full week at a time.

When reunited with Olivia back at Purewa, Purchas's priority was the design of his new Onehunga church. At the same time he drew up plans for a single-storey house on the other church site nearby and a small wooden schoolroom to be erected on land beside the church itself.

Known as one of the very first 'Selwyn' churches, the overall design of St Peter's Church is attributed today mainly, if not solely, to Purchas, working in close collaboration with Thatcher. Thatcher's biographer, Margaret Alington, states that "the only churches attributed solely to Thatcher with any certainty were St Mark's, All Saints [Howick] and St Barnabas [Parnell]". As further evidence supporting Purchas's main role, she said: "It was unusual for Thatcher <u>not</u> to introduce a pointed window at least in the gables; nor was it his practice to use buttresses … there is a strong likelihood that the design of St Peter's was influenced by the unusually gifted first minister, Dr Purchas …"

Further underlining the Purchas hand is the fact that many other design details which appeared in this first St Peter's design would resurface later in his other church projects. He would also supervise its construction by the college carpenters in early 1848 and later managed a major alteration and then enlargement for which close familiarity with design and engineering details would have been needed.

Thatcher was under considerable pressure himself at this time anyway, finalising the design of the Howick church (All Saints), which opened late in November 1847. He surely would have welcomed any lead from Purchas on the Onehunga project, and any additional ideas or tips Purchas may have picked up from his time with the architect Blacket in Sydney. The late Cyril Knight, professor of architecture at Auckland University, former president of the New Zealand Institute of Architects and perhaps still the foremost authority on the subject, confirmed Purchas's design involvement. He also suggested that St Peter's Church was prefabricated at Purewa – like All Saints – and shipped to the site, because this was how the building department at St John's worked.[58]

The Onehunga church was larger and more elaborate than Howick's All Saints. It was a 300-seat building with an octagonal tower in the centre topped by a tall spire with hooded louvres. Purchas was to favour a spire in all

---

58   Knight, p 28.

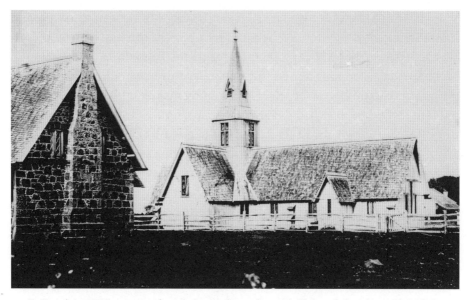

St Peter's in 1856, was significantly larger than other early 'Selwyn" churches with its lofty central spire. The partly showing stone building also built by Purchas, was used as a Fencible library and Onehunga school for many years.
AUCKLAND MUSEUM IMAGES PH ALB 88 P52-1

his later designs, although never again in a central position as in the original Onehunga design. Externally the building did not share the same Thatcher exterior diagonal bracing as the Howick church, or the St Stephen's and St John's chapels – but it did incorporate the same vertical windows with diamond panes, vertical inside buttressing, the gable roofs on the entrance porch and chancel, and pleasing exterior proportions, thus giving it the same "Selwyn look".

Frederick Thatcher was an engaging character with whom Purchas shared much in common apart from an obvious interest and skill in architecture. He was seven years older than Purchas and had come to New Zealand from England after enduring the economic depression of the late 1830s, which was probably the worst in British history. He was a professional architect and major buildings that bear his name are still standing today. One such example is a large brick building in the town of Battle – so named after the nearby Hastings battle of 1066 – originally designed by Thatcher as a workhouse for paupers. Today it is a luxury apartment block.

Soon after marrying, he lost both his wife and first child, and decided to emigrate to New Zealand to start afresh. He was originally employed as a Superintendent of Public Works before joining Governor Grey's staff and working with Selwyn in his spare time on the original "Selwyn" concepts and Purewa buildings. By the time he first met up with Purchas, he had already been supervising the Purewa programme for about 18 months and was seriously contemplating becoming a priest himself. He eventually took up residence at Purewa and began his own theological training in August 1848.

Thatcher, like Purchas, believed it was "character rather than a man's work which distinguished the great and the good from the common-place". They both agreed with the Selwyn ethos of habitual self-discipline, although neither were enamoured with their superior's propensity for impatience and frustration. Both men were kind and generous, with a calm, unruffled manner, and unfailingly courteous. They also believed strongly, as did Selwyn, in racial equality. Māori and European were always to be treated the same.

By the time Purchas and the college carpenters had finished erecting St Peter's – watched all the time by curious Fencible onlookers – he had already made a start on his house. The church was finally opened on June 29, 1848, by which time Olivia was pregnant with their second child. Purchas was still away from Purewa more often than not, returning with stories of people met and visits made to Mauku, Waiuku and Epsom – and even the missionary station at Taupiri where the CMS had established a mission in 1842 under Benjamin Ashwell. It was on these visits that Purchas first began to establish his significant contacts with Māori and gain his great proficiency in their language.

Then, slowly but surely, his overnight presence in Onehunga, and visibility on the church and house construction site, began to attract growing interest from locals wanting medical attention. Word of this kindly doctor's excellent medical reputation had spread rapidly, despite the fact that another doctor, Henry Weekes, also lived nearby. Weekes had been brought to New Zealand as the doctor for Wakefield's New Zealand Company in New Plymouth and had similar qualifications to Purchas. After leaving New Plymouth in 1846, he bought Puketutu Island and built a home there. But after he and his wife almost lost their lives in a boating accident when returning from Onehunga, he decided to resettle on the mainland, setting up practice early in 1847.

However, Purchas seemed to have a far more engaging and sympathetic manner than Weekes, and patients warmed to him quickly. Unfortunately Selwyn had forbidden Purchas to charge for any of his medical services. It was the root of a further conflict of principles set to last for the next 12 to 15 years ... and brought him into immediate unwanted and direct competition with Dr Weekes.

The Purchas-Te Wherowhero connection

Māori tribes in the areas south of the Auckland isthmus, and in the Waikato area, had hardly seen a Pākehā before the mid-1830s. Contact with Europeans developed quickly, however, particularly after the great chief Te Wherowhero and his Ngāti Mahuta people began trading from the Onehunga area in 1835 and the missionaries began their work. By this time Te Wherowhero was at the height of his power and probably the pre-eminent chief in New Zealand – after 20 years of war with Ngā Puhi from the north, Te Āti Awa from Taranaki, Ngāti Hāua and others.

But the Treaty of Waitangi was largely negotiated with the northern tribes, despite Te Wherowhero possessing the greatest chiefly mana in the land and Ngā Puhi being his traditional enemy. When it was finally signed, however, Te Wherowhero had already tired of war and was living across the Manukau Harbour at Awhitu, on its western shores. Although unwilling to sign the Treaty himself, he nevertheless had developed a certain empathy with the European and missionary messages of conciliation and development; was hopeful of better living conditions for his people via greater trade; and was looking to take advantage of the benefits which European goods, schools and the growth of the Māori language could bring. He had even allowed his daughter, Tiria, to marry an early European settler and trader. This son-in-law had built up a large flax, timber, food and arms business in the 1830s using predominantly Māori labour and was later based at Ngāti Mahuta headquarters near Ngāruawāhia.[59]

Te Wherowhero also realised early, says historian Vincent O'Malley, "that Christianity was the passport for Māori literacy". It was this period – the late 1830s and early 1840s – which probably saw the peak of Māori enthusiasm for the missionary message. After this "the two worlds became increasingly differentiated by language, culture, race, politics and land conflict"[60] and missionary influence slowly declined.

Te Wherowhero had then come to live even closer to the new capital – on land near Onehunga, at Mangere,[61] offered to him as a gift by Ngāti Whātua chief Āpihai Te Kawau when his own tribe began moving back to their ancestral land on the shores of the Waitematā. Te Kawau also wanted "a good relationship with Waikato tribes in the new order which now existed

---

59 M King, *The Penguin History of New Zealand*, p 126.
60 A K Davidson (ed), *A Controversial Churchman*.
61 At least one early historian noted that the name "Mangere", meaning "lazy", was given to the area by Government surveyor Ligar. Māori immediately argued against it, preferring the name Queenstown after Queen Victoria. E Soar, *Old Onehunga – History of St Peters*, p 54.

..."[62] and the added protection Te Wherowhero offered against their mutual adversary in the north, Ngā Puhi.

Governor FitzRoy even built a house in Auckland's Domain for Te Wherowhero and he subsequently became heavily involved in many of the arguments and discussions about land issues arising out of the Treaty signing. He was to move between this humble raupō home in the Domain, known as Pukekawa, and a whare at Mangere for the next six or seven years ... looking to consolidate the relationship with Grey's officials and often helping to settle tiresome disputes involving land titles, law and order issues, and altercations with settlers.

He took every opportunity to reassert his mana, including the organisation of the "great Remuera feast" or hākari, in May 1844, inviting iwi from all over Auckland, Hauraki and the Waikato. "Te Wherowhero's status as guardian and protector of Auckland was well and truly confirmed as a result ... Auckland's fate now rested in his hands as the northern war broke out ... an attack on Auckland would be an attack on Te Wherowhero."[63]

So it was inevitable when Purchas first arrived in Onehunga and started moving about his parochial district that he would quickly come into close contact with Te Wherowhero's Ngāti Mahuta people, their chiefs such as the rangatira's cousin Tāmati Ngāpora, and eventually Te Wherowhero himself, his niece Te Paea and her father Kati Takiwaru. The Ngāti Mahuta had also welcomed the CMS mission at Taupiri which Purchas began to visit regularly, usually to stand in for Benjamin Ashwell when he was away.[64] On his trips to the mission – often just to swap duties with Ashwell for a few days while the latter spent some time in town – he would also visit Māori villages from Ōtāwhao (near today's Te Awamutu) to the Waikato Heads or Port Waikato (Maraetai).

Living expenses

In between the regular walks to Mauku and beyond, taking services in Onehunga and Epsom, school classes in the little wooden schoolroom and working on his house ... when Purchas returned to Purewa, he continued to be dismayed at the 'unease' there. He was also having difficulty making ends meet on the meagre deacon's stipend – meant to be £90 per annum but usually far

---

62   V O'Malley, *The Great War for New Zealand*, p 47.
63   Loc. cit.
64   Ashwell was not ordained deacon until after Purchas in late 1848, by which time he had been a catechist at Taupiri for six years.

less. He took the matter up with Selwyn on two or three occasions, suggesting it could be supplemented by his medical services, but without success or satisfaction. Selwyn would not compromise. He had bigger headaches at this time, not just in trying to retain senior students for his schools, but in finding and paying people to teach them.

The junior school for local children, mostly the offspring of college staff, was run initially by J D Dale, a theology student training for the ministry – apparently a gloomy individual with a bad temper. Jane Williams wrote of him that "his bad temper resulted in such free use of the cane that his supply was soon exhausted. He then used equally supple quince sticks." When Dale resigned less than a year later and left St John's to join the Roman Catholics, the school was in danger of closing down. It was left to Olivia Purchas and Sarah Selwyn, both pregnant at the time, to step in and take over the classes. Despite all their efforts, it seems the school was later left to just fade away.

While Purchas was relieved not to be in the middle of such problems, he was still decidedly unhappy about the situation, especially for Olivia's sake, let alone being earbashed by all and sundry whenever he walked back into the college. He was still the hospital doctor and surgeon at Purewa and his time there was usually fully occupied by his medical and musical duties. The CMS central committee had also resolved that their group would have only one doctor, specifying Dr Purchas, and would allow each missionary £10 per annum for "medical attendance and advice" – money which went to hospital maintenance, not Purchas himself.

As a result of his new position in charge of the large Onehunga parochial district, his musical responsibilities, and his architectural and building prowess, there was now plenty of opportunity for everyone to discuss their particular problems and seek his counsel. When Selwyn returned to Purewa from his own travels around the country one day in mid-November 1848, it seems Purchas made a conscious decision to set aside any qualms and attempt to broach various subjects with him on everyone's behalf.

William Williams noted in his journal at the time – a couple of days after arriving in Auckland from Hawkes Bay – that "Purchas walked in on his way from Onehunga … he has been in hot water with his superior and carrying matters to some length". Purchas told Williams that he found it "convenient to have the time occupied in a five-mile walk for rumination".[65] His rumination this time was on how best to approach Selwyn on a number of issues.

One of those issues might have been the possible discovery by Selwyn of

65   F Porter (ed), p 505.

a recent land acquisition by Purchas – although from the Government, not Māori. Just before this meeting, in September 1848, he acquired about 15 small lots of rural land which today is the corner of Mt Eden Rd and Watling Street.[66] He bought them from the Registrar of the Supreme Court very cheaply – maybe just £1 an acre or even less. He onsold four lots immediately, followed by another six the next year and the rest between 1850 and 1852. He retained one small lot almost certainly for his own or his children's future. He still owned this lot at his death.

If Selwyn had known of such a transaction, it certainly would have been a major issue between them. But it also happened to be the start of a lifetime of experience and expertise in land purchase and disposal – mostly, it must be emphasised, in various trustee roles on behalf of estates he was subsequently called on to manage. When the opportunity arose later, however, he would buy more land on his own and Olivia's account, mostly as a means of providing for his own family.

We don't know what was discussed between the two at that November meeting at St John's. Whatever was said, however, would be forgotten or completely overshadowed a couple of months later when matters came rapidly to another head. Selwyn issued a proclamation to everyone at Purewa that his capital was almost depleted, the college's financial state was grim and that, in future, "all errors and deficiencies arising from neglect or incorrectness in the management of the college business, will be charged against the fund out of which the salaries will be paid". Even the normally mild-mannered Purchas was angry and other students and staff were "all in a commotion".

Responding, he thought, to Selwyn's invitation for some discussion on the matter, Purchas decided to put his objections to such a plan in writing and wrote up a draft. This original protest must have been a strong one since another letter – described by student Thomas Smith as "less contentious" – was then substituted in its place, signed by virtually everyone at St John's and handed to Selwyn. Apparently it innocuously asked the Bishop how the signatories might raise the issues with him. But, unhappy with this softer approach, Purchas, Smith and fellow student Frank Gould then went ahead and again wrote separate letters specifically explaining their issues, which mainly concerned their own very difficult financial situations.

Unfortunately, Selwyn took immediate offence and refused to soften his stance. His dictatorial management style meant he remained "determined to follow his own course", as William Williams put it, and take the consequences.

---

66   Deed 1675 25/9/1848 Reg 2D1139, L Cocks records.

It must have been most upsetting for Olivia – and Sarah also. Williams described a few days later, when Purchas had gone back to Onehunga, how he visited Olivia in her home upstairs above the hospital for tea and "heard her account of collisions". These were tense times. Smith later described Purchas, possibly a little too floridly, "as a red-hot radical who had lots of rows with the Bishop."[67] In spite of all the fuss, protest and consternation, a showdown was again averted. But the issues remained unresolved – for the meantime.

Purchas the chemist

For his own little school next to the new church in Onehunga, Purchas hired 49-year-old Scot Robert Lusk and a young assistant Sophia Bates, daughter of a Fencible corporal, to teach the local children on his behalf – despite Selwyn's rule that deacons themselves must teach at least three hours a day. But Lusk was soon also complaining that the trifling fees paid by the Fencible families and other settlers did not cover his salary and expenses. Within a year he had resigned. To Purchas's relief, the admirable Miss Bates stepped up to the plate and became the sole teacher for the next seven years. She may, perhaps, have been one of the very first 'sole-charge' female teacher principals in New Zealand.

Amidst all this hullabaloo – and while continuing his Greek studies, learning Māori, writing sermons and conducting services, taking music classes, designing and building a church and a house, travelling miles by river and harbour, and providing free medical services to Māori and settlers alike – Purchas's scientific interests had also come to the fore. What happened next was his first main entry in an extraordinary catalogue of scientific achievement, which he would expand and consolidate in the next 50 years of his life.

His love of botany and horticulture, and an interest in building materials arising from his study of New Zealand timbers for use in his church and house designs, led him to closer examination of the native puriri tree in particular. Over the winter of 1848 he became fascinated with the peculiar bark and chemical makeup of the puriri. He began tests – 26 different experiments in all – with what he thought might prove to be a useful substance and product from the puriri bark.

That new product was a dye. Over several months he concentrated production of various different-coloured dyes via his own secret process, which included treating the bark with chemicals such as "potash or the sulphate of lime". Further experimentation produced other colours particularly favoured by Māori (black, red and crimson), all "easily worked and fast colours".

Purchas submitted his dyed samples of plain calico cloth or canvas to the newly formed New Zealand Advancement Society for their consideration. The samples were all "ticketed with details, examined by members of the society and much admired". Newspaper coverage of the society's following meeting in Port Nicholson concluded by proclaiming him to be "one of the best chemists in the colony".[68] As Christmas approached, the accolade would certainly have given him much quiet satisfaction after a very busy and somewhat turbulent year.

Within four or five weeks of this success, his second child, Agnes Olivia, was born at St John's and christened in the chapel on February 2, 1849. Arthur and Olivia had also decided by now that they did not want to remain at Purewa one day longer than necessary. As soon as the baby was settled, and with their Onehunga house still 12 months or more from completion, the small Purchas family made a temporary move into accommodation in Epsom. The details of their residence here are unknown but Epsom at this time had an estimated population of only 150-200 people, some still accommodated in old raupō huts, others in smaller, but newer, timber dwellings.[69]

Most of the land had been divided into five- to 50-acre blocks, growing wheat, oats, barley and potatoes. And there were also residents who would become well known in Auckland – men like Dilworth, Greenwood, Potter and Willamson who, no doubt, were both willing and able to provide decent accommodation to the young couple helping at the local church. William Williams wrote about their move to Epsom that "it was a change he [Purchas] has long been wishing for … although you will then inquire who remains to take charge of the stone walls on the summit of the hill" – meaning St John's.

Apart from wanting to disentangle himself from the difficulties at Purewa, Purchas could now walk more easily and quickly to Onehunga from Epsom after first conducting the Sunday service and school there. He could do the same on Sunday afternoon at Onehunga, and then spend a day or two working on his house and attending to medical matters.

Once a month on a Wednesday, he would set off on his long walk to Mauku or Waiuku to hold services in various sawyers' huts before attending to the sick. Other weeks he would walk from Onehunga along the northern shores of the Manukau Harbour, past places like Little and Big Muddy Creek to Cornwallis. Here, at the various isolated huts and settlements of both Māori and European, he would also hold services and provide medical help.

For the moment at least – even though life must have been very tough for

68   Papers Past, *Nelson Examiner and New Zealand Chronicle*, Dec 16, 1848.
69   G Bush (ed), *The History of Epsom*, pp 20-21.

Olivia living much of the time on her own with two infants in probably a very small and basic dwelling – Purchas was very happy to be away from any further friction with the Bishop. Things on that front were still no better. William Williams wrote again: "Our poor bishop is in the midst of perplexities and will yet be more troubled unless he alters his course. Every individual clergyman in the country is against him ... our church is in a crippled state for want of men fit to carry on the work and of friends to support it ..."[70]

Meanwhile in Onehunga, two more Fencible ships had arrived (the *Berhampore* and the *Oriental*), with another 150 soldiers, plus wives and children, all ready to dress up and parade to St Peter's Church on Sundays. With their arrival, by the end of that year (1849), the Onehunga village population was recorded as 867 people, including nearly 100 other independent migrants and settlers, all busily engaged in fencing off their sections and working on their land. That land was fertile and their crops, like those in Epsom, were well received in the markets of Auckland. Onehunga was off to a promising start.

Ngāti Mahuta connection grows

The events up north in 1845 and the violence which had threatened to spill over into Auckland, had other serious effects on Māori-European relationships. Not only had the links between missionary and Māori been severely tested in the last couple of years, but also the flood of European immigrants was bringing new pressures to bear on a somewhat stressed Māori society.

New sicknesses like skin diseases, scarlet fever, influenza and typhoid were taking their toll. Intoxicating liquors were even more readily available, sold by unscrupulous Europeans to undiscerning Māori, often in exchange for crops, pigs or artefacts. The older Māori chiefs – whose traditional power bases and authority revolved around centuries-old tikanga and practice – were struggling with new problems among their people, particularly those younger Māori exposed to and tempted by some of the worst features of European society.

Te Wherowhero and his family within Ngāti Mahuta were just one of many tribal groups now extremely concerned at the decline of chiefly mana within Māoridom and the daily threats to their systems of law and order. The whole matter was still largely rooted in issues of landownership and disposal, and the fact that disputes over who actually held "customary ownership" of blocks of Māori land were so difficult to resolve when Europeans were involved and when not all Māori wanted to sell.

---

70   F Porter (ed), April 1849.

While the settler government of the day was theoretically in charge – with its developing legal system watched over by people like Selwyn's colleagues Sir William Martin and the colony's second attorney-general William Swainson – for Māori, the British system of justice was, for the most part, a completely new and often unintelligible and perplexing hotchpotch of ceremony, rules, speeches and punishment. It often made no sense to Māori, used to their own principles of customary law and order, developed and practised over the past 500 to 600 years. When it came to land, for example, Europeans then – and even today – found it very difficult to understand that, as far as Māori customary tradition was concerned, a man had no further right to enduring 'title' over any section of land, than he had over any section of the sky or the sea. The concept of 'permanent alienation' of land in large or small blocks remained a mystery to most Māori. For Europeans, their view of land was that every parcel was owned by someone as their private property to use or improve as they saw fit. The Māori concept, however, was that all land was "an indivisible communal inheritance to be named, known and cherished".[71]

In 1848 Tāmati Ngāpora wrote to Governor Grey about his and Ngāti Mahuta's great fears about the decline in chiefly authority and the impact such decline would have on their own tribal law and order systems, especially when it came to land. The letter made its way back via Grey to the desk of the secretary of state for the colonies in London, who took the matter seriously enough to suggest by return to the Governor, that chiefs simply be given the title to their tribal land and their own jurisdiction over any dispute.

Grey felt this would be a step too far. Besides, under the earlier 'pre-emption' rule, if Māori had wanted to sell land, they were required to do so first to the Government ... and Grey was well aware of the problems he would have again in establishing clear titles. But he did have another idea which he hoped would eventually lead to better understanding on both sides.

It involved capitalising again on Te Wherowhero's standing among Māori and the influential Waikato tribes. Grey's plan – which bore all his usual hallmarks of a wider agenda at play – was to have Te Wherowhero and senior chiefs reside closer to the capital and the European centre of influence. As a result, Grey reasoned, Māori could have more involvement in tribal disputes and problems over land matters – and also provide additional military protection for Auckland if events in the north got out of control.

Te Wherowhero previously had a whare on land near the Onehunga beach where he had lived for part of the year (usually in summer), to preserve mana

---

71   F Porter (ed), p 366.

or customary title over the area. This land had then been sold in the mid-1840s by other chiefs to Robert Forbes, whom Purchas had first got to know when he moved to Onehunga.

In April 1849, Te Wherowhero and more than 100 others of his tribe signed a new Mangere land agreement with Grey, similar to the deal made for the Fencibles. They were reallocated some 486 acres in Mangere on which about 70-75 families were to live – led by Ngāpora and eight other chiefs – with the same long-term rights of possession as those given to the Fencibles. Ostensibly it was justified as a friendly Māori militia settlement, on specially surveyed and allocated land at Ihumatao, linked to Onehunga across the short stretch of water today by the Mangere Bridge.[72]

Grey then asked Purchas – who he knew by now was very familiar with Te Wherowhero and Ngāpora, and who could also speak Māori – to supervise the relocation and let him and government officials know of any issues or difficulties that might arise. In what could be described as a 'semi-official' capacity, Purchas was to continue in this communication role for the next 15 years, right through the later birth of the Māori King movement and Te Wherowhero's eventual accession. Only in 1863 would the events that led to the Great War, launched by Grey and involving the entire Waikato, bring about an unavoidable interruption in that relationship.

Before long, Purchas was invited to take services in whare at Ihumatao for Ngāti Mahuta and other local Māori like Ngāti Tamaoho. After the services he would try to attend to some of their many and varied health needs. Māori children were then among the very first people he baptised in St Peter's after the church was finally opened. Ngāpora's first son, Tāmati, was also baptised in St Peter's by Purchas a couple of years later, reflecting another personal relationship which was to last for some 35 years.

It was at this time that Te Wherowhero first began calling Purchas "Rata (Doctor) Patiti". Various letters written by Te Wherowhero to Grey in 1850 refer to conversations between himself and Rata Patiti, in particular following the death of the chief's younger brother, Takiwaru. He mentions that Rata Patiti had told him Grey had gone to Wellington and if he had not been so distressed over the death of his brother, he would have gone to Wellington himself and visited Te Rauparaha with Grey.

Anxious at this time to build as much goodwill with Māori as possible, Grey asked Purchas to organise some "horses and a cart" for Te Wherowhero and his chiefs, authorised via a Purchas request to the Colonial Secretary.

---

72 The land at Ihumatao had previously been settled and farmed by Ngāti Whātua. Refer R C J Stone, *From Tamaki-Makau-Rau to Auckland.*

This was an expensive purchase in those days for Europeans and especially for Māori.[73] In another letter Te Wherowhero refers to Purchas having mentioned that Grey had also promised to get a plough for him.[74] Grey was obviously keen to establish a good relationship with the chief, which Purchas became instrumental in maintaining.

Over the next couple of months, while Purchas advised on and assisted in the rangatira's move – watched on by somewhat bemused European settlers and soldiers – businesses around the Onehunga waterfront and beach were developing quickly. In no time there were shops, warehouses and licensed accommodation, and, of course, the pub – a two-storey wooden building known as the Royal Hotel. This quickly became a makeshift government office because it had a large 'long room' with stage and auditorium big enough to accommodate 200 people. Here a diverse range of activities took place, including inquests, land discussions, public meetings and judicial hearings, all attracting officials from Auckland and curious spectators boosting the small local economy.

While Purchas regularly conducted services for Māori in the whare at Ihumatao or Mangere, special Māori occasions such as Ngāpora's family baptism and later his son's wedding, were conducted at St Peter's. Purchas took special care to ensure their inclusion on an equal footing, always under the suspicious gaze of the locals. But the Ngāti Mahuta settlement, and Tāmati Ngāpora in particular, had a strong commitment to the Christian message. With Purchas's encouragement, he took up a new role as an Anglican lay preacher and then assessor – helping the resident magistrates resolve matters within the local community. Ngāpora's other common interest with Purchas at the time was trying to control the spread and availability of alcohol, and the increasing problems both races were experiencing with it.

Then, after a few months eyeing the Pākehā church in Onehunga, Ngāpora asked Purchas if his people might have their own church at Mangere. Purchas offered to design one for them if the money could be found and land provided. Te Wherowhero did not take much persuading and carved off a three-acre site below the Mangere Mountain on which to build a church and a house for the priest. While Selwyn approved the idea in general, he was not ready to make it a priority and the plan was put on hold.

By now the Onehunga district population had swelled to about 1000 and Selwyn, no doubt, would have been hoping that more reasonable contributions to Purchas's stipend might have been forthcoming from the Sunday offerings – particularly since the locals were benefiting from his free medical services.

73   Purchas's receipt, given to the Colonial Secretary in 1849, is held in Archives New Zealand Title 1934.
74   AKL, Grey Special Collections, GNZMA 327/328.

This, however, was not to be. The Onehunga Fencible community of the time was generally of very poor means, unlike the typical English parish. Purchas's financial situation remained difficult.

Back at St John's, no improvement was in sight. The stand-off between Henry Williams and Selwyn continued, as did the missionary body's frustration over the Bishop's unwillingness to train or ordain enough Māori clergy. The fact that theological students, Māori and Pākehā, were still required to learn Latin and Greek as part of their training in the English church tradition, was also hugely perplexing to both missionaries and Māori families.

Relatively petty incidents, therefore, were blown up out of all proportion – such as one in 1849 involving Wiremu Tāmihana, the son of the great warrior Te Waharoa. Tāmihana was chief of the Ngāti Hāua, a man of great mana, and strong Christian beliefs … and, like Te Wherowhero, a supporter of Grey and the Government. He was also a keen pipe smoker and when he tried to enrol at St John's while smoking his pipe, he was bluntly told that smoking was prohibited at the college. He withdrew and returned to Matamata immediately.

CHAPTER 5

Making a Mark

At the end of that tumultuous decade, which had begun with the Treaty of Waitangi, Purchas received the news from England that his father, Robert, had died, aged 68. Although his passing would have yielded some form of financial legacy, the far more important inheritance for Purchas from his father, apart from a love of engineering, was a consuming passion for geology and minerals – first conceived in his time at Tintern and now to be exercised in the fields near the Taupiri mission station.

Coal had fuelled the Industrial Revolution in Britain, propelling it into an entirely new age of transport and economic development. The early settlers in New Zealand were aware of the urgent need to find their own viable local source of this wonder fuel. While it is recorded that the first European users of coal were whalers on the Otago coast, the first big discovery in New Zealand was made by Thomas Brunner on the West Coast in 1848.

Only weeks after Brunner's find, Purchas was on one of his trips south to Benjamin Ashwell's Taupiri mission, when he learned from some local Māori contacts of the presence of coal in the area. On a couple of subsequent visits, he began prospecting. On February 23, 1850, the editor of the Auckland newspaper, the *New Zealander*, broke the news the whole town had been waiting to hear.

"That coal exists in various parts of New Zealand has long been a fact … but we were scarcely prepared for such a gratifying disclosure of the great capabilities of the Waikato district in this respect, as will be found in the following communication with which we have just been favoured by the Rev A G Purchas, to whose ability and enterprising diligence in conducting the investigation, the public are indebted for the information …"[75]

Purchas had delivered a full report on his discovery late the previous night to the paper and the *New Zealander* published it in full with the assumption "that it will receive the attention to which it is so obviously entitled". A scoop

---

75   Papers Past, *New Zealander*, Feb 23, 1850.

was a scoop – even in those days!

Purchas described how he had found worthy seams of coal in four or five places along the banks of the Waikato. The first site he described was on land belonging to Te Wherowhero, about half a mile from the northern bank of the river and nearly opposite a little village called Kupakupa. He said there had been a large landslip many years ago which had uncovered the edge of a coal seam, but it was only recently that Māori had become aware of it. He also described finding fine specimens of kauri gum here. The other site, which proved to be a far better grade of coal, was on the south side of the river, called Papahorohoro, again on Ngāti Mahuta land.

Purchas reported that he had "separated" about half a ton of coal and he dropped off a couple of samples to the editor with his report. He called it superior to New South Wales coal, being "clean and perfectly free from sulphur" – and entirely suitable for domestic purposes and as fuel for steam boilers. A third site had also been examined, this one in the company of another chief as a guide, who Purchas said was the only person who knew its exact location.

He concluded his report by suggesting the mines could be worked with no machinery and the coal would be easily transportable being only a few hundred yards from the Waikato River, with access to the Manukau Harbour and Onehunga.

Thus our history records that 28-year-old Arthur Purchas was the first European to discover the great Huntly coalfields.[76] And it would by no means be his last scientific triumph. His outstanding work over the next 10 years, in a variety of scientific fields, would see him eventually being elevated into the top ranks of the local science community.

The Huntly coal discovery, however, took some years to gain traction. A furious debate immediately arose in Auckland about what should happen next, foreshadowing similar debates which still rage today. While there was little argument about the quality of the coal, there were many questions that needed to be answered. Who owned it? Did Māori understand its value? Would they sell the coal or the land, or both? Who should then own the asset – the Government, the city of Auckland or a private company? For his part, Purchas simply stood back and left them to it. In his profession at that time, he simply had to. Other events then overtook the debate. All this Huntly land was eventually confiscated by the Government after the later Waikato War, and was then allotted to British soldiers. It would be another 20 years before development and mining of the great Huntly coalfield finally began.

---

76   W E Clark, Background to Huntly, *Auckland-Waikato Historical Journal*, Sept 1988.

Purchas was encouraged a year later, probably by friends and acquaintances like Captain Haultain, to send samples of the new Waikato coal to London's Great Exhibition in 1851 – as part of New Zealand's modest display of about 40 items. The exhibition was organised by Prince Albert and housed in the Crystal Palace, a temporary structure erected in Hyde Park. As well as the coal specimens, Purchas also displayed some samples of iron ore and limestone.[77] Only a few years later, he was to discover another coalfield even closer to Auckland, sealing his reputation as one of the province's leading men of science.

Family tragedy

By the autumn of 1850, with discussion about Purchas's Huntly coal finds still buzzing around Auckland, Olivia was pregnant with their third child. Some of the settlers' general anxiety about possible Māori 'pushback' over the steady alienation of land was being partially offset by a vibrant social scene in the town. Its population was growing fast – heading towards 9000 and now larger than Wellington's – fuelled by a growing military presence with all the ancillary opportunities for employment and profit, notably food, horses, transport and administration.

The entire mood within Auckland at this time was considerably lighter and there were plenty of diversions for those looking to resume or replicate the more familiar aspects of English social life – levees, receptions, concerts, parades, and theatrical and musical events. Even at St John's, in spite of the ongoing financial worries, it seemed like some of the cares had eased with many references in letters and journals of the day indicating staff and students knew how to celebrate.

In April, Purchas was called on by Selwyn to assist at one of those celebrations, which happened to be Auckland society's wedding of the year. His role, however, was not as a priest but as a waiter, serving tables with other clergy including Thatcher. This was not an unusual request from Selwyn. As part of his 'egalitarian' approach, he had variously made use of friends like George Grey's wife, Lady Martin, his wife Sarah and the Williamses to wait on special guests at large social functions in his giant tent at Purewa. One such event had been a welcoming party for some 300 Fencible soldiers and their families.

This Easter occasion, however, involved two weddings. The main event was the marriage of Edward Eyre, appointed by Grey as Lieutenant Governor of New Munster (one of the two New Zealand provinces at the time, and

---

77   Refer Te Ara, Exhibitions and world's fairs.

which covered the entire South Island, Stewart Island and the bottom half of the North Island). His bride-to-be was Miss Adelaide Ormond, a recent and apparently somewhat reluctant arrival in New Zealand. Eyre was a dashing character, an intrepid explorer and pioneer of that vast tract of Australia west of Adelaide. He was a very wealthy man, having amassed a fortune from his sheep farming enterprises.

Miss Ormond seemed a little doubtful about the impending marriage, which prompted Selwyn to invite her to stay with him and Sarah at Purewa while she thought it over. Her doubts allayed, the wedding duly took place and involved some 200 guests who kept Purchas and Thatcher busy, scurrying back and forth between courses.

The other couple married at the same ceremony were Henry (Hēnare) Taratoa and a young Māori woman from George Kissling's native girls' school. Enjoying the same reception, they sat down at the other end of the wedding table chaperoned by Sarah Selwyn, who later complimented Purchas and co. for "ably performing the honours". Taratoa was a protégé of Henry Williams, after whom he was named, and both he and his wife were very familiar to Purchas from his music lessons.

A couple of weeks later on May 4, Olivia gave birth to another daughter, Mary, and at first all was well. She was baptised in the same month at St Andrew's in Epsom as Purchas and his helpers put the final touches on the family's new single-storey house in Onehunga in preparation for their move. Ironically, the street had just been named Selwyn St. Even so, it must have been an enormous relief when they finally moved in about June 1850.

Unfortunately that mix of relief and happiness was short-lived. Within weeks the baby became ill with a fever and rash. To his horror, Purchas soon realised it was diphtheria. There had been another outbreak of some size around Onehunga and in Auckland itself soon after the baby was born – and in those days there was no real cure. The baby Mary died with a badly ulcerated throat in the new Onehunga house in September and, at only five months old, was buried in the small cemetery next to St Peter's. It was the first family tragedy faced by Arthur and Olivia, but it would not be the last.

There are no family documents to shed any light on the Purchases' life at this time, but it could reasonably be assumed that Arthur curtailed any visits too far away from his church and medical duties in Onehunga and Epsom. He probably spent more time in the little wooden classroom down the road next door to his church. He also began the practice of holding a morning service every day of the week, immediately after his breakfast – the only church other than St John's at Purewa to do so. Although Selwyn had required the deacons in his chapelries to teach in the schools between 9 and 12 each morning, the sheer impracticality of such an order meant that, in normal times, Purchas could only fulfil a semi-supervisory role for the principal, Miss Bates, and hope that Selwyn would turn a bishop's blind eye.

References to the Purchases' household life do, however, exist in other journals and notebooks. They indicate that Purchas's routine, when home in Onehunga, was generally to meet his pupils in the mornings whenever possible, walk to Purewa in the afternoons and attend to hospital, church and music matters, and then walk home via Epsom to see more local patients there and in Onehunga in the evenings. He was always known as a brisk walker – he had to be, since there was no possibility of buying a horse. In those days a reasonable horse would cost between £40 and £50 – almost a year's income for Purchas at a time when his stipend was so often short-paid and unreliable.

It was also about this time that Purchas gained support and encouragement from a new priest in town – the gloriously named Vicesimus Lush,[78] who had taken charge of the Howick parish and, like Purchas, was struggling to meet his expenses. At least Selwyn had warned him beforehand that it might be tough. In a letter to Lush before he left England, Selwyn wrote: "My own income is altogether precarious … our laity are by no means rich nor willing to give even in proportion to their means … if you come to New Zealand, let it be to help me and not to lean upon me for help!"

By coincidence, an old friend of Lush's from Britain was the same Robert Lusk – the former Onehunga school headmaster – who by now was farming on the outskirts of the Onehunga district near Three Kings. Lush would often visit Lusk on his way to Epsom or Onehunga where he would take an occasional service in either church – deputising for Purchas when he was away. They would become good friends.

The Gundry connection

Late in October 1850, only a month after baby Mary's death, Lush was astonished at the sight which greeted him when he walked into the Purchas home. He was welcomed as usual by Olivia "with much kindness and hospitality". But in addition to the Purchas offspring, there were another five small children in the house – all clearly of mixed parentage – and three young Māori women helping with the domestic routines.

Lush soon learned the 'extras' were the children of Makareta Rautangi, the

---

78   Meaning 'twentieth' from Latin because he was the 20th child in his family.

daughter of the principal chief of Ngāi Tupoto from the Hokianga area. She had been living with an English settler there, William Gundry, who had bought 500 acres from Māori before moving to Auckland with his family when the capital was established on the Waitematā. Gundry was very well connected to senior figures within both northern Māori and European political circles – and also to many in Selwyn's church administration. Nevertheless, because he was unmarried and cohabiting with a Māori woman, life would have been difficult for him and his mixed parentage children in the centre of Auckland town.

Having built up considerable means and with a main address in Albert Street, Auckland where he had a chemist's shop, Gundry had also acquired some property in Onehunga. While there he attended St Peter's occasionally and soon got to know Purchas. A mutual interest in chemistry, and the fact that Purchas believed so strongly in education for Māori children, quickly led to Gundry becoming a trusted friend of the Purchas family. Olivia and Arthur very generously agreed to take Gundry's children into their new home and educate them alongside their own two children.

One of the Gundry children had even been christened Olivia, after her sponsor, Arthur's wife. Another Gundry child, six-year-old Arthur, soon displayed a rare talent for drawing. Purchas recognised it as being well above the ordinary. When he could, he gave him some home tuition before later introducing him to local artist Albin Martin.

A year or so later, Purchas agreed to marry William Gundry and Makareta Rautangi in his Onehunga church – even though their children were born "out of wedlock". A formal marriage therefore – although an unusual event for such couples and not particularly acceptable to most clergymen of the day – would have enabled them to move far more easily as a family within their own St Paul's parish and town community.

Meanwhile the young artist in the Gundry family progressed so rapidly that it wasn't long before Purchas felt compelled to introduce him to Auckland's other great artist of the day, John Kinder. Kinder and Purchas shepherded him through school and on to St John's where all were agreed that Gundry's talent was exceptional. It was arranged next, via contacts in London, for him to be enrolled at the Royal Academy of Art in 1863.

There, within a couple of years, he took high honours, not only exhibiting in the academy three times but also contributing some work to *Punch* magazine. Such was his fame that he was even asked by Queen Victoria to do a sketch of her in pencil. On its completion, she is said to have given him a signet ring with her crest on it.[79] Then, at the age of just 23, Arthur Gundry contracted tuberculosis and peritonitis, and died in Penzance where he is buried. Auckland's *Southern Cross* newspaper said: "His artistic talents were of a very high order and had he lived he would undoubtedly have attained great eminence in his profession." Visitors to the church of St Andrew's today can still see a memorial there to Arthur Gundry in the form of the baptismal font. Kinder had it made in London and shipped out to New Zealand when the original old church in which Purchas first served, was replaced in 1867.

The Purchas-Gundry connection, however, was far from over with the death of young Arthur. In fact it was just the beginning. For Purchas, the work and responsibilities which resulted from the friendship with Gundry were to keep him occupied for many years to come.

Network expands

Despite having been in Auckland himself for barely a year, Vicesimus Lush was also now very troubled by the situation at St John's, calling it "that refuge of the afflicted".[80] He appeared to have much in common with Purchas's own ideals and interests, and struggled even more with the same vexing issues of living expenses and the precarious stipend. Lush learned quickly of his new friend's medical reputation and soon came to rely on Purchas's medical services for himself and his large family. And he was forthright in praising his friend's abilities … "he being a deacon being considered by far the cleverest doctor in the colony". He once rode over from Howick to see Purchas while in great pain from a chronic abscess in a cheek which was impacting on his teeth. Purchas duly lanced it, extracted two teeth in the process and repaired the wound, to Lush's intense relief.

It wasn't only Purchas's medical expertise which impressed him. A couple of years later, Purchas visited Lush in Howick to check and dress an injured leg for him. After completing this and prescribing his next round of medicine, Purchas cleaned and tuned the Lush family piano, "taking it entirely to pieces and dusting it thoroughly. I need hardly add the instrument is infinitely better," Lush recorded.

Lush was one of the few clergy at the time to own a horse. He greatly enjoyed telling a story to illustrate the often significant difference in financial circumstances between Selwyn's men like himself and Purchas, and so many others including Māori, in the bustling capital at that time. He described

---

79 Gundry family documents.
80 A Drummond (ed), *The Auckland Journals of Vicesimus Lush*.

meeting a Māori on horseback speaking excellent English, who offered Lush £40 for his own horse. Lush turned down the offer but asked him where he kept his money. The Māori replied "in the bank". Lush asked him if he would be going to Australia to convert it to gold. "No," he said with a grin. "I bought two horses, a cart and a plough and I sowed 100 acres in wheat. I worked little and sent my corn to Sydney. The English worked very hard picking the gold which they sent me for my corn. So Pakehas work hard, I work little and I pocket the gold." He ended with a grin saying, "kapai, kapai – it's good!"

Purchas also began another lifelong friendship at this time with a 21-year-old English aristocrat, Robert Cecil. He was the second son of the Marquess of Salisbury and was destined for a life at the top echelons of British politics. After the obligatory Eton education, he was sent away in 1848 for a couple of years to serve on a Royal Navy frigate, the HMS *Havannah*, on station in New Zealand waters. On his first shore leave – and most likely armed with a note of introduction from Gladstone – he met up with Selwyn and others at St John's, including Purchas, with whom he immediately developed a strong rapport.

On regular occasions subsequently, Cecil would walk out from his ship to the Purchas home in Onehunga "to have a yarn and shakedown on a colonial sofa," which a later newspaper recorded "was all Purchas could offer him in those primitive days of early colonisation".[81] Cecil had a great interest in Anglicanism and events in the colonies, and clearly enjoyed conversing and learning all he could from an interesting character like Purchas.

A few years later, Cecil duly went into Parliament, succeeded his father as the 3rd Marquess of Salisbury, became a peer and rose to become foreign secretary before eventually succeeding Gladstone as Britain's Prime Minister. It was an office he would hold three times between 1885 and 1902. Purchas would catch up with him again much later in life.

While such interludes would certainly have brought Olivia and Arthur some respite from the grief of losing their baby daughter, Arthur's normal routine of travel and parochial work could not remain neglected for long. Early in November 1850 it was again time to visit the mission station at Taupiri to relieve Benjamin Ashwell for a few days. Just before leaving, Purchas happened to bump into two brothers, and recent immigrants, Francis and Harold Fenton. The pair were on the lookout for land and were keen to investigate the areas south along the Waikato River. Purchas invited them to accompany him on his trip to Taupiri, an offer they gratefully accepted. A letter which Harold Fenton later wrote to his mother described the trip in detail, giving a fascinating insight

---

81   Papers Past, *Observer*, Jan 11, 1896.

into the routine perils and hazards of those early days.[82]

Fenton began by reassuring his mother that "Mr Purchas, the clergyman of this parish, is one of the nicest men I ever met in my life!" He went on to say, "We started from Onehunga on a small vessel, which is kept at the expense of the Government, to Waiuku where we arrived at 2am. We waited until daylight and after having our breakfast in the 'bush' style, we collected our natives to carry our baggage ... before walking four miles to the Awaroa River where we hired a waka (canoe). ...

"We soon came to an immense forest which the river meandered through. I cannot describe to you the effect when first entering, fine trees that excel all that I have seen in England, beautiful birds of all descriptions. We went for 14-15 miles and then entered the Waikato and set sails of two native blankets bound with flax to a pole ... before coming to a village where we put in for paddles. Mr Purchas bought the paddles while we took our guns and shot two or three pigeons."

That night, the trio slept in a smoke-filled raupō hut in a pā with some of Purchas's Māori friends. By morning all three were seized with severe dysentery. "Mr Purchas and myself were not so bad as Frank and fortunately for us," Harold wrote, "Mr Purchas had studied medicine and so was able to give us some relief." They left at 8am and sailed all day up the Waikato River before finally landing at 9pm to stay in another Māori village ... rising again at 6am when Purchas conducted prayers with the natives.

"We decided to go on again immediately because Mr Purchas says if we don't get some medicine very soon, it will end very seriously," Fenton wrote. It took them until midnight to reach Taupiri where Purchas went up the riverbank to Ashwell's house to wake him. After some tea and food, the three were in better health by morning. Fenton described how Purchas went immediately after breakfast to "give the native school a lesson in singing and we were astonished to find them take parts so very nicely".

Purchas and the Fentons stayed there recovering for two days before setting off again for Ōtāwhao (Te Awamutu), where missionary John Morgan resided. They went as far as possible further up the river "near to Kihikihi before we had to walk back about 28 miles which we did in a day".

Fenton continued: "The natives wanted us very much to buy land there and settle amongst them but their character is no inducement for one to go and settle amongst them, they are very covetous and try to get all they can out of you ... the love of money is so strong rooted in them that I think it will be

---

82   ATL, MS3273.

two or three generations before they lose this vice."

The next day they returned to Taupiri. Francis Fenton remained in that area while Arthur and Harold started back for Onehunga, initially in a canoe. "We had some very hard walking through the bush after leaving the canoe but we reached Onehunga after walking about 60 miles in two days."

Fenton ended his long letter explaining how he had been introduced to the "first families" of Auckland by Purchas. "I spent the other night with Mrs Selwyn and several clergymen. The society is quite as good here as in England and much more hospitable. I'm much pleased with everybody."

Purchas had unknowingly performed a good deed on behalf of the colony. Francis (Frank) Dart Fenton, who was the same age as Purchas, and a "tall, aristocratic looking barrister and accomplished musician," soon came to the attention of George Grey. He appointed Fenton as a magistrate and later Secretary of the Native Department, and subsequently Chief Judge of the Native Land Court. The Purchas-Fenton friendship – which began out of an act of kindness in the forests and rivers of the Waikato – again proved significant later when both became separately embroiled in the events during and after the dreadful war in the Waikato.

Medicine, gold and water

Christmas 1850 came and went, and while money in the Purchas household remained extremely tight, happier times resumed with Olivia newly pregnant and weddings, baptisms and other events continuing apace in both Epsom and Onehunga. In fact such was the activity at Epsom, even the busy Purchas was struggling to stay on top of things there. A large part of the problem was that his medical practice – although completely informal and 'unofficial' – had expanded, particularly after the other Onehunga doctor, Henry Weekes, had left Onehunga for the Californian goldfields a year or so earlier.

Apart from always being available for routine general practice matters, Purchas was also the obstetrician in Onehunga – or, as he was known in those days, the 'accoucheur' or male midwife – on call day and night. Similarly, when accidents or poisonings occurred, as they did frequently, or any sudden or tragic death was reported, Purchas was called out like the 1850s equivalent of today's paramedic. And he would never refuse.

The Auckland population was now expanding faster than ever, to the great benefit of all new commercial enterprises, while military and government expenditure was also helping to create a new class of wealthy immigrants. For the capitalists and entrepreneurs in town – men such as John Logan Campbell and his partner Brown – the early 1850s were boom times. They made Campbell in particular, an extraordinarily wealthy man while Brown spent large sums of his own fortune on his pet projects, politics and his newspaper, the *Daily Southern Cross*. Even the phenomenon we know as 'urban sprawl' had begun to take effect with fern and scrub being turned into grass and crops, producing more wheat, potatoes, cheese, butter and oats. Breweries and pubs, flour mills and bakeries, sawmills, boatyards, brick kilns, retailers, leather goods manufacturers and carriage makers dotted the town landscape.

Māori were also enjoying the growing opportunities for trade. They built their own flour mills and also their own ships to replace the canoes that transported their goods, becoming increasingly competitive in the process. In fact Māori ships and mills soon became the new status symbols for iwi. The price of land rose accordingly, with some section prices in the town quadrupling in the space of five years. Mortgage money was fetching rates of 15% or more.[83]

Then the discovery of gold in New South Wales and Victoria resulted in another great surge of business activity and profit. With the Australian economy unable to meet the demand for food, goods and timber, new exporters in New Zealand stepped in to supply rope, bricks, timber, dairy products, potatoes and oats, profiting enormously along the way. Māori trade into Onehunga from the Waikato tribes was also booming, and included potatoes, onions, chickens, pigs, flax, timber, fish, maize, kumara and cabbage.

Enterprising Māori took advantage of the gold discoveries on both sides of the Tasman, not only as exporters of commodities but as diggers themselves. Lush gave a colourful description of how he met "half a dozen Maoris who had just returned from the Australian gold fields with £1000, swaggering around Auckland, dressed in the height of fashion with gold-headed canes in their hands, cigars in their mouths – a fine, handsome set of men who had also adopted the European custom of wearing a long beard".[84] Times were definitely a-changin'.

At St John's, however, and among the less affluent settler and Fencible communities in Onehunga, Howick, Otahuhu, Mt Eden, Mechanics Bay and Parnell, the situation was somewhat different. After the death of his daughter, Purchas became increasingly worried about the multiple risks to public health following the expansion of the economy and population. Dysentery and other enteric fevers were rife and had been a scourge in the towns for the past eight to 10 years. Every immigrant ship brought the risk of new outbreaks of measles, scarlet fever and tuberculosis. Queen St was an open sewer, and offal and human

83   R C J Stone, *Young Logan Campbell*, p 168.
84   A Drummond (ed), *The Auckland Journals of Vicesimus Lush*, p 135.

excrement littered the back streets. Everywhere the sights and smells were as bad as the back streets of any large Victorian city in England.

Purchas was still medical chief at St John's and, as in Onehunga, Epsom and his country areas, was dealing every day with adults and children suffering continuing bronchial, respiratory, stomach and skin infections. He could do nothing when George and Sarah Selwyn's only baby daughter also became afflicted and died in February 1851. But he was convinced he could do something about the cause of the problems. Purchas believed a ready supply of good clean water was fundamental to improving the poor state of public health.

Onehunga was better off than Auckland in this respect, with several discoveries of apparently endless supplies of clean, naturally filtered water from the very substantial Onehunga aquifer. This was water which drained down from the lava fields around Maungakiekie, often finding its way to the surface and thence to the Manukau Harbour. Purchas and others calculated that the water being 'wasted' in this fashion amounted to some eight million gallons a day!

The idea of supplying the entire town with clean water from this source – including Epsom, Onehunga, Auckland and Remuera – now began formulating in Purchas's mind, including the thought of making use of a crater-reservoir on Thomas Henry's farm around Maungakiekie, later to become One Tree Hill. He began discussing the possibility with others, in particular one of the city's more prominent and able engineers, James Stewart. Specifically, it was the height of the One Tree Hill land – nearly 200 metres above sea level at its peak, midway between Onehunga and Auckland – which Purchas saw as the perfect answer for the gravity-fed water pipeline he envisaged. He walked all around the area, choosing the lower crater of One Tree Hill as a likely reservoir.

For the next three or four years, however, his plan for Auckland's water supply remained a work in progress because for Purchas, other things were happening. Olivia had safely reached the final stage of her next confinement and their fourth child, Emily, was born in the Onehunga home that year of 1851.

But within days of this event, the daily newspapers' coverage of progress on the goldfields in Australia, California and down south – and even a new gold find on Waiheke Island – was suddenly bumped to the back pages by news of a different sort. It was a serious incident which reminded every European settler just how tenuous the relationship with Māori could be. Excited and inflamed by a wrongful arrest and insult to one of their chiefs by a government official, a large group of Ngāti Pāoa (Hauraki) iwi, said to be 250-300 in number, arrived in the Waitematā from various parts of the Firth of Thames. They were intent on making a major statement to the European authorities and demanding some form of redress. Rumours quickly spread of a likely attack on the town.

The warriors assembled near Waiheke in five or six large canoes and 14 or 15 smaller ones, and then paddled up the harbour before landing at Mechanics Bay in a furore of traditional war cries and haka. The bugles were sounded and Grey called out the 58th Regiment. Fencibles formed up on the Parnell slopes above the bay looking down on the scene below, while the artillery swung into readiness. The Royal Navy frigate HMS *Fly* came back up the harbour and trained its guns on the beach while angry exchanges began between Grey and the chiefs.

After a long day of intense argument and discussion, Grey gave the chiefs an ultimatum to withdraw while the action which had caused the initial problem was reviewed. Eventually the Māori accepted Grey's commitment to the review, dragged their canoes back into the receding tide and returned home. The matter was later settled satisfactorily but Māori had made their point. The European government might be in charge and the Hauraki tribes, at least, were prepared to accept Governor Grey as dispenser of justice fairly to all. But they also wanted him and his Pākehā officials to respect and take into account Māori protocol and tradition in applying the rules of British law and order equally and fairly.

Problems mount for Selwyn

Meanwhile at Purewa, Bishop Selwyn was pushing ahead quickly with the other crucial part of his 'master plan' – the establishment of a new constitution and governance structure for his New Zealand diocese. He still wanted it to be part of the English church but with a couple of key variations of ecclesiastical law. There had been a significant meeting on the subject the year before in Sydney between the Australian bishops and Selwyn had gone there with the support of powerful laymen like Governor Grey, Martin, Swainson and others, all pushing for the separate New Zealand church constitution.

Selwyn then set out his key proposals in letters to all his clergy. The main variation from the established English constitution, he explained, was to be a three-way division of control involving bishops, clergy and, most important, laypeople. Significantly, there was also discussion at this early stage about allowing women to have greater involvement in church matters and decisions.

Purchas attended all the various local meetings on this major constitutional topic, which kicked off in Auckland in May 1852[85]. Discussion continued for

---

85   Papers Past, *New Zealander*, May 8, 1852.

the next five years. At that very first meeting, he put aside any of his earlier differences with Selwyn by actually leading the debate and demonstrating his support. Purchas proposed that Selwyn's first clause (about having three "houses") should stand as is, since "he [Selwyn] had not introduced it without considering the question". Debate on the fine points of church and common law continued in Auckland and around New Zealand. At the Auckland meetings, newspaper reports of the day reveal that Purchas was in the thick of the discussions throughout.

In between times, most likely over cups of tea in various foyers, Purchas and his colleagues had been introduced by Selwyn to two new arrivals at the college. It seemed that the Bishop had finally acknowledged the long-standing teacher and management problems, and was confident that the two senior newcomers he had recruited from England would be able to resolve them. One was Charles Abraham, another Eton and Cambridge man, who was married to a cousin of Sarah Selwyn, while the other was the affable John Lloyd. Abraham had been called in as college principal to "put some of that Eton spirit into the young men at St John's". Selwyn had written to his brother-in-law many months earlier, in September 1850, about his hopes of soon having Abraham and Lloyd's help to reform the college, saying he would now be able "to leave it with comfort and satisfaction in their hands".

No one was to know it yet but neither comfort nor satisfaction was heading Selwyn's way. Purchas and his colleagues, however, would probably have been positive and pleased that, finally, things at the college might be changing for the better. Selwyn had even expressed the desire that, with Abraham in charge, he might be able to spend more time in the southern settlements, and on his mission activities. As soon as Abraham and Lloyd had settled in, Selwyn went off to do just that.

Within months young Melanesian students were being invited to St John's, but they really only added to the ever-growing financial burden. Despite the best endeavours, nothing much changed. The determined and single-minded bishop was still having to provide money for his beloved college out of his own salary. Even with new men in charge, William Williams wrote that it seemed to him "as if the whole fabric is crumbling to the dust".

But Selwyn's building programme could not be held back. He returned from one of his trips with word that he was urgently commissioning a church for Otahuhu and its new Fencible community. No definitive record exists of who the specific architect was for this project. However, it seems almost certainly to have been Purchas – based on the particular features and style later apparent in churches confirmed as having come from the Purchas drawing board. The new building was prefabricated again at Purewa and assembled by Fencibles on the site of the present cemetery in Otahuhu's Church St in 1851.[86]

Ten years later, however, this church burnt to the ground – although by then it was deemed too small to cater for the needs of Otahuhu's growing militia community. Purchas was asked to draw up new plans for a replacement church, as referenced again by Professor Cyril Knight. Remarkably this second Otahuhu church is still in use today, having been shifted to a new site in Mangere East in 1928 after it had also become too small for the Otahuhu community.

College crisis

Just before Christmas 1852, less than 12 months after the Otahuhu Fencibles had opened their first church – and Purchas, the architect, doctor, builder, priest and music teacher had perhaps been reflecting on his usual hectic calendar of daily activities – came news of shocking events at St John's, which rocked the Auckland establishment.

It was the unfortunate newcomer John Lloyd who apparently first learned of a "storm of evil" involving homosexual practices among staff and students at St John's. It had apparently begun much earlier among English students but later included some Māori. Once confirmed, it was Lloyd's sad duty to inform Abraham and then Selwyn himself, just as he was about to set sail on New Year's Day for Porirua and the South Island.

All students at the college were immediately suspended. The college council was called together and began a disciplinary hearing. Some students who wanted to leave and who had not been implicated were given clearing testimonials. In April, when all the talk had ended, and apparently with little retaliation or heavy accusation, Selwyn simply took the opportunity to disband his college and instruct that its affairs be wound up. The sheer weight of such accusations and proof was too much for him to take. Lush recorded the happenings matter-of-factly in his diary, saying only that he had learnt via a conversation with Purchas that "the place was going to be broken up ... it has for some time past struck me as a failure".

Sadly for them, George and Sarah Selwyn moved out and never lived at Purewa again. The steadfastly loyal Charles Abraham, still happy to remain

---

86   Heritage architect Peter Sheppard attributes it to Purchas in his 1993 article for *Historic Places* magazine. The only photo known to exist of this first Holy Trinity Church in Otahuhu is in the Auckland Museum Library's 'Richardson Collection'. It shows the same buttresses, entry porch and familiar tower used in later Purchas-Selwyn designs.

in New Zealand and help Selwyn, was made an archdeacon and given the authority to oversee the large Purewa 'estate', its farm and buildings. Lloyd took on a new role as a parish priest in Auckland town.

Historical opinion since has mostly regarded the scandal as being the straw that broke the camel's back. The education system Selwyn tried to implement had failed long before this sordid event finally marked the school's demise. As Davidson put it, Selwyn's larger college picture was a "bold but unsuccessful attempt to bring together the CMS, the Maori constituency and the needs of the colonial church into one institution" – and it had not worked.[87]

The closure of St Johns in early 1853 – or *Bishop's Auckland* as it was referred to – clearly brought about a "line of separation" for men like Purchas and the rest of the missionary group and clergy. The college never became the cathedral institution Selwyn had wished for. His influence in the daily lives of his priests diminished because he could no longer oversee so tightly the theological direction, the supervision of so many impractical ideas, the training and ordination of Māori students, or even the running and production of the Purewa farm. This was now left to the faithful Abraham who, for the next six or seven years, would still invite Melanesian students to Purewa each summer to study and be trained.

As far as Purchas was concerned, and also his colleagues, it seems individual relationships with Selwyn mostly changed for the better from this point. The stipend issue certainly remained but Purchas just had to accept and understand better that Selwyn was simply unable to do anything about it – at least not until the endowment programme he had been working on could provide an adequate income stream. 1852 records show that in that year, a salary of £65 was approved for Purchas in the "general estimate" or church budget, compared with £100 for his friend and fully ordained priest Vicesimus Lush.[88] The paltry size of such stipends could easily be seen when compared with the cost at that time of a horse and cart. At around £100 it was known then as the "rich man's toy" and for good reason!

One compromise the Bishop and his church funds committee did eventually make, however, was the offer of a cash equivalent for produce or labour given by inhabitants of any parochial district in support of their priest or schoolmaster. They also tried to encourage greater offerings at the time of the Easter harvest.

Unjust as it may have seemed to him, Purchas realised that if he was to play any productive long-term role in the settler or Māori communities from

---

87   A K Davidson (ed), *A Controversial Churchman*.
88   AAA – *St Peter's/St John's Notebook*.

now on, he would have to ensure there would be no further confrontation with Selwyn. Both seemed plainly to have taken stock and almost separately moved on at this time. The same could be said for most of Purchas's colleagues who had themselves been tangling on occasion with the Bishop for the last four or five years.

It appears that Purchas determined at this time not to allow himself to be buried by the non-resolution of his stipend issue. Possibly he reasoned that his five- or six-year 'contretemps' with Selwyn on the matter, if left to run, could end up ruining an otherwise happy and productive career … or at least cause a serious upset as exemplified by the tribulations suffered by Henry Williams. Purchas did not want to allow the issue to get that far, out of respect for Selwyn's office and perhaps also Olivia's and his own friendship with Sarah Selwyn. As far as his future finances were concerned, he simply decided that, thenceforth, he would take matters into his own hands and take whatever steps were necessary to organise a more permanent solution for himself and his family in Onehunga.

At the end of 1852, the name of A G Purchas appears once again on land documents, this time as owner of three separate lots in Onehunga.[89] How he paid for them or exactly why he bought them is not known – although, as before, it is most unlikely to have been a case of straight speculation and profit. The land was relatively cheap at the time and such a purchase may well have been possible with a 10% deposit – using part of an earlier inheritance from his father and via an easily available local mortgage or loan. Most likely his reasons for such an investment were still to do with making long-term provision for his growing family and thoughts of a full-time medical career if things in the church did not work out.

In February 1853, while Selwyn and Abraham were tidying up the mess at St John's, Purchas decided to call a meeting of the senior Church of England residents of Onehunga in his little schoolroom. Seventeen of its leading citizens turned up. Purchas explained his financial situation to them, basically saying that if they wanted him to remain their local priest, the time had come to conclude some formal arrangement with regards to the church finances, its school and the cemetery he had established for them. After some positive discussion, those present agreed to establish a parochial trust board to run the church, cemetery and school, and to get its finances, including the priest's stipend, on a firm footing – initially under the care of four new, competent trustees. It had now been five years since the church was built and Purchas's

---

89   Onehunga Fencible & Historical Society records – Lots 5, 6 and 9 on Allotment 10 of Section 13 of the Town of Onehunga Plan 352, granted 24/12/1852 under the hand of Henry Wynyard.

endeavours in the Onehunga community no doubt stood him in very good stead. Not only did he have a growing reputation as a community and civic leader, but also as a doctor, scientist, architect and teacher. The Onehunga gentry listened to his plans and, persuaded by his eloquence, agreed to do all they could to secure the Purchas church and school for the long term.

Captain John Symonds[90] – younger brother of the unfortunate Cornwallis Symonds, whose family name was later given to Symonds St in Auckland and Onehunga – together with the former schoolteacher Robert Lusk, were two of the four new trust board appointees. The meeting also agreed, with the backing of Fencible commander Major Kenny, that the three local Fencible divisions would make monthly subscriptions from now on to the church trust board. Finally, a new set of school fees was published – 9d a week for children writing on paper and 6d a week for those who used chalkboards.

Purchas no doubt would have returned home to Olivia that day with some far more positive news about the likelihood of at last receiving a 'living wage'. While the older Gundry children were no longer with them, except for Olivia and Helen, who remained as household help, there were three young Purchas children to feed – Arthur Jnr, Agnes and Emily. Olivia was also pregnant again, with their fifth child – another daughter to be named Elizabeth, or Lizzie, when she arrived a few weeks later in March.

It seems the birth of this child – combined with the establishment of the trust board and hopes for a more positive relationship with the Bishop – galvanised the 32-year-old Purchas as he entered a period of unbelievable activity on several new fronts. With his striking good looks and a commanding but kindly 'presence,' he was already a person of some authority in the town. The only photograph of him at this time reveals a young man with rugged features and dark beard, combined with a determined gaze.

Within the space of the next six or seven years, as Purchas took control of his career and developed his many divergent interests, he came to be widely identified as much more than simply Onehunga's parish priest. His drive and exceptional talents were to bring him recognition as one of the most versatile and accomplished citizens in Auckland.

---

90   Another interesting friend of Arthur Purchas, John Symonds was earlier responsible for purchasing much land from Māori for the Government and later became a private secretary to Governor Grey.

CHAPTER 6

Civic Contributions

By 1853 the population of Auckland, between the Waitematā and Manukau harbours, had grown to about 10,000 people[91] – some 10% of whom lived in Onehunga and its surrounds. Another eventful year for Purchas on a domestic level was more than matched by the public drama following the introduction of the first stage of greater representative government for the colony. The New Zealand Constitution Act of 1852 had divided the colony into six provinces, overseen by a general assembly and a Legislative Council, requiring leaders, superintendents and representatives to be elected and new bureaucracies to be established. Only individual property owners or leaseholders could vote, which of course excluded all but a tiny minority of Māori.

For the next four years, the many various elections saw Auckland, in particular, consumed by political squabbling, shouting and scandal – or as historian Stone called it, "an intemperate political spirit which seemed to intoxicate the whole community". The problems which Selwyn and his men in Auckland had been grappling with became insignificant, given the political bitterness and denunciation being splashed across the news-sheets almost every day.

For the last year or so, in between everything else, Purchas had quietly renewed his friendship with the up-and- coming Francis Dart Fenton. The pair had been cajoled into helping with teaching duties at Robert Maunsell's mission at Port Waikato, where he had established a native boarding school. Fenton had purchased his first parcel of land further up the river and, when asked by Purchas, gladly agreed to help out at the school. They were also joined by the young James W Stack who Purchas had befriended at St John's when Stack's father had become seriously mentally ill.

When Purchas returned home to Onehunga after two or three days midweek at Port Waikato – taking that same strenuous route by foot and canoe via Mauku and Waiuku, and then by government vessel across the Manukau

---

91   R C J Stone, *Young Logan Campbell*, p 204.

– there was little time for rest. He was always immediately on call as a doctor, and was often kept busy with family matters. And he also had an increasing number of additional duties to attend to, much of them stemming from the contacts made after the formation of the trust board.

One such role was as surveying advisor and advocate for the construction or upgrade of two local roads. The first involved major improvements to the road linking Onehunga to Auckland town, via today's south Penrose area and Epsom – a route which he had regularly walked over the previous five or six years.

The other far more difficult project was the construction of an entirely new road running from Onehunga eastwards to join up with the Great South Rd – today's Church St. The significance of this road was to become very apparent a few years later as a strategic part of the Government's plans for easier access by troops from the Auckland military camps into Drury and the Waikato heartland. Probably completely unaware at that stage of this longer-term plan, many of the local Onehunga townspeople, including Purchas, donated money towards its construction.

More pressing than these matters, however, was the controversial topic being raised more and more frequently in his regular contacts with Te Wherowhero, his niece Te Paea, Ngāpora and other Ngāti Mahuta chiefs in their settlement at Mangere – that of land. In the bigger picture of Māori-European relationships – amid all the political electioneering and bickering that continued in the settler community – not only had the issues of land sale, exchange and alienation not been solved, but they were also taking a worrying new turn. In his conversations with these Māori leaders – before and after his regular church services and consultations around Mangere and Ihumatao – Purchas became privy to the unease and ill feeling now spreading quickly among many of the powerful Waikato and Hauraki tribes regarding the Māori-Pākehā relationship in general and land alienation in particular.

While the growth and speculation led by firms like Brown & Campbell in the Auckland province resulted in relatively good economic times for Māori, the benefits were offset to a large degree by regular outbreaks of disease, drinking and gambling, lawlessness and confrontation, often between chiefs of the same iwi or hapū. It was the key gestation time leading to the birth of the Māori King movement or Kīngitanga, which in its infancy would not only involve Purchas so heavily, but would define the course of later New Zealand history.

The focus for the issue of land loss at this particular time was mostly centred on the Taranaki area. More and more settlers had been arriving there, with many promised blocks of land in advance, the ownership of which was

much in question. Unbeknown to them, such land had often been purchased
from chiefs already in dispute with other hapū over who held customary rights
of ownership. The situation was further exacerbated when European settlers
tried to acquire seemingly abandoned or unused blocks of Māori land from
owners often settled hundreds of miles away, but who refused to sell. It was
the start of the so-called "wastelands" injustice, which would eventually rear
its ugly head some 10 years later.

For Selwyn and many of the missionary group, the issue of land repeatedly
came under the microscope in their relationships with their many long-term,
trusted Māori leaders and friends – men like Wiremu Tāmihana, Te Hāpuku
of Ngāti Kahungunu and others, who forcefully expressed their concerns to
the missionaries at every opportunity. These were often the same men who
had been so active in promoting the missionary and Selwyn's messages of
conciliation, peace and respect for government and Christian values, and who
for the most part were trusting supporters of the Treaty.

Selwyn meanwhile still had his own nagging issues to resolve at this
time – notably Henry Williams's five-year break with the CMS and the
overriding need to restore some credibility with the public generally regarding
the missionary church's land ownership and policies. In the north and on the
east coast – where the Williams brothers had built such strong relationships
with their Māori communities – real fear was building that the European

St Peter's c1855-6 before Arthur Purchas dismantled its prominent spire and relocated it by the
transept to stop it moving in the strong south-west winds and squalls.
AUCKLAND LIBRARIES HERITAGE COLLECTIONS 957-192-1

St Peter's in 1858, with the spire in its new position, clearly illustrating the job entailed in Purchas's dismantling and re-erection – a job he supervised and carried out largely by himself with the help of a few Onehunga locals.

AUCKLAND MUSEUM IMAGES PH NEG C11407

domination and relentless advance on land could even result in the eventual extinction of all things Māori.

The closure of St John's gave Selwyn the opportunity to rearrange his agenda, and he next confirmed plans for a round of ordinations starting in May with the colony's first Māori deacon, Rota Waitoa. Waitoa's elevation, with all the mana such an appointment brought him, was long overdue. Then, as if to underline that changes were in the wind, Selwyn advised that he would be leaving in June for Australia – to consult with church leaders there about his constitutional plans – but would be back well before the end of the year. Following this, he announced further ordinations would be held, including that of Arthur Purchas, this time as a priest. Then he would take a year's furlough in England and see what he could do about reinstating Henry Williams.

Events were moving quickly for Purchas. Learning of his imminent promotion, he immediately took the opportunity to ask Selwyn to relieve him of his responsibility for the Epsom parish, since he was simply unable to perform all the duties now required of him there as well. Selwyn agreed.

When he got back to Onehunga, however, his new trustees had some slightly disconcerting news. Someone had discovered that the four main posts supporting the church tower were moving slightly and the tower itself was showing signs of instability in the strong south-westerlies which occasionally tore across the Manukau Harbour. The tower and its spire were located in the middle of the church and while such positioning may have been satisfactory in the earlier and smaller Selwyn designs, on the much larger Onehunga building it was clear to Purchas that different forces were at play.

He decided fairly quickly that some major redesign would be necessary and that if the tower could not be braced well enough, it would have to be shifted or removed in its entirety. Meantime, he assured his trustees of its safety by attaching some additional temporary supports and then set about designing a more permanent fix.

At the same time, he drew up plans for a new drystone wall for the church boundary and asked the trust board to formalise the new cemetery next door with the appointment of a permanent sexton. Just a few weeks later Olivia greeted her husband with the news that Dr Henry Weekes had returned to Onehunga from the Californian goldfields and was apparently reopening his medical practice a few streets away – and with a new list of consultation charges. Purchas had little time to worry about this. In between his continuing visits to Mauku and the Māori community at Ihumatao, he remained in constant demand to conduct weddings, baptisms and funerals. The original church registers show he had officiated at no less than 181 christenings and 20 weddings at St Peter's since the church opened – plus many more at the churches and chapels in Epsom, Purewa, Remuera and in Auckland. As Selwyn's music precentor, he continued to be in charge of organising the church music and choirs at all the main public events in Auckland.

Purchas had also taken a leading hand at the regular monthly archdeaconry meetings at Purewa, called by Abraham, where Auckland's shocking record of "drunkenness and immorality" was high on the agenda. When asked next by his friend Tāmati Ngāpora if he could do anything for Māori – specifically, curbing the flow of liquor that was having such a detrimental effect on them as well – Purchas decided to take the bull by the horns. He set up and led a campaign with his Auckland colleagues to petition the local magistrates' bench to impose restrictions on outlets selling "ardent spirits", except for medicinal purposes.

A couple of meetings later and this campaign had also attracted the attention of many other worried leading citizens including solicitor Thomas Russell and the editor of the *Daily Southern Cross*. A public meeting was called in the new Mechanics Institute building in Shortland St, which was addressed by Purchas. Elected to head a new public committee tasked with finding some answers, he was to spend the next several years organising petitions and advocating possible solutions to the problem by talking to various provincial council members, political figures and friends.

Ordination at last

Selwyn returned from his visit to Australia and his Pacific missionary diocese, and plans were made for Purchas's ordination the Sunday before Christmas 1853 in St Paul's in Auckland town. At the same time, preparations were being made not only for Selwyn's departure to England immediately after the ceremony, but also for the large public farewell to Governor Grey. His first term was ending even though no replacement had yet been found.

Purchas would have been completely unaware that Selwyn intended to use his ordination service to provide a detailed summary of his work in New Zealand since arriving way back in 1842. For Selwyn it was a key opportunity and perfect timing. St Paul's was crowded when the service began at 11am on Sunday, December 18. The newspapers reported that "the ceremonial was an unusually impressive one and St Paul's was crowded to excess in every quarter".

All the town's leading citizens were present, together with senior Māori figures such as Tāmati Wāka Nene. He also spoke, paying tribute to Selwyn, "his faithful and generous ally". Selwyn's address showcased his substantial oratorical skills. He talked of "the great war canoe of the savage which had sped on its career of death, desolation and cannibalism … down to its present period when peaceful industry and Christian fellowship are uniting the native and European races in working out the happy destiny of both". It was an impressive event, even if the messages conveyed may have seemed a little too glowing for those in the congregation, including Purchas, extremely conscious of the fast-developing Māori discontent.

Within a couple of weeks of Purchas's somewhat overdue elevation to the priesthood, Grey and Selwyn had left the country to its own devices. In their respective fields, they were arguably two of the most significant figures in that first decade of colonial history following the signing of the Treaty of Waitangi. Departing on the same ship for England on December 29, 1853, each would return at different times but to a very different New Zealand. In the meantime, Robert Wynyard was sworn in as the interim administrator, leaving the colony governor-less until the late arrival of Grey's replacement, Thomas Gore Browne, more than 18 months later.

The departure of Grey and Selwyn almost seemed to generate a sense of even greater freedom or personal responsibility for Purchas and many others in the wider settler community. They appeared to accept that a new era of authority and initiative was upon them and that it was up to them to get on with building the society they wanted for themselves and their children. And it was their children's education which received the most immediate attention. Only days after Selwyn sailed for England, Purchas and his fellow Auckland priests met in town to discuss the establishment of a brand new grammar school to replace the earlier feeble and failed effort at Purewa.

It was decided that the new school should be set up in Parnell, on five acres of land the church owned and in buildings to be designed by their colleague Frederick Thatcher.[92] They needed to raise £400 a year for at least the first three years – £300 for a clergyman-teacher from England to run the school and £100 a year for the interest on the loan needed to build it.

The money was quickly raised by a small group of enthusiastic and well-heeled Aucklanders, who kicked things off immediately with lessons organised in a house known as St Kevin's in Karangahape Rd. It had previously been occupied by Governor Grey after his government house had burned down[93].

Selwyn got wind of the school idea before he left and when he arrived in England duly identified a suitably qualified principal, the Reverend John Kinder, whose services were secured. Arriving in Auckland in October 1855, Kinder proved to be a man of considerable versatility and expertise in a number of fields and was soon very successful in attracting the sons of many prominent Auckland families to the school. Among his teaching staff were fellow artists Charles Heaphy and J B C Hoyte. Thatcher's buildings were completed by mid-1856 when everyone moved from Karangahape Rd to the new site in Parnell.

With his own small school in Onehunga now well established and staffed, Purchas's next move was to set up a library for the town. When the Fencibles had first arrived, the British Government arranged for a collection of books to be assembled and despatched to New Zealand for the edification of the troops. These books had been housed in a room at Major Kenny's house and then in a small cottage nearby ... probably New Zealand's first free library.

Purchas suggested to Kenny that perhaps the books might be made available to all the citizens of Onehunga, not just the soldiers. He offered, on behalf of the church trust board, to organise a library. This was duly set up in Purchas's wooden schoolroom a couple of months later. The soldiers' books, supplemented by other publications provided by various citizens, were available on the payment of a small subscription.

---

92   The site was on the corner of Parnell Rd and today's Ayr St, known as Grammar School Lane when the school was opened.

93   Alington.

This small but important initiative by Purchas was the first of many on his part over the succeeding years to enhance the educational well-being of the wider community. This work would bring him recognition a few years later as one of Auckland's leaders in the field.

Local politics

Purchas was now being called on regularly to attend – and increasingly take the chair at – various social and local government events, many still hosted in the town's Royal Hotel, owned by Elizabeth and Edward George. Its 'long room' was also the venue for coroners' inquests, and meetings of various committees of inquiry or commissions. The hotel acquired a prestigious reputation, which the town guarded jealously, and attracted a flood of curious spectators, guests and officials coming into the town.

When the new provincial councils were established a couple of years earlier, only property owners were invited to elect the council members. Vigorous opposition had been raised to the idea of Fencible soldiers having the same voting rights, because they were seen as only 'nominal' property owners at that time. Also, opponents believed the soldiers were not educated well enough to understand the importance of their vote! The soldiers' case was taken up by one of Purchas's friends and parishioners, a Captain William Powditch – a man who clearly shared Purchas's belief in racial and social justice, and fair play.

Many years earlier, Powditch had assisted Purchas by acting as a witness at an important Māori baptism in Epsom. A few months later, Purchas officiated at the marriage of Powditch's daughter – the very first marriage at St Andrew's in Epsom. Now Purchas stood by him again as he took up the Fencibles' cause. Powditch won the argument and then found himself elected to the Provincial Council. It was seen as an important and principled stand, and a significant step forward in local government politics.

Members of the Council and the House of Representatives came to Onehunga in October that year, 1854, joining with the citizens of the town to hear the views of Edward Gibbon Wakefield on the land ownership question. Powditch chaired the meeting and it was reported that Purchas delivered "a lengthy speech". The content of the speech was not disclosed but the presumption might be that it was a polite dissertation on the need for all settlers – no matter on what basis they landed in the colony – to follow strictly the Treaty of Waitangi in recognising Māori rights of security of tenure and undisturbed possession.

Another John Kinder photograph of Purchas outside his new St James church in Mangere, soon after its opening in 1857. With him are his wife Olivia and two Māori assistants, including Rota Waitoa (George Selwyn's Māori priest) and possibly members of the Gundry family.
BROOKFIELD FAMILY FILES

By the end of 1854, Olivia had produced their sixth child, Edith,[94] while Purchas had his hands full dealing with another serious outbreak of scarlet fever. This time his friends, the Haultains,[95] had a son in extreme danger and Purchas attended to him and other children day and night. Teddy Haultain survived but only just, dying a few years later from the inevitable heart complications which the disease often induced.

As the year turned, Tāmati Ngāpora – by now a very active man, not just in promoting Christianity among his people as a lay reader, but also in continuing contact with other leaders on the land alienation problems – began pressing again for his church. Three or four years had passed since he had

94   Christened Sarah Edith, she was born on December 16, 1854.
95   Captain Haultain, later Colonel, rose to become Minister of Colonial Defence. He was a staunch supporter of the temperance movement and served for many years on various key Church of England institutions and boards.

first asked Purchas to design it, just for Māori.[96] The three-acre site given by Te Wherowhero was still available and set aside – and now Selwyn, having appointed an Auckland Māori missioner, was also happy to give it his blessing. He even donated £10 to the cause before leaving for England. And he endorsed Purchas as the man to design it and his missioner, Richard Burrows, to help with overall construction and project management.

Knowing the cost of timber would be a problem, Purchas and Ngāpora agreed to use stone, sourced free from the Mangere mountain crater and a perfect fit again with the Selwyn Gothic Revival style. Purchas went straight back to the drawing board to finish his design while Ngāpora stepped up the fundraising. The final amount was almost entirely raised by his local Māori people and, before long, the go-ahead was given. The work of cutting and transporting stone to the building site continued under Burrows' supervision for the next two years.[97]

The little Purchas church of St James and its cemetery in Mangere have lived through some remarkable times. It remains one of Auckland's architectural treasures – "a monument to the friendly co-operation of the Maori and British people which existed before … the disastrous warfare of the 1860s".

Catastrophe on the water

The eternally busy Dr Purchas would have had little time to rest as the Mangere church project got under way. His was a seven-day-a-week job, which never seemed to concern him. The final hearings on liquor licences and the associated problems with drunkenness, or what today is meekly called "unacceptable social behaviour", were due to begin any day. Purchas was still walking to other settlements like Epsom, Otahuhu and Howick to gain support and signatures for his committee's submissions at the upcoming hearings. Even Wakefield, having heard of Auckland's problems in this regard – and seeing the similar effects of hard liquor in his own southern settlements – gave £10 to help with the committee's expenses in preparing its case.

Lush describes Purchas arriving at his home in Howick one Friday evening to ask if he (Lush) could conduct the service at St Peter's that Sunday while he walked around the Howick district all weekend to collect signatures. Lush agreed to the request, while Purchas obtained another 200 signatures to place

---

96   Refer to the Heritage New Zealand website for confirmation of Purchas as the architect. Also Knight, p 67.
97   Opened in 1857, St James is the only surviving Selwyn church built of stone.

before the magistrates in a few weeks![98]

Perhaps it was Olivia who encouraged her husband to have a break a few weeks later in mid-April 1855, with their five small children. Purchas agreed, suggesting the family have a couple of days at a small bay he had in mind, near Nihotupu on the Manukau Harbour.

The plan was for himself and his son Arthur (whose family name was 'Agape' – Greek for 'love') to go up there first and check the exact spot out, before returning a few days later with the rest of the family. Purchas and the eight-year-old Agape were no doubt excited at the prospect and one of Purchas's Onehunga friends, Henry Smythies, agreed to take them there in his sailboat.

They sailed from Onehunga up the northern coast towards Nihotupu, towing a small flat-bottomed dinghy and no doubt exploring some of the little inlets, possibly even doing some fishing, before finally heading into Big Muddy Creek. This was an inlet beside land very familiar to Purchas from his regular visits there to settlers and Māori families during the past seven years.[99]

Purchas later described what happened next: "When we reached the creek … the tide was too low to admit the boat reaching the landing place. We therefore anchored her outside and went ashore in the dinghy. We there lighted a fire and cooked our dinner and by the time we had finished our meal the sun was going down."

The two men then organised their sleeping place, laying down some fern before setting off back to the boat to get their bedding. "I asked Agape if he was afraid to be left alone while we went for the boat," said Purchas, "and to this he said 'no'. I preferred leaving him on shore for fear of any accident which I thought might have happened if I had taken him in the dinghy with us, as it was dark."

Purchas and Smythies then headed back out into the channel, rowing hard against the incoming tide. But for Agape, a small eight-year-old boy, probably unused to the strange noises of large crabs scuttling in the mud around his feet – and birds and creatures settling for the night in nearby bush – it must have been a somewhat unnerving experience.

He ventured a short distance from the safe spot where his father had told him to wait. Purchas was almost halfway back to the boat when he heard his son call out. At first, he couldn't make out what he was saying. He shouted back in the dark to tell him to wait quietly and that he would be back in a few minutes. But then Agape called back distinctly: "Papa, I want you to take my boots."

By this time, Purchas and Smythies had reached the bigger boat. "When I

98   A Drummond (ed), *The Auckland Journals of Vicesimus Lush* (Mar 28, 1855).
99   A large tidal bay near today's Laingholm, below where the Lower Nihotupu Dam is situated.

heard these words, the terrible sense of impending danger came over me," said Purchas. "I did not lose a moment but pulled back as fast as I could, calling to tell him I was coming and also to reassure him."

But Agape had already stepped down through the mud to the water's edge. Purchas was within about 40 metres of him by now and, as he got closer, he called out again in the dark: "My dear boy, whatever made you come down to the water?" Agape answered in a voice of terror: "Papa, I was frightened!"

Before he could reply, Purchas heard the dreadful sound of the boy's splashes as he began wading towards the dinghy. The horrified father swung his dinghy around in the direction of the noise. But by the time he got back somewhere near the spot, calling out all the way, there was nothing but an eerie stillness. The boy had inadvertently stepped off a steep edge into deep, fast-flowing water, disappearing beneath the surface without a word.

Frantically, Purchas called out to Smythies that his boy had drowned. But Smythies could do nothing but shout out to some woodcutters camping nearby in the bush. One of them rushed down to help. After hours of furious searching, Purchas realised it was in vain. He trudged back to the dinghy in the pitch black. In his utter despair, he described how he climbed back in and knelt down inside it, alone in the dark, to "commend my son to God and to pray for strength".

They found Agape's body the next morning "in such a peaceful attitude that it quite struck those who saw him", Purchas said later. It is difficult to imagine the distress endured by Arthur and Olivia when he finally returned home to Onehunga the next day with the body.[100] The funeral followed quickly as friends rallied around. The boy was buried in the cemetery next to St Peter's beside his sister Mary.

Once the initial grief subsided – and possibly prompted by the terrible tragedy – Purchas busied himself with the nagging problem of the church tower, for which he now had a solution. Perhaps the thought of some strenuous manual labour and testing project management might have helped relieve a little of the crippling responsibility or even guilt he must have felt for his son's death.

As Professor Cyril Knight explained in his expert commentary on the Selwyn churches, the central bell tower was too difficult to brace inside at the church floor level, being in the middle of the building between transept and chancel.[101] It produced too much strain on the roof joints around the tower itself and the drainage points. Purchas realised he needed to take down and

---

100 Purchas family records – the account is from an 1855 handwritten document, believed to be Arthur Purchas's statement given a few days later for a coroner or police record.

101 Knight, p 29.

shift the entire tower, which was a wooden structure with louvres and a spire on top, about six or seven metres high. It needed to be moved from the centre of the building to the angle outside the transept and chancel, where it could be braced securely on the ground and against the side of the main building.

In those early days, with such limited tools and equipment, this was no easy task. On asking around the town, Purchas had great difficulty finding a competent builder to take the job on. So he decided to do it himself, helped by a few local volunteers. It is recorded that on the Sunday night before he was due to start, a violent storm raged over Onehunga. But on Monday the weather was calm and fine. It was also said that the entire job of dismantling the tower, removing it to the side and securing it, and then closing in the gap in the roof where it had been, took "just one week".[102] When it was finished, another storm broke and the word around Onehunga was that "providence approved the Purchas alteration".

In Auckland meanwhile, the family bereavement had spared Purchas the necessity of attending the hearings on the hotel licence approvals – on which he and others had been campaigning for weeks. Thomas Russell, appearing for the Purchas committee, made the case that nearly 300 people in Auckland and another 93 in Onehunga had been convicted of drunkenness in the past year and the granting of licences for selling liquor needed to be curtailed.

At that time, for its European population of about 10,000, Auckland had 28 pubs! Russell painted a grim picture of "scenes of debauchery and drunkenness continually enacted before the open bar of the Osprey Inn in High St". The bench of magistrates listened in silence. Purchas, his colleagues and a large slice of the citizenry of greater Auckland, were to be bitterly disappointed. In scenes still being repeated 160 years later, also often against public wishes, most licences were renewed at this hearing.[103] For Ngāpora and other Māori leaders, it was an even bigger blow ... softened not a jot by Selwyn writing letters to his parish priests and trustees asking them to warn "those living in open and notorious sin" that it was time to mend their ways!

There was some better news to follow, however, from the local Provincial Council, on the subject of education and schools. Up until now, education had been almost entirely directed by the churches and the slow transition towards it becoming a state responsibility was only just beginning. The council decided to make some grants to a few of the "established schools" in the region. Having built one of the first in Auckland, Purchas worked on his own application, hoping he could make a strong case. In September 1855 the good news came

---

102 Soar, p 5.
103 *Daily Southern Cross*, April 21, 1854.

through – a grant for Onehunga of just over £93, to be paid annually in two instalments.

The school's status changed overnight to that of a public school. Purchas and his trust board next found a new headmaster to oversee the spending of the grant and undertake further development, including plans for a larger, more permanent school. Another architectural assignment loomed for Purchas – to design and build the new school. Even though he was still completing the design of Ngāpora's new St James Church at Mangere, he was delighted to take the project on.

New governor arrives

In the same month, the new governor, Colonel Thomas Gore Browne, finally arrived from the island of St Helena to take over the administration of New Zealand and "with precise instructions to introduce responsible government".[104] At first, the community at large and the clergy, including Purchas, were full of optimism for the future. Bishop Selwyn had returned in July from England where he had impressed many attentive audiences with his ground-breaking plan for a new form of church governance in New Zealand.[105] His addresses at the University of Cambridge were said to have been particularly persuasive and he had 'sold' his vision of effectively subdividing the New Zealand bishopric into smaller dioceses extremely well.

He had also been successful in reinstating Archdeacon Henry Williams to the CMS, much to everyone's great relief. Purchas – together with most of the senior clergy and distinguished citizens and military personnel of the day – attended the welcoming ceremonies for Browne, and life in the increasingly bustling and bawdy townships of Auckland and Onehunga resumed its normal course.

In the same year, 1855, the next chapter in Purchas's musical life would be written. While his involvement with secular and church music in Auckland had continued apace on a variety of fronts, a new challenge and opportunity suddenly appeared out of nowhere. Purchas had met up with a Joseph Brown, a highly qualified music teacher and organist from Windsor, near London. He had come to New Zealand to find a better living and apparently, sometime earlier, had been offered a role as an organist and librarian at the vastly different St John's College.[106] Arriving in Auckland, he found (since the scandal at the

104 R C J Stone, *Young Logan Campbell*, p 213
105 Selwyn was away from New Zealand for 18 months.
106 A Simpson, *Hallelujahs & History*, p 8.

college a couple of years earlier) neither library nor organ, save for an old harmonium, and his job prospects suddenly disappeared. Instead Brown set up some singing classes, no doubt encouraged by Purchas, and the pair soon established a great rapport. With Purchas's experience of helping to set up the choral society in Sydney a few years earlier, the idea of a similar society in Auckland quickly took root.

When fellow music enthusiast John Lloyd also became interested, he joined Brown and Purchas in seeking expressions of interest from other leading citizens. They included Governor Browne, who was asked to take on the role of patron. Keen to build early relationships, he happily agreed.

With the Governor's patronage, public response was instant. In September and October 1855, the first advertisements appeared in the *Daily Southern Cross* announcing practices. These were followed by the formation of the Auckland Choral Society under the initial chairmanship of Purchas, whose musical organisation and reputation were already well known. Honorary membership was to cost one guinea per annum, payable in advance, which also allowed the member to bring one lady to public rehearsals!

Practices were held under Joseph Brown's baton every Thursday evening in the Odd Fellows Hall, a venue even in those days with seating for about 600. Amid much excitement and public interest, the new society's first performance took place in early December with about 100 singers and musicians, including members of the Army's 58th regimental band.

A couple of weeks later, on December 20, 1855 – while Purchas, Brown and co. were still basking in the positive reviews and congratulations from friends and colleagues – Purchas was jolted back to reality by the death of his close friend, William Gundry, at the age of only 41. He had been ill for some time, looked after at home by his Māori wife Makareta. Before his death, Gundry had asked Purchas, together with Frederick Thatcher, to be his trustee and children's guardian.

It is very likely that neither man quite realised the amount of work that would be required over the next 20 years to fulfil these roles. Gundry had built up a sizeable portfolio of property in Auckland and Onehunga to add to the 500 acres he and his wife had acquired in the Hokianga. The administration and management of this land was to be the main means of support for Gundry's wife and children for the rest of their lives.

While having benefited greatly from the Purchas family's generosity and kindness in raising his children, Gundry had always shown full appreciation and had proved a loyal and generous friend. He had supported Purchas on numerous church matters, including a donation on the formation of the Parnell

Grammar School.

A couple of years earlier, he had gifted five small blocks of land in Onehunga into Purchas's care – just after he had bought some himself – for him to do whatever he wanted, so long as it was for "divers good causes".[107] This land remained an important gift to the Anglican Church, which Purchas had leveraged well via a £400 mortgage to provide desperately needed funds for his church trust board.

Now, just a few days before Christmas, Purchas's job was to comfort Gundry's widow and seven children, organise and conduct the substantial funeral, and see to his burial in the Symonds St cemetery.

That same year, 1855 – apart from the ongoing christenings, weddings and funerals, including the burial of his own son – Purchas officiated at a particularly significant marriage. It was that of Te Wherowhero's nephew, son of his younger brother and chief, Te Kati Takiwaru, to a young Māori woman in Ngāpora's family.[108]

While Olivia looked after her own four children at home and kept an eye out for Makareta and the Gundry youngsters, a steady stream of patients with their varied ailments continued to knock on the front door. A few streets away, Dr Weekes was becoming somewhat disgruntled because so many of the locals still preferred going to Dr Purchas – mainly, Weekes believed, because service there was still free. Weekes, in fact, quickly came to resent the implication he felt Purchas left him with, that he [Purchas] was still compelled to see these patients and not refer them on. Purchas had been seeing most of them for a long time, both before Weekes transferred to the town from Puketutu and for the four years he was away in California. Purchas could not turn them away now just because Weekes had set up shop again, and with his new set of charges.

A medical colleague, Dr J Giles, wrote later that Dr Weekes eventually lost most of his practice "through the greater popularity of the parson". Although Giles found nothing to object to in Weekes, he said: "I could easily understand the difference between the two men in point of popularity."[109] Purchas and Weekes did, however, collaborate effectively at a later date in an operation which would make medical history in New Zealand.

---

107 Gundry family files. Lots 1 & 3, Sec 21. Deed 3527.
108 Significant in Māori tribal politics because the Ngāti Mahuta chief Te Kati Takiwaru had married the daughter of a Ngā Puhi chief, Matire, 30 years earlier in a powerful alliance between the two former warring tribes. Kati is buried at St James, Mangere.
109 Auckland Medical History Society – EMDML – Giles notes.

CHAPTER 7

Momentous Times

From advocacy and architecture to music and medicine, the sheer scope of Arthur Purchas's activities, innovation and expertise – in so many fields and across so many disciplines – is sometimes hard to comprehend, especially given his relative youthfulness at this time. There seemed to be little that failed to attract his attention, curiosity or enthusiasm. It was the new technological wonder of reproducing photographic images which next captured his imagination.

The birthdate of what the world regards as "practical photography" had occurred in 1839 with the first somewhat hazy images. The chemical development of the original daguerreotype process continued over the next 10-15 years, with small improvements in the quality of those usually facial images. By the early 1850s, linked with the demand for portraiture from the narcissistic Victorian gentry, photographic development involving both camera equipment and collodion chemicals began to attract growing interest from all sectors of the community.

It was probably Purchas's own knowledge of and experience with chemicals – and the fact that his new friend, John Kinder, had become passionately interested in the phenomenon – which sparked his interest in early 1856. By March of that year, Purchas had acquired a "photographic machine" and was busy experimenting with portraits – one of the first among a very small group of pioneer photographers in New Zealand.

In another visit to the Purchas home in Onehunga, Lush recorded one day finding his colleague "busy trying to take portraits with his photographic machine". He was having difficulties apparently with the quality or combination of his chemicals – still at this time an imprecise and demanding skill. But despite issues with retrieving perfectly clear images, Purchas's work and occasional successes inspired several others to take up the art and within a couple of years, amateur photographic houses were set up in many parts of the country. Kinder, of course, went on to establish a considerable reputation for his photography, with many of his subjects being his own and Purchas's churches, homes and surroundings.

As Purchas finished the design of the new Onehunga School – which he had decided to build in stone like St James – Olivia gave birth to their sixth daughter, Amy Charlotte. All was well in his own home, but on each of his resumed trips south to Taupiri, Mauku and Mangere, he heard more of the growing discontent in Māoridom through his various Māori contacts.

Meanwhile, his stipend continued to be frustratingly irregular or in arrears from the Bishop, while the question of reimbursement for materials used in the construction of the Onehunga house and the original wooden schoolroom was still unanswered. What little money Olivia and Arthur had been able to acquire from family legacies or loans had mostly been sunk into the few vacant plots of cheap land or the buildings in which they now lived and worked but did not own – such as 'their' house, which was on church land.

Purchas was therefore greatly appreciative of the occasional opportunity to swap duties with Lush at Howick – in return, no doubt, for medical services rendered – and to have the chance thereby forfeited by Lush, of retrieving a slightly more acceptable offering from that congregation. But even this arrangement sometimes ran into trouble. In the middle of the winter of 1856, Lush was surprised one Saturday evening – having ridden over to Onehunga to swap services the following day – to find Purchas still at home. Purchas apologised profusely, saying he was "so pressed with medical work" that he hadn't been able to leave yet. But at 6pm he borrowed Lush's horse and set off for Howick to do his promised duty the next morning. Only a very fit, determined and committed individual would manage such a journey at that time on a winter's night. And, of course, he needed every penny he could find.

Spoiling for a fight

The following four years, 1857-1860, were to be momentous ones not just for Purchas, but for Auckland and New Zealand, Pākehā and Māori, settler and missionary. The bigger picture involving the build-up to the Taranaki and Waikato Wars, the beginnings of the Kīngitanga and other events – the consequences of which we are still trying to resolve today – is the main subject of chapters to follow. But the chronicle of all the activities Purchas was involved in during these next four decisive years, was compiled against a backdrop of deep uncertainty and concern over the future of Māori in the new 'European' society.

Purchas and the vast majority of his fellow missionaries and clergy could sense that they were being drawn slowly but surely into a web of conflict from which neither settlers nor Māori would be able to extricate themselves successfully. Many in the settler community – government officials included – were spoiling for an inevitable fight with the natives. The preliminaries were already well under way, beginning much earlier with the arrival of the Fencibles, most of whom believed they were there to "fight the natives if necessary".[110] It developed to the point where any Māori even slightly protective of his land, goods or culture, was deemed to be "against the Queen" or, in extreme cases, a "rebel".

Māori had begun their conversion to Christianity under missionaries from three main denominations – Church of England, Wesleyan and Roman Catholic. They had watched while the early missionary ways of interaction had been overtaken and replaced by Selwyn and other settler church leaders, who had also generally been slow to train and absorb Māori into their church hierarchy. Māori had also seen their missionaries – who initially brought great mana to individual tribes, among other things – gradually lose their influence on the new generation of political leaders and representatives, in so far as upholding some Treaty principles, controlling the worst of European vices and protecting traditional chiefly authority.

There had, however, been some positives. Literacy rates among Māori by the mid-1850s were surprisingly very similar to those among Europeans. The Government had even helped to produce a version of *Robinson Crusoe* in Māori, which proved extremely popular. This was followed a couple of years later by a translation of *The Pilgrim's Progress*. Given that there had been no written Māori language just 30 years earlier, this was remarkable progress.

One single event in January 1857 perhaps typified the extent to which the relationship between European administrators and Māori leaders had broken down. Wiremu Tāmihana, chief of Ngāti Hāua – and well known to Selwyn and other church leaders from his early conversion to Christianity and his strong efforts over the previous 20 years to promote peaceful co-existence – came on a long trip to Auckland to make a special visit.

His aim was to talk to Governor Browne about the problems resulting from the accelerating land sales and ways to set up good government for Māori "being led astray by the wicked ways of too many Pakeha".[111] He was met at Browne's office by a clerk and asked to wait. There he sat for several hours, while others came and went, with Browne refusing to come out of his office

---

110 ATL, MS4280, Williamson, H. *Brave Days in a Young Colony*, regarding Fencible Isaac Fletcher. "Volunteers being called to go to New Zealand to fight the Maoris."
111 K Newman, *Beyond Betrayal*.

to greet him. Eventually, late in the day, the proud Māori chief returned home by way of Mangere, where he met Te Wherowhero. It was there, at a major conference at Ihumatao not long after, that he convinced Te Wherowhero to take up the Māori kingship so they could attend to the problems themselves.

At the very same time, Bishop Selwyn was preparing final details for his own triumphant conference planned for May when he would formalise his New Zealand church constitution. As church historian H T Purchas noted some 50 years later, it was somewhat ironic that a Christian law was the object of both conferences. "While the infant kingship was still a sorry enough thing in outward appearances, its flag even bore the Cross ... its objects were to bar intoxicating liquors and other introduced European evils and keep them from unwholesome contact with the white man."

Aside from the continual local political skirmishes in the towns, Selwyn's upcoming constitutional meeting was a much-debated topic. The establishment of a separate New Zealand 'church of England' – independent of state governance and financial support, and the first in the British Empire – was a matter of great interest to many, from the Governor to the man in the street. Before he left New Zealand, and while confined to his bed with some illness, Governor Grey had even drawn up his own draft of the new constitution for Selwyn. That draft was examined in detail by constitutional law experts in England, both church and state, since there could be no room for error. Key elements, such as retaining links with the English church and participation in governance by laypeople, had been debated and anguished over for several years. Purchas and his colleagues had attended countless meetings, not only involving the clergy, but also leading laymen from the Army, the professions and the Government.

Selwyn convened his final major 'summit' in the newly built chapel of St Stephen's, Parnell, on May 14, 1857. Even Premier Edward Stafford was invited to attend the main sessions, along with all the other key figures involved in the process – Sir William Martin, Attorney-General Swainson, Frederick Whitaker, Archdeacons Williams, Hadfield and Abraham, and all senior clergy.[112] The debate and final discussions continued there for a month. Nearly 50 years later Purchas was asked to recall the event for a newspaper, being the only person still alive who had attended the entire conference.

It was in many respects, he wrote, a remarkable assembly. "The men of whom it was composed were men of renown ... it was a privilege to listen and

---

112 In spite of the summit's relevance to New Zealand social history at the time, *Michael King's The Penguin History of New Zealand* strangely makes only one reference to George Selwyn in his entire work – in a small footnote.

watch their expressive faces … the picture that remains most vividly impressed on one's memory is that of the two archdeacons [Abraham and Hadfield] one standing at the south-east corner and the other at the south-west corner … often holding opposing opinions but setting them forth with remarkable energy and force.

"Their wordy duels were not lacking in vigour, attack and defence and on both sides were keen and lively and when looked on and listened to, afforded a treat of no uncommon kind.

"Signs of astonishment occasionally appeared, sometimes a smile of conscious victory and perhaps a cloud of reproving dissent for a brief space … then the clear, calm tones of the moderator [Selwyn] would be heard, peace would prevail and no bitterness be left."[113]

The conference was Selwyn's big moment. When success came with the final adoption of the constitution, it helped some to put aside all the failings of the earlier St John's College 'experiment'. It can be assumed that Selwyn would still have been in a buoyant mood a little later in the year when he and Purchas met again, this time for the opening of the latest Purchas church, St James in Mangere. It would also have been an immensely pleasing moment for Purchas as the keys were handed over to his friend Tāmati Ngāpora. A very rare and early photograph in the family archives shows Purchas, his wife and children standing proudly outside the church alongside Rota Waitoa, Selwyn's first Māori priest.

A short time later, Purchas's new stone school next door to St Peter's was completed. It was not a moment too soon. The original old wooden classroom had blown down a few weeks earlier in a violent storm. The stone building cost just over £250, much of which was raised locally. Purchas himself raised about £17 by delivering a well-attended lecture on music to a local audience.

But there was still a deficit in the school accounts on opening day – either from the new build or the cost of the earlier wooden classroom – which was subsequently made up somehow by Purchas, out of his own pocket. While he was happy to contribute his own design work, supervision and labour free of charge for the church on behalf of the community, he felt this final deficit should still be settled by the diocese. The school was authorised by church officials and built on church land, although its operation was also subsidised by the annual government grant. Purchas could also have reasonably argued – although no record exists of him having done so – that even though he had been ordained as a priest, he was still not receiving the larger stipend for which he had qualified. The reason was that St Peter's had not been granted full parish status. That was still some four years away!

The Purchas stone school remained in constant public use for the next 50 years – a testament to its design and construction. Olivia would act as superintendent there for many years. Apart from also serving as the first Onehunga public library, it became home for a variety of charitable lodges like Freemasons and Odd Fellows, music groups and bands, and local benevolent societies – and was even used as shelter in times of disaster.

The problem of money, or Purchas's lack of it, was quickly put aside, however, when a new medical crisis arose in the town. This time it involved the Filmer family – well known to Purchas and most of the town – William Filmer being Onehunga's first Postmaster. Purchas had been caring for Filmer's wife during her latest pregnancy and had also been concerned for some time that she was suffering from a form of serious cancer. He consulted other Auckland doctors – Robert Curtis and Thomas McGauran, as well as Dr Weekes – and it was agreed by them all that a ground-breaking Caesarean operation was the only way to save the baby. The procedure had never been attempted in New Zealand before.

Weekes proposed that he act as lead surgeon ... so with Purchas and the other two doctors assisting, New Zealand's first Caesarean section was carried out on November 26 or 27, 1857 in Onehunga. The unfortunate Mrs Filmer was sedated with chloroform and the result – the community was told the next day by the press – "was the extraction of a fine healthy female child, which we are glad to hear is doing well".

The poor mother, whose death from cancer Purchas knew to be inevitable, survived briefly to see her baby before passing away. The reporter simply closed his story by adding that "the saving of the child is, however, a sufficient reward for the performance of a very rare and dangerous operation, without which its life would have been sacrificed with that of its mother."[114]

The dangerous surgery performed in such primitive conditions clearly revived Purchas's determination to make more use of the operating skills he had acquired at Guy's, but which up until that point he had few opportunities to practise. Over the next 30 years, he would develop a reputation as one of the country's finest pioneer surgeons.

The Purchas family continued to grow as George Henry entered the world just before Christmas 1857, the eighth of 14 eventual offspring. Things in the household remained extremely tight financially. The stipend issue – or "clergy

---

114 *New Zealander*, November 28, 1857. See also R Wright-St Clair, *Auckland-Waikato Historical Journal*, 40 & 41, Sept 1982.

maintenance" as it was euphemistically called – remained unresolved. Selwyn tried to be sympathetic, arguing that church communities could not get away with paying their priests peanuts while also expecting them to operate to the highest possible standards. Olivia and Arthur's skills in their garden helped to reduce some costs – but earlier hopes that the St Peter's trust board might be able to find ways and means of extracting greater contributions from their fellow churchgoers towards their priest's living expenses, proved in vain.

A month or two after the latest meeting of his Onehunga trust board in January 1858, Purchas walked into Auckland to attend a meeting on the subject called by half a dozen of the town's key clergy. Things must have been tough because Purchas spoke strongly at the meeting of his hardship in "not having any salary from his parishioners". He must have also spoken firmly at the earlier trustee meeting because, apparently, he gave them notice that "he would leave the country if they left him unpaid any longer". Lush suggested – as he himself had done – that they all give notice, to their congregations the following Sunday, that services would be suspended, adding that "as they don't or won't pay anything to their clergy, they must not grumble if he occasionally goes elsewhere!" Yet despite the strong words, the matter remained unresolved.

Two months later, Purchas was busy again in yet another new role – this time as a local inspector of schools, walking around the Howick and Tamaki areas looking for a site for a new government school.

He had also been appointed by the local Auckland magistrate's court as a public trustee to look after the settlement made for Harriet Austin by her husband John, who had died suddenly. It involved Purchas in the management and letting of yet more property – in particular a large warehouse in Shortland St in the city.[115]

Second coal discovery

In Auckland, the commercial boom times and the growing domestic demand for fuel, specifically coal, continued to exercise everyone's mind. The long arguments over how the earlier Purchas discovery of coal at Huntly might be exploited had been stymied in the meantime due to the issue of Māori ownership. The pressure was now on to find coal closer to the town. Auckland's main source at this time – the late 1850s – was Newcastle, New South Wales, but the imported coal was expensive.

On another trip to Taupiri, midway through 1858, Purchas took some

---

115 This property burned down just seven years later. Purchas would then be involved in yet another time-consuming redesign and rebuild.

time out to back his hunch that further seams of coal might be found on land between the original Drury Hotel (where today's Jolly Farmer tavern stands) and the foothills of the Hunua Ranges. Some settlers living in the area, mostly growing wheat and barley, had reported finding traces of coal in some of the local streams. Once again, Purchas opened the eyes of the local provincial council and public with news of his latest discovery. This time it was a fine bituminous brown coal, which burnt with such heat that "it could melt metal within nine minutes". Also exciting was the fact that this Drury coal, although bulkier than Huntly's black coal, was lighter and therefore more economical to transport by rail or ship. The newspapers were full of optimistic reports about what this new discovery could mean for Auckland and even the rest of the colony.

Purchas immediately got a group of other experts involved – including Onehunga friend and engineer Captain James Ninnis – and their opinions excited even more interest. After another month or so of tests, they pronounced the resource to be better than Newcastle coal and even better than the black gold from the north of England.

But Purchas also knew he needed someone else – an independent geologist or engineer of significant authority and reputation – to confirm the real worth of his find. As it happened, one of the world's great scientific research expeditions of the day – the Imperial Austrian Government's Novara Expedition around the world – was under way at the time and, better still, the ship was in Sydney, on its way back to Europe via the Pacific.[116]

The massive scientific research project was being carried out for the Natural History Museum of Vienna and among the seven eminent scientists on board was the geologist Ferdinand von Hochstetter. Purchas sensed an opportunity and immediately suggested to his friend Charles Heaphy, Auckland's surveyor at the time, and provincial superintendent John Williamson that he (Purchas) should approach von Hochstetter as soon as the Novara berthed in Auckland with the idea of getting him to assess his Drury find.

The Auckland provincial government had been impressed with Purchas's earlier findings and report – so much so that he was asked to extend a warm invitation to von Hochstetter, on behalf of the provincial government, to inspect his Drury-Hunua coal and limestone fields. Von Hochstetter was also asked to consider remaining on for a few months to conduct a geological and natural

---

116 A report in the New Zealander at the time also mentioned that Purchas had earlier "been on the point of joining the Australian expedition of the German explorer, Leichhardt", subsequently lost on this trip. His remains were never discovered. The Leichhardt Oval in Sydney was named after him.

The signed portrait of Ferdinand Von Hochstetter, given by him to Olivia Purchas in thanks for the hospitality extended to the great explorer and geologist when he stayed with the Purchas family in 1858-59.

AUCKLAND LIBRARIES HERITAGE COLLECTIONS 881-2 J CROMBIE

history survey of the entire province.[117] He agreed to inspect the coalfields but wanted time to think about the much larger assignment.

Arthur and Olivia accordingly hosted von Hochstetter over Christmas 1858 and the two men spent the next two days scouting the area between Otahuhu and the Whau River. Then, on December 28, von Hochstetter, Purchas, Heaphy, Ninnis and others set off for the Drury-Hunua district "to examine the coal which had recently been discovered there by the Rev A G Purchas".[118]

Purchas remained with the group for the next eight days as they tramped throughout the area between Drury, Opaheke and the Hunua Ranges. Then, in early January, Purchas and von Hochstetter returned to Auckland for a meeting with the Government at which von Hochstetter would reveal his decision to either stay or return home. "It was on the 5th of January," von Hochstetter wrote. "Accompanied by my friend the Rev A G Purchas, with whom I became so intimate, I entered the council chamber of the Colonial Government office, resolved to state to the assembled ministry my special reasons for <u>declining</u> the proposition made me by the NZ Government and preferring to continue my travels on board the *Novara*."

The government officials that day, Attorney-General Whitaker, Treasurer C W Richmond, Superintendent John Williamson and Postmaster Henry Tancred, listened to von Hochstetter's explanation of why he could not accept the proposition. He cited the extraordinary territorial difficulties, the lack of any maps, no knowledge of the Māori language, etc. Then Purchas spoke and it was "the eloquence and amiability of my friends, Mr Purchas and Dr Fischer, as well as the obliging disposition of the ministers present", which

---

117   Refer *Journal of the Royal Society of New Zealand*, 6:3, 1976. Michael Hoare.
118   Dr F von Hochstetter's Report – *Government Gazette*, Jan 13, 1859.

finally persuaded von Hochstetter to change his mind and stay.[119] He was given permission to leave the *Novara* at that point to begin what would turn out to be the first geological survey of significant parts of New Zealand.

As government and public interest in the forthcoming expedition surged, Purchas introduced him to various other geologists and explorers such as Julius von Haast who would accompany von Hochstetter on the major surveys around the North Island and Nelson.

Von Hochstetter's first report on the initial Drury coalfield trip was greeted with great enthusiasm in Auckland – not only because of his very favourable initial assessment of the coal, but also because of his positive comments about the quality of pottery clay and limestone which Purchas had also shown him.

The reports from such an eminent geologist as von Hochstetter led very quickly to the establishment of a new company specifically to mine the Drury coal. Purchas, however, had no money to invest in it and, even if he did, would almost certainly have declined because of his clerical responsibilities and the criticism that might have ensued if he, as a member of the clergy, were involved in such a transaction. The Waihoihoi Coal Company was accordingly established[120] with enough initial capital subscribed to open a shallow mine, collect the first 200 tons and investigate the building of a rail line from the mine to the Drury port for onward shipment by water transport to Onehunga and overland to Auckland. Ninnis was given the contract by the company directors to "execute all the works required". For the next few months Purchas's role in the Drury coal business was limited to regular visits to the site, writing up progress reports for the Auckland newspapers and inviting Aucklanders to go and see the project for themselves.

Back in town, von Hochstetter, accompanied again by Purchas or Heaphy or both, as time allowed, began his more detailed assessment of the Auckland volcanic field. The discoveries in von Hochstetter's name were many and significant, and are well documented elsewhere. One particular twin-cratered cone, about 50m high on the northern side of Mt Wellington – having erupted before it about 10,000 years ago – was even renamed by von Hochstetter, after his friend, as Purchas Hill. Originally named Te Tauoma, it has since been mined away as part of a suburban development although still remembered on the original site today as Purchas Hill Drive.

While von Hochstetter proceeded on his work elsewhere around New Zealand during 1859, the development of the Waihoihoi mine continued

---

119 Refer F von Hochstetter, *Nine Months in New Zealand*, p 11, Auckland University, ENZB.

120 It is thought John Logan Campbell was one among a group of prominent Auckland shareholders. The company was set up on June 28, 1860 with a capital of £10,000.

and a couple of small ships were put into the colliery trade to Onehunga and work began on a two-mile railway extension. It seemed the discovery might indeed provide a long-term answer for Auckland's fuel problem, especially after later reports commissioned by von Hochstetter from scientists and experts in England confirmed his own findings on the quality of the coal – with a couple of minor qualifications regarding its sheer bulk for the weight involved.

As von Hochstetter completed his task and his time in New Zealand drew to a close, numerous testimonial dinners and farewell 'thank you' events were held for the most famous scientist New Zealand had ever welcomed to its shores. Purchas shared the stage with him at the key Auckland functions, including a large settlers' dinner for the entire Papakura district. Toasts were made to the "continuing prosperity of the district" and prolific thanks were extended for "the eminent services rendered to the Province by both Dr von Hochstetter and Dr Purchas".

At the final official event in the Mechanics' Institute in Auckland, a huge crowd attended with hundreds unable to get in. As was the custom in those days – and after Purchas had introduced his friend and Superintendent John Williamson had made his opening speech on behalf of Governor Browne – von Hochstetter was presented with a handmade woven purse, containing several hundred gold sovereigns. In his generous reply and lecture to follow, von Hochstetter went out of his way to give great credit to those who had preceded him in the geological exploration of the province of Auckland, specifically naming Purchas and Heaphy.

The next day's report of the big occasion spoke of the province's great indebtedness to them both. The newspaper thanked them for the help they had given von Hochstetter and concluded its report by saying, "they will feel themselves amply repaid for their past labours by having their names for the future ever associated with that of Ferdinand von Hochstetter in the geological history of New Zealand".

Von Hochstetter presented a signed portrait of himself to Olivia and Arthur with a special message of thanks to Olivia for her home hosting on many occasions. Purchas now had just one task left – to check the English version of von Hochstetter's official report for the New Zealand Government. The English translation was done by another member of the *Novara* party, Dr Karl Scherzer. He and von Hochstetter asked Purchas "to kindly check the English and detect any 'Germanisms' in the final version". Purchas replied that he "found but little occupation for his critical pen".

The later failure of the Waihoihoi Coal Company – due to a combination of lack of capital, difficulties with the rail line, the beginning of the Waikato

War to follow and the fact that the brown Drury coal proved less than ideal as steamer or boiler fuel, mainly due to its bulk – did nothing to harm Purchas's reputation as "a doyen of local scientific culture".[121] From this time on, he would be sought after by people from all walks of life for his advice on all manner of engineering, mineral and geological matters.

More new projects

Purchas had been busy hosting, and travelling and working with von Hochstetter over a period of many months in 1859. But, typically, he was still busy with other matters. Every minute of every waking hour for Purchas was filled with work on a number of different projects.

While Selwyn was busy planning his first general synod in Wellington, followed by his major constitutional synod, Purchas found himself having to undertake an unavoidable trip north to sort out some important land matters in his role as William Gundry's executor and trustee. He and Olivia took their first visit together out of Auckland – sailing north to Russell on the passenger steamer *St Kilda* – for three weeks. The job was to confirm titles for the Gundry land in the north, which had been given to him and his wife at Paraoanui through her chiefly Māori relatives.

On his return – having met the Māori chiefs in question and sorted out the title issues – Purchas learned that his name had come up at the Wellington synod in connection with a proposal for a new New Zealand hymn book. It was an important means, and one of many, that would help to consolidate the autonomy of Selwyn's church in the colony. The proposal failed to win total support at the time, although it would emerge again a couple of years later. However, it was enough to spur Purchas into some preparatory work, which included writing words and music for two new hymns.

Purchas was also working on something obviously inspired by his studies with von Hochstetter. While walking over the very fertile Hunua and Drury lands, von Hochstetter had commented to Purchas on the quality of the soils and the lushness of certain plants growing naturally in the area, such as the flax and green vegetables. It got Purchas thinking. As a student in England, he had learned a little of the chemical makeup of certain vegetables and the oils they contained, and had retained an interest in the subject ever since. He had also learned of the apparent health benefits which peoples of other European countries, and the Mediterranean in particular, seemed to derive from using

---

121   M Hoare, *Journal of the Royal Society of New Zealand*, 1976, p 388.

vegetable oils in their diet in place of animal fats. He counted such things as rape seed, linseed oil, various earth nuts, olives and castor oil among these new and possibly very valuable food sources.

Accordingly, he spent many late nights preparing a detailed paper on his ideas for presentation and publication – initially presented to a meeting of the Otahuhu Agricultural Association in November of 1859. It was to be another completely revolutionary and far-sighted proposal, and probably the first promotion in this part of the world of the health benefits obtainable from vegetable oils.

His presentation was again listened to intently and reported in full by an eager press, intrigued by Purchas's recommendations – and encouragement to anyone who would listen – to use a little less of the pig and duck fats in such common use in the colony and to take up more vegetable oils in their place.

He highlighted, in particular, four oleaginous plants – linseed oils from common flax, rapeseed or colza, *Brassica oleracea* or the various cabbage species including broccoli and kale, and earth nuts like peanuts and other legumes. Purchas suggested Aucklanders should start growing castor oil plants and olive trees, and particularly recommended that interested entrepreneurs should investigate the soils around Papakura, Drury, Pukekohe and Waiuku. Unfortunately we have no idea how his audience reacted on the night. However, it must have sounded strange to a largely English audience, used to butter and lard, who were mostly unaware that green vegetables and seeds could produce valuable oils – let alone that they should be suitable for cooking and eating!

Purchas's talk that night in Otahuhu may also have been the first inkling of the great crop-growing potential that would be exploited many years later in those now highly valued market garden areas of Pukekohe and Franklin. The newspaper report the next day quoted Purchas as saying: "It is my hope that vegetable oils may, ere long, be reckoned amongst the staple products of the colony, both for home consumption and for export." It was an astonishingly accurate forecast.

Auckland water engineer

Purchas's interests and concerns, given his medical background, naturally extended to include Auckland's major water and sanitation problems. The all-too-common recurrence of water-borne diseases and fevers, and the death rate among children in particular – even the serious fire risk due to the lack of water storage – all weighed heavily on the minds of many Aucklanders. The urgent problem of sourcing clean water for the town became something of an obsession for Purchas, heightened even further when his colleague and Choral Society friend John Lloyd's six-year-old son died, probably of diphtheria. Arthur and Olivia invited Lloyd's devastated wife and her four other children to share their grief in the Purchas family home for a couple of weeks, when Lloyd was called away on business with Selwyn.

Unlike other settlements such as Onehunga, Auckland had no ready source of fresh water from its local rivers and streams, given that most were tidal. Although fresh groundwater did collect in ponds or small lakes, it was soon badly polluted. As we learned earlier, Purchas's idea of supplying Auckland town with water from Onehunga had first taken root in 1851. His interest was revived two years later when John Logan Campbell purchased the Mt Prospect estate from Thomas Henry in a mortgagee sale, before renaming it the One Tree Hill estate.

Then the great Auckland fire of August 1858 prompted Auckland Superintendent John Williamson and other leading figures in provincial government, to raise the water question again – this time with real urgency. The massive fire had started in the notorious Osprey Inn in High St, the very same place Purchas and others had complained about at the earlier magistrates' hearings on liquor licences. Between 40 and 50 businesses, shops and houses were destroyed as citizens, armed only with buckets, tried to put out the blaze in a howling north-east gale.

Prompted by Campbell and others who had been seriously worried by this fire, Purchas immediately revived his earlier plan. He discussed it with local engineers and planners, and, encouraged by everyone's response, arranged for well-regarded local engineer James Stewart to take up the project. (Stewart had been the main engineer employed on the Waihoihoi coal project.)

The Purchas scheme involved drawing water from the Onehunga springs and pumping it to a large natural reservoir on Campbell's One Tree Hill estate – in fact a small crater. Natural gravity would then be used to feed the water to another reservoir he planned to build at the top of Symonds St. From there, the water could flow simply and easily, with some pressure, downhill to the main Auckland town.

Official discussion and planning with government and town officials went on through the late 1850s. Arguments mainly raged not over whether the Purchas idea would work, but over who should own the eventual project – the local provincial government, the national government, or a private waterworks company. A committee of inquiry was established to solicit any better ideas and a £50 prize was offered for the best scheme. Besides the Purchas-Stewart plan, another five proposals were eventually submitted, including one to pump water from the Domain springs, another to take water from the Waikato River, and yet another to use Remuera's Lake Waiatarua. By now, Purchas had also secured Campbell's ready agreement to provide access to his land for the One Tree Hill reservoir and pipework.

Stewart's preference was to use "the old crater to the west of the higher one … which is 68 feet lower than the other and with a 12-inch main will discharge one million gallons a day at the Khyber Pass road".[122] With Purchas's help, he put together their proposal with detailed costs, engineering and construction calculations, pressure calculations and pipe route. A lot of the planning was based on information from similar projects under way at the same time in England and Australia. Other town engineers and officials agreed it could work and were keen to implement it. The public also favoured the plan, given that the risks of fire and disease were very much top of mind.

The Purchas-Stewart scheme seemed to have it won, confirmed when the committee awarded them the cash prize. Most of that money went on repaying expenses incurred by both men. But, at the last minute, one member of the local Provincial Council – unable to be convinced about the costs – vetoed the proposal and, to everyone's anger and frustration, stopped the Purchas plan in its tracks. Instead water was taken from the Domain springs for the next 15 years. It would be 1875 before Western Springs and its new lake was established. Purchas, who had always been against the Domain scheme because of pollution worries, was a strong backer of the Western Springs alternative, even though it was always, for him, a second-choice solution. However, his original proposal for a reservoir at today's Symonds St-Mt Eden Rd intersection was eventually taken up and still stands there today.

Purchas was later thanked publicly and acknowledged once again in the press for his major contribution towards getting the ball rolling on such a vital public utility – even if it did take some 15 years to come to fruition. There was probably no other public issue as critically important to Auckland in those days as the supply of clean water. Purchas's role in advancing a long-term solution, and its impact on improving public health, was a major one.

Back to architecture

It must be highlighted once more – lest any impression be gained that Purchas might have been tempted to neglect his parish duties at this time in favour of science, architecture and engineering – that he was still taking services,

---

122 Stewart Report on the Purchas scheme presented to the Committee of Inquiry on November 15, 1859.

providing free medical care, burying the dead and conducting christenings and weddings. In fact in the period 1858-59 alone, he performed no fewer than 75 baptisms and eight weddings, and hosted Bishop Selwyn again in September 1858 for the consecration of St Peter's after the relocation of its tower and spire.

Except for the brief time he was away with von Hochstetter, Purchas's regular Wednesday walks to Mauku, near Patumahoe – returning on Thursday via Waiuku and Mangere – continued as usual. It was probably inevitable that the Mauku settlers – having heard about the wonderful churches Purchas had designed at Onehunga, Otahuhu and most recently at Mangere – would start making noises about having a church built for them.

Purchas intimated he would be happy to take the project on if they could find most of the money in advance. So just three weeks before extending his invitation to von Hochstetter, and only a week after he had been enlightening Aucklanders about vegetable oils, Purchas met the Mauku residents again in late November 1859 and, with promises of funds available, agreed to design their new church.

The settlers were thrilled. Even today their descendants still admire the original Purchas church of St Bride's, which remains the historical centre of the area and is arguably one of the most beautiful of all the Selwyn churches. While the residents decided on the site[123] and then battled for the next couple of years to collect the funds on promises made, Purchas drew up his plan. It was for a perfectly proportioned and detailed native timber building, with familiar 60° gables and shingle roof, unusually with no side aisles or transept, but with an entrance porch beneath a 20-metre-high bell tower. Knight comments that this feature was intentional because, in addition to standing on high ground and housing the bell, the tower was intended "to give the local people a sense of safety and comfort by its presence". The familiar diamond-paned windows with foliated Gothic heads also reprised the similar Purchas detail from his St James and Otahuhu designs.

Worryingly, at several points it looked as if the people of Mauku were not going to be able to come good on their money pledges for the church's completion. A suggestion was made to leave out the bell tower and spire because at least one intended subscriber did not want a spire and would not make a donation if it was kept in. To Purchas, this was an impossible demand. He offered to find the £25 needed himself to accommodate the spire … otherwise, in his mind, the design would be ruined. In August 1859, despite the risk of some final debt hanging over the project, construction began using the best

---

123 Knight, p 68. The site was eventually secured via a government grant, with help again from Selwyn.

heart totara and kauri logged from the nearby bush.[124]

As the Mauku foundations were laid and having just waved a final farewell to Ferdinand von Hochstetter sailing down the Waitematā on his way home, Olivia announced she was pregnant again. Arthur's response was to start work immediately on yet another project – the enlargement of their Onehunga home.

For Purchas and his extremely resilient young wife, both still only in their thirties, the last two or three years of the decade had, at times, been frantic, difficult and challenging. But for Arthur, they had also been immensely satisfying. The main frustration, and his biggest disappointment, was still the inability to relieve the family's financial pressures. Although it was never his focus, he had also acquired a significant personal reputation in the last few years with his many scientific and architectural accomplishments, and undoubtedly would have been looking forward optimistically to far more productive times.

As for the bigger colonial picture, he remained deeply concerned at the state of the European-Māori relationship and the direction it was taking. The underlying suspicions felt by the settlers towards Māori and their growing belligerence as a result of the Kīngitanga foundation had grown worse. Purchas knew well from his contacts with Ngāpora and others that the land issue from the period of accelerated selling was at the heart of it all. But he also knew that the Kīngitanga and men like Te Wherowhero and Tāmihana were seriously against any military confrontation with the Government as the means of settling the matter.

If people like Olivia and Arthur Purchas did entertain any hopes of a calmer family life over coming years – perhaps even hope for a greater understanding of the Māori King movement – those hopes were already dashed in the emerging climate of distrust. As more dark clouds rolled in, their third son, another Arthur, entered the world safely.

His birth was quickly followed by Selwyn's confirmation of St Peter's finally being granted the status of a full parish – theoretically resulting in a small increase to Purchas's inconsistent stipend. But there was a catch. The Bishop also required Purchas to take back responsibility for the parish of St Andrew's, which, by and large, had remained a small mission station in the intervening years – woefully strapped for cash and lacking parishioners. It seemed as if nothing much was going to change after all.

Selwyn would remain in Auckland for another seven or eight years – but for Purchas and most of the original clerical pioneers, the "Selwyn years" as they knew them, were now all but over. Purchas's relationship with Selwyn

---

124   The church was finally opened by Purchas with some celebration, on July 14, 1861.

had probably not been much different from that of the rest of the clergy – with the exception of a few of Selwyn's closest colleagues like Abraham, Thatcher, Lloyd and Cotton. While Selwyn was trying to establish his self-sufficient "cathedral" system at Purewa – and attempting at the same time to merge two quite different clerical groups into one cohesive body – it was inevitable there would be clashes along the way.

As has been well documented by so many others, Selwyn's aims were basically unrealistic and led to the inevitable failure at St John's. Apart from those regular irritations which often arise in any close working relationship between two strong individuals, Purchas's main beef with Selwyn had really been the scant attention paid to the problem of basic living expenses. For his part, Selwyn clearly expected his men to readily accept, if necessary, the almost monk-like virtues of discipline and forbearance. His error of judgement lay in probably never realising that not all – especially those with wives and children – were ready or able to live on such difficult terms.

When Purchas's patience finally wore thin and he understood Selwyn's inability to fix the stipend issue, he showed the necessary resilience and strength of character to put it behind him without bitterness and simply take greater charge of his own circumstances. Several others, like Williams, Maunsell, Grace and Lush, were far more critical and sometimes seriously bitter towards Selwyn, despite their often better personal means or resources. But in some pretty tough circumstances, Purchas managed mostly to tread a diplomatic line and to maintain empathy and respect for Selwyn, even when his ambitions for St John's could not be realised.

Arthur and Olivia's somewhat difficult "Selwyn years" of the late 1840s and 1850s would evolve into more troubled times – the 1860s being described 140 years later by historian Michael King as "the most volatile decade in the young nation's history". It was a decade involving an even more dramatic sequence of events for Purchas, arising from his intimate contacts with the Ngāti Mahuta family at the very heart of the Kīngitanga.

These events would exert immense pressure on Purchas's personal loyalties, his ethical decisions and his theological convictions. They would also be an extreme test of his physical and mental courage. He would not only survive the test, but would go on to accomplish even greater deeds.

PART II

WAR YEARS

CHAPTER 8

Seeds of War

July 9, 1863. Three years later. The resident Auckland magistrate, Henry Halse, was on an important mission, via Onehunga, to the Māori settlements at Ihumatao, Pukaki and Mangere on horseback.[125] One of several local magistrates acting on instructions from Governor Grey, his task was to ensure every Māori resident in those settlements swore allegiance to Victoria, Queen of England and her government in New Zealand.

Halse and the other magistrates were, in effect, asking Māori living anywhere between Auckland and south to the Waikato River, to identify themselves as 'Queenites' or 'Kingites' – to state whether they recognised Queen Victoria's sovereignty or that of Matutaera, the second Māori King. For these particular Māori, it was an impossible undertaking.

Halse rounded a corner on the rough road and came across two people walking the same way, engaged in earnest conversation. It was Ngāti Mahuta chief Tāmati Ngāpora and his friend Arthur Purchas. Halse stopped, dismounted and greeted the pair. He told Ngāpora of his mission and asked the chief if he could read the oath of allegiance to him, before he went further and presented it to his people. Ngāpora agreed.

Halse read the oath in English a first time. There was the usual Māori silence. Ngāpora asked Halse to read it to him a second time. There followed another long silence. Then Ngāpora turned to Purchas and asked in Māori: "Rata Patiti – is the time of harvest close at hand?"

Purchas simply nodded quietly and answered: "Yes."[126]

Both knew instantly that not taking the oath meant inevitable separation, relocation and banishment of Māori from all the native settlements south of Onehunga – from Mangere, Pukaki and Ihumatao to Awhitu, Waiuku and Tuakau. Both also knew this was surely the beginning of their worst fears coming true, a stroke of doom – the final, hopelessly uneven and dreadful

---

125   Halse (1819-1888) was later appointed Assistant Native Secretary and, in 1875, a judge of the Native Lands Court. He was regarded by some as "ineffective".

126   V O'Malley, Choosing Peace or War, *New Zealand Journal of History*, Vol 47, No 1, 2013, p 48.

collision between Pākehā and Māori.

Only a few miles to the east, at exactly the same time, the next corps of British troops to assemble – comprising some 1500 men – was already preparing to march down the Great South Rd heading for Drury. The British invasion of the Waikato was under way.

* * *

The seeds of the dreadful harvest of the 1860s, which Ngāpora was warning about, had in fact been sown in the late 1840s and early 1850s. Back then, however, Māori and European were in that first real phase of "economic interdependence", living in their own respective territories, trading with each other freely, but cautiously, and with a fair amount of co-operation and goodwill.

But the continual arrival of ships from Britain, loaded with families and goods and men with ambition and capital – all speaking of new lands, opportunity, development and industry – soon began to tip the uneasy balance in the relationship. Most new European arrivals took it for granted that, although still heavily outnumbered, they were the ones now in charge of the new colony and its future. The natives, a 'conquered' race it was assumed, would submit quietly, gratefully take the few pennies per acre offered for their land and retire graciously somewhere else – away from the Europeans.

As the 1850s progressed, many Europeans even began speaking openly of the eventual possible extinction of the Māori race. For the original missionary group and men like Purchas, backed by their leaders Selwyn, Martin and others, this was always an appalling thought. They relayed their concerns about such an outcome to the colonial administration, members of the British Parliament and the British public, including any friends in high places. Those concerns did help to bring about changes in public opinion there about the perceived benefits of such colonisation, but not enough to alter the process.

Māori chiefs from many North Island tribes, particularly in the rich Waikato lands – including those who had willingly signed the Treaty – also sensed the change and the threat that unchecked arrivals presented to Māori institutions and customs. Many of these chiefs and their respective hapū and iwi had built strong relationships with the European Government since 1840, taken on Christian values, renounced many barbarous ways of the past and even offered military and economic support against 'renegades' or troublemakers in their midst.

While, on the face of it, many Māori were enjoying what Europeans offered in the way of attractive new goods, cash and lifestyle, chiefly concerns were increasing over the threat to their tikanga (customs and laws), and their systems of land tenure and harvesting, history and justice, built up over several hundred years. The most obvious threat, and the very heart of it all, was the incessant pressure on their land, despite the Treaty's guarantees of "undisturbed possession". It was written in one early account of Wakefield company settlers landing in Port Nicholson, that Māori stood on the shore weeping at the sight of so many foreigners or "Pākehā" coming to occupy their land – never realising it could be overrun so quickly despite the provisions of the Treaty.

As more and more Māori leaders tried to come to terms with the new order, it seemed to them that if they were going to buy some time for their race – even prevent it being wiped out – the first thing they needed to do was to slow down the sale and permanent dispossession of their lands. The mechanism which they believed was needed to achieve this was a single, unifying authority – a monarch, just as the Europeans and the British had.

Who it was, or where the first conversations took place on how to achieve this, is still a matter of conjecture among historians. Ngāti Mahuta chief Honana Te Maioha[127] – who was quoted in a detailed and widely circulated story later in 1882 – said talk of a king had actually begun among Kawhia Māori only four or five years after the Treaty signing, as early as 1845. He said the original objectives were to find a way to unite the tribes with some kind of bond, perhaps their own Māori king; to form a land "league", not to stop all land sales but mainly the "reckless alienation" of the most valuable land; and to prevent further fighting and bloodshed among Māori.

The other, more commonly quoted story, says that it was two former students of St John's, Tāmihana Te Rauparaha, son of the fearsome Ngāti Toa chief, and his cousin Mātene Te Whiwhi, who first began convincing their elders they had to do something about slowing this "land grab" and proposing that a Māori king would be the best way to achieve this. Tāmihana Te Rauparaha had attended St John's for a couple of years in 1846-47 and Mātene Te Whiwhi for a few months at the end of 1846. Arthur and Olivia Purchas would have known both men well following their own arrival at the college. But, like many of their fellow Māori students at the time, neither Tāmihana nor Mātene reached Selwyn's ordination standards, despite the mentoring and encouragement of Henry Williams and others. While benefiting from some education at St John's, they had not been candidates for the priesthood.

In 1851, a couple of years after leaving St John's, Tāmihana Te Rauparaha visited England and returned thoroughly impressed with the mana, power and

---

127 He was a cousin of the second Māori King, Matutaera Tāwhiao. Refer Papers Past, *New Zealand Herald*, Feb 18, 1882.

prestige of the British monarchy – and the fact that the British people seemed so unified under their reigning monarch, Queen Victoria. To Tāmihana, the monarchy appeared in stark contrast to the divided, incohesive Māori tribal system – despite their common cultural traditions and the uniform view of Māori land ownership, use and transfer.

In 1852, Tāmihana and Mātene were based among Ngāti Toa and Ngāti Raukawa people in the Ōtaki region, and had been instrumental in persuading Henry Williams to send them their own missionary. This was Octavius Hadfield, a man of great influence and mana among Māori who shared their vision of Māori integrity and desire to preserve their race and customs. Tāmihana and Mātene's plan was to first promote peace in the Māori world and then bring the more powerful tribes together in a new kind of confederation and authority similar to the British monarchy.

Neither saw such a move as being a challenge to replace or overthrow the British Queen. Instead the objective was to promote what historian Michael King described as the natives'"sense of 'Maoriness'"[128] by preserving traditional lands, customs and authority among their own people. They saw the divisions existing within Māoridom at this time as being all the "incentive" a united English settler force needed to take advantage of and pressure Māori into selling their land – before absorbing them into European culture and thereby reducing Māori chiefly authority.

The pair took a big risk going first to the South Island with their message … straight to the Ngāi Tahu heartland to tribes which, only a few years earlier, had been invaded and decimated by their father and uncle, Te Rauparaha. But their message of concern over the rate at which ancestral Māori land was disappearing into British hands was well received – underlined with warnings about the widespread associated decline of tino rangatiratanga and chiefly mana.

From suspicion to anger

By 1853 ordinary Māori people were also learning fast that British settlers and government officers had a vastly different attitude towards the acquisition and possession of land. For the British, acquiring land through war, or a relatively silent 'conquest' as it had been in New Zealand up to that point, was a 'reward'. This was never the case for Māori who might raid, invade, kill and plunder, but would then withdraw, sometimes taking slaves. Māori would not usually

128 M King, *The Penguin History of New Zealand*, p 212.

take possession for ever. To do so invited severe retribution and loss of their own mana and mana whenua.

Māori tribal lands were imbued with their own identity and whakapapa, and permanent alienation via a piece of paper called a 'title' was an altogether foreign and misunderstood concept. More simply, the European concept of a title for a piece of land made no more sense to Māori than having a title for a piece of sky or an area of sea. It is the essence of the misunderstandings and disagreements over land which exist to this day.

Word of the discussions about a Māori "king" – not as an alternative to Queen Victoria, but as the possible means of binding tribes together on the land question – filtered back into European conversations. In Purchas's case this most certainly occurred via his regular contact with Te Wherowhero and Ngāpora at Ihumatao and Mangere. Unfortunately the European and settler mood of the day was not conducive to promoting any reasoned discussion on the subject. Settlers wanted access to land and simply saw a Māori king as a hindrance to achieving this objective. The result was immediate confusion and suspicion on the part of most colonial leaders about the real intentions of a kīngitanga.

One exception, however, was Minister of Native Affairs C W Richmond, who did his best to allay that suspicion in an early report to Governor Browne. He pointed out that many respected Māori tribal chiefs – otherwise well disposed towards the government of the day – were cheerfully lining up in support of the king proposal with no thought of rejecting or challenging the British Government or Queen Victoria. The Māori King movement's raison d'être, he wrote – as envisaged in its early days by Tāmihana Te Rauparaha and Mātene Te Whiwhi – was simply to seek from the colonial government (an institution established completely without Māori participation) a concession of equal standing to the Queen, so Māori might gain greater control over the disposal of their land.

Wherever the Kīngitanga movement started – Kawhia or places further south – by 1854 many Māori minds in the Waikato had come together on the concept. At the first of several hui on the matter – with the influential Christian chief of Ngāti Hāua, Wiremu Tāmihana, now directing them from his Matamata base in the Waikato – it was underlined repeatedly that there was no suggestion the sovereignty of Queen Victoria would be replaced by that of a Māori monarch. Nor was it apparent then that in promoting the Kīngitanga, Māori were indicating any form of hostility towards the Crown. Tāmihana went out of his way to explain to both Māori and Pākehā leaders that a Māori king or a British queen would never be an "either-or" option. There was room for both.

But despite all the assurances and overtures, the initial settler confusion and suspicion was soon replaced by anger at what they regarded as signals of disloyalty and gross ungratefulness. In turn, Māori increasingly refused to sell their best lands as they were eyed jealously by more and more entrepreneurial settlers.

Tāmihana, often viewed later as the Māori "kingmaker" – and cruelly misjudged by European leaders of the time – was also seriously misunderstood by many early Pākehā writers and historians who saw him as an almost semi-tragic figure. Today, however, he is regarded as one of the most outstanding statesmen of his day.[129] With his fearsome tattoos and appearance he was not well known personally to many Europeans of the time and did not "put himself about" as some other Māori leaders did. Yet he had great authority and mana in the missionary world and among the Waikato and Hauraki tribes for his loyalty and honesty. Sir John Gorst wrote of him later: "The members of the government in Auckland did not like Tamihana. It was the fashion to believe him insincere."

The great Ngāti Hāua chief Wiremu Tamihana, well known to Purchas, both mutual supporters and advocates for each other in the days leading up to the outbreak of the Waikato Wars in the early 1860s
AUCKLAND LIBRARIES HERITAGE COLLECTIONS 661-6 – KINDER

So when he was deliberately made to wait that hot January day in 1857, in the foyer of Governor Browne's office – as he attempted to set the record straight once again about Kīngitanga objectives – it is perhaps not surprising that his first stop on the way home was to talk again to Te Wherowhero about accepting the kingship. Not in great health, the old man resisted at first, mainly because of some unavenged incident involving Tāmihana's Ngāti Hāua people. Tāmihana himself had been pressed to take it on but had no desire to do so. Discussion also involved Te Hapuku of Hawkes Bay's Ngāti Kahungunu, a man also well respected by the Government; Te Amohau of the Arawa tribes; Te

---

129   Nearly 140 years after his death in 1876, a *New Zealand Herald* special feature on 150 "great New Zealanders" named Tāmihana its retrospective "Man of the Year" for 1863. *NZ Herald* 'Celebrating 150 Years' November, 2013.

Kaniatakirau of the East Coast; and Te Heuheu Tukino of Ngāti Tūwharetoa, with whom Ngāti Mahuta had always retained the strongest links.

After further hui at Waiuku and then Paetai near Rangiriri in May 1857, it was not until a final meeting late in 1858 that Te Wherowhero finally agreed to accept the kingship. [130] Waikato Māori, Ngāti Kahungunu, Arawa, Ngāti Tūwharetoa chiefs from Taupō, and some Ngāti Porou and Hauraki tribes were all utterly convinced by now that the settler government had no sensible solution for either race to the land problem nor was actively searching for one. A unifying Māori king was the only way they would find specific Māori answers to their problems and control the disorder among their own people.

In Auckland and in other towns, men like Purchas were still working hard lobbying their own politicians to deal with the same rapidly rising problems – alcohol abuse, poor public health and racial intolerance – all upsetting the delicate social balance between Māori, settler and government.

Without doubt, there were other Māori tribes and hapū, particularly in the upper Waikato area, such as Ngāti Maniapoto, who even at this early stage saw a Māori king as giving them the best opportunity yet to somehow restrain or confront the Europeans in their inexorable advance on Māori land. Their leader, Rewi Maniapoto, viewed the growing settler encroachment – so often into areas of long-standing significance to local Māori and in total ignorance of tribal customs and traditions – with serious frustration and anger. In addition, the breakdown of tribal authority had meant that many land deals – either in the early days directly to Europeans or later to the Crown – were being made by Māori in a cloud of disputed ownership, or worse, with no customary authority to sell.

Commercial life in the towns in the late 1850s nevertheless continued to grow with the discoveries of coal, the construction of new buildings, and the daily arrivals of ships unloading new products from Australia, the United States and England.

The only major interruption to progress was the great fire of 1858, a possibility Auckland townsfolk had been dreading for years. Down south in Christchurch, the New Zealand Company was laying down plans for more new settlements, while the local news in Onehunga was that Bishop Selwyn was finally arriving to consecrate the Purchas church and dedicate the plot of land next door as a cemetery, as it remains today.

---

130 S Oliver, *Te Ara – The Encyclopedia of New Zealand*, Vol 1, 1990; Pei Te Hurinui Jones, King Pōtatau. Refer also M King, *The Penguin History of New Zealand*, p 212, who says Te Wherowhero agreed to become king at the earlier Pūkawa Taupō hui in 1856. But various events suggest it did not occur until much later.

But settler talk, opinion in the streets and the underlying sentiment of almost all Europeans was that the institution of a Māori monarchy – even if not supported by all natives – would still be a deliberate attempt to undermine the authority of Queen Victoria. Worse, as far as the settlers were concerned, it would surely mean even greater restrictions on land sales.

In spite of the settlers' mistrust, the 'king-in-waiting', Te Wherowhero, finally left his home at Mangere in late April 1859 and was taken by his people to Ngāruawāhia. There, on May 2, in a simple but dignified ceremony, with Wiremu Tāmihana placing a bible on his head, he was installed as the first Māori King, taking the name Pōtatau. The coronation was marked with a new Kīngitanga flag bearing a cross and with hymns and prayers for the Queen. As he had done for years previously and would continue doing until he died, Pōtatau Te Wherowhero ended them all with a loud "Amen". In his place at Mangere, he asked Tāmati Ngāpora to deputise for him – again with the assistance of Rata Patiti (Purchas) – as a main channel of communication between the Kīngitanga Waikato tribes and the Government.

While Selwyn and several of his Auckland colleagues did not like the idea of the Kīngitanga, others such as Sir William Martin saw no real harm. Donald McLean, chief land purchase commissioner and native secretary, expected the entire movement would simply die out. In Selwyn's circle, Purchas surely would have known best, from his intimate connections with Pōtatau and Ngāpora, that the Kīngitanga's main priority was land preservation and that they harboured absolutely no warlike intentions. His only concern might have been whether Pōtatau, Tāmihana and others could control the hardliners from some of the more aggressive Waikato tribes like Ngāti Maniapoto and their chief Rewi.

Reaction to Kīngitanga

For most of the 16,500 European settlers then living in Auckland and the thousands in other settlements around the country, the predictable reaction to the Māori King's coronation was the instant confirmation that it was indeed a deliberate threat and "rebellious even traitorous conduct followed by talk of consequences".[131]

Tāmihana again countered immediately that any ideas of Kīngitanga rebellion couldn't be further from their minds. He was supported in the sincerity of this assurance initially by Selwyn, despite the Bishop's antipathy

---

131 R D Crosby, *Kupapa*.

towards the movement, and his genuine concern about how Governor Browne might react. After his return from England in mid-1855, Selwyn had learned first-hand of the thinking at some of the kīngitanga hui and reported at later government select hearings in 1860 that "whenever I asked the natives what the use of the King was, they always answered – 'to take care of their land for them'".

Purchas's long-standing Māori friends and families living around Ihumatao, Pukaki and Mangere,[132] and the lower Waikato-Tuakau areas, were aghast at the reaction of most settlers. Here Māori had been living peaceful, co-operative and productive lives, happily co-existing alongside European farmers in the area for many years, with little or no apparent friction. Purchas had also spent a lot of time among both races in the late 1850s while designing and supervising the building of the new churches at Mauku and Mangere – and, in between, when working with von Hochstetter on his geological projects. Many conversations had taken place between Purchas, settlers and Māori friends from several different iwi over the direction future events might now take.

To make things even more difficult, Purchas's missionary colleagues began to come under fire from their European congregations for supporting Māori who opposed development and the release of tribal land, even when so-called "wasteland" was involved. The aggressive settler press further inflamed the situation. Selwyn tried to ward off some of this criticism by gently suggesting to Māori that perhaps they should sell land they didn't actually want to live on or farm, and to follow strictly the legal European title system when doing so.

Suddenly it became a tough time to be a clergyman like Purchas. The European congregations' natural expectation was that their priests would support them against these Māori "rebels" and stand up for Queen and country – especially since the congregations were supposedly paying a proportion of their salary. The consequent drop in financial support from many congregations at this time stemmed partially from the mounting anger over what they perceived to be the unwillingness of the clergy and missionaries to speak out loudly enough over the Māori shunning of their Queen. They simply expected Māori to accept gratefully that they were now Her Majesty's protected subjects. However, the settlers were still not prepared to extend all their privileges to Māori, particularly the vote.

So by 1858-59, it was quite clear that the Pākehā minority shared the belief that *they* had assumed true power and initiative in the colony. Governor Browne also began insisting that any subsequent "rebellious act" by Māori would inevitably result in them being taught a "short sharp lesson". While he and his administration had been happy to make some concessions to Māori with the setting up of rūnanga or councils – to hear and adjudicate on Māori

---

132   The name Mangere did not actually come into use until later in the 1860s.

land disputes and local law and order incidents – these had often proved to be indecisive and marred by confusion over varying loyalties and rights. The rūnanga were increasingly being seen as the impotent mechanism of patronising Europeans.

In a wider context, the contemporary attitudes and reactions of Europeans regarding any expressions of indigenous 'independence' – or attempts by natives to better manage their own problems – were also being influenced by events in other colonies. This was particularly the case in South Africa, where George Grey had ruthlessly dealt with the natives, and in India, where the British had faced the 1857 Indian Mutiny. Vincent O'Malley explains the significance thus:

"The Indian Mutiny marked the end of the two decade period in which humanitarian ideals were a prominent and perhaps even dominant feature of the imperial project ... the British Empire thereafter took on a harsher, more militaristic and racial tone. In this context, military confrontations with recalcitrant subjects became that much more permissible and likely ... this shift in thinking inevitably influenced Colonial Office attitudes towards war."[133]

While some Māori may have expected confrontation, later historians have argued that the establishment of the Kīngitanga – supported as it was by about two-thirds of all the major tribal groups in the North Island – effectively gave the New Zealand Government all the justification it needed for subsequent military action. The argument and confusion over sovereignty and loyalty, which the Kīngitanga gave rise to, was quickly reshaped into a reaction against a supposed "rebellion", the later violent suppression of which was then used to justify the confiscation of vast areas of land – notwithstanding the Treaty.

Waitara conflict begins

While Purchas was drafting his plan to add a few more rooms onto his Onehunga home for his growing family, the pressure to acquire more land for the latest settler arrivals was increasing, this time in Taranaki. Wakefield's company had done a great job selling the vision to intending migrants from England, but its agents had consistently over-promised and under-delivered. When new settlers arrived, they often found that the best land talked up earlier by company agents was simply not now available for them to buy. Much of the remaining land in Taranaki was also either "abandoned" or wasteland – far away from safe, main settlements. In other areas, the real owners were hard to find, or the land was in some kind of dispute – sometimes as a consequence of the

---

133   V O'Malley, *Beyond the Imperial Frontier*, p 141.

Musket Wars of the 1830s when tribes like Te Āti Awa, with long-standing customary occupation rights, had been driven away towards the Wellington area.

Grey had actually investigated many ownership claims in the area in 1847 and concluded that Te Āti Awa had, in fact, abandoned many of those early customary rights in some of the best parts of Taranaki. He also agreed that factions within the Waikato Tainui tribes now held many of them by right of their own somewhat sporadic occupation. However, Te Āti Awa chief Wiremu Kīngi Te Rangitāke never accepted this assertion. Under growing pressure from disgruntled settlers wanting land and probably without the best advice from Land Purchase Commissioner Donald McLean, Governor Browne signed a deed in 1859 for 600 acres of prime land near Waitara with another Te Āti Awa chief – Te Teira.

The problem was that Kīngi had actually been a supporter of the English in earlier days and the Waitara land in question was regarded by him as traditionally belonging to his own tribe. To make matters worse, Te Āti Awa had split into a couple of factions – landholders and land sellers and Te Teira was strongly in the latter group. The feud over which Māori tribe owned the Waitara land ignited when Te Teira offered it for sale to the Government. It was to be the defining act leading to the forthcoming wars.[134]

Kīngi immediately and forcefully made known his opposition to this sale to Governor Browne who responded by ordering a survey of the land in January 1860. Although Kīngi politely maintained he did not want a fight, the Governor still found it necessary to warn him that any disruption to the survey would have serious consequences. For Browne, trying hard to appease angry settlers, this was now a test of who was in charge. For Kīngi, it was a case of an unjustified permanent alienation of land which, more significantly, now lined him up precisely with the views of the Kīngitanga movement and some of his Waikato allies.

Unfortunately, a small group of Kīngi's supporters did subsequently disrupt the survey. In late February, Browne seized the opportunity to show who was running the country by declaring a state of martial law. Wiremu Kīngi's people were forced from their pā while government troops and ships moved in. Almost before anyone knew, the first Taranaki War had effectively begun ... on March 4, 1860.

Selwyn, Abraham (now Bishop of Wellington), Sir William Martin and Octavius Hadfield with his pamphlets about the "little war", were all vociferous

---

134   For an excellent summary of this background, refer to A Parsonson, Te Rangitake, Wiremu Kingi, *Te Ara – The Encyclopedia of New Zealand*, 1990.

in their protests to the Queen and the colonial secretary of state about what they saw as an "over-the-top" and far too drastic response from Browne. They were backed up in England by the CMS committee who also wrote to the British secretary of state asking for an inquiry to determine the rightful ownership of the Waitara land. His pride wounded, Governor Browne's response was simply to issue an order to the church to stay away and not interfere.

In Ngāruawāhia, King Pōtatau and Wiremu Tāmihana – neither of whom had any previous sympathy for Wiremu Kīngi – now saw the Waitara situation aligning with their own objectives of obtaining better control over Māori land. A short time later, they were even more strongly united with the overall cause following the pointless burning down of Kīngi's impressive Waikanae Church by government forces. The Kīngitanga next sent a party to Taranaki to determine for themselves who indeed was the rightful owner of the Waitara land and concluded it was Kīngi. While hardliner Rewi Maniapoto and his Taranaki tribal allies pushed the Kīngitanga hard to make a stand there and not wait until the British came to the Waikato, Māori views on land alienation became even more entrenched and widespread.

For the Government the Waitara issue may have been about sovereignty and "who was in charge", but for Māori and church leaders at the time, including Purchas, it was nothing of the sort. To them it was, purely and simply, a breach of the Treaty of Waitangi relating to undisturbed possession, particularly in circumstances such as these where rightful ownership of the land was so obviously in dispute and needed clarification.

Settlers prepare

At home in Onehunga, Arthur and Olivia were welcoming their latest child, Arthur, to the world, preparing for their first AGM as a full parish and starting work on the house enlargement. Purchas had already climbed up on the roof and removed the two chimney pots in preparation for his "master plan"[135]. He intended jacking up the entire house and building new rooms underneath. While this was going on, he ensured the family could continue to live upstairs for the next several months. So careful was his work that not even the family clock stopped. To minimise noise from banging doors and to make it easier for the children passing through, he set them with springs so they could swing open and shut on their own. He rebuilt the chimneys, made and fitted a new staircase, and prepared additional strengthening and supports for the upper

---

135   Brookfield family notes 1991 and Gertrude Stevenson (nee Purchas).

storey and verandah.

In the streets of Auckland and Onehunga, as the news of the government action in Taranaki filtered back, the general atmosphere took a decided turn for the worse. The open talk among the locals was that the time had indeed come to teach the natives a lesson. That should include forming local militia to defend the towns against possible full-scale Māori invasion under their new Kīngitanga flag (without the slightest hint that any such thing was in the wind). Browne, of course, had no wish to persuade the settlers otherwise.

In the first week of March 1860, a meeting was called of all Onehunga residents to discuss the setting up of volunteer military corps in support of their ageing Fencible force. Purchas was not going to be able to cry off from this important gathering in the face of his own very personal and excruciating moral dilemma – how to front his fellow townspeople with integrity and credibility while remaining on good terms with Te Wherowhero, Tāmati Ngāpora, Tāmihana and those in the Kīngitanga, people he had always known to be peaceable and basically supportive of the Government.

From the press reports in the *New Zealander* the next day, his speech at the meeting appears to have been masterly – a skilful combination of diplomacy and honesty. A motion was first presented and quickly accepted to form a volunteer corps in Onehunga "to fight the Maoris". A couple of other senior townspeople addressed the crowd before all eyes turned to their priest. Purchas opened his remarks by saying he was "glad to see the spirit shown by the Onehunga people and that it was right to form a corps to defend their families – if necessary".

Then, with considerable calculated risk, he said: "There is little to fear from natives in our neighbourhood … it is true there is some slight disturbance in the Waikato from a small section … but Te Wherowhero is one of our staunchest friends," he reminded them. "Our very existence has for a long time depended entirely on the good will of the natives."

He went on to say he had heard that very day that the chief now supposedly taking up arms against Governor Browne (Wiremu Kīngi) was the same man who had just helped quell a native disturbance of his own people in the Hutt in support of the Government. And, using his most diplomatic language, Purchas suggested that "the best way to keep the natives quiet is to show we are prepared".

Finally, perhaps relieved at the attentive reception from his local audience and knowing he might be the only man who could say such things, Purchas gave his fellow Europeans a polite but firm admonition. He referred to the single main cause of any discontent among Māori as being "the insults they are subject to when they come among Europeans. The Maori," he continued, "is a man like ourselves, after God's own image, and so deserves respect. And we may depend that the Maori never forgets and will remember those who put an indignity on him."

It was a courageous public stance for Purchas to take at this time and, happily, it appeared to enhance his standing in the community. Confidence was such that he was still able to be the mover of a final motion, limp as it was – a "memorial" to Governor Browne "that the Onehunga community viewed with some anxiety the disturbed state of our relations with Maori". It was then signed by the 46 newly signed-up volunteers of the Onehunga Defence Corps – allowing Purchas to return home to worry about the next stage of his home improvement programme.

CHAPTER 9

More New Hats

It was also around this time that Selwyn finally relented on his long-standing opposition to Purchas accepting any payment for medical services rendered. Almost certainly it was due to the fact that Selwyn's archdeaconry fund was now in an even more parlous state. And there was the realisation that the settlers were never going to increase their offerings enough, especially in the light of so many new uncertainties. Selwyn's consent, however, did not make much difference financially to Purchas, who understandably found it very difficult to start levying his long-standing patients after nearly 12 years of free service. The only real opportunity, except where wealthier residents may have offered to pay for medical advice, lay in fuller reimbursement of the medicines and drugs he was prescribing for his patients.

Purchas had also, for some years now, accepted responsibility for attending accidents and treating local trauma victims – and for providing expert medical advice to coroners and police as to cause of death or serious injury. Such time and advice could be more easily accounted for and paid by local government officials now and Purchas established a strong reputation early on for his reliability and excellence in this area.

The inevitable result was a request from the superintendent of Auckland Hospital for him to accept a new role as the hospital's main surgeon. This work, while not full time, not only drew Purchas into the heart of the medical community in Auckland, but also meant an additional small source of income.

And the work came at an opportune time because he now had some extra funds to help pay for the second storey on his house. Although he avoided the expense of employing someone to prepare all the detailed drawings and engineering calculations by doing the work himself,[136] the extra income from his surgical employment meant he was able to engage additional local labour for any heavy lifting required. On Sundays he was still busy taking services

---

136 The house itself was not his, of course, it being on church land and therefore technically "owned" by Selwyn's diocese.

at Onehunga and, later in the day, in the small 50-seat church of St Andrew's on the hill in Epsom.

Yet, incredibly, Purchas's active and enquiring scientific mind had also seen him begin work on a completely new project involving a particular interest of his – *Phormium tenax*, the New Zealand native flax or harakeke. This interest may have been sparked by his earlier botanical studies of vegetable and plant oils. And while he would not have known the precise chemical makeup of flax oil, he certainly knew enough to understand its possible value. More likely, however, he was excited by the idea of inventing a simple machine which might eliminate all the drudgery involved in the manual stripping and beating of flax leaves to extract, not oil, but the fibre itself. It was the flax fibre within the simple flax leaf which was the real item of value.

The process of extracting the fibre had been a laborious and labour-intensive job for centuries. Purchas first wanted to speed up the stripping process, almost always done by Māori hands with very basic tools such as sharpened mussel shells or obsidian, where it was available. Since first coming to Onehunga, Purchas had become very familiar with the natives' flax preparation methods and was excited by the fibre's many uses – for cordage and fabrics, and even as stuffing for chairs, cushions and soft toys, to say nothing of the Māori skill in using the flax leaves for plaiting and weaving.

Demand for the treated flax product in British, American and Australian markets was also growing rapidly at this time. New Zealand flax had first been exported to Australia in the 1820s where it was used in sizeable quantities for lashings on wool bales. Ngāi Tahu also exported significant amounts of South Island flax, and used the proceeds to obtain guns and ammunition when they were fighting Te Rauparaha's Ngāti Toa invaders.

The opportunity, which Purchas was now keen to exploit, lay in finding a faster, more efficient method of extracting and preparing the fibre for the varied product range including rope. The main problem with flax ropes was that, although strong and reliable, they were susceptible to excessive dampness, humidity and changes in temperature, which could induce early rot. Purchas hoped that a partial answer might lie in faster stripping of the fibre from the green leaves and better drying. He discussed his idea for a new flax stripping machine with James Ninnis, the Onehunga engineer with whom he had worked on the Drury coal mining project. Ninnis agreed the idea had great potential.

For the next six months, throughout the winter of 1860 and during all the Taranaki troubles, the pair got to work – Purchas drawing and designing, Ninnis manufacturing and building, and both of them testing, reworking and adjusting the design of their first working model.

It comprised a large wooden cylinder, revolving on a central axle and mounted on a solid iron frame. Above the revolving cylinder was a row of iron plates, each one grooved at one end. These plates were raised to a height of about 30cm, dropping continuously onto the green flax leaves as they passed over the rotating cylinder. The green waste produced by this mechanical beating of the leaves was taken off by running water. Their machine, driven by a water wheel designed by Ninnis, was capable of producing about 250kg of fibre a day from about 1500kg of flax.

Purchas's work, however, was interrupted by several serious incidents and the further deterioration in North Island race relations. While the raids, sieges and assaults carried on in Taranaki between Browne's supposedly significant British imperial forces and their small but seemingly unconquerable foe, the news came in June of the death of Te Wherowhero Pōtatau. He had become increasingly unwell in the short time since becoming king and died on June 25, 1860 at the age of about 85, according to Māori historian Pei Te Hurinui Jones.

Te Wherowhero had known Purchas for some 13 years – since the time the latter had organised horses, a carriage and a plough for him when the famous rangatira first came to live at Mangere. He had become known from those days on "for the peculiar dignity of his manner, a tall and graceful-looking man" who conversed with quiet ease with those he met in the drawing rooms of Government House. It was also said no one would have guessed then that he was the same Māori warrior who had sat naked on the ground at Pukerangiora years earlier, smashing the skulls of hundreds of defenceless prisoners, "until almost smothered with blood and brains".[137]

The great Te Wherowhero Pōtatau was buried on Taupiri Mountain and succeeded by his son Matutaera (38),[138] ahead of Pōtatau's niece Te Paea – both remaining in close contact with Purchas. While Purchas and others surely would have contemplated the effect of the King's death on the future turn of events in Taranaki, he would also have been somewhat relieved knowing that both Matutaera and the influential Te Paea (his cousin)[139] shared Te Wherowhero's strong commitment to peace. Purchas knew they would do everything they could to avoid any escalation of trouble with Governor Browne.

Optimism in this respect was even boosted a little further when the great Kohimarama Conference opened in Auckland about two weeks later. Organised by Donald McLean for Browne, it was a chance for a large invited

---

137 W T L Travers, *The Stirring Times of Te Rauparaha*, p 161.
138 Matutaera did not take the name Tāwhiao until 1864.
139 Often mistakenly referred to as Tāwhiao's sister. She was the daughter of Kati, the younger brother of Pōtatau. Refer M King, *Te Puea – A Life*, p 36.

group of senior New Zealand chiefs to again discuss the entire land question and hear the Crown's position on land acquisition. A secondary objective – at least for McLean and some others in the Government – was to persuade the Kīngitanga against any possible thought of attacking the Europeans in Auckland, at that time still the seat of government.

Among the 112 chiefs assembled – although only six came from the Waikato – were many staunch government supporters, like the great Ngā Puhi chief Tāmati Wāka Nene. Tāmihana Te Rauparaha was also there and asked, during the final sessions, that the conference be made a permanent institution so both sides could clear the air regularly and continue trying to find solutions to "the evils affecting both European and native".[140]

Tāmihana was no doubt thinking that a regular conference – well attended by Māori chiefs in good faith and with good intent – might well provide the perfect forum for Māori and European to find some other way of retaining their rangatiratanga and sorting out the land issues. Why the senior Pākehā leaders of the day – Browne and McLean, and Grey soon after – did not take up what seemed such an eminently sensible proposal has been interpreted since as a gross error of judgement or, more likely, as a deliberate tactic on a path to the intended military confrontation, Browne's "short, sharp lesson".

The fact that the proposal came from the very man so heavily involved in the creation of the Māori King movement six or seven years earlier, should have been significant for the Government. However, the golden opportunity to find a peaceful resolution was lost for ever. If men like Purchas, with an understanding of both sides of the argument, had hopes at this late stage that Governor Browne might desist from his seemingly one-eyed pursuit of all-out military confrontation and victory, those hopes would soon be extinguished.

Even though the Kīngitanga was not well represented at Kohimarama, some communications between its representatives and Governor Browne did continue. Most of it was initiated from the Māori side and underlined the desire of Matutaera and Tāmihana not to engage the Government in military action.

At the same time this was playing out, Purchas was working long hours on his flax machine but, in conjunction with Ngāpora, was still managing to remain intimately involved with the communication lines originating with the Kīngitanga.

Warnings begin

Three or four months later, by late September 1860, the tension and spasmodic

140 R D Crosby, *Kupapa*.

Arthur Purchas, was
a man of striking
appearance in his mid-
40s, this photograph
taken about the time
of his significant
involvement in the long
period of uncertainty
and build-up to the
Taranaki and Waikato
wars.

PURCHAS FAMILY FILES

skirmishes between settler and Māori unfortunately continued to escalate. Many were over relatively trivial issues, but often with deadly outcomes. Purchas met with Ngāpora regularly to assess their impact and to keep a gauge on wider Kīngitanga feelings and report back to the Governor in the hope of avoiding any wider conflict. In the weeks preceding an important select committee meeting on the Waikato situation, the three of them had also met, with Purchas translating. Ngāpora was again anxious to relay to Browne his observations and assurances that he (Ngāpora), King Matutaera and Tāmihana remained resolutely opposed to any conflict. How far Ngāpora was prepared to go to keep good faith with Browne and avoid conflict was evident a day or so later, September 27, when Purchas wrote the following urgent note to the Governor:

"Sir, Tamati Ngapora has begged me to return to tell you one thing which he forgot to speak of. He says the natives are watching for an excuse to seize the military stores at Raglan and he thinks that the establishment of a military post at Maungatawhiri or any other place in the immediate neighbourhood of the native districts would be looked upon as furnishing a 'ta-ke' [reason] for such seizure."[141]

Browne also referred to another warning from Ngāpora in a letter he wrote about the same time to Donald McLean saying: "Purchas was here last night, after you left, with a message from Ngapora saying that the upper Waikato had written to him desiring him to fix the day for an attack on Auckland but that he wrote back declining the honour." The "upper Waikato" referred to here by Ngāpora was mostly a reference to Maniapoto.

The Governor was then warned by missionary John Morgan at Ōtāwhao (Te Awamutu) that various Waikato hapū were now dividing into their clear tribal groups, usually with each individual rangatira's opinion determining the feelings of the entire tribe or group. The three strands of opinion that emerged involved the Queenites, who still wanted to sell land freely; the Kingites who were totally opposed to such sales; and a third group willing to let the Government have the Waitara lands in return for stopping sales within the broad Kīngitanga boundaries of the Waikato. These boundaries included the very rich Hauraki lands from Coromandel and Te Aroha to Morrinsville and Matamata, across to Raglan in the west and today's King Country, and south to Taupō.

Within days of these exchanges, Purchas found himself right in the middle of the most serious incident yet in what was now becoming a fast-developing crisis in the Waikato. In Auckland, most of the senior politicians and officers not involved in the Taranaki conflict, were taking part in the "Waikato Committee" inquiry. Ostensibly it was set up to investigate the circumstances of the earlier establishment of rūnanga – Māori councils as institutions of civil government among the Waikato Māori – and their spectacular failure after only a couple of years. The inquiry had focused to a large degree on how Purchas's old friend Francis Fenton, as the Government's resident magistrate in the area, had set them up and the reactions from the different Kingite and Queenite factions as to how he had been conducting them.

Waikato Māori chiefs, missionaries, Bishop Selwyn, other senior churchmen and government servants all participated in the hearings which continued for nearly three weeks. The final report, comprising some 200 pages, is still the best summary of the key factors that led to the establishment of the Kīngitanga, and the feelings on both sides immediately before the "Great War of the Waikato."[142]

Halfway through the proceedings, word came through that a man named Eriata, of Ngāti Tamaoho, had been found shot in the head in bush near Patumahoe. Ngāti Tamaoho lived mostly in the Tuakau, Pokeno and Patumahoe areas, had strong links to Ngāti Mahuta and other Tainui tribes, and were all staunch Kīngitanga supporters. Within hours, McLean, Selwyn, Robert Maunsell from the Port Waikato mission station and Purchas were immediately involved as the news spread. The initial Māori assumption was that Eriata had been shot by a Pākehā settler for trespassing.

Eriata's allies, the Ngāti Hāua, immediately assembled a 400-strong war party or taua, which set off for Patumahoe under their chief, Wiremu Tāmihana. In Onehunga, a hastily assembled settler force on horseback was called up by Governor Browne under Colonel Marmaduke Nixon, with an order to prepare to leave early next morning for Patumahoe. Alarm on the part of the settlers – not only in the Mauku-Patumahoe region but also in Onehunga and Auckland itself – was considerably heightened because, at that time, most of the British forces previously stationed in barracks in Auckland and ready for just such emergencies, were far away ... involved in the battles in Taranaki.

---

142 Appendix to the Journals of the House of Representatives, 1860, *Report of the Waikato Committee.*

The evening before Nixon's party was due to leave for Mauku, one of Purchas's many reliable Māori friends living at Mangere got word to him at home in Onehunga that Tāmihana's Ngāti Hāua party would not attack the settlers unless the British attacked first, and that Tāmihana would communicate with him (Purchas) again shortly. Knowing of Tāmihana's moderating influence and trusting his native communication links, Purchas borrowed a horse and rode straight to Government House in Auckland to alert Governor Browne and his Executive Council, and warn him not to despatch Nixon or make any kind of move against the Ngāti Hāua war party. This done, about 9pm Purchas headed back on the 10km ride home to Onehunga. Just before midnight there was a tap on the window of one of his new rooms downstairs. The messenger gave him the confirmation he needed, direct from Tāmihana, that Ngāti Hāua would certainly not be the first to start a fight, but they needed to know quickly how Eriata had been killed.

At 1 or 2am that morning, Purchas saddled up his horse again and rode as quickly as he could back to Auckland where Donald McLean, Richmond, Whitaker, Pollen and others of the Executive Council met him at Browne's front door, the Governor apparently still "in the undress of the bedchamber". Purchas was asked to report his information which was listened to in complete silence. A further lengthy period of quiet followed as the council members pondered the extremely delicate situation. Eventually the silence was broken by Purchas himself, asking that he might be excused for what he was about to say, but that the situation was urgent. He knew that in Mauku, both Selwyn and Maunsell were trying to calm the settlers down and to talk also with Tāmihana about the dangers of any sudden response by a wayward or overly aggressive member of his taua. The Governor asked Purchas to continue.

He advised that two things needed to be done immediately to avert a catastrophe. Firstly, Colonel Nixon's planned departure for Mauku must not proceed. Secondly, the settlers should be told to stay in their homes in Mauku and certainly not flee, something which would easily have been interpreted by Māori as an admission of guilt. But Browne had already ordered a ship to be sent from Onehunga the next day to collect them. Besides, said one of the council – apparently Frederick Whitaker – "we have no means of communication".[143]

By now it was about 4am. Purchas offered immediately that, if the Government could supply him with a fresh horse, he would personally relay the message directly to Tāmihana and the others, including Browne's promise

---

143 Brookfield family notes, E H Roche (Purchas's grandson).

of an inquiry. This agreed, Purchas rode from central Auckland to Tāmihana's camp near Patumahoe where, as dawn broke, he was met on arrival by Te Paea. She escorted the exhausted Purchas through groups of hostile warriors to meet with Tāmihana.

His mission proved successful. Selwyn and Maunsell managed to calm the settlers, who had all packed and assembled quietly in a nearby house to wait for the ship. Tāmihana, very pleased on behalf of the Kīngitanga to avoid a major confrontation – but still sensing many of his men's real reluctance to withdraw – agreed to let a proper inquiry determine the true cause of Eriata's death. A day or so later, the taua withdrew quietly to their homes in the Waikato, while the settlers relaxed a little and resumed their daily lives.

The subsequent inquiry, held in conjunction with the respected chief Ihaka Wirihana Takanini of Te Āki Tai, proved without doubt that the unfortunate Eriata had accidentally shot himself, apparently when trying to climb over some obstacle while hunting. But the overall level of tension between Pākehā and Māori had still risen considerably as a result.

The key question left for Purchas and the missionary group was whether Tāmihana and Matutaera's moderating influence within the Kingite movement could continue to restrain the increasingly belligerent factions gathering around Maniapoto and now spreading down through some of the other smaller Waikato tribes as far as Taupō and the east coast.

Some historians have speculated that influential chiefs like Rewi Maniapoto were probably more intent, at this time, on provoking the major confrontation they wanted with the British in Taranaki – thus avoiding what they expected would be a far more destructive conflict if it were to happen in the Waikato. It has also been suggested that Maniapoto and his allies believed the Kīngitanga had not only been far too passive already, but would likely be an easy foe for the British in a war on their "home patch," even with their many allies. If nothing else, besides being a shrewd tactician and strategist, Rewi Maniapoto was a realist.

Flax machine success

Amid such a worrying episode as the Eriata business, continuing random violence between native and settler, and the grave position in Taranaki, the last two or three months had still been a time of good progress for Purchas and Ninnis with their flax machine. While Ninnis was nearing completion of the first working prototype, Purchas began drawing up the documents in preparation for what was to be a New Zealand "first". Others who had seen the first working model, and analysed the results, had been so impressed that the talk now was of the Purchas machine having the potential to provide a major breakthrough for the entire New Zealand flax industry.

Purchas was savvy enough to realise that in the machine's simplicity also lay its greatest commercial risk – the ease with which it might be copied. On October 10, 1860, his detailed plans and specifications "for an invention for the preparation of the fibre of phormium tenax and other plants for manufacturing purposes" were lodged at the Auckland office of the Colonial Secretary. Purchas and Ninnis wanted a patent to protect their invention.

Their problem was that at this early stage in the colony's legislative history, there was no patent law or process established to grant such a patent. But the Government was keen to promote innovation and enterprise, and the Purchas-Ninnis machine and proposal became generally credited with spurring the authorities into action. In a matter of weeks, special legislation was drawn up while Purchas went to ground at home, waiting nervously lest someone else might produce a similar machine.[144] To his great relief, the final bill was presented and passed into law as the Purchas and Ninnis Flax Patent Act 1860 – the founding document of the New Zealand patent system.

The Letters Patent for the flax machine were subsequently issued in March 1861 – thus Arthur Purchas had his name on the first patent to be issued in New Zealand. It was for a period of 14 years and the initial wording gave Purchas and Ninnis the "exclusive right of manufacturing machinery for preparing flax by percussion". Subsequently this wording had to be amended because it effectively precluded any improvement to the Purchas-Ninnis method of beating flax, which was obviously not the intention of the original drafters of the law.

Their flax machine immediately created huge interest, and not only in New Zealand. Inquiries came from Australia, England, India and Sri Lanka, or Ceylon as it was. A story appeared in the *Ceylon Observer* about three months after the patent was granted, describing the Purchas machine. A British investor, Samuel Harland, wrote to Purchas saying he was keen to import a machine to help with his new business of growing aloe fibre and "wished to have the best and most economical mode of working it".

Purchas, the clergyman-doctor-scientist-architect-musician-geologist-diplomat and now inventor, must have been pleased with the acceptance and success of the project. He might also have expected that the new machine would help to ease some of the pressure on his finances. As he and Ninnis

---

144 Designing the Future – Celebrating the Past, *WIPO* Magazine (World Intellectual Property Organization), June 2011; Brookfield family papers; *Heritage New Zealand* magazine, Winter 2011.

dealt with the flood of inquiries from all over New Zealand and elsewhere, a group of Auckland investors began putting together a proposal to capitalise on the new machinery. A sum of £400 was promised to build a new flax mill and conduct a full commercial trial. While Europeans enjoyed the finished fibre products, they were not keen on the laborious work of cleaning and dressing the flax – seen purely as a job for the natives. Hence, a machine which could efficiently perform this role – and do it 200 times faster than the best native cleaner – was of great interest to the entrepreneurs of Auckland town who suddenly smelled money.

The Waitangi flax mill, built for Purchas by Auckland investors, to house one of his new flax machines.
AUCKLAND LIBRARIES HERITAGE
COLLECTIONS 7-A2820

There is no specific evidence to confirm the architect of the mill building – but logically, and most likely, Purchas would have chosen to design it himself. The site selected was familiar to Purchas and Ninnis – a large flax-growing area beside the Waitangi stream, near Waiuku.[145] While the planning went ahead, the two inventors were encouraged to exhibit some of their dressed fibre at the 1862 London International Exposition. They were awarded a medal as was fellow Aucklander Neill Lloyd, who had submitted samples of rope made from the same Purchas-Ninnis fibre.

War clouds gathering

Putting aside their concerns about conflict in the Waikato, the future would still have looked a little rosier to Arthur and Olivia Purchas at this point in their lives. With their seven little children – now all aged between six months and 11 years – and another baby on the way, Olivia was also enjoying the extra space her husband had provided for her downstairs in the Onehunga home. The news that many prominent Aucklanders now wanted to invest in the new flax project was also extremely heartening. Purchas's church affairs were in relatively good shape at both St Peter's and St Andrew's under the parochial trust board, families were still coming forward regularly for baptisms and a

---

145 The exact location is near today's Waitangi Falls Rd, off Glenbrook Rd.

steady line of couples, including Māori, continued to present themselves for marriage instruction and ceremony. St Peter's remained a focal point in the community, its church bell ringing out across the township every Sunday morning for half an hour as a constant reminder.

As the main Gundry trustee and executor, Purchas was now heavily involved in a detailed plan of reinvestment for the Gundry estate on behalf of its family beneficiaries. Olivia Gundry continued to live with the Purchas family as a helper with all the children – and perhaps she was now of an age when a small wage for her services was thought appropriate in addition to her free lodging. In the busy 12-month period up until June 1860, Purchas inspected, checked and then authorised, on behalf of the Gundry estate, the purchase (for £415) of another three separate lots of land in Onehunga, which were then leased. His fellow trustee Frederick Thatcher was finding it difficult to be of much help – being heavily engaged with Selwyn in establishing a pension fund for the clergy and working on other long-term endowment and property projects, which would later form most of Selwyn's enduring legacy in New Zealand. With his growing experience and confidence in the buying and selling of land in Onehunga, Purchas sold two of these lots a couple of years later at a tidy profit, reinvesting the proceeds into a 10% mortgage.

Somewhat ironically, Thatcher was also privately advising clergy at this time to consider carefully their own land or stock purchases wherever they could, as investments to "make moderate provision for themselves".[146] Times had clearly changed in this respect, given that 15 years earlier such transactions had been expressly forbidden. Purchas had certainly been thinking ahead in this particular game.

Inevitably though, as the British failures in Taranaki against the small Māori forces became known, the wider public mood in Auckland grew decidedly less cheerful and more anxious as the year wore on. Purchas's friend Vicesimus Lush noted that he had called on Selwyn about this time and found him "very angry with the government for bringing about the native war in Taranaki ... the very fact of there being an insecurity to life and property will throw the colony back fearfully ..." A week or so later he added: "There seems more and more certainty of war. The militia are being called out and there will soon be 4000 civilians under arms, besides soldiers. Poor Maoris! What numbers will perish."

The skirmishing in Taranaki continued, easing only briefly when some of the Maniapoto allies – East Coast tribes like Ngāti Porou and some Te Āti

146 Alington.

Awa warriors – returned home to plant crops for summer. Ngāpora, and a couple of fellow chiefs still living at Mangere, wrote again to Donald McLean while Tāmihana also wrote once more to Browne. They requested an end to the war in Taranaki while a proper investigation was conducted into the Waitara land controversy and specifically the entire background of customary land entitlements there. Selwyn and his new group of bishops also took the opportunity to tackle Browne again, this time claiming "on behalf of the New Zealanders, an investigation of all questions relating to their title to land before a regular tribunal".[147]

With the British forces failing in any recognisable way to crush the Māori spirit in Taranaki, the settlers themselves turned on their senior imperial officers for failing to get the result they all expected – a clear-cut victory in the field. While a kind of truce was eventually established at Waitara by May-June of 1861, Browne still put the pressure back on the Kīngitanga. He blamed the movement for escalating the trouble by sending various small war parties into the Taranaki to raid and kill, and then withdrawing to parts unknown.

Even if Browne was agreeable to the British troops lowering arms in Taranaki, he still appeared nowhere near ready to give up on his long-held belief that the Kīngitanga remained, by its presence alone, a deliberate challenge to the Queen's sovereignty. He saw its involvement in Taranaki, no matter by which tribe, as being an obvious sign of rebellious intent. With some of the Kīngitanga involving themselves in the Taranaki conflict without Matutaera's consent and still claiming rights to land there, Browne reasoned the British would never be able to develop a satisfactory plan for land purchase and economic development would be permanently stymied. He was fixed in his determination to take on the Kīngitanga in the Waikato heartland.

At its inception, the winning of what was expected to be a relatively quick fight in Waitara was almost certainly seen by Browne as the most expeditious way of extracting concessions of sovereignty and land from the Kīngitanga. Even when the military approach failed so miserably, his view only hardened towards the "obstinate and notorious Kingitanga rebels, interfering law-breakers, violent and extremist". Despite some attempts – including by Rewi Maniapoto himself – to make peace with Browne, the Governor and his allies remained convinced that the British cause could never be advanced while the Kīngitanga remained standing.

Browne quickly wrote to Tāmihana to tell him he would be calling on the Kīngitanga immediately to ask if they would now accept the "mana" of

147 Morrell, p 73

Queen Victoria, knowing full well what the answer would be. He went further – preparing a set of terms he now wanted all Waikato chiefs to accept and sign. And he set a date, May 21, on which to meet the Kīngitanga chiefs and present his ultimatum. He required Māori to submit, without reservation, to the Queen's sovereignty and the authority of British law – and he wanted both return of and compensation for plundered goods. Browne threatened that if Māori did not accept British law, they would forfeit the protection which the Treaty guaranteed them, with their land "remaining their own, so long only as they are strong enough to keep it". There could not have been a clearer or more threatening signal of intent, especially since the British had not "won" the war in Taranaki. In fact, neither side had won.

The Māori reaction was predictable. Matutaera, Tāmihana, Ngāpora, Te Hapuku and Kīngitanga supporters from many North Island tribes were deeply offended and outraged. Their reaction was summed up perfectly by Ngāti Kahungunu chief Renata Kawepo, a deeply Christian supporter and also long-term government loyalist who – a little earlier in a letter to the government superintendent in Hawkes Bay – had written: "The Treaty of Waitangi has been broken. It was said the Treaty was to protect the Maori from foreign invasion. But those bad nations never came to attack us. The blow fell from you, the nation that made that same treaty. Sir, it is you alone who have broken your numerous promises."[148]

Even so, in spite of Browne's aggressive words, Kīngitanga leaders continued to declare their unwillingness to go to war. But in the towns, the mood of the British settlers remained pugnacious and defiant, and fully supportive of Browne's threats. The talk was all about stockades, new redoubts being built, guns, cavalry and militia. Few had any hope at this stage that the fight might be averted. Browne believed he was now ready for the final showdown despite a serious underestimation, it turned out later, of the size of military force needed to accomplish the task.

Although Purchas and most of the other church and missionary leaders were strongly opposed to war, even they acknowledged there was now a sense of the inevitable. Lush wrote: "There is I am sorry to say, a desire on the part of many Europeans to force a war with the natives, knowing that ultimately the latter must be exterminated and that therefore the quicker will be the whole country opened up for occupation by Europeans. It is generally supposed that the Government fully intends to attack the Waikatos …"

He was right, but one more interesting turn of events was to come. Only

---

148   J Caselberg (ed), *Maori is my Name*, p 91.

eight or nine weeks later Governor Browne would no longer be in charge. Concerned about the direction he was taking and possibly even stung a little by the trenchant criticism from church and other leaders in New Zealand, the British Government simply took the decision not to renew Browne's contract. The Taranaki War had been a slow, inconclusive and frustrating military effort against a foe which would often just "disappear in the night" leaving the British forces with severe costs in time, lives and materials. So the news that Browne would be replaced by an earlier governor of the colony – the very same George Grey – actually came as a welcome surprise to many on both sides and another faint ray of hope for the Kīngitanga leaders and churchmen like Arthur Purchas, watching on from the side.

Grey, of course, had developed close and friendly links with many of the Kīngitanga, particularly the late Te Wherowhero Pōtatau, when in his first term as Governor. He was still strongly supported by the northern chiefs, who wrote him warm letters of welcome. But there remained a very large section of the settler business communities in Auckland and Wellington growing increasingly frustrated at the impasse – hungry for land, development and profit.

In their confidence and arrogance, they simply wanted the Government to get on with the showdown with Waikato Māori. The often repeated quote of the time – said to have come from one prominent Auckland banker – was that "nothing could be more ruinous for Auckland now than peace". But for the Māori leaders like King Matutaera, Ngāpora, Tāmihana, Te Hapuku and Wiremu Kīngi, there was still hope that Grey might yet be able to broker a compromise on the land alienation issue.

Return to architecture

In the lull before Grey's arrival, Purchas's attention turned back to architecture and family matters. The final touches were put on St Bride's at Mauku and a large crowd attended the first service, conducted by Purchas, on July 14, 1861. No sooner had the praise and congratulations for his efforts died down than, out of the blue, he received a request to design yet another new church – St Peter's – this time for the people of the Canterbury township of Akaroa.

The first church had been built there in 1852 but had proved far too small. Purchas's reputation and skills for designing cost-effective churches – using a relatively uncomplicated construction method as per the 'Selwyn' style – were now well established and word had spread quickly about the pleasing looks of St Bride's. His design for a new building on a slightly elevated site in Akaroa used the same nave and outside tower configuration as St Bride's – later to be enlarged with transepts and a sanctuary extension. Purchas again specified vertical totara timbers and a three-tiered spire. Today, as a Grade One Heritage New Zealand building, it is still in full use, "greatly admired for its architectural qualities … one of New Zealand's finest".[149]

The 10th Purchas child[150], Claude, was born in September, just four weeks before the large swearing-in ceremony in Auckland for Governor Sir George Grey, attended by the colony's leading citizens, including Purchas, and about 20 selected senior Māori guests. Grey was generally welcomed back with some warmth. The decision to shift the capital from Auckland to Wellington had been taken a few years earlier and was due to be implemented sometime soon – so the Auckland business community were collectively very glad of the opportunity to present their credentials to the Governor before his likely move south.

Within days, Ngāpora had also taken the opportunity to meet with Grey, attended by several other representatives of the Kīngitanga, including Rewi Maniapoto. It was not to prove a very promising event. Maniapoto told Grey their Māori King *had* to be independent. Grey immediately took this as a direct threat to British authority – similar to his recent dealings (as Governor of Cape Colony) with native communities in southern Africa who were also looking to preserve their lands and identity. His response in New Zealand, therefore, was unlikely to be any different from that of his predecessor, Browne.

Within weeks, Grey had written to his British superiors requesting that those British regiments sent to New Zealand to help with the war in Taranaki, be kept here for now. Perhaps one of the most telling and explicit summations of what Grey was thinking at this time came from Thomas Gore Browne's wife, Harriet, who expressed a couple of months later in a private letter to the native secretary: "I heard Grey with my own ears tell my husband that he hoped the natives would not submit, as it would be much better for both races that they should be conquered."[151]

At home, Olivia Purchas was becoming increasingly concerned about her father, Charles – still practising as an accountant in Liverpool, but suffering greatly from poor health. Letters from Olivia's mother, Eliza, refer to "bad times", her husband's poor breathing and "distressing cough", while inquiring also about Olivia's trouble with a very sore knee. She also asked, quite directly, why Olivia and Arthur had named their latest child Claude, saying: "It seems

---

149 Refer to the Heritage New Zealand website (www.heritage.org.nz). St Peter's was opened in 1863.
150 Named after Claude Guyon, Purchas's grandfather.
151 V O'Malley, *The Great War for New Zealand* – H Browne letter to C Richmond, former Minister of Native Affairs, 10/1/1862.

a curious name … I wish you had called the new one Charles." A second letter, at Christmas 1861, contained better news of a different sort. It was a reference to a copy of her uncle's will, which the Challinors were hoping Olivia had received and which, when it finally did arrive, contained some welcome news of a small inheritance.

On separate drawing boards in his Onehunga house, Purchas was now working on his two current architectural projects – the new church for Akaroa and the design and set-up for the flax mill near Waiuku. His Auckland investors had stumped up the money for the mill's construction on land leased beside the Waitangi stream. The plan was to undertake some experimentation on the machinery and the process before looking to establish a company and begin a full commercial operation.

However, in spite of some early optimism that Grey and the Kīngitanga might yet find a peaceful solution, the calls for war rose again, this time even more loudly. By the beginning of 1862, when Grey ordered extensions to the Great South Rd beyond Papakura and Drury to Pokeno, it was clear to everyone what the new governor's purpose was. The area from Pokeno to Mercer was sparsely settled and there could be no other use for such a road than a military one – especially when a new telegraph line was installed along its length. Continual movements of ships, soldiers and equipment into Auckland and Onehunga filled in the military picture. This 'build up', however, was presented by Grey to the settlers and the British Government as a sensible protective measure and self-defence to counter a possible a Māori invasion, and a demonstration to the Kīngitanga that the British were determined to stand fast on the question of "who was in charge".

Purchas's position – as for so many of his colleagues – involved the most perplexing matter of coming to terms with his conscience. His understanding of the complex Māori belief systems and traditions, his proficiency in their language and his years of personal interaction with people like Te Wherowhero, Ngāpora, Te Paea and others, meant he obviously understood the Kīngitanga's stance and the deep sense of mana associated with their land. On the other hand, he also understood the British Government's aim to be a progressive and hopefully generous instrument of change in concert with a willing indigenous race. He was much less impressed however, with the British settlers' sense of entitlement – that of "a conquering race with all rights to land and whatever it contained".

Given his understanding and perspective, it seems he came to the decision to take the middle ground and do his utmost to prevent any miscommunication by either side which might unjustifiably lead to war – and to provide honourable and fair support where he could, with neither fear nor favour. Some of his CMS missionary colleagues, notably John Morgan of Ōtāwhao, while initially standing alongside Māori in their quest to uphold Treaty principles, sadly now found themselves strongly on the Government side. The change of heart often came as a result of the increasing incidence of brutal raids, killings and attacks on defenceless settlers by small groups from belligerent Māori tribes – acting mostly on their own outside the direct control of the moderate Kīngitanga leaders like Tāmihana and Matutaera.

Purchas's reputation as an engineer threw him into just such an early personal quandary, as the road south to Pokeno was being built. Out of the blue, he received a letter from the senior British soldier in the field, Colonel Sir James Alexander, commander of the British 14th Foot Regiment. Alexander's men were building the road and establishing the new redoubt at Pokeno, and were under real pressure from Grey to get the job completed.

Alexander wanted Purchas's advice on a more efficient way to break up large rocks into metal for the road. He needed smaller, more portable machinery in place of sledgehammers and picks. Purchas felt he could hardly decline such a request without raising the question as to which side he was on. He replied a short time later with a design based on a tripod arrangement, using a simple block and tackle pulley system with a large weight being lifted and dropped continuously by a team of soldiers onto the smaller rocks below. The beauty of such a design lay in its portability and efficiency of construction, using equipment which Alexander would have immediately had at his disposal and which was quick and easy to assemble. [152]

Back in London, the British Government was collectively squirming more and more uncomfortably in its seat of power over the expensive military bills being incurred in New Zealand. The strain started to tell on Grey himself as he increasingly exaggerated, obfuscated and even deceived in his reports to his political masters – extravagantly justifying the military activity and expense. Platoons of well-armed troops were now being stationed at various outposts along the Great South Rd and nearby farms, while the large Queen's Redoubt at Pokeno was finally completed (it housed nearly 500 men by the middle of 1862).

Grey's reports to London still spoke of the need for preparations to defend the town of Auckland and for readiness against a Māori attack, which he said

---

152 Refer Te Papa PH000847, Letter from Alexander to Purchas. Alexander, later General Alexander, was a very senior British military officer who had earlier led his regiment in the Crimea at the Siege of Sebastopol and who was later instrumental in the erection of the famed Cleopatra's Needle on the Thames Embankment.

was imminent. As historian James Belich wrote: "The conclusion [that Grey planned the Waikato War well in advance] does not necessarily mean that Grey was an inhuman warmonger – though he could certainly have taught Machiavelli a trick or two in methodology."[153]

As settler attitudes hardened even more and war against the Waikato tribes appeared an inevitability, even some of the most peaceful Māori tribes began to accept that a major collision could not be avoided. Amid such deep uncertainty – and "with the Taranaki area still seething with discontent" – Selwyn and his team of bishops, priests and senior laymen, including several senior government leaders, nevertheless proceeded to Nelson in February 1862 for their second general synod.

For Purchas, the assembly resulted in another large assignment. The suggestion at the first Wellington synod in 1859 that he be asked to compile an all-new *New Zealand Hymnal* was declined, but came back onto the table in Nelson. This time the commission for Purchas to produce it was agreed upon.

It took him the next 18 months to compile a first edition, published in 1863, and comprised more than 220 hymns, including the two or three he had started composing earlier. While he was at it, he also put together a special 'tune book' of more complete music scores to go with the words of the most popular tunes in his hymnal, all in four-part harmony for choirs.[154] In the process, his reputation as the colonial church's 'master of music' was confirmed. While it was all in a day's work for Purchas, this project alone might have been half a lifetime's achievement for a person of more modest ability.

Purchas the artist

In early 1862, Purchas completed his design of the new Akaroa church of St Peter's – his fifth such building – and also handed over his preliminary plan for the flax mill to his partner James Ninnis to supervise its construction. Then, a few days later, he received a note from Frederick Thatcher confirming his wish to stand down as a Gundry trustee.[155] It wasn't a major surprise, although still an irritation at a very busy time and one that Purchas could well have done without. With the help of lawyers and the approval of Gundry's widow, he found another trustee – an experienced insurance manager named George Pierce.

---

153   J Belich, *The New Zealand Wars*, p 120.
154   The first copy of this *Tune Book*, especially bound and inscribed by Purchas for Olivia, is held in the Auckland Museum Library.
155   Family files – R Williams Letters 22/1/1862.

No sooner was this matter settled, than another request was made for his services as a trustee and executor. This time it was for long-time Epsom friend William Coldicutt, unfortunately now terminally ill and anxious that his wife and young son be properly cared for. Purchas had been involved in earlier land dealings with him as a Gundry trustee and now Coldicutt asked him to take care of his own estate. It comprised about 55 acres close to the church of St Andrew's in Epsom and Coldicutt's instruction was to sell it all within 12 months, put the proceeds out on mortgage, reinvest if and when necessary, and look after his wife and son. The generous and kindly Dr Purchas couldn't say no. He was now acting as trustee for three separate estates – and was regularly involved in the acquisition and disposal of land, with all the responsibility and judgement this entailed during a time of the utmost uncertainty and risk.

Perhaps it was a need to relieve some of the stress of these daily responsibilities or his concerns about the Waikato situation, which gave rise to another of his extraordinary talents – art and painting. His architectural work had seen him develop an instinctive ability to sketch quickly and accurately. A very early pen and ink drawing of the completed interior of Thatcher's St John's Chapel, done soon after it was opened, underscores his special talent.

Over the next couple of years, during his many travels to Waiuku, Ōtāwhao and the Waikato, Purchas took the opportunity to complete a number of new works. All in pen and ink, they include many different subjects – individual, unidentified Māori figures, travellers resting in the bush (dated February 24, 1862), and scenes of nature and recreation, including a detailed and expert rendition of Māori warriors launching canoes for the Auckland regatta.[156]

All Purchas's activities at this time – even if they did help to relieve some of the stress he might have been feeling – could not help but be overshadowed by the grave discussions he had each time he met up with Ngāpora, Te Paea and occasionally King Matutaera. Remaining a resident in Mangere, Ngāpora was still the man entrusted with keeping the main line of communication open from the Kīngitanga, through Purchas, to the Governor about the Waikato situation. Grey's road into the heart of the Waikato, right to the Kīngitanga boundary at Mercer, had provoked further hostile reaction and there was now a steadily building catalogue of retaliatory theft and violence. Each act of plunder against a European settler was reported in detail in the press, adding to the Māori reputation for lawlessness and sabotage. Ngāpora and Tāmihana, despite their meetings, letters and assurances, were fighting a losing battle and seemed to know it.

---

156 See illustrations elsewhere. Originals are held in family files and there are copies in the Auckland Diocesan Archives.

Purchas, the artist – a selection of his superb original sketches, many drawn between the years 1860 and 1870.
(Top:) St Andrew's church in Kohimarama.
(Above:) Girl in the Bush.
(Right:) Maori figures.

Launching the waka on Auckland regatta day.
COURTESY OF ALISON KISSLING

Earlier, in something of a mild concession to Kīngitanga demands for greater self-government and control of their own affairs, Browne first and then Grey had introduced the rūnanga system – Māori councils presided over mostly by senior Māori leaders and paid by the Government to act as assessors and magistrates within specific Māori regions.

But Grey, with some initial support from the moderates within the Kīngitanga, was also keen to have experienced Europeans involved as senior magistrates and commissioners working alongside Māori. He eyed, in particular, the regions close to the Kīngitanga headquarters in Ngāruawāhia and also Kihikihi-Ōtāwhao (Te Awamutu), where he felt the Europeans could teach some of the British principles of justice and balance, while trying to establish a system of local law and order, possibly acceptable to both races.

In other areas earlier on, specifically the north and east coast regions of the North Island, the rūnanga system had worked moderately well and was initially well received. But in the Waikato, as the special Waikato Committee was to hear later, it was a different story. As the Māori mood darkened over unresolved events in Taranaki, the rūnanga system did not fare well and soon began to collapse under the weight of suspicion concerning British intentions and what was perceived as more unwanted interference in the Māori world.

One single event in the implementation of the rūnanga 'experiment' in

Travellers resting in the bush.
COURTESY OF ALISON KISSLING

the Waikato was to catapult Purchas right into the heart of the inevitable collision to follow. It was the appointment of John Gorst as the British resident magistrate in Ōtāwhao, Te Awamutu, in February 1862.[157]

157 Gorst initially came to Te Awamutu a year earlier as a senior official under Premier Fox, recommended by Selwyn to try and soothe Māori agitation and introduce some gainful local employment.

CHAPTER 10

Ōtāwhao Crisis

The events that followed Gorst's appointment were what finally stoked the embers that burst into a conflagration only 18 months later, completely changing the course of New Zealand history.

The land at Ōtāwhao had been bought by Henry Williams and the CMS back in 1839 or early 1840, before the Treaty, as a site for a mission station. Back then, Māori warmly welcomed the idea of a mission station in their midst. The CMS first bought 100 acres and another 70 acres was added in 1852 – a gift from Te Wherowhero as an endowment for a Māori school.[158] The original CMS missionary in charge at Ōtāwhao was John Morgan, whom Purchas had visited frequently from the time he first moved to his Onehunga parish. The station comprised a house and farm outbuildings, a school for Māori and mixed race children, other hospital accommodation and facilities for the sick and the frequent visitors, together with the farm including crops and stock.

Initially, Morgan had also been a vocal advocate, along with Selwyn, for the appointment of a Māori-speaking senior British official to Ōtāwhao within the rūnanga system. But by 1862, with so many disaffected Waikato Māori increasingly antagonistic towards further European incursions, Morgan became somewhat disillusioned about the mission's future. When Selwyn raised the possibility of leasing back the entire property and school to Grey and the Government, Morgan gave his approval. That resulted in many formerly friendly and loyal Māori turning against Morgan and others of the missionary group who they now believed were working hand in hand with the Government to undermine the native race.

Māori mistrust reached new heights as Grey "took over" the activities and buildings at the Ōtāwhao mission station – a place which, from the start, had been "for Māori" on land endowed and given over "by Māori". At its height, the Ōtāwhao school under Morgan had averaged about 70-72 pupils annually for several years. By now, however, the roll had dropped to less than a dozen, mainly

---

158   Appendix to the Journals of the House of Representatives, Commission of Inquiry 1869, A-5.

mixed race children. Grey wanted to convert it into some kind of industrial school, where young Māori could be trained to be officers of the law, and to turn a couple of other buildings into a local police station and courthouse.

When Gorst was appointed and he moved into the mission station, it was already too late. Māori chose to ignore or blatantly disregard him. Highly suspicious and increasingly tense, they saw him as just another government agent engaging in an even higher level of interference in their own activities, proceedings and disputes.

The unfortunate result was that the very people who had stood by Māori for so long – the Anglican and Wesleyan missionary group – also began to believe that Māori were "just turning their backs on the great gifts of civilisation … acting contrary to the best interests of both the country and themselves".[159] The missionaries were offended and discouraged by the Māori action and Grey took full advantage of the missionary change of heart to further justify to his political masters in England the need for action.

Where did Purchas sit in all of this? While there is a telling lack of comment on, or reference to, the situation in any family or other files, it is clear that this missionary about-face would have presented Purchas with one more head-shaking moment when it came to the events at Ōtāwhao. His dilemma was likely compounded further by great personal exasperation and sadness that the bond between Māori and the church, especially in the Waikato, was increasingly under threat. For his part, he had befriended Te Wherowhero and Matutaera, and had known the family since 1849; he had helped them settle alongside Pākehā at Ihumatao, designed and helped to build their own church; served them as their doctor, as faithful intermediary and priest; and had explained to them so much that was new and strange about the British system of rule, of landownership, titles and justice.

While Purchas was confident his personal relationships with Ngāpora, Te Paea and the other Kīngitanga leaders would be unaffected, he could only watch while almost all of Selwyn's missionary group fell into line with Grey. Among them were several of his own close friends – George Kissling, William Williams, Ashwell from Taupiri and John Morgan. It could be interpreted that his quietness on the issue indicated a serious lack of conviction about the wisdom and the real intent of Grey's actions. Purchas would have been well acquainted with the Kīngitanga view that Grey's positioning of Gorst in Ōtāwhao would always be seen as just more provocation – the consequences of which would likely be even greater levels of subjugation under the Europeans

---

159   A K Davidson (ed), *A Controversial Churchman* (K Howe).

as their occupation intensified and land alienation continued apace.

Whatever Purchas thought, however, he was not about to run away. In fact he seems to have taken the view that he should stay even closer at hand, attempt to do his very best by Tāmihana, Matutaera, Te Paea and Ngāpora in particular, and try to stay the hands of the most belligerent parties on both sides. He knew the moderates in the Kīngitanga needed a voice to communicate their position to the Government now more than at any other time – someone they could trust and who understood them. So when Grey decided to establish a full native hospital on Crown land just outside the Ōtāwhao marae and settlement, and to appoint a Medical Commissioner for the Waikato, the Kīngitanga asked for Purchas. He was also recommended separately for the post by Wiremu Tāmihana, considered by Grey to be a powerful endorsement.[160]

Purchas did not think about it for long. His financial situation was still extremely difficult. While Selwyn had organised for his stipend to be supplemented in recent times via a couple of small grants from two British mission funds, one of those had expired a year earlier and the St Peter's congregation was providing only about half the sum required under Selwyn's salary scale.[161]

Purchas immediately went to consult Selwyn. With the church unable to provide further, Selwyn advised him to accept the Government offer as one "of great usefulness, in which without departing in any way from his clerical character, he [Purchas] might obtain an adequate maintenance for his family". Selwyn sent a young priest out to Onehunga to stand in for him, presumably on a far smaller salary.

In various times of gloom that Purchas might occasionally experience, there would often appear out of nowhere a bead of encouragement to return him to his generally optimistic and positive approach to life. So it happened in the winter of 1862 when a letter arrived on his front doorstep (postmarked Vienna) from the Natural History Museum no less – which Purchas must have thought was from his old friend, Ferdinand von Hochstetter.

On opening the letter, he learned to his great delight that one of his discoveries on the expedition with von Hochstetter three years earlier had gained him international recognition. That discovery – officially now recognised as a world-first – was of a new species of small land snail, found mostly in the North Island around Hunua and the Waikato, in moist, sheltered bush conditions. Believing at the time that he may have discovered something entirely new, Purchas documented his find in detail before giving the specimen to von

160   AKL, Grey Letters, GLNZM44.9.
161   Notes from the Auckland Synod meeting, AAA, May 1863.

Hochstetter to take back to Vienna for verification. This done, the experts in Vienna had decided to name the species after Purchas – *Omphalorissa purchasi*.[162] His scientific reputation had taken another major leap forward. After sharing his excitement with Olivia and family, Purchas prepared to leave her once more – to travel south and settle himself into the new role at Ōtāwhao.

Grey's Government meantime – and the New Zealand public – suddenly had something else to worry about. The planned shift of the capital from Auckland to the more central location of Wellington had been delayed because of the Taranaki War. Nevertheless the premier and his officials proposed to make a start by holding the next parliamentary session in Wellington and, at the same time, to begin moving many of the government records and files to the new headquarters.

In July, the ship *White Swan* – carrying Premier Fox, government ministers, wives and officials, plus a significant proportion of those files – hit rocks off the Wairarapa coast on its journey from Auckland to Wellington. Everyone got ashore safely, but the hundreds of wooden boxes containing paperwork covering the previous 20-25 years of colonial history were left on board. As the ship broke up, they were last seen floating on the ebb tide towards Chile, to be lost for ever!

Soon after, Wiremu Tāmihana and his Kīngitanga leaders convened a meeting at Tāmihana's base at Peria near Matamata, on October 23, 1862. The purpose was to review the evolving situation, try and gather together the various tribes into a more cohesive unit and put a stop to the inter-tribal quarrels weakening the rūnanga system and slowing their peace efforts. Tāmihana also invited Selwyn and other missionary leaders. They delivered a joint message to Wiremu Kīngi to go to arbitration with the Government about the Waitara lands. Underneath it all, Tāmihana was concerned that Kīngi's influence was on the decline and that, increasingly in his place, the more strident voice of Rewi Maniapoto was now being heard.

It is likely that Purchas was also at Peria – although there is no specific record of this, other than references to him having attended various hui in the Waikato at this time. His fluency in the Māori language would certainly have benefited both sides. A photo does exist from this time of Tāmihana with a group including, apparently, Purchas with Auckland businessman J C Firth (also a friend of Tāmihana's), which may well have been taken around the time of the Peria hui.[163] The group is posing, seemingly deliberately, among some

---

162 Purchas's original snail specimen remains in the Vienna Natural History Museum. Refer H Suter, *Manual of the New Zealand Mollusca*, p 175.

163 AML, Ph-aklb-93.

flax bushes – which might indicate that Purchas was taking the opportunity to discuss his new flax machine with Tāmihana and Firth.

Disaster at sea

The meetings were held and the long discussions continued in both camps, late into 1862. Despite it all, Grey's military build-up continued, with more regiments being deployed down the Great South Rd. At the same time, Onehunga was virtually turning into a full-scale naval port. Smaller steam-powered ships and paddle steamers were ferrying British military equipment and supplies across the Manukau Harbour to Waiuku and Drury, and further south to Port Waikato, to support the new redoubts and militia settlements. There were fortifications at Waiuku, Patumahoe, Papakura, Pukekohe east and Ramarama – and at Purchas's new church of St Bride's at Mauku. Other fortifications spread across from the main Queen's Redoubt at Pokeno below the Hunua Ranges as far as Miranda in the Firth of Thames.

Meanwhile, Māori were smuggling in arms and ammunition to Onehunga and shipping them by canoe across the Manukau and into the Waikato heartland along the many tributaries and streams feeding into the Waikato River.

Despite all the military activity, the residents of Auckland still went ahead with preparations for the usual Anniversary Day Regatta in January 1863. Although Māori participation in the regular waka races and onshore social activities had dropped off in the previous two or three years, Ngāti Whātua and Ngāti Pāoa crews turned up to race alongside the smaller European sailboats and whalers. The 23-gun British warship HMS *Miranda* overlooked the scene, acting as a marker and, later in the day, as a congenial venue for some "interaction between the races".[164] As the regatta organisers relaxed late in the day over a well-earned tot or two, none could have envisaged the scale of a tragedy about to unfold only days later on Auckland's other harbour – almost within sight of Arthur Purchas's upstairs windows in Onehunga.

Firstly however, on February 2, Olivia Purchas, now aged 38, delivered another son – their 11th child. Mindful of her mother's earlier quizzing about names, she dutifully called him Charles. Arthur was able to celebrate the occasion by presenting her with one of the first copies of his *New Zealand Hymnal*, straight from the printers, costing 1/6d with a cloth cover and 2/6d for one bound in calf skin. The hymnal was an immediate success with the first

---

164 P Monin, *Hauraki Contested, 1769-1875*, p 186.

2000 copies selling within days to churches all over the colony. Just five days later, Purchas was back at Ōtāwhao when the terrible news hit.

February 7, 1863. Soon after 3 o'clock on a calm, sunny day, news reached Onehunga of a ship in distress out on the Manukau Bar. It would be the next morning before anyone really knew much, but the word was that a human tragedy of epic proportion had occurred. The stories involving the wrecking of HMS *Orpheus* still grip the imagination today. She was a 225-foot Royal Navy corvette, powered by sails and a two-cylinder steam engine – sent to New Zealand from Sydney with extra troops for Governor Grey and to help relieve HMS *Miranda*, lying in the Waitematā.

Her skipper, Commodore Burnett, was supposed to go to the Waitematā Harbour but had left Sydney a little late and was behind schedule. He decided to cut his journey short by sailing directly to Onehunga, across the Manukau Bar, thus avoiding the longer route around North Cape. On board the *Orpheus* were 259 sailors, many of them young teenage boys, literally "learning the ropes". Only two of the crew had ever been across the bar. Using an old chart, the *Orpheus* missed the narrow channel and struck one of the sandbars, immediately heeling side-on to the rollers and filling with water.

As the young men began abandoning ship, others climbed the rigging to await rescue. The Onehunga harbour master Edward Wing, who was guiding the *Wonga Wonga* out over the bar, eventually tried to come back from some distance away to effect a rescue and managed to pick up some sailors from the surrounding waters. By 8pm that summer's evening, the *Orpheus* was in a hopeless situation. Her masts and rigging finally came crashing down, men and all, and in the gathering darkness what was left of the remaining crew became resigned to their fate. The Captain gave his lifejacket to the cabin boy and remained on board to eventually perish. The cabin boy and another sailor drifted down the harbour to Puketutu Island and survived. Over the following days, Wing collected more bodies from the sea and buried some on the northern shores of the harbour below Titirangi, eventually returning to Onehunga to talk to reporters from the *Daily Southern Cross*.

It remains New Zealand's worst maritime disaster with 189 men drowned. The 70 survivors were brought to Onehunga and on to Auckland, where a massive funeral service was held for one young sailor as the single representative of all those who died. Neither Purchas nor Bishop Selwyn was able to attend. Both were heavily engaged in respective peace and support efforts in the Waikato and Taranaki – Purchas on his medical commissioner assignment at Ōtāwhao. Governor Grey was also absent, confined to his sick bed. Purchas, however, made it his business to return a few days later to preside over two individual *Orpheus* funerals – in particular that of the ship's young chaplain, whose body had just been found. He was buried in the St Peter's cemetery.[165]

A far more pleasant duty followed – the wedding in St Paul's of the Māori widow of his old friend William Gundry. It was Makareta's second marriage, this time to a fellow Māori. Purchas's presence would have been warmly acknowledged by all the Gundry family.

Then he made a quick visit to Waiuku where his newly completed flax mill was almost ready to begin operation. It is very likely that Purchas had some genuine concerns about the business, knowing that war could intervene at any time. But his Auckland backers/entrepreneurs were in no mood to delay proceedings because of possible military action, which they believed would be over quickly anyway. Purchas's partner, James Ninnis, advertised for six young men to work the mill and all was ready to go.[166]

After confirming the start-up and making sure that Olivia and the children, including the new baby, were settled again, Purchas headed straight back to Ōtāwhao. The mill ran well under Ninnis for the next several months, producing nearly 100 tons of fibre before having to close for the first time as a consequence of the impending war. However, Purchas had little time or even inclination to celebrate because far more serious trouble was brewing in Ōtāwhao.

Trouble at Ōtāwhao

As part of Grey's semi-dysfunctional rūnanga system, a decision had been made to build a simple structure, another courthouse, at a place called Te Kohekohe – near where Mercer is today but on the other side of the Waikato River. Grey's men could not have picked a more provocative site. The building would be erected right on the Kīngitanga's unofficial boundary line or 'aukati', and the immediate Māori suspicion was that it would actually be a military post. This was confirmed in their minds only weeks later when John Gorst unwisely decided to house some local Māori policemen there, theoretically to support the rūnanga in its decisions.

The original plan for this courthouse, in fact, was that it would mainly serve a couple of iwi loyal to the Government, led by Wiremu Te Wheoro – a long-time Crown supporter, also closely connected to Ngāti Mahuta and other individual Kīngitanga leaders. However, in one of the more confusing clashes

---

165   The grave of the 33-year-old chaplain, the Rev Charles Haselwood, remains prominently marked in the St Peter's cemetery in Onehunga.
166   Papers Past, *Daily Southern Cross*, Feb 24, 1863.

to occur between Waikato tribes over this period, the Kīngitanga tried to warn off Te Wheoro from building the courthouse, which led to some potentially dangerous disagreements between the two groups. Fortunately they came to nothing and the timber was finally taken back to Te Ia further downstream and the construction programme aborted.

Within days, attention switched back to Taranaki and a block of coastal land known as Tataraimaka – about 20-25km south of New Plymouth. When Governor Browne had occupied the block at Waitara with his soldiers, local Māori had themselves occupied Tataraimaka as a kind of tit for tat or insurance policy of their own. But on March 12, 1863, and contrary to the advice of several of his advisors, Grey ordered the largely Taranaki-based 57th Regiment to clear the block of its Māori 'squatters'. About 300 troops moved in and forcibly retook the Tataraimaka land, evicting all Māori in a move which immediately ratcheted up the tension.

Worse, rightly or wrongly this single action was interpreted by Māori as a resumption of the Taranaki War by the British, despite the earlier truce. The Kīngitanga began to realise that this aggressive attitude – when added to the build-up north of the Waikato River – meant the front line for any battle to come would likely be on their own patch and would be a fight for survival.

By now, Rewi Maniapoto's impatience and aggression towards the British was proving to be more than just a thorn in the side of the Kīngitanga. He wanted the British removed from the Waikato "king country" immediately, starting with Gorst and his school, the courts, the hospital and anything else introduced at Grey's behest. The dozen or so children remaining at the Ōtāwhao School – orphans and otherwise semi-destitute half-caste minors, apparently connected to various Ngāti Hāua iwi – were of no consequence to him. He threatened to come and close the place himself and send Gorst packing, back to Auckland with his family, along with everyone else. And he did not have to look far for an excuse to do just this.

A year or so earlier Grey had authorised the establishment of a Kīngitanga newspaper, Te Hikioi, to help disseminate news and information among their Waikato tribes – much of it emanating from the decisions of the rūnanga directly affecting them. The paper was based in Ngāruawāhia, and edited and printed by Patara Te Tuhi – an early convert to Christianity and another senior member of the King's Ngāti Mahuta family well known to Purchas, but also, as it happened, friendly with Gorst. The printing press Te Tuhi used was a gift from the Austrian monarch to two Waikato Māori who had travelled back to Austria from Auckland on von Hochstetter's Novara in 1859.

However, annoyed with some of the editorial content of Te Hikioi –

strongly promoting the relevance of the Kīngitanga cause to Māori – Grey set up the Government newspaper *Te Pihoihoi* to counter those Māori kingship messages, and edited by Gorst. *Te Pihoihoi's* editorial line was that only one government could rule in New Zealand with authority over both races. One such story not only angered the Kīngitanga, but also incensed the more aggressive leaders in their midst, particularly Rewi Maniapoto.

On March 23, 1863, a war party under Maniapoto came to Ōtāwhao and entered Gorst's *Te Pihoihoi* printing office. After some brief scuffles and threats, they took the press and papers, and Gorst was eventually ordered to leave the area.[167] The Kīngitanga leadership, via Matutaera – understanding the ramifications of expelling such a senior officer in Grey's Government, and the serious challenge to Grey's authority that this represented – ordered Maniapoto to return the press and leave the matter of Gorst's continuing presence or otherwise for King Matutaera to handle.

But Maniapoto, with backing from some other Waikato chiefs, not only wanted Gorst gone but also set out a claim to take back a large part of the land on which the Ōtāwhao school stood – and with it the entire station, including the children sheltering there under the care of Purchas and two Māori teachers. Maniapoto based his claim on never having received due payment when the land was originally sold to the CMS in 1839.

As Vincent O'Malley noted: "The debate about Gorst was caught up in much bigger arguments about who could exercise rangatiratanga over the Te Awamutu district." Maniapoto was ready for war but Ngāti Hāua, Ngāti Mahuta and the Kīngitanga leadership were still not spoiling for a fight. Maniapoto was frustrated that the Kīngitanga leaders, who he knew did not want Gorst there either, had simply not done enough to stand up to Grey and force a withdrawal. And Maniapoto was not the type to sit around and wait.

April 1, 1863. Gorst wrote to Grey, via the native minister Dillon Bell, to tell him it seemed Tāmihana and Matutaera had lost their influence over Maniapoto ... and while they had told him (Gorst) they "would never consent to any attempt to drive me from my place", they also did not like him being in the district. He added that it seemed he was now "abandoned to the mercies of Rewi" and that the Ōtāwhao station was at an end. He concluded by saying that if the Government wanted to carry on there for a while longer, "the Rev A G Purchas will make the attempt".[168] While Gorst realised the danger facing him (and his family), he clearly felt Purchas's standing would allow him a measure of safety, at least for the time being.

---

167 Refer S Oliver, *Te Ara – Dictionary of New Zealand Biography*, Te Tuhi, Patara.
168 Appendix to the Journals of the House of Representatives, Appendix E, No 1-15.

Meantime, Tāmihana wanted to send Kīngitanga warriors to Ōtāwhao to protect Purchas and the property at the station, but this was rejected for fear of upsetting Rewi and losing his allegiance to the Kīngitanga altogether. In letters written over the following days, while awaiting Grey's response, Gorst reported that "the rapidity and violence of Rewi had frightened everybody … and the Waikatos were in a state of great perplexity as to what was to be done".[169] He advised that Te Paea and Te Tuhi were arriving at the end of the week to meet Maniapoto – and that Te Paea would leave the Waikato and return to Mangere if they wouldn't listen to her. The Ngāti Mahuta people, he said, seemed favourable to Purchas remaining but had no more power to protect him than they had Gorst.

April 10, 1863. Purchas, Gorst and James Fulloon, a half-caste government official and interpreter-conciliator working with Gorst, rode over to the Kīngitanga headquarters in Ngāruawāhia where they were met and "most hospitably received" by Te Paea, Te Tuhi, Wi Karamoa and other Kīngitanga leaders. Te Paea told them that the trouble over the Gorst newspaper and printing press had not been Rewi's main 'ta-ke' or 'cause'. For him, it was still the Taranaki land, Tataraimaka, and the forcible eviction of defenceless local Māori by the British forces. She said Maniapoto had tried to "get up a war in Taranaki" and now was just trying to do the same in the Waikato.

April 11, 1863. James Fulloon went separately to meet with Rewi Maniapoto and proposed to him that the boys at the school should be left with Dr Purchas. Maniapoto replied that he did not know whether Purchas should stay. He would discuss this with his rūnanga and then come "in person and not with a taua [war party]" to let Purchas know the decision. But he added that he didn't think his tribe would consent to Purchas remaining. In such imminent danger as he was, Purchas must have endured a few sleepless nights in his bed at Ōtāwhao while waiting for a decision. He was acutely aware that with Tāmihana and Matutaera now unable to restrain Maniapoto, and with their influence among the wider Waikato tribes on the wane, his own position could change for the worse at any time.

Purchas warns Grey

April 16. Wednesday. In his room at Ōtāwhao, Purchas wrote a crucial letter addressed to Bell, with information specifically for Grey.[170] Firstly, Purchas advised that the Ngāti Kahungunu chief, Te Hapuku, who was a friend of

---

169 Ibid., 1-17.
170 Ibid., E-1 No 19 Appendices.

the influential Donald McLean and also well-known to Grey, had visited him that day to notify him that Rewi Maniapoto was leaving on Monday 21st for Taranaki with about 600 warriors. It seemed likely from this news that Māori were rejoining the war in Taranaki in force. Secondly, Te Hapuku had told him that Wiremu Kīngi was also going and Te Hapuku "was greatly afraid lest they should succeed in their intended attempt to take the life of Sir George Grey (absit omen)".[171] Apparently, Purchas said some Māori "seers" had prophesied that if the natives could shoot the Governor, they would then be able to drive the Pākehā out of the country and that "it is therefore no longer safe for the Governor to travel about".

Te Hapuku asked Purchas to warn Grey that he would not now be safe, even in Ngāruawāhia, and that Gorst should leave because Rewi still intended to take possession of the Ōtāwhao station and land. Just as Te Hapuku was leaving Purchas to return to Napier, Purchas told him that he and Fulloon intended remaining after Gorst left. Te Hapuku advised Purchas to be careful not to offer any opposition or "they would be likely to kill us". Purchas's letter ended with the familiar warning to Grey, this time from Te Hapuku, and one on which he (Te Hapuku) laid great stress ... "viz whatever happens, the Pakeha should be careful not to fire the first shot".

This particular letter may well have been the final prompt and justification Grey needed on the drawn-out pathway to beginning a war. Two days later, just as Tāmihana and Maniapoto wanted – and no doubt with that personal and serious threat to him as the Queen's senior representative still ringing in his ears – Grey recalled Gorst. This "forced recall on account of the rebellious Waikato tribes", as Grey called it, would indeed be used by him later as the ultimate justification for an invasion – the final plans for which he had already started drawing up.

April 21, 1863. As Gorst packed his belongings to return to Auckland, the decision was made to close the school and not wait for any of Maniapoto's men to arrive unexpectedly. Purchas took charge of the operation and over the next two or three days completed a full inventory of those goods to be taken out to Maungatawhiri and Auckland, and what to leave behind. All the boys at the school, except two, had no choice but to stay behind – none of their "friends" allowing them to leave, presumably because they were not wanted. Purchas placed the nine or 10 staying under the care of two trusted Christian Māori teachers, who bravely volunteered to Purchas to remain. They were also charged with looking after some sheep and other property, and continuing the

171   Absit omen – Latin for "may this not come about" or even "perish the thought".

lessons in one of the buildings – for which they would still receive a small salary. Purchas also secured a willing undertaking from Te Paea and the Kīngitanga to prevent any of the grounds or buildings being occupied by Rewi Maniapoto or others. The last official 'European presence' in the Kīngitanga area was about to be totally removed, just as Maniapoto wanted.

April 25, 1863. Purchas reported to the native minister that he would be leaving Ōtāwhao in a few hours. He said a party of about 200 Ngāti Maniapoto warriors (not the 600 previously reported), had now left for Waitara and "would endeavour to drive out all they found there". Purchas went on to describe in detail the lengthy discussions that had been taking place over the last few days at Kihikihi between Rewi Maniapoto, Reihana (another Maniapoto chief) and their followers on one side and Matutaera, Te Paea and Te Tuhi on the other.

Maniapoto was now vigorously arguing for a Kīngitanga attack on the government redoubt at Te Ia, by the junction of the Waikato and Maungatawhiri rivers. If Te Paea and Te Tuhi were able to dissuade him from this, Purchas said, Maniapoto was proposing to attack Raglan instead. "If Rewi should not succeed in silencing the opposition of Te Paea and Te Tuhi," Purchas added, "I believe I shall have immediate notice and shall either ride into Auckland as quickly as possible or send off a messenger at once."[172]

The split between the Kīngitanga leaders and Rewi Maniapoto and his followers had widened. Purchas sought to reassure Grey and the Government that the Kīngitanga leaders were still trying desperately to prevent Maniapoto taking them all to war. "Wiremu Tamihana and Tioriori [of Ngāti Hāua] have expressed their entire disapprobation of the proceedings of Rewi and his people and I believe, will prevent Ngati Haua taking any part in the conflict which appears to be impending," he said. "The Potatau family are also deeply mortified at what has been done and said by Rewi and his companions."

Te Paea had also told Purchas that "if Rewi and the violent men" should win the discussion, she would quit Ngāruawāhia and return immediately to Mangere. In this case, Purchas noted, he wouldn't be surprised if King Matutaera followed her. Both of them, she said, were very upset that so many of the Waikato tribes were disregarding Te Wherowhero's dying words to "live in peace with the Pakeha". In private conversations Purchas had with some of the Māori King's other near relatives, they now admitted despondently that Matutaera had no power to restrain Rewi and others who "professed to be his own subjects".

As a result of the angry discussions between Rewi and Kīngitanga leaders,

172   Appendix to the Journals of the House of Representatives, E-1, No 25.

some local European farming friends of Māori still in the Waikato area were also advised to pack up and leave immediately or, as Purchas said, they would have to put themselves under the protection of the King and pay "tribute". He told the Government that some of them would probably stay and pay, "having the choice of two evils, becoming either rebels or beggars".[173] Te Paea did the decent thing by making it part of her business to warn the European settlers in the area that the Kīngitanga could not now protect them from Maniapoto.

April 26, 1863. As Purchas completed the arduous task of packing up, he engaged in conversation with Hohaia, one of the Māori men he was leaving behind in charge. Hohaia had met with Rewi Maniapoto that same day and was told that Ngāti Maniapoto chiefs were going to Matutaera to demand that the Kīngitanga should take over the property for the proposed barracks at Te Ia, and that Matutaera himself should go and live among the Ngāti Maniapoto. Then, Purchas listened in horror as Hohaia said that Maniapoto believed all the mixed-race children in the entire Awamutu area should be "seized". Horror turned to disbelief the next morning when Purchas learned that, during the night, two girls of mixed-race descent (aged 17 and about 10) had been taken from the European house in the settlement where they were living. There was nothing he could do.

Final countdown

April 27, 1863 (Monday). Purchas and Fulloon finally left Ōtāwhao by river, using a few canoes loaded with the goods he didn't want to leave behind (he had sent some horses and cattle on ahead to Auckland). Two boys and one other schoolmaster were also in the party – Purchas having arranged for them to be taken in to St Stephen's School in Parnell. Before leaving he posted notices all around the property at Ōtāwhao, in Māori and English, warning any intruders about trespassing. He completed the large inventory of goods left behind, from a bullock belonging to John Morgan, to bedsteads, tools, paint, salt cellars and teapots – and about 13 tons of potatoes.

The party stopped at Ngāruawāhia for the night where long conversations resumed with Te Paea, Te Tuhi and others. At the end of the evening, Te Tuhi asked Purchas to pass on to Grey the suggestion that some Kīngitanga chiefs should go to Taranaki and negotiate a period of truce with him. During such a period, Te Tuhi proposed that all government officers and other Europeans should withdraw from the native districts including Tataraimaka, that

---

173   Ibid, 1863, E-1, No 25.

the Waitara should remain unoccupied, and that Māori be left entirely to themselves for three or four years. Then, if Māori were still unwilling to submit to the law, Grey could declare a "paeroa" or general war, as Te Tuhi called it, to settle the question for ever. Purchas said that Te Tuhi's idea – which he himself clearly thought was unworkable – was that the natives would be "so thoroughly miserable for want of the comforts and help they have hitherto enjoyed", they would be glad to submit to anything!

April 29, 1863. The next morning Te Paea joined Purchas in his canoe and the party proceeded to Taupiri. Here, on the riverbank, Purchas was approached by Māori who begged him to ask Grey to set aside some land where all those who didn't want to fight could go and wait out any conflict. Further on down the river they also met up with King Matutaera, still "greatly vexed at the proceedings of Maniapoto". He told them he was going to make one more effort "to bring Maniapoto back to their senses". He also gave Purchas a copy of a letter which Te Tuhi had just written to Tāmati Ngāpora, setting out the somewhat forlorn hope of reining in Maniapoto. But Rewi had now won extra support from the Urewera Tūhoe chiefs, with both demanding the Kīngitanga let them take back Te Ia. Matutaera also confirmed to Purchas that the smaller war party under other Maniapoto chiefs had gone to take back the Waitara land.

May 2, 1863. Safely back in Auckland, Purchas left Te Paea at Mangere and organised the transfer of the Ōtāwhao schoolboys to Parnell. He saw to it that all the government goods from Ōtāwhao were secured in an Auckland storehouse and then walked back to his Onehunga home to be reunited with Olivia and the children. It must have been a time of great relief for both, even though he would have to confront the stipend issue again with the Bishop and his church trust board. Knowing also that a bloody and unnecessary war was probably only days away, Purchas went to bed that night with a heavy heart. On waking the next morning, he returned immediately to his desk and wrote a long report to the native minister, describing all the events of the last few days.[174]

May 4, 1863. He had scarcely finished posting this report when news arrived of a deadly ambush by Māori of a British unit at Oakura, in Taranaki. The unit had been taking a native prisoner back to New Plymouth. Nine British soldiers were killed. Ngāti Maniapoto were immediately suspected of having masterminded the act, even if their 200-man taua had not been involved. To Grey, it mattered not who had actually killed his soldiers. He blamed the Kīngitanga.

---

174   Ibid., E-1, No 28.

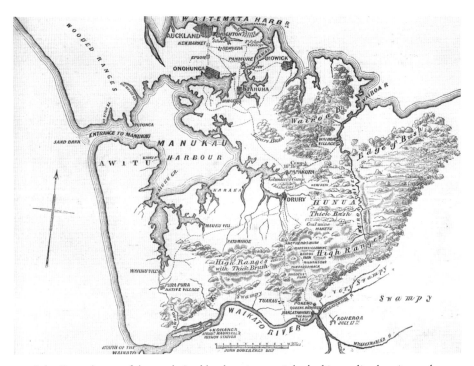

John Dower's map of the south Auckland territory as it looked immediately prior to the outbreak of war and first published for the benefit of English readers, in the *London Illustrated News*, November 1863.
AUCKLAND MUSEUM IMAGES G9083.F7

These lead-up events to the war that followed now seemed to be in an unavoidable and unstoppable sequence. The debates about the degree to which the British and Grey were content to let them happen – whether the moderates in the Kīngitanga could have found some way of isolating the more extreme elements in their midst, or whether some kind of lengthy truce might have led to a long-term solution – will never be resolved. That Grey and Browne before him were intent on war from an early date, no matter what, is an argument that is difficult to refute. Individuals like Purchas and Ngāpora, trapped in the whole sorry affair, must have been so distraught that their two peoples should have let it come to this. And now they could only seek to protect and preserve their own from the physical dangers looming.

In early May, Māori marauding parties were increasingly active beyond the northern Kīngitanga boundary line into parts of South Auckland, Hunua and the lower Waikato River regions. Pākehā settlers were being "insulted and reviled and their homes looted" as Auckland readied itself for full-scale action. In Otahuhu, the centre of military preparations, the regular forces now numbered in their thousands and were bolstered by some 400 or 500 men of the volunteer Auckland militia. The fear was – although completely without foundation as Purchas knew only too well – that an invasion from the Waikato could come at any time.

John Gorst, back in Auckland and certainly of the same mind as Purchas, did not believe the Kīngitanga had ever been serious about attacking Auckland – even though they would not have put it past Rewi Maniapoto to do so, but for the restraint shown by Tāmihana, Ngāpora and others. Ever intent on finding a peaceful resolution, Tāmihana even wrote at this 11th hour to the Government, urging that "Tataraimaka be handed back to the Crown to bring the fighting to an end" – despite angry opposition to his action from Maniapoto and Wiremu Kīngi.[175]

In an effort to prevent needless slaughter by either side, Purchas picked up his pen again on May 9, this time writing to Captain Francis Bulkley, one of the senior officers of the British 65th Yorkshire Regiment of Foot,[176] whose men were now assembling north of the Kīngitanga border near Mercer. Purchas reminded him "and other high officers not to disregard the warnings which have been received" that great efforts would be made to kill those in highest command. Although he didn't mention names, Purchas was simply passing on the warning from Ngāpora and Te Paea who both knew the Māori battle tactic. "Nothing but the strongest conviction that extraordinary precautions are necessary would induce me to write in this manner," he wrote to Bulkley.[177]

It may have been the weather – in what later would turn out to be one of the worst autumns and winters on record – but for the next three weeks an ominous silence descended over the entire region. In the middle of June, after more conversations with Tāmati Ngāpora in Mangere – who had told Purchas he would remain there as a "hostage for peace" – Purchas again wrote to Governor Grey. This time it was to ask him to ensure safe passage for Ngāpora who was wanting to travel in his own canoe to Waiuku, across the Manukau from Mangere. Purchas did not state the reason for Ngāpora's trip, knowing Grey would understand without asking that, in Ngāpora's case, it would not be for anything other than peaceful purposes. In fact, Ngāpora was looking to retire into exile in the King Country.

June 20, 1863. General Cameron, commander-in-chief of the British forces, returned from Taranaki to Auckland and sat down to discuss with Grey the final plan for the invasion of the Waikato. Most of his forces also returned

---

175 R D Crosby, *Kupapa*, p 188.
176 Known as the "Royal Tigers", but called the 'hickety pips' by Maori.
177 AKL, *Grey Letters*, GLNZ, p 24.

to Auckland. The overall objective of the plan, it was later disclosed, was to "clear the area between the Waikato River and Auckland of all potentially hostile tribes".[178] Fed up with what they deemed to be Māori "insolence and contempt" towards the Pākehā, settlers readied themselves for what they believed would be the long-overdue fight with "the rebels".

CHAPTER 11

War

In the context of both Browne and Grey's public obsession with "toppling the Māori king" – and the profoundly negative impact their stated intention had made on various Waikato tribes – it is not difficult to conclude that matters had reached the point of no return many months earlier. Only a single flashpoint was needed for the big issue to be settled by force – the British settlers wanting "to teach the natives a lesson" and the Kīngitanga feeling utterly betrayed by the Crown for not honouring Treaty undertakings in respect of their land. There had been several flashpoints along the way – but Grey also knew he would need a watertight case if and when he might be asked to justify his war to the British Parliament.

As Grey and Cameron plotted the invasion, Premier Alfred Domett – in a memo, the tenor of which still shocks many historians today – called for all hostile natives on the Auckland isthmus to be cleared out and their lands confiscated, and for them to be "settled on military tenure to provide for future security". In Domett's proposal of June 1863, he marked out the territory he wanted, being an east-west line from the Firth of Thames near Miranda across to the west coast – studded at intervals by military posts, and even a battleship permanently moored at Ngāruawāhia. Rumours of when either side might actually start a war, invade, or otherwise engage the other, circulated throughout June among both races and all persuasions.

For today's students of this "great war", it is worth considering at this point the sheer weight of forces Grey assembled for his campaign, versus the strength of the Waikato tribes lined up against them. Apart from the 10 British regiments which Grey had at his disposal within a few months of the invasion, every able-bodied European male between the ages of 16 and 55 was eligible for conscription – except "priests, lunatics and members of the general assembly".

Estimates of the imperial forces in toto vary among historians, from a minimum of 4000 in 1863 to a more likely 12,000 in late 1864 – noted by James Belich as "still more than was available at the time for the defence of all

England". Even though a large part of the overall force was always engaged in road building, transporting supplies or other logistical work, it was still sizeable by any standards of the day … and four or five times that of the comparatively ill-equipped Kīngitanga tribes ranged against it.

Some 3000-4000 Māori warriors from various North Island tribes were available to fight if called upon. The general consensus today, however, is that no more than 2000 Māori actually fought in the Waikato War.[179] They were grouped in small parties, often numbering 200-300 at most, but more usually were in raiding groups of 10 to 60. The Māori force was mainly led by Rewi Maniapoto and Tāmihana, using basically the same guerrilla tactics which had earlier been effective against superior forces in the northern and Taranaki conflicts.

General Cameron also had at his disposal a British 'mini-navy' – four steam-powered battleships including armour-plated paddle wheelers. One of them, the 300-ton HMS *Pioneer*, had been built especially in Australia for the war. They made their way, laboriously, down the west coast to Port Waikato and up the river as far as Meremere where they could engage the Māori guns and bring in supplies.

On July 7 came one final letter from Purchas to the Government. His intent, in co-operation again with Ngāpora, was to give a balanced and up-to-the-minute account of the sentiments expressed within the Waikato tribes. He was not to know that Governor Grey would use this last-minute report when underlining again to the British Colonial Office that his decision to go to war was absolutely justified.

In the report[180] Purchas said he had been visited by Ngāpora at his home in Onehunga that day, following Ngāpora's own briefing with Waikato representatives at Pukaki 24 hours earlier. Ngāpora told Purchas the "talk of Waikato was very bad and that many of the people were proposing to kill the Europeans without delay". Those who were still arguing for peace, he said, were doing their best to defeat what he called such "murderous designs".

Ngāpora told Purchas there was to be a large gathering of the tribes at Rangiriri or Ngāruawāhia on July 8 or 9, and that he "had urged the people to think quietly before they rushed into war … and to take care to let the Europeans know before any acts of violence were committed". Purchas said Ngāpora believed that if no murders or attacks were made before the following Sunday, July 12, he would be greatly relieved because he would feel

---

179   Refer M Wright, *Two Peoples, One Land*, p 123. Belich, in his *The New Zealand Wars*, gives a detailed summary and analysis of both European and Māori forces, and says total mobilisation of British forces was in the order of 18,000 men.

180   Appendix to the Journals of the House of Representatives, E-3, Encl No 6.

Gottfried Lindauer's stunning portrait of Purchas's friend Tamati Ngāpora, a peace-loving man of great compassion and wisdom, admired and respected by all colonial leaders including Governor Grey.

GOTTFRIED LINDAUER, TAMATI NGĀPORA MANUHIRI, 1882, OIL ON CANVAS. AUCKLAND ART GALLERY TOI O TĀMAKI, GIFT OF MR H E PARTRIDGE, 1915

the "advocates of peace" would have gained a good hearing. If, on the other hand, the aggressors on the Māori side won the day, then he would be afraid of the consequences.

The Purchas report from Ngāpora would have been music to Grey's ears.

The Manukau natives, Purchas added finally, were selling off everything they had, including animals, so they "could leave at a moment's notice if necessary".

July 8, 1863 (Wednesday). As soon as the Purchas report had been received – and combined with other similar intelligence acquired about Māori intentions – Grey and Cameron took the decision to begin the invasion. It was a few days earlier than had originally been planned but Cameron immediately instructed his officers to bring their troops up to the Maungatawhiri border and front line. Cameron later reported that this was because of the Purchas report and the other intelligence – but historian O'Malley, for one, believes they may simply have been a little ahead of schedule in their preparations anyway.

July 9, 1863 (Thursday). Within 48 hours of the Purchas communication to native minister Bell and Governor Grey, a proclamation aimed at clearing all 'hostile' Māori between Auckland and Onehunga and the Waikato River was issued. The presumption was that 'every' Māori was hostile. This was the proclamation that Henry Halse, the local resident magistrate, was ordered to present and have signed by all the natives in his Mangere jurisdiction. Other magistrates went into the rest of the territory. By the very wording of the proclamation, therefore, any Māori aligned directly or indirectly via immediate family ties, long-term tribal links or casual friendships with Ngāti Mahuta, Ngāti Hāua or the other Kīngitanga tribes of the Waikato or Hauraki – or with preferred loyalty to any Waikato whānau or iwi – was automatically to be declared 'hostile'. Grey's proclamation said:

> (i) "All persons of the native race living in the Manukau district and the Waikato frontier are hereby required immediately to take the oath of allegiance to Her Majesty the Queen, and to give up their arms to an officer appointed by the Government for that purpose.
> (ii) "Natives who comply with this order will be protected.
> (iii) "Natives refusing to do so are hereby warned forthwith to leave the district aforesaid, and retire to Waikato beyond Maungatawhiri. In case of their not complying with this order, they will be ejected."

Tāmati Ngāpora, on the road to Mangere that day in the company of Purchas, happened to be the first Māori to hear the proclamation. When Purchas quietly nodded to his rhetorical question about the "day of harvest", Ngāpora's ensuing silence might have disguised a thousand words. Shortly after, when Ngāpora had fully digested the news, he pointed out to Halse that he had "dear friends living in the midst of the English and dear friends living with the Maori". Why were they now to be killed, he asked.

Later again, he was to query why Grey had not instead put the Waikato on a "trial" at least, to judge the rights and wrongs of things like the Gorst expulsion. Resorting to a full-scale war – contrary to everything the British missionaries had taught Māori for the past 40 years at least – made no sense at all to him, especially when both sides knew the British possessed by far the greater military strength.

Māori exodus

The consequences for the local Māori were severe. They had been living and working alongside Europeans here for years. Many were elderly and could not possibly be seen as a threat to the British forces. For them to be cast as "hostile rebels" would have seemed almost laughable to Purchas, if it were not for the very proclamation he had just heard read aloud once more to Ngāpora. A superb account of these moments on the road to Mangere (as written later by John Gorst), concludes with these same Māori a day or so later, thanking the Pākehā via Purchas and others for their kindness in giving them timely warning of the war to follow and of the chance to escape. "All the old people," Gorst wrote, "showed the most intense grief at leaving a place where they had so long lived in peace and happiness, but they resolutely tore themselves away."[181]

As the Governor's proclamation circulated, Ngāti Tamaoho Māori in the areas of Pukaki, Ihumatao, Te Kirikiri (near Papakura) and Patumahoe, plus Ngāti Mahuta around Mangere, mostly accepted their fate and prepared to leave for the Waikato "to where they must go and die with their fathers". However, the Ngāti Pou in the Tuakau area did not, defiantly advising the magistrate James Armitage on July 10 that they would not take the oath, leave their lands or give up their arms, but would resist. A day or so later when 300 soldiers of the 65th Regiment suddenly appeared out of the bush behind their peaceful flourishing settlement on the edge of the Waikato, they had no choice but to go, "moving mournfully to their canoes, and with many tears and deep sighs" paddling south to find a place of safety beyond Maungatawhiri.[182]

They had not been "rebels" on the day of the proclamation. But the very act of this expulsion of whole whānau, children, cousins and grandparents from their own lands, turned them into "rebels" the next day. Some Europeans expressed great surprise at how restrained the Māori tribes had been in their reaction to literally being driven out and away in an instant – with no provision made for their future other than to go "somewhere south into the Waikato".

Robert Maunsell, despite his support for the Government's stance on the

181 J Gorst, *The Maori King*, p 381.
182 J Featon, *The Waikato War*, 1863-4.

sovereignty matter, deplored the expulsion of peaceful Māori. He wrote that the Government's proclamation actually drove them into rebellion. "In expelling them, they [the Government] indicated no place to which they might go or what course of conduct they must adopt ... they just sent them south among rebels who of course feeding them, would expect them to fight for them."[183]

Over those couple of days – while Purchas and others like Selwyn and Maunsell moved among them – Māori made arrangements for some of their property, such as churches and burial grounds, to be handed over to the Anglicans and Wesleyans for safekeeping. Ngāpora also asked a personal favour of Purchas – to take care of his land at Mangere and in the Remuera area for at least the next seven years. Purchas, of course, agreed. No legal agreement was made or needed. It was a matter of trust.

July 11, 1863. Mohi te Ahiatengu, chief of the Ngāti Tamaoho – at the head of about 150 of his people from Pukaki – led a great "Mangere Exodus" down the Great South Rd, towards Papakura, Drury and beyond.[184] With them came some 50 or 60 horses, shepherded along with about 15 flat-deck drays, carrying the tribe's most valuable household possessions – all the while accompanied by platoons of soldiers and their leaders, marching towards the Waikato battlefields. It must have made for a bizarre and sorry sight.

For the next few months, throughout the winter of 1863, the road became a "highway for refugees" as the exodus continued. Ngāti Mahuta from Mangere and Ihumatao were followed by various remnants of Ngāi Tai and Ngāti Te Ata, and even families and individuals from assorted iwi who had been living in or around Onehunga and Auckland. In fact so many refugees were on the long march, sharing the road with the British forces, that they seriously slowed up the military advance towards the Waikato. Many drays, horses and other animals or livestock left unattended were often plundered by soldiers. The Māori refugees became alarmed at the close contact with their enemy who hurled insults at them as they passed by on the road.

There were reports, later questioned by some, of British soldiers looting and burning the Māori settlements after the occupants had left – destroying canoes and whare, and stealing animals and crops. From a military point of view, it would have made little sense to leave intact any resources that could have been used by the future enemy. On the other hand, some European writers and citizens lamented the destruction of property for what they felt was no good reason.

---

183 Garrett.
184 B Ringer, What Happened at Mangere in 1863? AKL. First published in *New Zealand Legacy*, Vol 22, Issue 1, 2010.

Invasion

The British invasion of the Waikato began in the early hours of July 12, 1863 when Cameron and his troops crossed the Maungatawhiri River, the actual spot being approximately halfway between Pokeno and Mercer on State Highway 1. It was the act both sides always knew would serve as the formal declaration of war. Grey, however, persisted in his claim that the river crossing was a response to the actions of the rebels – European settlers having been driven from their own lands in the Waikato, property plundered, soldiers murdered in Taranaki and crimes committed under Kīngitanga authority. He didn't tell the Colonial Office of the advance until more than two weeks later, by which time he had also published a second proclamation.

Claiming he needed to protect peaceable settlers, and "the lives and property of all well-disposed people", he advised that he was compelled to establish posts at several points along the Waikato River and take the necessary measures to protect people inhabiting "that district". Perhaps, it was argued, the wording of this proclamation was purposely vague to enable the troops to advance anywhere in a southerly direction.

But the veiled assurance of security for "well-disposed people among you" was only for those Māori who remained peaceably in their villages or in areas nominated by the Government. And then came the rub. "Those who wage war …" the proclamation said, "or remain in arms, must understand they will forfeit the right to the possession of their lands guaranteed to them by the Treaty of Waitangi."[185]

With this one sentence the whole issue of raupatu or confiscation of land for the later benefit of European settlers only, was well and truly justified and settled in Grey's mind and for generations of Pākehā ever since. The propensity to view an automatic reward of permanent ownership of a defeated race's land as sacrosanct – that race having been overpowered by superior force with little or no reference to any previous Treaty agreement – is still a moot point. Present generations of New Zealanders are still trying to come to grips with this "might is right" principle as the Waitangi Tribunal hopefully nears the end of its 45-year quest to settle the controversy.

The wise and old would-be peacemaker Wiremu Tāmihana possibly explained it best when he said as the invasion began: "It is now a war of defence. Nothing is left but to fight." Indeed, as has been stated many times before, Māori had no option but to fight, if they wanted to preserve their lands. But Tāmihana also warned Grey to make sure any defenceless settlers were taken

---

185 Appendix to the Journals of the House of Representatives, E-5, p 5-6.

into the towns "lest they be killed in their farms or in the bush".

The question of when this second proclamation of Grey's was actually given to Māori has also been under serious scrutiny ever since. Several Europeans saw the injustice of it immediately, including Gorst, who first claimed Māori did not even know of the proclamation until three days after the Waikato River crossing. How then could Māori have complied with Grey's demands in time as O'Malley carefully, and in detail, also concluded 150 years later?[186]

In just one example of the consequences of the proclamation, only one week after it was issued, 400 armed soldiers arrived at Te Āki Tai settlement at Kirikiri, near Papakura – home of the elderly and sick chief Ihaka Wirihana Takanini. While the rest of the tribe had complied and gone south, the chief and 22 mostly elderly men, women and three children who had stayed behind to look after him, were arrested without charge and locked up in the Drury prison for nine days. They were then transferred to Otahuhu and finally exiled to Rakino Island in the Hauraki Gulf. The old chief died just six weeks later and of the 22 others with him, only six survived.

After the war, much of their land at Kirikiri was disbursed to other claimants.[187] The tribe spent the next 150 years trying to retrieve the chief's remains and to have some of the land issues given a fair hearing. Such matters, and their consequences, are critical to every New Zealander's most basic understanding of our history and the modern reconciliation process.

Purchas's only involvement from this time on was as a helpless bystander. The country churches, virtually requisitioned by the military, became part of the settler defence system. That included St Bride's, which had a stockade of half-round logs built around the outside – and rifle slits or loopholes in the outer walls of the church itself. It was right in the middle of the supposed 'war zone' and some estimates put the number of troops encamped around the immediate church area at up to 2000. Purchas could only watch and listen as British soldiers in smaller platoons were despatched to round up the remaining Māori in Manukau and Patumahoe, and the surrounding areas – and then to have them acknowledge the Queen by taking the oath or instantly send them on their way south to "king country".

There followed the first serious military confrontation a few days after the crossing of the Maungatawhiri River at Koheroa on July 17, 1863 as Cameron sought to establish control of the Meremere area, and thereby protect his supply routes down the river to Port Waikato and Onehunga. The Māori resistance was led by Ngāti Mahuta and the first casualties were recorded on both sides,

186   V O'Malley, Choosing Peace or War, *New Zealand Journal of History*, Vol 47, No 1, 2013, pp 52-53.
187   See Te Āki Tai website www.teakitai.com. Also AKL, *Manukau's Journey*.

although favouring the British who, says Belich, had 12 killed or wounded. Some reports said that up to 30 Māori were killed, although Belich, quoting Māori sources, says only 14 or 15 Māori died there.

In a conventional British war strategy of the time, General Cameron would have then expected to press any initial advantage and advance on the Māori strongholds to the south. But here the vastly outnumbered Māori forces stunningly turned the tables on the Imperial Army. At virtually the same time as Cameron was engaging Māori at Koheroa, a small group of warriors from Ngāti Pāoa broke out of the bush in a murderous attack on a British convoy – supposedly safely going about their business at Martin's Farm, a few kilometres south of Drury, well behind the British lines. Sixteen of Cameron's men were killed. This was followed by a drawn-out series of similar attacks and raids by small groups of young Māori fighters who "infested the bush like wild animals". The sporadic attacks that occurred between Hunua and Pokeno, and to Papakura and Alfriston, on the smaller, less-well-defended military posts, supply convoys and farmers in their fields, panicked the settlers in the countryside, who previously believed themselves to be safe, miles behind Cameron's main forces up ahead.

For the rest of the winter of 1863 – as the intermittent raids, bloodthirsty skirmishes and random attacks and withdrawals by Māori raiders continued – Cameron was forced into a new type of unconventional conflict. While his army still had superior rifle and gun power, every raid and skirmish forced him to divert precious manpower into more protective backup, including communications, extra patrols, escorts and redoubts. Big British guns which could fire from hilltop, shore or riverboat had little impact prosecuting this type of warfare.

Many of these "guerrilla operations", as Belich described them, were probably masterminded by the Kingite leaders Tāmihana and Maniapoto, and proved extraordinarily effective, tying up a large proportion of Cameron's troops for most of the winter of 1863. But through sheer weight of numbers – as Cameron and Grey's mighty military force expanded and built up to re-engage and threaten the Māori line at Meremere – the Kingite leaders were eventually forced to face reality.

Olivia's charity

Inevitably, it was the impact on civilians on both sides which mattered most. For Māori families, it was also a time of withdrawal to settlements well away from the main pā sites – to places across the Waikato River towards Raglan

Olivia Purchas, who bore 14 children in 21 years from 1847, and who – like many other early New Zealand women – played such a large part behind the scenes in her husband's significant life.
JULIET McKINSTRY

and Kawhia, or other isolated places where food could be more easily grown and supplied.

For the British settlers forced from their homes by the threat of a miserable death at the hands of a Māori warrior party, times quickly became even more stressful. Many of the menfolk were already away in the militia or being called up. In late July and early August, wives and children from the settlements across the Manukau and further south were ordered to evacuate immediately to Onehunga "as the natives were reported to be on the warpath". No time was given for them to collect bedding, clothing or provisions, and they soon started arriving by the score in small boats on the Onehunga beach at the foot of Princes St, fearful, bewildered and with nowhere to go. No arrangements had been made by government authorities for the 'Pākehā exodus' – an unforeseen consequence of the advance into the Waikato. The flight of the settlers was not on the same scale as for Māori, but the result was the same. They were ushered first into the old customs house to sleep on the bare floor, "cold, hungry and miserable".

While attending to some of the sick, Purchas made contact with Frances Fletcher, the wife of a soldier, whose wedding ceremony he had performed some 10 years earlier. Frances was quickly enlisted by Purchas to act as his nurse for the next couple of years. "Whenever there was an epidemic of fever or measles, Frances was 1st lieutenant to Dr Purchas and he often referred them straight to Frances, replenishing her medicine chest and advising her what to do."[188]

Within a couple of days of the first settler refugee arrivals, the trickle had become a mini-flood and the now-widowed licensee of the Royal Hotel, Elizabeth George, asked Purchas, her friend, to convene a public meeting which she then chaired. The result was the formation of what became the very first institution of its kind in the country – the Onehunga Ladies Benevolent

Society – with Olivia Purchas as its first president.[189] There were no charitable aid organisations or other government relief agencies in place at this time, other than the churches. For the next few months, and supported by her husband, Olivia led the effort to find housing, food and clothing for more than 100 British refugees, all the while caring for and feeding her own family.

By October – when Cameron was in a position to turn his attention to the Meremere line from the hard-won security of the Waikato River – the main Māori forces had already started to retire south, in their tribal groups, back into their various pā and other strongholds. The British mounted a concerted gunboat and land attack on Meremere, a place which Māori chose to now abandon, sustaining few casualties. Instead their new 'line' was drawn at Rangiriri. This was basically an unfinished pā site, not yet fully garrisoned. Nevertheless it featured a commanding ridge facing north – the direction from which they expected the next British assault would likely come.

In that same month, in the safety and warmth of comfortable leather seats in the panelled rooms provided for members of the New Zealand General Assembly, the first steps were being taken to validate, by statute, the anticipated and imminent confiscation of Māori land. Led by Frederick Whitaker, the process began with the Suppression of Rebellion Act, copied from earlier Irish legislation and very much written with senior military officers in mind. They were the ones given the immediate power to arrest or capture "rebels" – to be held pending later trial or court martial if deemed necessary.

Coverage even extended to settlers, missionaries and clergymen who might have openly sided with any Māori who had not sworn allegiance to the Crown. With the act swiftly in place, for men like Purchas the final barrier to co-operation between the races was up. The "guilt by association" label meant he would have to cease contact with the likes of Ngāpora and Te Paea – now among the thousands of Māori uprooted and resettling in Kīngitanga country. All were awaiting a hopelessly negative and destructive outcome in whatever shape or form it might arrive.

The New Zealand Loan Act followed, which confirmed the borrowing of £4 million from London sources to fund the war – scheduled to be repaid by the sale of confiscated land after the "rebellion had been suppressed". The final major piece of war legislation was the New Zealand Settlements Act. It basically allowed officials to decide later which of the best Māori land to confiscate and which land Māori tribes would be allowed to retain and resettle on after hostilities ended.[190]

---

189   Papers Past, *New Zealand Herald*, April 27, 1930.
190   D Keenan, *Wars Without End*, pp 260-261.

Life in the Purchas household at this time was a constant mix of charitable work, business, medical service, church and family. Olivia, pregnant with their 12th child, was working next door in the stone schoolroom, directing operations for the benevolent society every day. The latest task she had picked up with the help of her friend Elizabeth George, was to organise local builders to fix up some temporary accommodation for her "refugees". There was a run-down old building opposite the Royal which was quickly turned into basic accommodation for them.

Meanwhile Arthur had received some bad news from James Ninnis. After running so well for the last eight or nine months, their flax mill had suffered some damage caused by a group of Māori intent on mayhem and destruction. Apparently this aggressive group had turned up, scared off the employees with threats, roughed the place up and left the machinery running, which eventually caused major problems. The partners felt they now had no choice but to close the place down – and Purchas reluctantly did so on July 11, 1863. Any return on their investment would have to wait a while longer.

At night, he was still working on his final design touches for his new church at Otahuhu, being built on a half-acre block next to where the first one had stood.[191] He had designed this one to accommodate 200 people, bigger than St Bride's in Mauku and with provision to extend the western end to accommodate up to 325 people. It had a shingle roof, a kauri-lined interior, kauri seats and ventilation in both floor and ceiling. Built to the same basic plan as St Bride's, with slightly larger bays, it had large windows at either end and a private door to enter the vestry from the outside. The bell tower stood waiting for "an exceedingly good bell from Kororareka" to replace the old one which had unfortunately cracked. The dedication was set down for immediately after Christmas to be carried out by Bishop Selwyn.[192]

Throughout this time, apart from his absence in Ōtāwhau, Purchas had also remained in his subsidiary surgeon's role at the Auckland Hospital. Now relatively well settled at home in Onehunga, unable to move far beyond the towns, his medical services were once again in demand – particularly when accidents or serious trauma occurred, which seemed to happen frequently in those early days.

While reading his paper one morning – no doubt catching up on the proposed legislation to be introduced at the General Assembly meeting starting

---

191 Refer to the Heritage New Zealand Pouhere Taonga website, Selwyn Church, Otahuhu.
192 Further attribution to Purchas as the most likely designer is given on the Heritage New Zealand website – see Construction Professionals link. Also refer to Papers Past, *Daily Southern Cross*, Sept 21, 1863, where specific reference is made to this church "being built on the same plan as the Mauku church".

the next day – Purchas was called out to one particularly shocking emergency. Madeleine Stewart, the two- or three-year-old daughter of a prominent Mangere farmer, had died an excruciating death. By the time Purchas got across the water to Mangere by the ferryman's dinghy, it was all over. The toddler had found a small glass bottle containing some white powder and taken it outside to play. A few minutes later the child's mother asked her young domestic servant to bring the child in. She found the girl on the ground, her hand so rigidly clasped around the uncapped bottle she was unable to break the grip. The frantic mother poured castor oil down the child's throat producing violent convulsive fits for an hour. When Purchas arrived, he found the dead toddler in a state of "immense and rigid extension, her belly purple and distorted and frothy mucus exuding from the nostrils in considerable quantity", and her teeth clenched tight.

At the public inquest a couple of days later, Purchas explained how he had completed his tests of the white powder in the bottle – the process he followed "being sufficiently delicate to detect the millionth part of a grain" – and pronounced it to have been strychnine. The findings shocked the entire colony. Farmers and small landowners everywhere habitually kept the deadly poison to kill stray dogs, hawks, rats and other vermin. Newspaper editors forgot the war for a day or so to warn everyone about the dangers of keeping such deadly poison on their household shelves.

Rangiriri battle

The gruesome strychnine tragedy was inevitably and quickly overtaken on the front pages by the renewed activities of war, now focused on Rangiriri where Cameron launched his long-expected attack in November on "the last major bastion blocking British entry into the Waikato heartland".[193] His forces numbered about 1200 men, backed by Armstrong artillery with guns also in use from two navy ships stationed in the nearby Waikato River. Despite their firepower, the British had problems clearing the parapets protecting the main pā and still had not broken through when night fell.

Many Māori escaped through the rear under cover of darkness – including, we are told, the leaders of the Waikato resistance, Wiremu Tāmihana and King Matutaera at separate times.[194] Then, at dawn, Cameron saw a white flag and assumed it indicated a Māori surrender. For Māori, however, the white flag meant a wish to talk about a truce, fair to both sides. The British came

---

193   Keenan, p 223.
194   B Ashwell – *CMS Missionary Letters*; Belich, p 153.

forward to the pā, without hindrance. Hopelessly outnumbered, the Māori had no choice but to hand over their guns and be taken prisoner after the British interpreter had explained to each side the confusion created by the white flag. One hundred and eighty-three men and women were rounded up and transported back to Auckland, many ending up in prison on Kawau Island.

In a strange coincidence, the interpreter that day was none other than young William Gundry – the 21-year-old son of Purchas's old friend – who had only recently been released from Purchas's guardianship. His main role was as a surveyor – Purchas had organised an apprenticeship for him as a 15- or 16-year-old. Gundry's youthful enthusiasm probably got the better of him when he wrote to the native minister soon after the Rangiriri battle to tell him that, despite the misunderstanding over the white flag, the Kīngitanga still wanted to negotiate an end to the fighting. His message, although undoubtedly correct – including information that up to 40 Māori bodies had been found – was completely ignored.[195] Wiremu Tāmihana also sought peace with Cameron – but in response, Grey insisted that Māori first surrender all their lands and arms.

The action at Rangiriri had produced the war's first large casualty list, with some 45 killed on each side, and another 78 British and 50 Māori wounded by bullet, shell or bayonet. Although the British military claimed a great victory, the public were far less impressed, with some newspaper correspondents bemoaning the heavy cost – despite such clear advantages in manpower and weaponry. The small remaining Kīngitanga forces were still able to reassemble further south, trying to keep out of Cameron's way, but certainly no less determined to resist the British advance.

Nevertheless Cameron was easily able to move on and occupy the Ngāti Mahuta base at Ngāruawāhia and from there threaten the entire Waikato district. His only problem at this stage – or so it appeared to the settlers voraciously following reports each day from the more jingoistic newspaper correspondents – was to keep his large supply lines to the north intact. In fact, much of the army was involved in the defence and maintenance of supplies, up road and river, north to south and across the island from west to east. The great pretence involved in trying to assure the public that Auckland was protected, remained a key part of Grey's overall strategy.

---

195 Gundry family papers; V O'Malley, *The Great War for New Zealand*, p 264; Appendix to the Journals of the House of Representatives, E-5.

CHAPTER 12

Pain Continues

If the action at Rangiriri had not been so deadly, the war (after only six months) might have been called "phoney" – an early version of that period of relative inaction at the beginning of World War II. It certainly suited the Kīngitanga, who although effectively having to retreat, were also tying up vast British resources in terms of armaments, supplies and military men on full pay and high commissions, mostly in logistical support.

The increasingly frustrated British soldiers believed they were there to get on and fight the Māori in conventional battle – not to skirmish behind their own lines, carry hay to horses, water to billycans or potatoes to the peeling tents, or even guard settlers' empty homes. Grey's Executive Council met in Auckland on December 14, 1863 and forced Cameron to present a new plan – referred to in the minutes of that meeting as a plan to "bring the rebel natives to perfect subjugation". While the Kīngitanga continued to make moves designed to open the way to peace, the powerful Auckland financiers, landowners and business lobbies were pressuring Grey and his army officers to finish the Māori resistance once and for all.

Christmas 1863 came and went. In January, yet more troops arrived from England, including what was to be the last of the 10 British regiments brought to quell the "rebellion". Perhaps in a response to the agitation expressed by the Auckland settlers, Grey ordered another 500-600 troops, under Colonel Carey, to be landed at Tauranga – with instructions to head inland towards Ōtāwhau/ Te Awamutu and the Waipā River area. Back near Ngāruawāhia, Cameron's supply headaches and frustrations only got worse when one of his two ships on the Waikato River sank after hitting something solid beneath the surface.

Despite this setback, and with Carey covering his flank to the south-east, Cameron decided to push south towards Maniapoto's large fortified pā at Pāterangi, where almost 2000 Māori warriors were now stationed. For Māori, if there was to be a major battle, this was where they now believed they might have to engage the enemy. Pāterangi was well set up for both defence and attack. It was not far from Ōtāwhau, scene of the earlier Gorst expulsion and Purchas's involvement when medical commissioner.

But Cameron then determined not to attack Pāterangi. Instead he set off in darkness for Te Awamutu, marching silently past the Pāterangi pā about a kilometre away and on to the Māori settlement of Rangiowahia, a little further south in the centre of their rich food-growing areas. It was unfortified and home to many older people, women and children. Most of their menfolk were at Pāterangi. It was also a Sunday and the Christian Māori would not fight on that day.

Cameron's relatively small force of 80 or 90 men – under the command of Colonel Marmaduke Nixon from Mangere, and including some on horseback and a group of Forest Rangers – attacked the Rangiowahia settlement at dawn on February 21, 1864. Nixon's sergeant was shot in the initial attack, and when Nixon and others went to retrieve the body, he was also shot.[196]

The British encountered some serious resistance from Māori defenders in a couple of whare, which were then set on fire. In the mayhem, an old Māori man waving a white blanket came out to surrender. In what was apparently a mix-up of orders, he was also shot. Further burning and destruction followed, including the well-documented collateral deaths of women and children in the raging fires which followed and the attempted escape of the Māori inhabitants. It was a catastrophic morning all round. Twelve Māori died and five British were also killed. Another 33 Māori were taken prisoner.[197]

Te Awamutu now became the main British base for the entire campaign. When Māori heard of the Rangiowahia disaster, the large Pāterangi pā was quickly abandoned and the warriors simply dispersed – some went east to Maungatautari where Tāmihana had a fortified base; others went south to wherever they could find shelter. Cameron's men swarmed in to occupy Pāterangi before he turned his attention to the nearby settlement of Kihikihi – home of Rewi Maniapoto and the centre of a large and thriving vegetable and fruit growing area. It was to be Cameron's next target. But Maniapoto and his men had already gone, seemingly vanishing in the cool, autumn night air. The British assault there was unopposed.

Redoubts were soon established at Kihikihi and at other nearby centres with up to 200 British soldiers stationed at each. But Maniapoto and his Kīngitanga allies remained determined to resist the Cameron advance. He was encouraged in this by chiefs from various North Island tribes – including Tūhoe,

---

196 In 2017 a large monument of Nixon in Otahuhu, Auckland was the centre of further controversy arising from his action at Rangiowahia. He died later from injuries received that day.

197 J Cowan, *The New Zealand Wars*, Vol 2, p 35.

Ngāti Raukawa (his Maniapoto neighbours), Ngāti Tūwharetoa from the Taupō region and war parties from Tauranga and Hawkes Bay. Then, against his better judgement, Maniapoto was prevailed on to establish a new defensive pā site on land only four or five kilometres south of Kihikihi at Ōrākau. Behind Ōrākau was the Puniu River, a tributary of the Waipā River.

Matutaera Tawhiao, the second Māori King, a great Ngāti Mahuta leader and friend of Purchas, with whom he enjoyed a special relationship in the troubled times between 1859 and 1864.

ALEXANDER TURNBULL LIBRARY, REF: 1/2-050875-F

Little more than a month or so after the assault on Rangiowahia, Maniapoto was still seriously unhappy about the Ōrākau site – especially its lack of water and exposure on three sides. He next tried to persuade some of his allies to go and talk peace "rangatira to rangatira" with Cameron. But there was too much mistrust, especially after Māori had seen the way the British treated their prisoners.

When the British eventually learned of the Kīngitanga force amassing at the new Ōrākau pā, late in March 1864, the decision was immediately taken to attack. By now their main assault force was led by Carey who ordered a bayonet charge by three columns, hoping Māori would advance to meet them outside the fortified pā. Two or three such charges were repulsed by hails of rifle fire and Maniapoto's men remained behind their parapets. Again, we are told William Gundry was involved at Ōrākau, this time as a British scout and surveyor.

General Cameron – whose soldiers had been stationed further east to watch over Tāmihana's main pā at Maungatautari – arrived the following day and began a continuous bombardment with heavier artillery. By midday, the 300 or so Māori were running out of ammunition, but even when given the chance by Cameron to surrender, refused to give in. In the late afternoon, realising they were finally trapped, a mass evacuation was ordered. The entire force gathered as one and moved quickly out and over the south-eastern parapets without a word being spoken. When the British realised what was happening, a small group rushed forward into the pā to fire on the Māori as they escaped. In the ensuing chase and rout, about a third of the Māori were massacred – between 100 and 150. Another 20 or so were taken captive.

The later summary of the conflict concluded that, while the British finally overpowered the Māori force, neither side had really won. Most of the main

Kīngitanga army crossed to the other side of the Puniu River, while Tāmihana's Ngāti Hāua forces and allies remained safely ensconced in their fortified base near Maungatautari. The Kīngitanga had still not been dismantled, broken or destroyed despite their grievous losses. They had certainly been subdued by virtue of their retreat but could still regroup. While newspaper correspondents wrote of victory, it was more akin to the earlier Taranaki stalemate.

Yet again, a week or so after these events, a group of Māori approached Cameron about peace terms. Cameron refused to talk, insisting once more on absolute "unconditional surrender" of arms and land. Māori were given half an hour to decide. Rewi Maniapoto, back across the Puniu – now the new boundary line for the Kīngitanga – decided to wait a while. The British were unwilling to chase him further, so the war would soon be taken up elsewhere.

Gate Pā and Te Ranga

That "elsewhere" was Tauranga and the Bay of Plenty, from where, for the last several months, the Kīngitanga tribes had been fighting a rearguard action – well supported by men and supplies, ammunition and guns from other local tribes. When Carey had landed there in January, his orders were to neither provoke local Māori, nor open up another front.

Over the next two or three months, while the battles were being fought at Rangiowahia and Ōrākau, Māori warriors under Rāwiri Puhirake gradually moved closer to the British encampment at Te Papa outside Tauranga – finally erecting a new fortified pā at what became known as Gate Pā. A confrontation became inevitable and the first shots of this next encounter were fired on April 28, 1864, only three weeks or so after the Ōrākau tragedy.

This time the dice landed in favour of Māori. After withstanding an initial bombardment from Cameron's artillery, the British troops were met by tenacious resistance as they tried to storm the pā. The Māori were concealed in tunnels and trenches, and mowed down the unfortunate troops as they appeared in front of them. Cameron ordered a retreat on this occasion. About 35 of his troops died while Māori losses were estimated at 25.

Besides being noted in history as a defeat for the British, Gate Pā is also known for its many accounts of individual chivalry. In this context, perhaps no story has been told more often than that of another of Purchas's colleagues and friends, Hēnare Taratoa. He was the young man from the early days at St John's, whose wedding Purchas had served at and who had since become Bishop Selwyn's chaplain, accompanying him on all his travels.

But he had also become a victim of the war, forced finally to resume his place among his own people, stranded between two opposing forces. Shortly before the Gate Pā battle, he wrote a brief manifesto or document addressed to both Māori and Pākehā, setting out various principles to be observed to minimise needless slaughter on either side. Soldiers or warriors who offered the butts of their rifles to indicate surrender, were to be spared. The same went for unarmed Pākehā or Māori who surrendered. Other rules of simple humanity were set out in plain language. It is recorded that while Māori mostly adhered to Taratoa's requests, the British did not.

Other famous stories of Gate Pā tell of Māori offering water to a dying senior British officer, wounded soldiers being attended by Māori women, and bodies on both sides being retrieved and buried with honour. Selwyn himself was involved in such action, only to be roundly and unjustly condemned by settlers for supposedly supporting Māori and not the British. Māori, on the other hand, also turned from him, alleging that he was complicit with Grey in the plan to separate them from their land.

The final encounter in this wretched, indecisive and pointless campaign of invasion – which had begun with Cameron's crossing of the Maungatawhiri Stream in July the previous year – took place almost 12 months later on June 21, 1864. After Gate Pā, Māori had once again withdrawn to the south and had constructed another pā, this time at Te Ranga, not far from the ranges separating the area from Rotorua. The British attacked before the various Māori tribes assembled there had finished their preparations and the result was a complete reversal of the Gate Pā battle. Bitter hand-to-hand fighting took place with knives, bayonets, mere and patu. Māori losses were substantial with well over 100 killed, while the British casualties of dead and wounded amounted to about 50.

Where were King Matutaera, Te Paea and Tāmati Ngāpora in all this? None could offer any significant military expertise, even if they wanted to be involved – although Matutaera had been with his people at Rangiriri. The military leadership of the Kīngitanga had mainly been left to the experienced but peace-seeking Wiremu Tāmihana and his aggressive partner Rewi Maniapoto. The Kīngitanga leaders remained with their people in Ngāti Maniapoto territory across the Puniu River – Ngāpora staying near today's Te Kuiti where he took a new name, Te Manuhiri or "guest in the land of others". Matutaera, carrying a great sense of betrayal by Grey, came to live at Kawhia and took the name of Tāwhiao after converting to the new Pai Mārire faith. He continued to express principles of peace and goodness, always wanting to find a way to have his Waikato land returned but insisting that, for his people, there was to be no more killing. He then married Ngāpora's daughter, Hera.

Ngāpora remained Tāwhiao's closest advisor.[198]

The river effectively became the new northern boundary or aukati of Kīngitanga – the King Country – and for the next 20 years, Europeans avoided crossing that line.[199] Ngāpora, in particular, remained his usual courteous self, always making sure that any Europeans who did appear later in the King Country by invitation, were met with respect. Rewi Maniapoto continued to hold well over 1000 warriors under his command, just to remind the Pākehā that nothing had been resolved. By the end of 1864, it was estimated there were more than 2000 armed British settlers living on former Kīngitanga lands north of the aukati. As O'Malley wrote: "For many years after 1864, the Kīngitanga's ability to strike back at any time remained a source of considerable anxiety for many Europeans."[200]

The fighting did not stop elsewhere of course. Over the following 15 years, Māori resistance to the European designs on their land continued. Conflicts took place again in the Bay of Plenty, Taranaki, Wanganui, the East Coast, Hawkes Bay and Poverty Bay. Random atrocities were committed by both sides. The missionary Carl Völkner was killed, and other names like Te Kooti, McDonnell, Panapa, Te Rangihiwinui, Tītokowaru and Whitmore entered our history books via various violent exploits. Māori in many places developed split loyalties, giving rise to the kūpapa (Māori supporting the Government) and resulting in virtual civil war in some areas. Many native communities were crippled as a result.

The times following the Waikato and Taranaki wars were also fraught with other dangers for Māori. Poor diets and living conditions (worse than ever before), led to the alarming spread of influenza, pleurisy, measles, dysentery, tuberculosis and skin diseases. In the fracture of the post-war Māori society, the consequences of the increasing contact with Europeans were even more disastrous than those of the war itself.

As early as 1865, hunger, disease and despair were all experienced in the Kīngitanga countryside beyond the Puniu. Yet again the indefatigable Wiremu Tāmihana sued for peace in a famous meeting with Carey at Tamahere, where he laid down his taiaha and agreed that Queen Victoria's law would also be King Tāwhiao's law. His hope was that other Māori tribes might follow the example – but his act was once more met with suspicion, and nothing eventuated.

Unable to talk peace, even though they had not been "conquered" or their so-called rebellion finally put down, Māori now had to face an even worse

---

198 S Oliver, Ngapora, *Te Ara – The Encyclopedia of New Zealand*, 2013.
199 Appendix to the Journals of the House of Representatives, 1871, A9.
200 V O'Malley, *The Great War for New Zealand*, p 347.

prospect – the confiscation of their land. And Grey was in a hurry. He needed to sell a lot of it to repay his war loan.

Back in Onehunga

Just three days before the Te Ranga battle, Arthur Purchas had attended to Olivia while she delivered another healthy girl, named Gertrude. In the days before the birth, he had also been busy, advocating strongly as a member of Selwyn's standing committee – effectively a board of control – for a new public cemetery in Onehunga. The one next to the church there had little space left and the town authorities in those days expected church administrators to look after such matters on their own land on behalf of the entire community.

While on the lookout for a possible solution, Purchas became interested in an upcoming sale by auction of some elevated sites – small vacant lots on the corner of today's Harbour View Tce in Onehunga. The 43-year-old Purchas was still highly conscious of the need to somehow make provision for the education and future of his very large family. Investment in land, purchased by the Government from Māori many years earlier, was the only way he could see to achieve this goal and improve his situation in the longer term.

The lots were available on favourable terms of one-third cash deposit. He scraped together everything he could and decided to take a chance. The auction had to be delayed a day because of the large funeral for Colonel Marmaduke Nixon, who had died of his wounds sustained in the earlier battle at Rangiowahia. The entire Auckland and Onehunga area was in mourning with business houses closed everywhere for the full military funeral and burial.

When the auction resumed the next day, Purchas's bid on Lot 10 was successful, based on the one-third deposit and settlement in 90 days. We don't know the price paid but it was probably £25-£35 in what was by now a buyer's market – with the seller, Henry Hardington, funding Purchas's mortgage for the remaining two-thirds.[201] Purchas was to retain this small block until he died and it is believed the land was only ever used for grazing and crops, in conjunction with adjacent lots.

While the violence and troubles further south may have seemed a world away, by the autumn of 1864 the negative effects of the war on the economy were just starting to be felt in the settler community. Economically, the previous couple of years had been generally buoyant in Auckland, although the arrival of the refugees did create financial challenges. But after Gate Pā and Te Ranga,

---

201   Henry Hardington ran a successful coach business for many years out to Onehunga.

conditions changed almost overnight as the massive expenditure on items of war came to a halt. Times very quickly became tough everywhere and at all levels within the European community in Auckland.

The Māori food trade into Auckland had been decimated and because so many European settlers and farmers in the productive areas across the Manukau Harbour had left their farms to serve in the war, vegetables, fruit, meat and potatoes were soon in short supply. Business leaders and traders in Auckland, where the population had now increased to 12-13,000 – men such as Buckland, Firth, Daldy and Williamson – became concerned that Māori were no longer able to supply food to Auckland. The business community wanted their most productive land "by whatever means, to come more freely into European hands"[202] so the Pākehā could produce the food needed. The large Purchas family, including 17-year-old Helen Gundry – living again under their roof and helping Olivia with the children – was now, like everyone else in town, relying heavily on their own garden and the spirit of co-operation and generosity of others. That winter of 1864, although an increasingly bleak time for everyone in Onehunga – including the Purchas family – was alleviated a little for Arthur by a couple of satisfying and more pleasant duties arising from his trustee and guardianship roles. The dutiful and well-mannered Helen Gundry had set her eyes on a young man named Francis Young and came to Purchas, as her guardian, seeking his permission to marry.

Purchas was, in fact, well acquainted with the up-and-coming Francis, to whom he had sold a couple of Gundry estate lots in Onehunga about three months earlier. It seems that, despite her youth, Purchas had no reservations because, within days, not only had he consented to the marriage but also performed the ceremony itself in St Peter's.[203] It is not recorded how Olivia then managed with her 10 children – including two babies and eight others aged between three and 15 – but it is likely that Helen continued to help during the day at least.

A couple of days after the Gundry-Young marriage, Purchas the trustee was active again in the property market, this time for William Coldicutt. He asked local auctioneer Alfred Buckland to arrange an auction of the bulk of the Coldicutt property, as per the original instruction in Coldicutt's will two years earlier. Given the uncertain times, Purchas was clearly nervous about property prices and the economy in general.

In spite of his justifiable concerns, a total of 42 Coldicutt acres was nevertheless disposed of at the auction, advertised as "choice volcanic land,

---

202   R C J Stone, *Makers of Fortune*, p 9
203   Gundry family papers – L Cocks.

near the Epsom church of St Andrew's" – land which Purchas obviously knew well. It sold for £60-£61 an acre while the estate's herd of cows went for between £11 and £21 each. Purchas was under instruction to give £1000 to Coldicutt's son and to invest the remainder on mortgage for his widow until she remarried or died.

Purchas (and the auctioneer) did well, producing a very pleasing result. He must have been happy, for the moment at least, given that he had sold just in time. In the process, he was continuing to learn a lot about land, how to read the sudden ups and downs of a developing market, and how best to manage the various properties under his care. A property like the warehouse in Shortland St, which he leased out on behalf of Harriet Austin and her eight children, was her family's only source of income – so she also was totally dependent on Purchas's good judgement and conscientious oversight.

Helping him now with his trustee duties was a local solicitor, Frederic Brookfield, who had been serving on the St Peter's trust board since 1855, after establishing a legal practice in Onehunga. Their lives would be inextricably linked for the next 40 years. And their children would be connected by marriage for many generations to come.

Also depending on Purchas's good judgement and advice over the later part of the year (1864) was a dedicated group of businessmen and entrepreneurs from Dunedin. Since the discovery of gold at Gabriel's Gully in 1861, the town had been transformed and was now New Zealand's largest and wealthiest city with a population quickly approaching 15,000. A committee comprising Dunedin's most prominent citizens resolved to use the new-found gold wealth to create long-term institutions and benefits for their fast-developing town.

They decided to hold an international exhibition and asked Purchas if he would like to join their northern committee to help with planning and organising. After all, Purchas had some of the best geological and scientific contacts and knowledge in the world at his disposal – developed from his own experience exhibiting in London in 1862 and, more recently, including experts at the world famous Natural History Museum in Vienna through friends like Ferdinand von Hochstetter.

The idea was also greeted favourably and promoted by other Anglican Church leaders – also hoping to see some good transpire from the single-minded pursuit of gold in the south with all its accompanying evils. In his committee role, Purchas assisted in the efforts to attract exhibits from Austria and England, while other items came from France, Belgium, Germany and Australia. He despatched some items of his own, including flax fibre samples, cordage and finished goods to sit alongside the charts, stuffed birds, wood and wool collections, paintings, Māori artefacts and geological displays.

More than 31,000 visitors attended the New Zealand Exhibition in Dunedin in the four months it was open from January 1865. The only mishaps were the late arrival of the ship carrying the British exhibits and the absence of George Grey on opening day. He was still far too occupied with the fighting and confiscation program in the north. Nevertheless the event was pronounced a success and many of the exhibits later provided the basis of the collection for today's Otago Museum. Purchas's reputation in all things historical, scientific and educational increased immeasurably across the wider New Zealand cultural scene.[204]

Confiscation begins

As we have seen, repeated efforts by the Kīngitanga to seek peace had all been in vain. There was also nothing the movement could do when the massive programme of confiscation got underway in December 1864, under the New Zealand Settlements Act. A first proclamation, taking 1.2 million acres of land in Taranaki, was gazetted on December 17. But then – to Purchas's horror, since he knew Māori in these places to be among the most peaceable in the country – Grey issued an order in council for the seizure of Māori land at Pokeno (19,000 acres) and Tuakau (10,887 acres), and thousands more acres at Patumahoe, Pukekohe and Waiuku.[205]

Grey made a good start to repaying the huge loan which had funded the Waikato War by on-selling the Tuakau land fairly quickly to the Auckland province for £18,000. But his proclamation announcing the confiscation programme also stated: "….that where the Governor in council should be satisfied that any native tribe since January 1 1863 have been engaged in rebellion … it should be lawful to take possession of any other lands … and to define and vary as he should think fit". By this last clause in his proclamation – and despite the Treaty guarantee of undisturbed possession – Grey gave himself carte blanche with regard to land now open for seizure.

In the prized Waikato district, virtually empty between Pokeno and south of Te Awamutu, another 1.2 million acres was taken. A further one million acres was seized in the Bay of Plenty, between Tauranga and Opotiki.

For the modern-day generation of New Zealanders who may have wondered about or even questioned the process of land repatriation recommended since to successive governments by the Waitangi Tribunal, a

---

204 Refer J Phillips, Exhibitions and world's fairs, *Te Ara – The Encyclopedia of New Zealand.*
205 Appendix to the Journals of the House of Representatives, D-02.

couple of points need to be made.

The Māori land involved was mostly unoccupied or not yet surveyed. No titles, other than customary agreement, were in place. Many Māori, still living on ancestral land which the Government had now taken, remained completely unaware of their loss for years. The paperwork involving such dispossession sat in files in Auckland or Wellington since "owners" in the European sense were unknown, there being no British-style titles. In fact many individuals and iwi did not learn of the loss of their land until survey teams arrived, sometimes years later.[206] The $170 million Tainui settlement of 1995 is said to have returned only about 3% of the total land confiscated.

Grey had also confirmed by proclamation that any Māori tribes who had accepted the Queen's sovereignty would keep their land. He also offered to compensate Māori who felt they had been wronged in the confiscation process. But they had to prove their case in a new Compensation Court, which only began to hear cases in 1866 (presided over by none other than Purchas's friend, Francis Dart Fenton). The turn of events would obviously have disappointed Purchas, but he could hardly have predicted the 150-year nightmare involving land dispossession which was to follow.

Complementing the Settlements Act was the Native Lands Act, which established native land courts for the purpose of declaring exactly what was Māori-owned land – to be confirmed via a British title system. The Government's plan was that customary Māori land, including much uninhabited or "waste land", would then be available for Europeans to negotiate to lease or buy, without reference to the Crown.[207] The end result, unhappily, would be an even more rapid "dispossession" of Māori land over the next 20-30 years – involving long-damaging arguments again over who actually had the rights to sell; and characterised by the inability of so many Māori to challenge court rulings, having neither the financial resources to counterclaim nor knowledge of the process to effectively argue their case.

As Wiremu Tāmihana launched a petition to the Government to try and clear his name as a "rebel", planning got under way for the first sitting of the Native Land Court, early the next year (1865) in Waikato territory – mainly Tāmihana's own Ngāti Hāua land, only a few miles away from the boundaries of the million-plus acres of land confiscated just a few months earlier.[208] As the British slowly exacted retribution, Purchas could only watch from a distance

---

206 P Maxwell, *Frontier – The Battle for the North Island of New Zealand*, 1860-1872, p 98.
207 Monin, p 230.
208 By now Tāmihana was very ill and while he continued to attend further sittings of the Land Court, he died a year or so later at Peria on December 27, 1866.

knowing that for him, anyway, the war was over and little more could be done. One of the most eloquent summaries of the events of the previous five or six years was provided later by Sarah Selwyn.

"Land was at the bottom of it ... the desire and impatience of the English to possess land, the ignorance on both sides of each others' feelings and customs in the matter, the mischief made by ignorant or unprincipled men prevailed at the outset. As time went on things grew worse. The English judged the Maori by their own standards and the only recently converted natives ... under the impression that they were not justly dealt with, reverted to their former habits which were in some cases, barbarous. So they did evil things, then the English retaliated and so it went on and public feeling ran very high. Even our old friend Tamati Ngapora had to fly ..."[209]

Trials and Tribulations

Away from these shattering and dislocating confiscations, however, the next two years (1865-66) for Arthur and Olivia Purchas were without doubt the most severe financially they had ever experienced. The stipend issue remained, the church congregation was even less able to assist and, more worryingly still – with serious maintenance long overdue – their beloved St Peter's Church was falling into a state of disrepair. Local government spending had all but stopped, property prices had collapsed, buyers were non-existent and soup kitchens were opening up for those suddenly out of work. And, in between times, the Government had finally been fully re-established in the new capital of Wellington, where its fifth session got under way at the end of July 1865.

While a form of peace had come to some areas, fighting and atrocities continued in Wanganui, south Taranaki, the East Coast and around Opotiki. Particularly disturbing was the horrific hanging and barbarity inflicted on Lutheran missionary Carl Völkner, in March 1865. Most of this new violence had developed following the formation of the Pai Mārire religion – or Hau Hau movement – and its strange promises to unshackle Māori from European domination. This movement, in turn, led to the rise of another religious movement, Ringatū, and the ongoing battles with its founder, Te Kooti, once a government supporter. The Kīngitanga leaders remained supposedly in exile and while Grey and his army set about trying to clean up the damage caused by the Taranaki and Waikato wars, settlers and Māori alike were left to manage as best they could in the harsh recession that inevitably followed two or three years of war.

209 AAA, Sarah Selwyn, *Reminiscences*, MS273 Vol 4.

Regrettably, for the sorely pressed Purchas household, in between news of the continuing hostilities further south, there came a series of totally unexpected domestic shocks and highly unsettling events – all of which would test Olivia and Arthur's sense of hope and emotional well-being.

The first of these, in April 1865, was what turned out to be a highly controversial £1278 claim in the Compensation Court for losses Purchas said he had personally sustained in the Waitangi flax mill operation. The controversy centred on a number of matters. First, Purchas unfortunately entered the perfectly legitimate claim on his own behalf, without mentioning his partner Ninnis. It was an error of judgement (which Purchas accepted later), because with Ninnis having only contributed about £50 to the project (plus his unaccounted for time), Purchas was going to settle with him after any award was made.

Arthur and Olivia 'at home', circa 1865, typical of photos often taken for forwarding on to 'reassure' family and friends in England in the early days of the colony.
AUCKLAND MUSEUM IMAGES
PH NEG C14448

Second, the claim did not include compensation for any of the backers – first enlisted by Purchas and Ninnis – who funded the mill building itself. Presumably, at this stage, Purchas deemed it to be just part of the risk and misfortune associated with a one-off 'angel' investment – still, technically, an unrealised loss.

The third and far more personal issue arose later when settlers in Auckland questioned, via letters to the press, why churchmen supposedly with Māori sympathies (meaning Purchas) "should feel so little hesitancy about recounting the wrongs they have endured at the hands of their beloved protégés" in justifying their own case for compensation from those who they had previously called "land-grasping and covetous colonists".

Purchas quickly found himself in trouble with the Compensation Court Commissioner for entering the claim in his own name, without mentioning Ninnis – thereby leading the Commissioner to believe he was the sole occupier/operator of the mill and "that no other person had a right in the matter". Unfortunately, to further complicate matters, Ninnis had strangely put in a claim for the same amount (£1278), obviously without consulting Purchas.

Apart from this clearly unintended 'double dip', the Commissioner was left to state that if he did award anything to Purchas as the first claimant, legally Ninnis might still not be able to recover anything.

With Frederic Brookfield assisting at his side, Purchas explained that his intention was to make the claim and then settle up with Ninnis afterwards for his appropriate share, based on his £50 contribution. Unfortunately, a deed of partnership which had been drawn up originally between Purchas and Ninnis had never been signed, even though the flax machine patent had been drawn up in both their names. Further, Purchas argued, the flax mill had never been contemplated at that time.

The Commissioner severely scolded Purchas for causing him such great anxiety and putting him in such a difficult position – having to decide how to be fair to both him and Ninnis. Purchas had jeopardised the entire claim, he said. Arthur apologised profusely, saying it was certainly not his intention to deceive the court and that he fully intended to reimburse Ninnis and would rather "have nothing, than deceive the Court". After further hand-wringing and much discussion with Brookfield and others, Ninnis finally withdrew his own claim. Purchas then agreed to insert Ninnis's name on his original claim. The Commissioner pronounced himself finally satisfied with Purchas's explanations and made the award, leaving Purchas to settle a fair share with Ninnis. We don't know the details of this arrangement but it would be fair to assume that Purchas probably made a generous division on account of the trouble he had unintentionally caused.[210]

Purchas had been paying ground rent at £20 a year since the Waitangi flax mill had opened, and he had paid the resident engineer's removal costs when the place was closed down. The remainder sought was basically the interest on his own investment capital of time and expenses in a temporarily abandoned project. It was a sorry administrative mess which did not read well from anyone's point of view. But at least the mill was still more or less intact and would live to see another day. In fact, it was to resume operations less than a year later, which helped to resolve some of the original backers' queries.

No sooner had the dust settled on this controversy than Olivia and Arthur learned of the death of her father, Charles Challinor. He had suffered ill health for the last eight or nine years of his life. In family letters to Olivia four years earlier, her mother, Eliza, had written that her husband was already "unequal to use his pen any more than he can possibly help" and was obviously severely incapacitated at that stage. Olivia had not seen either of her parents since

---

210 Papers Past, *New Zealand Herald* and *Daily Southern Cross*, April 24, 1865.

she left England as a 21-year-old nearly 20 years earlier and would have been visibly shaken when eventually she received word of the family bereavement.

The news only got worse just weeks later when she and Arthur were informed by local police that they had received serious allegations of sexual misconduct against Dr Purchas. That news, so soon after the compensation claim, was also immediately all over the daily papers. About nine months earlier, Olivia had employed a new nursemaid, Matilda Craig. Now, it was alleged, she had conceived a child by Dr Purchas who had also urged her to take "medicine for an improper purpose" – explained later as being to procure an abortion. The allegations were first made in a letter by a 28-year-old farmer named Adam Elliott, who lived near Mt St John. He claimed that Dr Purchas "had tried the same with other girls and should be brought to justice".

The good residents of Onehunga and Auckland were briefly agog on hearing the news. Could this possibly be true? It sounded sensational. Many of the leading citizens of Onehunga had, only three weeks earlier, been listening spellbound to the same Dr Purchas delivering a lecture to a packed hall on the latest advances in telegraphy and electricity. He had been explaining the differences between electromagnetic and electrogalvanic machines, and the various telegraphic alphabets used around the world – accompanied by small experiments showing what electricity could do, complete with ringing bells, lights and clicks. Now this!

As always with people of some standing in the community like Purchas, many were ready to believe the allegations. Fortunately, however, most did not. With Purchas's lawyer friend, Frederic Brookfield, quickly on the case, the police were soon convinced that the allegation was malicious. After further interviews with Purchas, Matilda Craig and Elliott himself, they asked Purchas and the nursemaid if they wanted to press libel charges against Elliott. On Brookfield's advice, both agreed that, despite the ongoing publicity involved, the only way they could convincingly clear their names was to do just that. It took a week to 10 days but eventually on August 23, 1865, Adam Elliott was charged on two counts of maliciously and unlawfully writing and publishing a false and defamatory libel against Purchas and Craig.

It must have been a very embarrassing and testing legal action. Craig explained in the Magistrate's Court that she had met Elliott four years earlier in Ireland before they had both come to New Zealand and Elliott had been writing to her – approaches which she had spurned. The case was heard and then referred to the Supreme Court for Elliott's trial. Purchas and his family had to steel themselves for another few weeks of unnerving gossip around town.

Fortunately for them, however, Elliott finally realised that the game was up and on arrival in the Supreme Court a month later, he pleaded guilty. Chief Justice Sir George Arney wasted no time in sentencing him to 12 months' gaol on each charge, to be served concurrently. A year later he paid a £200 bond and two sureties of good behaviour amounting to another £200 and was discharged.

In between all this came the death of John Morgan, Purchas's friend and missionary colleague from Ōtāwhao. He died nearby in Mangere after falling foul of his CMS chiefs a couple of years earlier. His strong support for the Government at the start of the Waikato War went against the judgement and advice of his CMS superiors, and eventually brought about his resignation from the organisation he had spent a lifetime serving. In fact, historian K R Howe says he was even offered money by the CMS to leave the country, such was the fractured nature of the relationship.[211] But despite their differing views on various subjects, in particular the war, Morgan had been a hospitable host to Purchas in the early days.

In his capacity as Auckland Hospital surgeon, the year must have seemed a particularly trying one to Purchas with apparently no end to the continuing stream of death and injury accidents he had to attend. In October, he was called out to assist a young man, Alfred Dye, a recent immigrant arrival who had attempted to cut his own throat with a blunt instrument. The attempt failed and Purchas was there to stem the blood and dress the wound before being called to the Magistrate's Court on the following Saturday morning to help sort it all out. Purchas, with the assistance of another doctor, regretfully determined that the young man was of unsound mind and needed restraint. He was subsequently ordered "to be removed to the lunatic asylum".

Yet more tragedy followed in November when Purchas was called to another nasty incident, this time involving a small child – the 22-month-old son of a couple living in the local Onehunga camp for the poor. Apparently the mother had gone over to the camp cookhouse about 4pm to cook her husband's dinner, leaving the toddler alone. He wandered outside to find her and was set upon and badly gored in the head by a stray cow. The mother and her friend rushed the child down the street to Dr Purchas who just happened to be home that Saturday evening. In the Coroner's Court a few days later, he described the child's severe laceration above the eye "from which the brain protruded and there was considerable haemorrhage". Purchas cleaned and dressed the wound, and visited the child later that night and again on Sunday. Unfortunately the boy finally went into convulsions and died early on Monday morning.

And before that sorry month had ended, news came of the death of another,

---

211   K R Howe, John Morgan, *Te Ara – Dictionary of New Zealand Biography*.

even closer missionary friend, George Kissling. Since their very first meeting at Purewa in 1847, Purchas and Kissling had lived, worked and shared many interests together, from music and philosophy to education, art and science. Kissling had suffered a paralysing stroke a couple of years earlier while in the middle of conducting a marriage ceremony. His funeral was described as "one of the largest there has been in Auckland" and Purchas joined John Kinder as one of the main pall-bearers.

Despite it all, there were still some more pleasant occasions that year – notably the solemn induction of Purchas into the Provincial Grand Lodge of New Zealand as a Freemason in November, one week after the Kissling funeral. In between times, he enjoyed his continuing parish duties every weekend, usually weddings on Saturdays[212] and sermons on Sundays at morning and evening services in the churches at Onehunga and Epsom. But overall it had been a rough last six months for Arthur and Olivia, who was now expecting their 13th child.

---

212 Onehunga parish records show he conducted 16 weddings in 1865.

CHAPTER 13

Bridge and Arbitration

With a few small plots of land now secured in his own name, a lull in the fighting down south, and an inability to do anything of consequence to help his former Kīngitanga and Māori friends now living in the "king country", Purchas took stock and decided that the future direction of his own life now needed his full attention. The stipend issue was only getting worse and he had almost resigned himself to the distinct possibility that it might never be resolved. The Onehunga church badly needed repairs and the house they lived in – and on which he and Olivia had lavished so much care and attention, and whatever money they had spare – was not even theirs to call their own.

His trusteeship and guardian duties, his surgeon's role for the hospital, plus his local medical activities – to say nothing of his ministerial responsibilities at both St Peter's and St Andrew's in Epsom – were all satisfying, but completely unable to provide him with the money needed in the long term to fund the interest on his two small mortgages, let alone provide for things like his children's education.

A year or so later, when he commented briefly in public about this period, he was reported in the press as saying that "he would never willingly place himself again in a position of such anxiety and uncertainty such as he occupied while incumbent at that parish". Given his generally calm demeanour, this was a heartfelt expression of his situation – and probably still an understatement. He began talking to Olivia about their circumstances again, and then to a couple of his closest friends at St Peter's, before finally deciding to go once more to Bishop Selwyn. Purchas indicated to them all that his resignation from the ministry was inevitable, given his financial position, and that he would be forced to earn a living elsewhere, almost certainly as a doctor.

It seems that Selwyn may have intimated to him in the course of their discussions – probably at a church committee meeting or synod – that he would now willingly consider some means of making the long-overdue recompense for the personal costs Purchas had incurred since 1847. The compensation would possibly include some of the costs of building the parsonage and the stone school at least, some of the recurring maintenance costs for the church over the last 18-19 years, and even some salary arrears.

But Selwyn could still not give Purchas any guarantees of security with regard to future stipend improvement. And Purchas was not the only member of the Bishop's team repeatedly lobbying him about stipends. His good friend Vicesimus Lush (in Howick) had been even more forthright on the matter, bemoaning his £200 per annum salary and complaining about the Bishop's refusal to give him "a more desirable parish near town" where he might be able to rely on greater financial support.[213] Selwyn did agree, however, that it was time for Purchas to pass on his responsibilities at St Andrew's. Within a few weeks he had confirmed Purchas's friend John Kinder as the new man in charge of the now fast-growing parish of Epsom.

For his part, Purchas took it all in good heart as usual, but let his intended resignation from the ministry stand – while graciously volunteering to stay on in Onehunga until a replacement could be found. At least he had put a stake in the ground and something was now going to have to change. It was by no means a threat, since this was never a part of his character. Either Selwyn or his diocesan standing committee would need to sort it out, or he simply would have no choice but to make it official and take up a full-time medical practice – the only certain path to being able to educate his children and secure his and Olivia's future.

While Purchas left Selwyn to think about some kind of belated compensation, his life continued apace involving a multitude of activities in all kinds of disciplines. For much of 1866, it seems even the relentless reporters from the daily newspapers had difficulty keeping up with him. They found him first in February at an important public meeting in Onehunga, where, for the first time, the major local topic of a bridge across the Manukau Harbour, between Onehunga and Mangere, was to be discussed.

Ever since Purchas had arrived in Onehunga some 20 years earlier, he and everyone else had to use a local ferry service – a man rowing an open boat – at any time other than dead low tide, to cross to Mangere, Ihumatao or Pukaki, and even sometimes to Mauku and beyond if the weather was too rough on the Manukau Harbour itself. If the ferryman happened to be on the other side, a flag had to be hoisted to let him know he was needed.

For early Māori, however – before the arrival of the settlers – it was usually a matter of camping at the water's edge until low tide and then walking across

---

213 A Drummond (ed), *The Waikato Journals of Vicesimus Lush.*

… using a long sliver of rock extending across the mudflat where a shallow stream of salt water a few yards wide was easily traversed.

But about 1858, this rock was blasted away so bigger boats could get further up the channel. The ferryman took full advantage and upped his fare to a shilling, apparently demanded in mid-stream just to keep everyone honest.[214] No one needed persuading that far better access was now needed to avoid having to use the long way around – either via the Great South Rd or on a bigger ferry to the wharf at Drury.

Purchas, with his engineer's cap on, immediately entered the discussion with some vigour, purposefully explaining the feasibility of a certain kind of bridge, expanding on the benefits to Onehunga and Auckland, and trying to persuade the large audience at the meeting that funds must be found.

Further meetings ensued, involving local council members, Auckland administrators, bankers, businessmen and the farmers occupying the rich lands on the south side – recently confiscated from Māori. For them, especially, it was a three-day round trip to get produce to Auckland before returning home. A bridge was even more of a necessity if they were to capitalise on the huge demand for meat and vegetables, and to fill the food vacuum left by the Māori farmers – most of them now languishing behind the aukati (boundary) in the King Country.

The end result of all the discussion was a motion to form a company of all interested parties, with its objective being to call for a design, funds and an ongoing maintenance plan, using a bridge toll. The Mangere Bridge Promotion Company was set up to raise £10,000 and a contest for designs was launched. Purchas sat down at his desk in Onehunga and began to draw up his plan for the first Mangere Bridge.

Several others also submitted plans. While they were doing so, the bridge company representatives were out trying to collect money from the hundreds of wildly enthusiastic locals who had pledged to take up one or more of the £10 shares.

Purchas had something of an advantage in his participation. He was well known and regarded as a man of integrity and his engineering and design prowess was already acknowledged (after all, his father had actually designed famous bridges in England). Purchas's design, when he submitted it just five months later in July 1866, was declared the winner.

His plan is held today in the Auckland Museum Library. It comprises 20 or more foolscap pages, in longhand script, of specifications, materials and

---

214   N Borchard, *Untold Stories of Onehunga*, p 74.

costs. Purchas wrote in his proposal that it "was of the same general design as the Charing Cross railway bridge in London". The detail he included was impressive. For example, he compared the pressure on the proposed Mangere supporting piers as being similar to that of the Charing Cross bridge piers resting on London clay "at nine tons per square foot". He listed all the forces at play, the weights involved, the depth of supporting piers and piles, and the strengths and sizes of bolts, reinforcing and connecting beams.

The plan was for a stonework reclamation from either side, out to the low water mark with a hardwood (jarrah) cross-framed bridge linking the two. The bridge was basically single-laned but with passing bays for cattle and horses, at intervals across its span. His pages of detailed drawings included a cost estimate down to the last penny – 19,008 pounds, 2 shillings and 6 pence.[215] It seemed, therefore, that the Mangere Bridge Promotion Company would need to lift its sights a little higher than the original £10,000 estimate for the bridge.

Another new church

Only a couple of days after that first meeting about the Mangere Bridge, Purchas revisited the Waitangi flax mill accompanied by two of the other main investors from Auckland. Ninnis had left by now to set up a new flax mill (using their patented machine) at Kaiapoi in the South Island, which was the centre of another strong flax growing and cleaning industry. The purpose of Purchas's visit to Waitangi was to see if the mill could be restarted with some modifications and under a new manager. According to local press reports, it was soon under way again a couple of months later and continued to operate for another two years, relieving Purchas of the rent at least.[216] It is also likely that he was able to make a small return from the operation.

The flax mill at Waiuku and the similar operation in Kaiapoi were the first two of their kind in what developed into a large and very significant industry. By 1870, just 10 years after Purchas and Ninnis won their patent, there were 161 flax mills around New Zealand (many using the Purchas-Ninnis machine), employing about 1750 people.[217]

Perhaps the reopening of the flax mill did somehow provide a small lift to Purchas's income – or maybe it was an inheritance of some kind from Olivia's father. Nevertheless, in March 1866, his name appears as the new owner of

215 AML, MS1711/2.
216 AKL, B Ringer, *Manukau's Journey.*
217 Designing the Future – Celebrating the Past, *WIPO Magazine* (World Intellectual Property Organization), June 2011.

The stunning Purchas 'Selwyn' church of St Stephen's, Tuahiwi, photographed immediately after its opening. Today another Heritage NZ building, it was designed specifically for the Māori mission in North Canterbury with the foundation stone laid with great ceremony by Governor Grey in 1867.

CANTERBURY MUSEUM IMAGES 1957.13.219

some land at White Bluff, Hillsborough, overlooking Hillsborough Bay on the Manukau Harbour. He bought three small lots there, again via a deposit and mortgage. It cannot have been anything other than provision for his family's future because, although he remortgaged the land seven years later, it was still in his possession at his death some 40 years later.[218]

To add to the busy year, yet another architectural assignment arrived. It was a request for Purchas to design a new church, this time for the Kaiapoi Māori mission station in North Canterbury. Whether Ninnis in Kaiapoi had an initial hand in the request – or whether it was a recommendation from Purchas's old Purewa missionary colleague James Stack (now serving at Kaiapoi) – is a matter for speculation, but it certainly seems far more than just a happy coincidence.

---

218 Family documents, L Cocks, Deed 34754, Reg 22D.163.

Bishop Harper of Christchurch had established the mission in 1859 on land traditionally belonging to Ngāi Tahu, and Stack had been appointed to take charge soon after. In 1864, the decision was taken by Māori to build their own church. Ninnis, of course, was running his new flax mill at Kaiapoi a couple of years later, almost certainly using local Māori labour. The place where Māori lived within the Kaiapoi reserve was Tuahiwi and it was here that they and Stack wanted to build.

Ninnis and Stack were well aware of Purchas's architectural abilities. So it seems logical to conclude that when the decision to build was finally taken – after funds had been secured and when an architect was needed – each would have thought immediately of Purchas. Better still, the commission would earn him a modest fee – very useful for meeting his monthly interest bills.

Purchas spent the next six or seven months working on his design for the new St Stephen's at Tuahiwi. According to Heritage New Zealand, it is again "similar in many respects to both St Bride's and St Peter's [Akaroa] ... in particular, the square, three-tiered tower of St Stephen's is also characteristic of Purchas' work". St Stephen's is a simple colonial, board and batten timber church, "notable for its balanced proportions ... characteristic of its designer, Purchas". Heritage New Zealand also quotes art historian Jonathan Mane-Wheoki: "It is one of the most perfectly preserved of a group of later Selwyn Gothic churches ... whose architectural qualities are of national significance."[219]

St Stephen's remains the oldest Māori church in the South Island. Its foundation stone – for the seventh of Purchas's designs – was laid with great ceremony and fanfare by Sir George Grey a few months later, using a specially inscribed silver trowel. The building was completed and opened in 1867, and like St Bride's (Mauku), St Peter's (Akaroa), St James (Mangere) and the Selwyn Church in Mangere, stands today as one of the country's finest heritage buildings.

While working on the design over several months of 1866, there were the usual interruptions and duties, and new projects that attracted Purchas's attention. In his continuing role as hospital surgeon, he was often having to deal with some decidedly unpleasant cases. One such incident that shocked the entire community was the violent and horrific rape of a 10-year- old girl at Pukaki by a young European man. Purchas was required to attend to the victim first and assist the police, before supervising her recovery and providing detailed evidence on behalf of the Crown at the trial in the Auckland Supreme Court. As on previous occasions, the trial was accorded extensive press coverage

---

219   For more detail, refer Heritage New Zealand website. Also see A K Davidson (ed), *A Controversial Churchman*, p 136.

and must have been an ordeal, even for a professional like Purchas. Through his meticulous work and testimonies – by now so heavily relied on by the fledgling justice system and medical profession – Purchas continued to add to an already significant reputation as an expert in his field, a forerunner and early colonial equivalent of today's trauma and paramedic specialists.

More pioneer surgery

It was probably recognition of his great skill and calmness under pressure which next saw him being asked to assist in another New Zealand surgical 'first'. CMS missionary Thomas Grace, the 'vexatious' and strong-minded Liverpudlian – whose own disputes with Selwyn were well known – was in despair over the health of his eldest daughter, Bessie, just 19 years old. Purchas also knew Bessie well. She was engaged to be married to the son of his recently deceased friend, George Kissling. Grace himself had also suffered much in recent times, lucky just to survive the Opotiki raid which ended in the killing of his colleague, Carl Völkner. Purchas was glad to assist them both in whatever capacity he could.

It was determined, after further consultation, that Bessie was likely to be suffering from ovarian cancer – something which Purchas knew of from his initial training and midwifery experience. However, he had no surgical experience of the procedure.

It was eventually agreed that a leading army surgeon, William McKinnon, would perform an ovariotomy, the first recorded attempt in the colony. This was still regarded worldwide in those days as a hazardous and rare gynaecological procedure. Only a handful of such operations had been attempted in the United Kingdom up until 1866 and the mortality rate was high at 60%.[220]

Surgical instruments were brought in from Melbourne and the operation was set up by McKinnon and Purchas in Bishop Selwyn's library in Parnell. It must have made for an unusual theatre. Any differences Selwyn may have had with Thomas Grace were obviously put aside for such a groundbreaking and dangerous procedure, one which attracted wide medical interest. The operation was performed on April 11, 1866, and the tumour removed.

At first Bessie seemed to be recovering. In between his regular treks in from Onehunga to the Bishop's residence at Parnell to check on her progress, Purchas was still able to see, once again, to the safe delivery at home of another son. He was named Frederic Maurice, after his father's famous English mentor and friend. But on the 28th day after her surgery, amid the happiness at the

---

220   D Grace, *A Driven Man*, p 212.

arrival of a new son, the unfortunate Bessie died.

Despite the failure, McKinnon went on to become an honorary surgeon to Queen Victoria 25 years later. For Purchas, however, it was to be another pioneering surgical experience and clearly – from what we will learn later – a major advance in his own knowledge and skill in performing such difficult abdominal operations.

Then in June, the ever-alert daily newspaper reporters told their readers that Dr Purchas had fallen from a horse and broken his leg. He was luckier than one of his early Purewa colleagues Rota Waitoa, New Zealand's first Māori priest, who also had a bad riding accident at this time and tragically lost his life. After that funeral, when Vicesimus Lush called on Purchas a couple of days later, he was informed the injury was nothing but a badly sprained ankle. But even his restricted mobility did not stop the ceaselessly energetic Purchas from hobbling about the house as he prepared himself for yet another building task involving his Onehunga church.

While he was thinking about this, Selwyn finally came back to him with positive news on the stipend front. He had decided that Purchas's case did indeed warrant attention and he agreed to pass the matter over to his diocesan standing committee to discuss and make a decision. In the meantime, he asked Purchas to prepare the basis of a 'claim', covering salary arrears, the costs he incurred in building the Onehunga stone schoolhouse still in use, and monies spent on additions and improvements to the house.

It can be imagined that after living so long with this somewhat exasperating issue of money, the Purchas household must have finally sensed some real hope of progress. Things moved quickly this time. The standing committee met first in September 1866. After perusing the Purchas vouchers and claim, and unanimously agreeing he was entitled to some recompense, they decided to appoint two arbitrators to determine the sum. The men chosen were two of the most senior and respected people they could find – Sir William Martin and William Williams, the Bishop of Waiapu. It was agreed that Selwyn and the full Auckland diocese would honour any decision the pair made. The terms of reference also stated that if the compensation settled by the arbitrators should not be paid at the time Purchas was to resign (Selwyn already knowing of his likely intention to do so), a term of rent-free occupation of the parsonage would be established, equating to the total amount owing him.

By June the following year (1867), Sir William Martin and Bishop Williams had made their decision and reported back. Purchas then handed his resignation in writing to Selwyn and the diocesan trustees responsible for finding the compensation monies. They, in turn, signed the document confirming their commitment to carrying out the arbitrators' award. That award was for the not inconsiderable sum of just over £493: £182 for salary arrears; £161 for the school; and £150 for the house. It equated to about three-and-a-half-years' salary for Purchas.

The cheque was made out immediately. But then the standing committee had to recommend to Selwyn that – because there was still no replacement available – he should retain Purchas temporarily in charge at Onehunga and that he be allowed to continue living in the parsonage, but at a rental of £50 per annum. Effectively the entire process just confirmed the church's ownership of the parsonage, built and mostly paid for by Purchas on the original plot of church land.

There is no word in any family papers of Purchas's reaction to this resolution. But it has to be assumed he must have been extremely relieved and happy that the ordeal was finally over. His very long personal relationship with Sir William Martin and Bishop Williams would also have ensured his ready acceptance of their fairness and thoroughness in assessing the amount of compensation due.

For Purchas it was basically the end of the stipend saga. But unfortunately for Bishop Selwyn and his diocesan trustees, it was far from over. The money to pay Purchas had actually been appropriated from funds set aside for the Māori church, the "native pastorate". The question then remaining on the church table for the next five or six years, was how would that fund be repaid and from where?

The matter dragged on long after Bishop Selwyn had retired from New Zealand and returned to England. After many more debates, the Auckland synod finally agreed (in 1872) to charge the St Peter's parish £180 with the diocesan trust board, as property owner, meeting the remaining £320 from other endowment funds.

Bridge plans stall

Given that his bank account was now looking healthy, probably for the first time since he had arrived in New Zealand, Purchas could finally move forward with some certainty. The only disappointment was the delay in the Mangere bridge project following the failure of the Mangere Bridge Promotion Company to turn all the enthusiastic early pledges into actual cash. The £10,000 target was significantly underachieved and as the fund-raising drive dried up altogether – not helped by the lack of any central or local government support – the bridge promotion company finally had to call "enough" and wind up its affairs.

However, Purchas's plan, although consigned to the shelf for the meantime, remained ready to go whenever needed.

The building task he had been worrying about for some months meanwhile, involved overdue repairs to his Onehunga church. Some on his parish trust board were even suggesting that a new building was needed.[221] It was discussed again in September, but in the face of interest rates already approaching 10% on the loan needed to build it, Purchas was not very optimistic. He thought he could possibly make some repairs, even enlarge the church slightly and at least leave it in good shape for when the time came for him and the family to move on from Onehunga.

While money was available via a bank loan, the issue was complicated by the extremely tough times still affecting the Auckland province in particular. It would be difficult to justify spending money on a new church building in such circumstances. Calls for charity assistance from around the entire northern district, including the country areas vacated by Māori, reached a crescendo. Property prices had crashed and businesses were going bankrupt. The queues at the soup kitchens extended even further along the muddy roads and it was hard to escape the heavy mantle of gloom settling over the province. Letters and journals of the day tell graphic stories of deprivation and despair.

Many facing such hardships were new immigrants, fresh from places like Ireland, Scotland and England, and allotted new blocks of former Māori land in places like Tuakau and the areas south of the Bombay Hills. They had been told the New Zealand Government would give them 10 acres and a wage for a year – relying on local industry and businesses to back them up. "These poor people were worse off than any I have as yet seen," wrote Lush. "They are not yet on their own land – most of them have not even seen it and the few who have, say it is all dense forest: moreover there is no road formed to the block of land which has been allotted to them: altogether they are in a sad plight."[222]

With little or no capital of their own to sustain them – and the promises of work drying up everywhere they turned – the poverty from which they were trying to escape in Britain was again staring these unfortunates in the face in their new country. The annual report of Olivia Purchas's Onehunga Ladies Benevolent Society made for sorry reading in early 1867. "It has been a year of unprecedented hardship and distress," she said. "It has been utterly impossible to deal with or relieve the many cases of heart-rending destitution in the past year ... £90 has been collected and £86 disbursed ... much deep distress still prevails ... want and misery hold sway in many houses ... we

221 E Soar, Church Minutes, p 9.
222 A Drummond (ed), *The Waikato Journals of Vicesimus Lush*, p 87.

record our thanks to Drs Purchas and Nicholson for their gratuitous [free] attendance to so many cases."

Having already advised his parish trust board of his eventual resignation (but staying on until a new man could be found), Purchas was already formulating plans for a full-time medical career. But he was not looking to resign altogether from the ministry – instead fully intending to remain semi-active somewhere in the church.

While talk persisted about building a new Onehunga church, Purchas called a meeting to discuss the matter and in so doing unwittingly opened a small can of worms. Some wanted to start fundraising immediately, believing it might take four years to raise the £1000 Purchas had roughly estimated would be needed. Others remained totally opposed to the idea. Purchas diplomatically suggested to his trust board that, instead, they should start buying some timber for repairs while prices were so depressed and then canvass the community to see what funds might be offered.

Olivia and eldest daughter Agnes volunteered to join the committee. Their subsequent door-knocking at such a difficult time, perhaps not surprisingly generated mixed reactions. It included a couple of remarkably vitriolic letters in the press, aimed at Purchas himself. One writer, stridently opposed to the idea of spending money on a new building at this time, took him to task for spending more time on his "secular pursuits instead of parochial visitations". The same correspondent even claimed that "religious consultation to the dying" and conducting their funerals should not be done by the same doctor who gave "medicaments to the body". It was all water off a duck's back for Purchas. A couple of weeks later, he met again with his committee, strongly denying that he was now regretting his resignation, as had been implied. They advised that they could not procure the money to build a new church anyway, but did agree to start a long-term building fund.

Purchas prepared to get on with the repairs he had always advocated. Over the summer of 1867-68, with the help of a few occasional volunteers, he rolled up his sleeves and simply got to work. The subsequent repairs and alterations cost the trust board £283, almost all in materials. His intimate knowledge of the building, having been its main architect, was clearly a major advantage. It seems from references at the time, concerning the discussions about a possible new building, that one of the main problems was water leaks and the interior damage they were causing. The leaks may well have been connected to the earlier job – when Purchas shifted the bell tower, which required major reroofing and rerouting of gutters and drains.

According to Professor Cyril Knight, this latest work – a major undertaking at that – seems to have included the widening and lengthening of the nave (the main body of the church), thereby slightly reducing the pitch of the roof and probably helping to fix any drainage issues around the relocated bell tower. The results were to prove entirely successful and, amazingly, the church continued to be used in basically the same form for a further 60 years or more.[223]

In between his labours in Onehunga, Purchas was keenly following progress on the construction of the new church at his former parish of St Andrew's in Epsom, designed by the new man in charge, John Kinder. The opening was on November 30, 1867 and Kinder asked that Purchas take care of all the music for the special service. It involved a large choir and three rehearsals, with the best singers he could muster from around Auckland and Onehunga. Selwyn missed the opening at St Andrew's, having already left to attend the Lambeth Conference in England. The word casually spoken of around the opening ceremony was that he might be returning permanently to England anytime soon.

Change, it seemed, was in the air. For Purchas, of particular interest now was the passing of the New Zealand Medical Practitioners Act in October 1867. This provided for the first regulation of the medical profession in New Zealand under the supervision of a medical board and set out the qualifications required for general practice and surgery. Purchas was keen to be among the first newly registered doctors under this legislation and impatient to "hang out his shingle" just as soon as the Bishop had found his replacement.

The news that Selwyn had indeed been offered – and had accepted – the new role as Bishop of Lichfield soon followed. He remained in England for his consecration in January 1868 while Purchas cooled his heels, realising that the process of finding his successor was inevitably going to take even longer. He had no choice but to somehow retain some sort of decorum. Fortunately, relief arrived in the form of new interests and responsibilities.

One new responsibility arose from a surge of activity and discovery in the New Zealand scientific community, and plans in Auckland to form an Auckland Institute as an offshoot of the national body. One of Purchas's close contacts in the scientific and botanical world, Thomas Gillies – an Epsom resident and well-known politician and later judge – asked Purchas to join him and other Auckland 'notables' in establishing this first local institute.

Purchas joined Francis Dart Fenton, Charles Heaphy, John Williamson, Frederick Whitaker, Gillies and others (the initial foundation subscription was a guinea) and immediately found himself on the new Auckland Institute's first

---

223 This historic 172-year-old building remains virtually intact, but without its spire, sitting on a section at the end of a long drive in Onehunga. It should be preserved and sited in a far more prominent location.

council. It was the foundation of what would eventually become the Auckland War Memorial Museum. Purchas became a major contributor to, and supporter and administrator of the institute's activities – a passionate interest of his and what would eventually be seen by others as an enduring legacy of service. A particular pleasure was reacquainting himself with Fenton, who had led the revival of his Auckland Choral Society in 1866 after some early troubles, and who had always shared so many similar interests and cultural pursuits.

While indulging himself in this new interest, Purchas was also putting the final touches on his church repair and enlargement work. There was also revived talk in town about getting the Mangere Bridge project up and going again if some government funds could be provided.

But more than that, 43-year-old wife Livy needed him once more as she prepared to give birth to their 14th and final child. Another girl, named Ethel Mildred, entered the world on May 29, 1868. It was something of a double celebration. Just a few days earlier, Purchas had received confirmation of his official registration as one of the very first members of the New Zealand Medical Association.

Final choices

Although the "war years" were, unfortunately, still far from over, the country was experiencing rapid change. The great chief and would-be Kīngitanga peacemaker Wiremu Tāmihana had died 15 months earlier after a lengthy illness. King Tāwhiao and Ngāpora were living quietly in effective exile near Te Kuiti with Te Paea – who herself suffered a serious illness a year earlier but who had since recovered. The Māori agricultural economy in the King Country had picked up again after a period of stagnation. Politicians like William Fox and Julius Vogel were making their presence felt in opposing the indecisive and often weak Stafford administration. Even George Grey was finding himself caught up in change. His continuing procrastination over the return of thousands of British troops home to England – combined with the ongoing fighting and troubles involving Te Kooti and Māori tribes in the Taranaki and East Coast regions – finally provoked the British Government into terminating his contract.

It must have almost seemed to Purchas that the stars were somehow aligning. In some respects, his momentous decision to quit the professional clergy ranks and enter the medical profession full-time was a relatively easy one for him to make. He really had no choice in the matter because he needed to provide a suitable education for his children and also look after himself and Olivia in their old age. Earning a higher and more regular salary was the only answer.

He probably discussed his plans with close friends like Frederic Brookfield – recently appointed Crown solicitor in Auckland – and perhaps Kinder and Lush, who would have reminded him, no doubt, that finding a replacement for him at Onehunga was still, unfortunately, not an immediate priority for Selwyn. Even though Selwyn had been at the helm for 25 years, the province he was leaving still lacked new Anglican clergy able to fill such positions.

Amid the serious contemplation involved in such a decision came the upsetting news of the death in Cornwall in May, 1868, of Purchas's young artist friend, Arthur Gundry, [224] itself preceded by the earlier passing away (1867) of the old CMS "warhorse" himself, Henry Williams. As if to further underline a "changing of the guard," yet another of Purchas's friends, Auckland Archdeacon John Lloyd, advised Purchas and others that he too was planning to go back to England for good.

George Grey began his final round of farewells in September with a rousing ceremony in Wellington. At about the same time, Selwyn was on his own farewell tour, almost ending things for good when he was dangerously shipwrecked in the Marlborough Sounds while crossing from Wellington to Picton. He and about 100 other passengers had to evacuate their stricken ship in dinghies after it struck a rock coming into Picton. Having not only survived but also bravely assisted many other passengers to shore, he finally made it back to Onehunga and Parnell. He officially resigned at the fourth general synod which began in Auckland in October 1868.

In the late 1860s, with the institutions of church and state in the colony now properly constituted and representative, the time had arrived for a new generation of leaders with new objectives. There was much to be done in health, education and native affairs, the last mentioned being once more of particular concern as the Māori population declined and its future survival again came into question. Within months, there was a change of government in Wellington and an "expansionist programme of spectacular development"[225] began under a new group of ambitious and progressive politicians.

Purchas's own major change of direction now, at the age of 47, also raises the question – why didn't Selwyn simply promote him to higher office in the church? The senior position of archdeacon in Auckland (shortly to be vacant anyway) presumably attracted a higher salary and may have solved the problem of Purchas's inadequate stipend. The answer probably lies somewhere in

---

224   See pp 71-72.
225   M King, *The Penguin History of New Zealand*, p 228.

The home Purchas built in Onehunga, originally of single-level construction, but clearly showing the work involved when Purchas jacked it up and added a second storey himself in 1858-59.

ONEHUNGA FENCIBLE &HISTORICAL SOCIETY

between two possibilities. First, Selwyn may have proposed such a move and Purchas may well have declined – on the basis that, even with an increased salary, his extra responsibilities and duties in the role would severely limit his medical and scientific activities.

However, the more likely scenario is that Selwyn still harboured some misgivings about Purchas's "secularities" and possibly even doubted whether Purchas would be able to put aside his medical and scientific interests and fully commit himself to the church. He would undoubtedly have admired Purchas's exceptional talents in so many areas, and appreciated his wonderful contributions to church music, architecture and medicine. But he would also have been acutely aware of Purchas's involvement in many other city and commercial activities – his trusteeships and land dealings, the flax machine venture, his geological and engineering work, and his consultation and participation in so many local groups and institutions.

Whatever the reasons, Purchas was proven right in recognising that great changes were about to occur in colonial New Zealand and that he should be taking steps to move with, or stay ahead of, those changes. We can only speculate about his ambitions in life because he certainly never craved recognition or status in the public arena. Having made up his mind to embrace the changes, and increasingly keen to get on with life, his only problem was that he could

The Purchas home and garden in Selwyn St (numbers 50 to 52, on the right) was a prominent local landmark in the 1860s.

AUCKLAND LIBRARIES HERITAGE COLLECTION 957-53

not walk out on the people of Onehunga just yet.

In this respect, he may well have reflected a little on a similar situation 21 years earlier, when he and Olivia had been forced to cool their heels at Purewa and Epsom – before they could start their new life at Onehunga. Now, all these years later, they were having to sit it out again – waiting patiently in Onehunga for a suitable replacement, before they could once again get on with their lives. This time, the calling wasn't the pioneer church, but pioneer medicine. Unfortunately, this second wait would prove to be even longer than the first.

PART III

MEDICAL YEARS

CHAPTER 14

Transition

When the people of Auckland and Onehunga were given a half-day off in October 1868 to help farewell Bishop Selwyn, Arthur Purchas might have been forgiven for finding the whole situation somewhat frustrating. The one person who held the key to his departure date from Onehunga – thus enabling him to set up his new full-time, professional medical practice elsewhere in Auckland – was disappearing for good. Although pleased that he had settled his future course of direction, Purchas had absolutely no idea how long he, Olivia and family might have to stay in Onehunga. And all the time he was eating into his meagre capital, money he had carefully set aside from the earlier arbitration.

There was a large service at St Paul's on October 20, after which George and Sarah Selwyn were taken in a coach – drawn part of the way by admiring townsfolk – down to the wharf to board their ship, the SS *Hero*. Still in charge of the music for such major events, Purchas had a busy time preparing and rehearsing for the two-hour-long service, while Olivia said her own goodbyes separately to Sarah. They had been firm friends for the last 21 years since Olivia had first arrived on the Selwyn doorstep at Purewa in 1847, pregnant and exhausted. They had shared a few stressful times together, having to cope with the unfortunate deaths of children in both families.

Another three long months passed before Selwyn arrived back in England where – Purchas would have been hoping – his first task, after establishing himself in his new role as the Bishop of Lichfield, would be to find the replacement bishop for Auckland. The new appointee, Purchas surmised, would need several months to organise family, travel and the transfer to Auckland. Only then could he turn his attention to finding Purchas's replacement. He might also have considered the possibility that because Selwyn himself had not been able to find a replacement, the chances of any new bishop doing so quickly would not be great. No doubt justifiably frustrated, Purchas basically accepted that he might be in Onehunga for at least another 18 months.

Back home over the next few days, Purchas nevertheless wasted no time in letting it be known around Auckland that, since he had officially tendered his resignation as Onehunga priest, he was now establishing his medical practice on a fully professional paying basis. Significantly, ongoing reports in the daily press – covering his usual span of activities, including his continuing role of surgeon at Auckland Hospital – mostly referred to him as Dr A G Purchas MD in place of the previous clerical title, the "Reverend" A G Purchas.

Having taken this step, Purchas could have felt entirely justified moving out of Onehunga immediately and leaving the church and local parish trust board to their own devices. However, being the conscientious and principled man he was, the thought of doing so never crossed his mind. He continued his normal round of church duties at St Peter's on Sundays, prepared couples for marriage and conducted the usual family baptisms and funerals. But during the week, his new routine involved visiting, attending to and consulting with sick people who needed his help.

In between that work, often including night calls, he also threw himself into his new interest on the first Auckland Institute council and its workings. He began preparing lectures and addresses on a wide variety of scientific, botanical and geological matters. He had also acquired by now a sizeable collection of plants, seeds and specimens of various sorts, which he started donating to the institute for its first collections. One such item, reported at the institute's regular monthly meeting in July 1869, was a fossilised shark's tooth, which he had found in "the green sand formations in the East Hunua district" during his travels with von Hochstetter 10 years earlier.[226]

His presentation in the same year on the preparation of native flax and the various useful fibres available from plants and fruits, such as the pineapple, was full of typical Purchas foresight and innovation. He said the waste material from the recovery of flax fibre could be converted very easily into "useful brown paper", once the fibre gum had been removed. He also recommended that the copious quantities of this material, now being produced in many parts of the colony, would make an excellent food for cattle. And he strongly advocated that a rope manufacturing business, such as the one Ninnis had in Kaiapoi, should be established in Auckland.

His talks were well attended, attracted great interest and were fully reported. A few months later, at another of the institute's meetings, and armed with various careful calculations and measurements, Purchas brought to the attention of the town leaders that the harbour was silting up rapidly by the main wharf. An inquiry was quickly organised.

226 Papers Past, *Daily Southern Cross*, July 1869.

The Auckland Institute and Museum where Purchas served three terms as president, making
regular presentations and contributing many items to the first collections.
AUCKLAND LIBRARIES HERITAGE COLLECTIONS 35-R70 F G RADCLIFFE

The institute was widely acknowledged and applauded for focusing on
such matters and for contributing to the commercial, cultural and educational
development of the town. After the first 12 months of the institute's operation,
Purchas was nominated to succeed prominent lawyer-turned-politician
Frederick Whitaker as its next president.

Expanding practice

1869 was also important in Auckland's development for another reason –
gold. In fact, as Professor Russell Stone commented: "The discovery of gold
in Thames saved Auckland."[227] The province had gone from pre-war boom to
post-war recession and bust. But in the following two or three years the good
times returned, thanks largely to Coromandel gold. Within 12 months, Thames
had become the fifth largest city in New Zealand and Auckland became a
major beneficiary of all the associated new economic activity. Fortunes were
being made and lost. People were increasingly optimistic about Auckland's
prospects and even the problems associated with dissatisfied Māori were put
aside. In the space of three years, gold export receipts went from £18,200 to

---

227   R C J Stone, *Makers of Fortune*, p 9 ff.

£1.2m.[228] The gold rush in Otago was even more long lasting and spectacular.

For Purchas, the increase in his medical practice work at the time of the Thames 'gold rush' was also spectacular – and tiring. One of his closest medical colleagues in those days, Dr Joseph Giles, wrote that Purchas "soon acquired an extensive practice which ought to have proved very remunerating". But, Giles added, "Arthur Purchas had very little of the mercenary spirit in him and I suspect he was also careless in collecting his accounts".[229]

Purchas was obviously labouring long and hard – partly because he was now the only doctor in Onehunga, Dr Weekes having finally left. In one family letter at the time, written at 11pm one night, 50-year-old Purchas said: "I have just come home after a hard day's work and was up half the night last night ... it is the night work that tells most upon me but I am not in a position to decline any portion of the work that comes my way ..."[230]

It must also be remembered that the Purchas household now comprised 12 children, from two- to 21-years-old, plus Arthur, Olivia and, much of the time, the teenager Fanny Gundry, who was increasingly in very poor health. Unfortunately, they could no longer afford any domestic help, as Olivia lamented in one of her letters home to family in England. Meal times must have been a significant logistical exercise on their own. It is no wonder that Purchas was occasionally struggling to fulfil all his commitments.

It had been more than six years since Purchas last had any contact with his old friend Tāmati Ngāpora Manuhiri,[231] aged about 65 and living quietly at Pahiko near Te Kuiti in the King Country. Also living close by was Rewi Maniapoto. In November 1869, the pair agreed to a historic meeting with the new Minister of Native Affairs Donald McLean about the future course of events. The Government's focus had shifted to how Te Kooti might be captured and what steps could be taken next to get the European-Kīngitanga relationship back on some sort of sensible footing.[232] In particular, the new government was looking to open up the country further by extending its telegraph links and building a railway line – inevitably by the most direct route south, through the heart of Kīngitanga territory.

At the meeting, Ngāpora took the opportunity to ask McLean if he would confirm the status of two blocks of land he owned – one in Mangere and the

---

228   Ibid.
229   Dr J Giles, *Reminiscences 1921* – and Purchas family files.
230   ATL, MS5713 Letters.
231   Incorrectly spelled "manuwhiri" in some texts, e.g. Appendix to the Journals of the House of Representatives typescripts.
232   See published report of this meeting, ENZB, The Native Minister's interview with Ngāpora, Rewi, etc.; also published report by W C Wilson, Nov 1869.

other known as Te Pukapuka block in Remuera, above Orakei. Both had come into his possession on the death of Te Wherowhero. Ngāpora raised the matter now with McLean because when he was forced to leave his Mangere home at the start of the Waikato War in 1863, he feared the Government might have since confiscated both blocks under the 1863 proclamation. He wrote to McLean in early January 1870, explaining that he had been leasing the land since those early days, and that "Dr Purchas was the person who induced me to rent those lands, and I not understanding these sort of things, gave my consent".[233]

McLean duly checked with Purchas who confirmed that he had seen to it that both blocks were indeed rented out on Ngāpora's behalf. Further, he had collected the money for him at the agreed rate – £200 having already been forwarded and another £400 held in the bank for him. McLean then advised Ngāpora of Purchas's update based on the arrangement seven years earlier. Ngāpora finally responded that "Dr Purchas also knows about the land at Remuera – he has the deed in his possession".

This land at Remuera – and its deed, which Ngāpora had recently given to Purchas for safe keeping – was hugely significant for Ngāpora, Ngāti Mahuta and the Kīngitanga, and also Ngāti Whātua. Ngāti Whātua had been the original owners but had gifted the land to Te Wherowhero in the 1820s in an early alliance aimed at providing them with added protection against their mutual northern enemy, Ngā Puhi.

Te Wherowhero had then given this land to his younger brother Te Kati at the time of his marriage to a Ngā Puhi chieftainess, also as part of the protective alliance.[234] But when Te Kati died, Ngāti Whātua chief Āpihai Te Kawau sold the land via a legal transfer to the Crown. When he found out, Te Wherowhero was extremely unhappy. To conciliate him and keep the peace, the Crown promptly returned it to Te Wherowhero by grant, but mistakenly failed to register any new title or legal transfer. When Te Wherowhero Pōtatau died in 1860, the land was, in turn, gifted to Ngāpora. Neither had been aware that, without any such transfer or grant documentation, it was still legally Crown land. This was the "deed" or possibly letter of bequest which Ngāpora had given to Purchas to keep on his behalf.

Purchas may not have been told initially by Ngāpora precisely why Te Pukapuka block in particular was so important to him and Ngāti Mahuta. But he certainly would have been aware that some special historical value and mana was attached to it via the three tribes involved – Ngāti Whātua, Ngāti Mahuta and Ngā Puhi. McLean, on the other hand, may not have been aware

---

233   Appendix to the Journals of the House of Representatives, A-21, Nos 38, 39 and 49.
234   Refer also to page 99 regarding Te Kati.

of its significance.

So, for the past eight years – quietly and without fuss, and among all his other duties – Purchas had been looking after Ngāpora's interests by renting out Te Pukapuka and his Mangere block, and collecting some precious rental income for him. It is most likely that he had been helped in his administrative efforts by Frederic Brookfield – probably on a pro bono basis.

The block had also been the subject of an inquiry under Francis Fenton a few months before the McLean-Ngāpora meeting. At the enquiry, Purchas had testified – also unaware of the real story at the time – that, as far as he knew, "the Te Pukapuka block was always Tamati's land". The twist in the story of the land – which obviously Ngāpora, Purchas and McLean were unaware of in 1863 when war broke out – was that without a transfer having been executed, rightly or wrongly, the land still technically belonged to the Government. Ngāpora's worries, expressed to McLean and Purchas, were groundless because the Crown, of course, could not confiscate Te Pukapuka – it already owned the block.

To try and clean up the mess, Judge Fenton recommended the Crown simply formalise the earlier Te Wherowhero grant of Te Pukapuka in favour of his descendants, namely Ngāpora, King Tāwhiao and Matire, Te Kati's wife. This tidied up and resolved the matter of ownership, at least for the meantime[235] – but it had been a complicated and messy business, and Ngāpora must have been very grateful to Purchas for his helping hand.

Midway through the year (1869) news had also come of the appointment of William Cowie, a Scot, as the new bishop for Auckland. The 38-year-old Cowie was consecrated in Westminster Abbey in June and married in July. Arthur and Olivia must have dared to hope afresh that they were one step closer to being able to move away from Onehunga.

The usual whirlwind of activity that was Purchas's life continued unabated – from the Native Land Court hearings and his council responsibilities at the Auckland Institute, to regular meetings at his Lodge … interspersed all hours of the day and night attending to patients, trustee responsibilities, funerals and weddings.

One difference now, however, was that Purchas was earning a slightly improved living as a local doctor – despite still dispensing hours of charitable aid to the poor and, apparently, not exercising great diligence in chasing payment

---

235   The story of Te Pukapuka was, in fact, far from over. Ngāpora then initiated the gifting of the land back to its original Ngāti Whātua owners in 1872. Once again, the whole matter of its ownership came before the Native Land Court in 1889-90 when the Crown reconfirmed the earlier Fenton decision of three-way ownership, again in favour of Te Wherowhero's descendants, this time the individual grandchildren of Ngāpora, Tāwhiao and Matire Te Kati.

from others. He was also now paying £50 a year in rent to the Auckland diocese for living in the Onehunga house he had built. And it would be disclosed a little later, when Cowie eventually got to grips with local church affairs, that the St Peter's parish trust board remained in virtual recess over this period, under some financial pressure – mainly as a result of the £180 debt hanging over its head from Purchas's arbitration settlement.

A bridge and a holiday

More and more residents in Onehunga were now wanting to know what was happening about "the bridge". The revitalisation of the local economy had led to pressure being exerted once more on local politicians to do something about the proposed Mangere Bridge. A group of "300 irate Onehunga and Mangere people" signed a petition urging the Auckland Provincial Council to inquire into the failure of the bridge promotion company and to get the project back on the agenda. Auckland residents and retailers needed the Mangere farmers' produce and the incessant grumbling on all sides about the long round trip via Otahuhu and the Great South Rd to markets in Queen St could no longer be ignored.

An inquiry was held and a year or so later, perhaps unsurprisingly, it was agreed that the funds for a bridge could never be found entirely by the local population. Then, with the help of aggressive lobbying from the Auckland politicians, the project got a major boost with the promise of a £15,000 subsidy from the new Fox Government – keen to begin its new infrastructure programmes. Purchas's bridge design came back on to the table. The grant enabled planning and construction to begin on the bridge approaches and onramps with the idea, probably proposed by Purchas, that they use the same stone that had been sourced from Mangere Mountain for his St James project.[236] The contract was finally let for this initial work and everyone breathed a huge sigh of relief. The long-overdue project was finally under way on what would still prove to be a tortuous route to completion.

By the time William and Elizabeth Cowie arrived in Auckland in February 1870, the new Government – led by the determined William Fox and his treasurer Julius Vogel – had begun announcing more detailed plans for the most significant reforms and economic projects in New Zealand's short colonial history. The plans involved massive investment in buildings, railway lines, roads, communications and people. At the root of it all was a huge immigration drive,

236 S Maxwell, *Untold Stories of Onehunga*, p 74.

under a couple of different schemes of paid assistance, designed to attract more than 100,000 people over the next 10 years. Seventy-five to 80% of these people came from the UK – the rest from various European countries like Germany, Scandinavia, Denmark and Norway.

It was all funded via a bold, risky but calculated programme of loans amounting to about £20 million, from the huge pool of capital available in London at the time. One other important objective of the immigration drive, and vital for the long-term future of the colony, was to improve the ratio of European females to males. As Michael King recorded, the problem in 1871 was that about two-thirds of the white population were male and the chance of a "settled existence of married family life" was consequently very remote indeed for tens of thousands of working men.[237]

All the new projects which Vogel and the Government initiated in the early 1870s – telegraph innovations and extensions; road and rail developments; agricultural, meat, wool and food-growing projects; steamships and coastal shipping; bridge building; and large mining and timber activities – excited and energised men like Purchas.

In April of that year (1870) however, after 18-20 months of hard work attending to his medical practice (and having had little time off over many years), Olivia finally prevailed on him to take a brief holiday and rest in the Bay of Islands. It was also only a month or so before he was to take up his important new role of president, for the first time, at the Auckland Institute.

Another reason for the break was his and Olivia's worries about their eldest daughter Agnes – now 21 and not enjoying the best of health. Agnes and her sister Emily (19) went on ahead to Paihia to stay for a couple of weeks with Elizabeth Colenso, a very old friend of their father. Purchas had first met her in 1854 when she was teaching at Benjamin Ashwell's mission station at Taupiri. Some years after her very public estrangement from husband William, who had fathered a child in an extra-marital affair, she came to live in the Bay of Islands and was now running a school for Māori children at Te Tii, in Waitangi.

Purchas endured a very rough and sleepless trip in a noisy, single-screw steamship up the coast to Paihia, where he was very glad to get ashore by 1pm – only to be prevailed upon to take a service for the locals at 3pm! The next day they moved inland to Pakaraka, the site of the Williams's farm where they were hosted by the young Henry Williams and his wife.[238] Knowing of Purchas's great interest in geology and botany, Henry had arranged something

---

237 M King, *The Penguin History of New Zealand*, p 230.
238 Henry was the son of former CMS leader Henry Williams, with whom Purchas had remained in close contact over the years.

of a study tour over the next couple of days, including visits to some local coal mines and the springs at Ngawha.

Letters by Purchas's daughters refer to them hunting for quicksilver and digging a hole to find a "small stream of petroleum". They visited the coal mine and a flax mill – the daughters feeling sorry for the small boys sitting below the dripping flax, catching the leaves as they tumbled through the beating apparatus. Purchas hurried them off again the next day with Williams to inspect some special limestone rocks. There was a dinner and another service with the local miners, and a visit to the failing Captain James Busby and his wife.

In his absence, Purchas had managed to arrange for another Auckland doctor, Dr Watling, to visit some of his patients. Concerned for their welfare, he wrote to Olivia asking her to remember him kindly to Dr Watling and "hoping he is not getting fagged to death for my sake".[239]

He returned to Auckland with his daughters a few days later by coastal steamer, somewhat refreshed and keen to get an update from Cowie about his replacement. Instead, the only news for him from the church offices was that his *New Zealand Hymnal* had proved popular enough to warrant a second edition – including some updates and additions he had been working on. It was published that year (1870) by the Melbourne publishers, W Collins & Co.

Although Cowie had no news about a new man for Onehunga, he did at least decide to re-open St John's College as a theological training school and to address the problem left by Selwyn of a shortage of clergy. He appointed Purchas's friend, John Kinder, as the new Master. Unfortunately, Kinder, like Purchas, also had a long wait ahead of him before he could take up the new position, since a replacement also needed to be found for him at the Parnell Grammar School. That took until 1872.

At home, Olivia and Arthur were not only worrying continually about the poor health of daughter Agnes, but also that of 16-year-old Fanny Gundry. Like the other Gundry sisters, Olivia and Helen, Fanny was treated like another daughter in the Purchas family – helping Olivia at home in Onehunga and staying there for long periods. But now her chronic illness had finally got the better of her and it seemed even Purchas was unable to help. She died in the parsonage in July, probably from consumption or one of the many other respiratory diseases or illnesses prevalent in those days – often debilitating and/or untreatable.

Within a month, Purchas received a letter from the older sister, Helen, now living at Mauku with husband Francis. She politely asked Purchas if there was

---

239 Family letters, Arthur to Olivia 26/5/1870.

any possibility of him winding up her father's estate and making a distribution to eligible family members now that she, Olivia and her surveyor brother William – who had survived the Waikato War and was also inquiring – had all attained their majority. Helen added that she and her husband had started a new business and the money would be of more use to them now than seven years hence, when the last of the Gundry children, Henry, would finally turn 21.

Over the preceding three or four years, Purchas had pursued a relatively passive strategy with regard to the many Gundry properties. He had found new tenants for some and released a couple of others while concentrating on maintenance of the more valuable Gundry retail assets in Auckland's Karangahape Rd precinct – in particular the chemist shop which had proved to be a valuable business.

Trusting his own instincts, Purchas decided to wait a few more months, advising a disappointed Helen that doing so might be in her own and her siblings' best interests. The strong growth in the Auckland economy at the time and the improving demand for retail shops and property clearly indicated that Purchas was right to wait. Now halfway through his first term as president of the Auckland Institute, and regularly rubbing shoulders there with the town's leading citizens and businessmen, he would have been in an excellent position to make such a call.

Meanwhile his own book of medical patients continued to grow. His practical surgical skills were being tested and enhanced on a daily basis like never before. And he was deriving great satisfaction from it all, having the chance to read and learn, and to talk often with Auckland's other medical specialists and be consulted by them in return. There were new developments and techniques occurring regularly in England and the United States, particularly in the surgical field, which Purchas followed avidly and which he was keen to adopt and enhance if he could.

One of those medical colleagues in Auckland at the time (1870) was another British surgeon, Robert Tassell, with whom Purchas had established a close relationship. It began after Purchas had formed a medical section of the institute during his first role as president. Tassell was the chairman of this section and Purchas frequently stood in for him when he was unable to attend.

Tassell was also a pioneer surgeon, having first carried out some early operations in Australia, before moving to Auckland. He must have generated some serious interest that year when he advised his medical colleagues at the institute that he was proposing to carry out an ovariotomy in a week or two. In spite of what was described at the time as "a good deal of medical opposition",

Tassell performed the operation in April 1870.[240]

His unfortunate patient had been suffering from an ovarian tumour or cyst "the size of a large football". In the period of diagnosis undertaken by two other doctors (before Tassell had been consulted), the 4.5kg tumour had finally burst, releasing about four and a half litres of fluid into her abdomen. Tassell's operation to remove the tumour was successful and his patient was still alive 12 weeks later, with the help of sprinklings of carbolic acid and "three or four ounces of brandy a day". But it is not known whether she survived in the long term. The details of this particular operation – whether learned from doctors who attended or via Tassell's later reports to the institute and British medical authorities – were naturally of great interest to Purchas.

His own surgical experiences in the last few years in Auckland had all proven of great value, despite the restrictions of his continuing role as Onehunga priest. But it seems the Tassell operation may well have persuaded Purchas to take the first opportunity to carry out advanced abdominal surgery on his own account. He had always been known for his self-reliance and belief in his own natural ability, and he had some specific techniques and surgical treatments which he was now keen to implement.

Purchas was especially determined to emphasise the importance of hygiene, the treatment of surgical wounds via suturing and cleaning, and improved methods of sealing and bandaging in post-operative care. He had read much about the development and use of some revolutionary anti-microbial measures, the basis of what would soon be known as Listerism. And he would quickly become the colony's most prominent early disciple of Joseph Lister and his methods. Although once again in the middle of life at its busiest, Purchas was in a hurry to put some of these revolutionary new ideas into practice.

240   An ovariotomy, as recorded in an article by Dr R Tassell in *The Lancet*, October 8, 1870. See also the Auckland Institute report.

CHAPTER 15

Purchas – Surgeon

At the end of 1870, as Arthur and Olivia prepared to celebrate their 25th wedding anniversary on December 27, Purchas sat down late one night to write a long letter to his brother-in-law, William. He had some specific family matters to address, but these were combined with something of a Purchas status report and yet more bold plans for the future.[241]

"December 6, 11pm. My dear Will," he wrote. "I have just come home after a hard day's work and was up half the night last night so you will imagine I am not in a very bright state for letter writing ... hitherto we have had such a hard struggle to live with our very large family that all the help we got from home, though most gratefully received, did not enable us to put by anything.

"But this year I have ventured to insure my life for £1000 and trust I may have strength to earn enough to pay the premium besides keeping the house ... I am very happy and thankful that I am able to work and quite willing to work on as long as I have strength to do it ... it is the night work that tells most upon me but I am not in a position to decline any portion of the work that comes my way."

The first specific family matter addressed was the plan he and Olivia had for a legacy left by her Aunt Charlotte – which was to get two trustworthy friends to invest the money for her benefit. Then Purchas asked Will if he could send him a "good packet of seed" of each of the three mulberry trees known as *Morus alba*, *Morus morettiana* and *Morus multicaulis*. "With these seeds," he said, "I hope to ease my work as I grow older by making the silkworm produce a portion at least of my children's maintenance." He was deadly serious, believing the Auckland climate was very suitable for the growth of the mulberry and the production of silk. Nothing was beyond the imagination or scope of this extraordinarily clever man.

By now well into his first term as president of the institute, he reported to Will that although the duties of the office added to his work, "it is a pleasure

241   ATL, MS5713; also Purchas family letters.

to do what I can to promote intellectual culture in this part of the colony". Purchas and his council had already begun assembling collections for their new Auckland Museum, housed in small rooms at the institute's headquarters in Princes St. And he told Will: "We hope soon also to begin a free public library." This was a high priority for Purchas who had strongly promoted the idea of a library for Auckland when first accepting the presidency.[242]

It was probably well past midnight at this stage, but Purchas was also keen to brief his brother-in-law about the great progress the colony was making under Fox and Vogel. He described the agreement for a new passenger and mail service by steamer from England via San Francisco to the colony – the whole distance to be done in 40 days, and "the telegrams will bring us within 24 days of Europe," he exclaimed.

New Zealand's telegraph link at this stage also extended all the way from Auckland to Dunedin and was revolutionising the transfer of information. It had a uniform tariff of charges, he told Will, so that a 10-word message could be sent for a shilling to any part of the colony! Dunedin, in fact, was on the verge of becoming New Zealand's largest city with a population approaching 30,000 people (1874) versus Auckland's 28,000. Trading banks were becoming established, alongside new companies like Hallenstein Bros, Sargood and DIC, luxuriating in impressive new buildings. Dunedin was even building the colony's first university.[243] Such impressive progress was reinvigorating men like Purchas after the colony's decade of division and conflict. "We just want more both of capital and people and then it will be a grand country," he wrote.

As the New Year (1871) arrived, Arthur and Olivia's sense of well-being and confidence was lifted further when they were invited – along with friends Bishop Cowie, Sir William Martin and their wives – to be guests of Sir George Grey at his island home on Kawau in the Hauraki Gulf. After travelling there on the Government steamer, they spent a day or so enjoying the exotic trees, lawns, birds and animals.[244]

Purchas might also have made mention in his letter of another major effort – helping to establish the new Society of Artists as a foundation member in April that year. He was one of about 30 founding members, among them several notable local artists of the time, including his friend John Kinder, Albin Martin and Charles Heaphy. Their objective was "to encourage the cultivation of the arts, including painting and sculpture". Although the society originated

---

242 This was the beginning of today's Auckland Library. Refer *Daily Southern Cross*, "Auckland Institute", Feb 22, 1870.

243 M King, *The Penguin History of New Zealand*, p 209.

244 Grey's collection at the time included a variety of animals, from zebras and monkeys, to peacocks, wallabies and deer.

in Auckland, the founders did not originally see it as a merely provincial group and strongly encouraged nationwide participation from the beginning. This was the foundation of what later would become known as the Auckland Society of Arts.

Near tragedy

For the next two years – after Purchas had completed his term as president at the institute, and while his clergyman's role at St Peter's continued on Sundays – he looked to devote more time to his medical practice and the further upgrading of his knowledge and skills. He regularly attended the institute's monthly medical meetings, sharing his new findings and experiences. At one such session, he presented a paper on a unique and typically Purchas-style remedy for luxation – or complete dislocation of a joint. He told the assembled doctors that he had been called to attend to a patient suffering from a painful dislocated shoulder. He tried to put the poor fellow's shoulder back by the usual method of the day – using his own considerable physical strength and manipulative skill – but without success. Pondering his next step, alongside a patient in serious discomfort, he had an idea.

"The patient was lying on his back on a sheet at the time," he explained. "I knotted two end-corners of the sheet together by a reef knot; then introduced his head in the bight thus made." Purchas then described how he put his heel in the axilla – or underarm area – while others gently raised the body, "thus exerting great power on the dislocation". Very soon, he said, he had the satisfaction of feeling the head of the shoulder joint slip back into the socket. Purchas commended the method of treatment to his somewhat startled audience because "it enabled me to exert my full strength while at the same time leaving my hands free".

After some discussion, Purchas added that he had since used the same treatment on someone else, finding it both "expeditious and efficient". In those days, medical communication and updates from the United Kingdom involved at least a two- or three-week process by telegraph – so there was still plenty of scope to trial innovative treatments such as this, especially by men of intelligence and courage like Purchas.

It followed as a matter of course that this medical division of the institute – which Purchas initiated and established with fellow Auckland doctors Tassell, Stockwell, Hooper, Day and others – morphed a few years later into the first Auckland Medical Association. A group calling itself the Auckland Medical and Surgical Society had been formed in 1858, with the aim of protecting the public from the dubious services of unqualified medical men. But this group never found complete favour with the medical fraternity because of internal feuds and disagreements, and it appears that Purchas never joined.

Yet even experienced men like Purchas could still make mistakes. An incident the following year might have ended in tragedy were it not for the rapid assistance of two of those same medical colleagues, although their specific names are unknown.

Over the previous few years, Purchas had built up a relatively sizeable dispensary of chemicals and medicines at his home – kept downstairs in one of the rooms which served meantime as his consulting office. For a few weeks he had been treating himself for some minor complaint using a medicine from one of the many bottles on his shelf. The bottle he had been using was unfortunately removed one day by mistake, when he was absent – but was apparently replaced by his children with a bottle of similar size and shape, except that this one was filled with chloroform. Purchas came home on a Monday night, picked up the bottle from its usual spot and drank some of the contents. On swallowing the chloroform he immediately realised his terrible mistake.

Chloroform is a colourless liquid, smells relatively pleasant and has a slightly sweetish taste. As an anaesthetic it is effective in extremely small doses, but once ingested in full form, it very quickly metabolises to become highly toxic phosgene. The horrified Purchas gravely informed Olivia and his daughters that there was nothing to be done – it was already too late. But unwilling to accept his diagnosis, they immediately summoned other doctors and "with the usual remedies" – probably copious quantities of salt water and vomiting – he was fortunately restored to his usual good health and humour. The newspaper reports a few days later happily concluded that the town could "ill lose such a man who has been so useful in his ministerial and professional capacity among us".[245]

Business calls

In between attending to the sick and maintaining his role at St Peter's, there were also new matters of business to attend to – including the final reconciliation to the Government of some war expenses related to the closure of the Te Awamutu establishment some six or seven years earlier. Purchas was finally awarded £250 for his work over those dangerous months as part of the final settlement.[246] Then it was time to begin the complicated business of

---

245 Papers Past, *Auckland Star*, Nov 1871.
246 Appendix to the Journals of the House of Representatives, E-8.

winding up the Gundry estate, a process he began as soon as he had recovered from his nasty chloroform accident.

In April 1872 a notice appeared in the two Auckland newspapers advising of the two trustees' intent (Purchas and George Pierce) to dispose of the Gundry land. It was a significant event in the Auckland property market since the Gundry property portfolio, among other smaller lots, comprised large blocks in the valuable Karangahape Road area, and in Remuera and Onehunga. The Karangahape Rd land alone was large enough to be split, eventually, into 97 lots, while in Remuera the eight-acre block was divided into 28 lots.[247] The first single property advertised for sale by tender a couple of months later was the chemist shop on Karangahape Rd – a business which had been a valuable asset to the estate, and to Purchas and other Auckland medical men for its products and service for many years.

The terms of sale for the Gundry properties – a process which was to continue for the next six years – generally involved one third by cash, one third by promissory note 12 months later, and the final third by another promissory note at 24 months, all at an interest rate of 8%. Immediate conveyance was promised for full cash payment.

As the sale process continued, some of the money raised was paid out to the Gundry children, while other portions were retained by Purchas and Pierce to loan out again on short-term mortgages or to purchase other property on behalf of individual Gundry children – such as a small farm for Helen Gundry in Onehunga.

Of the seven Gundry children, three had since died. The youngest, Henry, had still not turned 21, so Purchas was conscious of ensuring that his fair share be readily available to him, in cash or equivalent property, when he attained his majority. Only when this was done later in 1878, could Purchas finally relinquish his guardianship of the children and with it a considerable amount of responsibility and care.

The overall extent of Purchas's involvement in land transactions, mostly on behalf of others between 1848 and 1906, was significant. During that time he signed off more than 230 individual deeds, transfers, sales or mortgage agreements, nearly 100 of them as part of the Gundry winding-up process in the 10 years from 1871.[248] Through the generosity of William Gundry originally, Purchas had organised the endowment of the Onehunga parish with land for both church and parsonage use… a permanent legacy.

---

247 The Karangahape Rd land involved was enclosed by today's Gundry St, Abbey St and Ophir St, bounded by Karangahape and Newton Rds.
248 L Cocks – detailed family research notes.

He had helped to settle complicated Māori land transactions in the Hokianga on behalf of Gundry's Māori wife and her youngest son Henry (who was now expected by the family to become a chief in his mother's hapū). And he had advised on, selected and purchased many blocks of land on behalf of various individuals and agencies – including land for government schools in Howick and Auckland, mission station land at Awhitu, land for church buildings in Mangere and Mauku, land for Ngāpora, and a couple of small blocks in Hillsborough and Mt Eden in Olivia's name for his own family. His knowledge of the intricacies of conveyancing, mortgages, the Land Transfer Act, deeds and financing was extensive and a match for most town lawyers, themselves specialists in the business.

It must have been disappointing in the extreme, however, when Purchas was called to Bishop Cowie's Auckland synod and the matter of the Onehunga parish debt came up once again later that year (1872). It was still not generally known by most of the clergy that the earlier settlement made to Purchas had to be 'appropriated' from a fund set aside for the Māori pastorate. Now it was all out in the open. Purchas had to sit in silence listening to some pointed questions while the arbitration settlement was brought up all over again.

Finally a motion was put with the aim of clearing him of any negative association and clarifying, once and for all, that Purchas had nothing to do with where the payment had originated – and "that Arthur Purchas himself had not been bound to ascertain from which of several church funds, the sum for his settlement was derived". After the fiery Robert Maunsell had made sure that Arthur and Olivia's monthly rent money was to be paid to the diocese's trust board – and not the Onehunga parish – Cowie and the synod reaffirmed the long-overdue St Peter's debt of £180. Further, this time they required that it be paid within the month.

The meeting closed on a happier note – confirmation of the promised reopening of St John's College. Cowie and his fellow trustees had finally found a replacement for Kinder at the Parnell Grammar school.

Serious surgery

In his book *Tangiwai – A Medical History of 19th Century New Zealand*, one of this country's most distinguished physicians and psychiatrists, Dr Laurie Gluckman, made the most interesting assertion that "it could be argued with some justification that [Bishop] Selwyn established New Zealand's first medical school".[249] Selwyn had brought two doctors with him in 1842, namely Butt and Davies, and the third medical man at his St John's College was Purchas. Gluckman argued that it was perhaps "unfortunate that all three were ordained" and therefore split between the two professions, church and medicine. Had Selwyn insisted, he said, that they should restrict their activities to medical work, but within the church framework, there could have been little doubt that the effect on Māori health would have been very beneficial. Some praise indeed.

Furthermore, Gluckman had no hesitation in stating that Purchas was one of the most gifted doctors ever to settle in New Zealand. So now, 25 years after his arrival, and armed with a formidable medical reputation and wide experience, the time had come for Purchas to demonstrate his pioneering skills in the high-risk and still relatively new field of abdominal surgery. He was 51.

In the mid-19th century, two of the biggest problems with surgery of any sort were how to "disconnect" the patient from the unimaginable pain associated with incision – in other words anaesthesia – and the great risks associated with operative hygiene and post-operative infection. Even though, as early as 1799, the inventor Humphrey Davy discovered that inhaling ether relieved pain, it was not until 1842 – when Purchas was studying at Guy's – that ether was first used as an anaesthetic.

The first person to be anaesthetised in New Zealand was a prison inmate, in September 1847. He chose to be sedated with ether so a tooth could be extracted. It worked so well that, later the same day, a second patient (apparently a Māori chief) also agreed to be knocked out with ether so a small tumour could be cut from his back.[250] Chloroform was introduced a few years later and would be the preferred anaesthetic for the next 40 years, while anaesthesia itself remained an inexact science.

The second problem – that of antisepsis and hygiene – was not nearly so clear-cut. The discovery and introduction of antiseptic surgery by Joseph Lister had only taken place in the Glasgow Royal Infirmary Hospital a few years earlier (1865). He began the practice of spraying carbolic acid over the patient during surgery. The results soon enabled much more complicated operations to be attempted. Then, surgeons in Germany began the practice of sterilising hands and clothes with carbolic acid before beginning an operation – while their instruments were also sterilised, using super-heated steam.

There is little doubt that several doctors in New Zealand, including Purchas, had read much about 'Listerism' and were very keen to adopt the new practices of sterilisation. A Dr J Ryley, practising in Hokitika, was said

249 Gluckman, p 95
250 Refer Thesis AUT 2006, Dr A Warmington.

to have used antiseptic surgery in early 1868; while a doctor in Invercargill, Francis Monckton, used the carbolic acid treatment in what is recorded as the first ovariotomy performed in New Zealand, in 1869.[251] That was followed by Robert Tassell's 1870 operation, in which he described using diluted carbolic acid on lint as a dressing for the wound.

For Purchas, who was always a champion of hygiene in his own surgical work and follow-up care – right from the days of dealing with typhoid at Purewa in 1847 – the Lister theories were common sense and music to his ears. His grandson E H Roche,[252] writing in the *New Zealand Medical Journal* in 1954, said this about Purchas's passion for cleanliness. "I remember on my 7th birthday when I was asked to see him in his study. There on his desk was a beautiful glistening pen knife but were my hands clean enough to receive it?" He described how Purchas inspected his hands and made him wash them thoroughly before further specks of dirt were discovered. "I had to wash them again and again before they would pass," he said. "After that experience I can well believe that neither his hands nor his instruments ever conveyed an overwhelming infection into any wound."

Late in January 1873, Purchas finally got the opportunity he had been preparing for – to carry out his own advanced abdominal surgery. J D Jackson, the clerk at Purchas's local Onehunga court and a senior member of his parish trust board, came to him in some distress asking to speak with him on a private matter. He was very worried about his 16-year-old daughter, Alice, in particular the "peculiarity of her figure". Alice was described in Purchas's notes as being very short in stature, large in waist and with a "very full and prominent abdomen". The girl herself claimed to be quite well and when meeting Purchas for an examination said she wondered why anybody thought there was something the matter with her.

Purchas, however, quickly diagnosed ovarian dropsy – or a benign cyst on her left ovary. After further examinations over the next two or three weeks – as poor Alice's girth increased still further and her left-side prominence became even more marked – Purchas thought there might be two if not three cysts altogether. By May, her girth had grown even larger – another 10cm – and she was having trouble breathing. Purchas advised her parents that it was time to operate.[253]

---

251 Refer D Dow, New Zealand Doctor article. The McKinnon operation in 1866 had been for ovarian cancer and was unsuccessful.

252 E H Roche was an eminent New Zealand physician, considered by many to be the founder of cardiology in this country at Greenlane Hospital, and former vice-president of the Royal Australasian College of Physicians.

253 Retired surgeon Pat Alley comments: "The distinction between benign and ovarian pathology is sometimes hard to detect, but the crude rule of thumb is that the bigger the cyst the more likely it is to be benign."

The circumstances of such major abdominal surgery in the early 1870s seem extraordinarily primitive in many respects. But a couple of the techniques and procedures used by Purchas in this and his subsequent operations were astonishingly modern in their application and remain a source of admiration and wonder amongst today's surgeons. Purchas describes how his colleague, Dr Day, sedated Alice with chloroform before Purchas and his two other helpers – Doctors Zinzan and Dowson – carried her into a "well-lighted room with a fire". The room with its simple operating table was almost certainly downstairs in the Purchas parsonage. Outside, the Onehunga day was cold and squally but as Purchas made his first incision – of about 12 or 13cm – with the fire crackling merrily in the corner, the temperature in the operating room was a cosy 70°F.

Arthur Purchas as he looked when about to take up his new full-time career as doctor and surgeon in 1875.

ALISON KISSLING

Purchas's step-by-step notes on the operation are precise.[254] The very thick subcutaneous fat caused some initial difficulty but when he finally got to the left ovary and had its extended cyst in view, he found it to be holding no less than "about 7 pints [just over 3 litres] of fluid"! This was slowly drained off using a trocar and cannula (a stout needle ensheathed by a steel tube), before the ovary itself could be carefully cut out. Here Purchas's innovative engineering skills came to the fore. Needing to clamp the pedicle (the crucial stalk-like organ carrying the main blood vessels to the ovary) before he could remove it, he reached for a piece of special equipment that he had designed and had made by none other than the local Onehunga blacksmith. It was an ingenious instrument, about 25cm long, consisting of two iron arms or parallel jaws, with three separate screws enabling different pressures to be applied at different points along the arms by means of a traveller, also fitted with a screw.

---

254 From Purchas family files; also copies in Auckland Medical History Society files. The Dr Zinzan mentioned here (spelled incorrectly as "Zimzan" in some places) is an ancestor of former All Black great, Zinzan Brooke.

The unique surgical clamp, an instrument Purchas designed and had built by a local Onehunga
blacksmith. Purchas used it with great success in most of his major ovarian surgeries.
TINA FRANTZEN – COURTESY MARION & ERNEST DAVIS LIBRARY COLLECTION

He was going to cut the pedicle through with a cauterising hot iron but
when one of the doctors passed the iron over, it was not hot enough to do the
job. Purchas then decided to use his clamp – slipping it over the pedicle and
tightening it up in just the right spot, so a cut could be made with little or no
blood loss and the stump could be easily cauterised. No problem, it seemed,
for the unflappable Dr Purchas. He noted, matter of factly, that there was "no
charring, no blood and therefore no sponging". The local smithy's clamps, he
reported, were "exceedingly convenient and efficient". One of these original
clamps is still on display in the Ernest and Marion Davis Library in Auckland.

Luckily for Alice, the right ovary was found to be in order. Soft iron wires
were used for the stitches, also with an innovative little process to make them
easier to manage. Purchas always kept two small pieces of soft leather in his
medical bag which he would place over the back of a nearby chair. Then he, or
an assistant, again only with thoroughly washed hands, would draw the slight
wire strands over the leather several times to clean and warm them, and make
them more pliable. He used three of these to close the wound, crossing the
ends and bringing them through the lips of the wound. Then three stouter
iron wires, similarly warmed up, were passed through the ends together and
gently twisted "so as not to exert much pressure". Finally another seven so-called
"superficial, fine iron sutures" were used to close the third layer of the wound
evenly on the outside.

Purchas would have relied on the abdomen having been stretched by the large ovarian cyst, says Professor Alley, so closure would have been a relatively straightforward exercise. The entire procedure, from sedation to final dressing, took just 70 minutes – "a very creditable performance", even for today's surgeons with all their modern equipment and facilities.

Then, the final and probably most significant procedure – antisepsis treatment – was undertaken. This was the key ingredient, Lister antiseptic putty, introduced in Glasgow in 1867. Purchas was among the very first anywhere in the world to use it, and certainly the pioneer in New Zealand (Lister did not introduce it to London for another 10 years). It was to revolutionise surgery everywhere.

Basically a glazier's putty, the dressing was made from carbonate of lime mixed with a solution of boiled linseed oil and carbolic acid. Lister recommended a 4:1 mix but Purchas began by using a more gentle 8:1 mix. The soft paste was laid evenly over the wound, about half a centimetre thick. Then a soft rag, dipped in the linseed oil and carbolic acid solution, was placed gently on top of the sutures, followed by a very light overall binding.

When Alice woke up following the operation she reported "very little pain" and, according to Purchas, was "much surprised to find herself comfortably placed in bed, having had no consciousness whatever during the operation". With that welcome news, Dr Purchas and his assistants celebrated by administering her a small brandy, no doubt sharing one themselves beside the glowing embers of the parsonage's fire.

Two days later, on June 1, Alice was enjoying some cold tongue and bread for breakfast. Purchas almost certainly had concluded before this operation that early feeding was, in fact, beneficial. Although she had experienced some pain over the previous 48 hours, she was doing well. Purchas removed the three upper stitches before serving his patient some of Olivia's chicken for dinner. Amazingly, by June 10, Alice was out of bed and standing up. The last two wire stitches were removed a day or so later and after another two weeks of recuperation, Alice walked to church on her way to a complete recovery.

The Jackson operation in Onehunga was technically the first fully successful procedure of its type in New Zealand[255] and the first of a series of major abdominal surgeries carried out by Purchas – 13 in all – between 1873 and 1894. All except one – where malignant cancer was already involved – were 100% successful. Alice Jackson herself lived a full and active life until the age of 77. Purchas's outstanding record, together with his many other

---

255 A complete removal of all or a major part of the organ, as distinct from an ovariotomy, where only an adhesion, tumour or other malformation is treated.

medical successes, prompted Cambridge University a few years later to confer on Purchas an honorary MD. Uncomfortable with such an honour, Purchas declined.

First Mangere Bridge opens

From surgeon's operating table to engineer's drawing board, it was all in a day's work for Purchas. By now, construction of the timber work, piles and framing on the long-awaited Mangere Bridge was about to begin. The stonework for the approaches on both sides had been completed to Purchas's and everyone else's satisfaction and the contractor, Martin Danaher, had sailed to Australia to buy the best hardwood he could find – jarrah, good enough to take the heaviest horses and carts. He had eventually won a contract let by the Government's "public works department" after a long political argument over whether the bridge was the responsibility of the provincial or national government. Danaher charted a ship for the job, which was first crippled in a storm on her way to Fremantle to pick up the timber. Then, when finally repaired and loaded with her jarrah cargo, she was wrecked on an island on her return voyage. All the precious timber was lost as well.

The delays continued for the rest of 1873 and into 1874 while new timber was sourced and as funds were slowly released. Purchas watched it all with a mixture of proprietorial concern and unwavering optimism. He remained on call to offer any special engineering or construction advice, and apparently retained his "consultant's role" as work progressed, including some rights of special access. At the time he had a small gig and pony, and one early summer's day in late 1874, he offered to take an elderly local lady, a Mrs Forbes, with him on one of these inspections as the bridge was nearing completion. The pair drove from Onehunga across the bridge, but on reaching the other side at Mangere, found the workmen contemplating how to close the remaining gap of about 10 feet.

Mrs Forbes, in a letter to one of the local papers a few years later, described how "Dr Purchas got out of the gig and had a few words to them". In no time the men were laying the planking as instructed and Purchas and Mrs Forbes continued their trip to Mangere. On the return home, Mrs Forbes was pleased and very much relieved to see that the unfastened decking they had trotted across a couple of hours earlier, had all been "well and truly laid and nailed".[256]

This must have been the very first full vehicle crossing of the original

---

256　Purchas family papers – notes from Mrs L M Hardy.

The first Mangere Bridge, looking toward Mangere mountain.
AUCKLAND LIBRARIES HERITAGE COLLECTIONS 957-136-1

Mangere Bridge. By the end of 1874, it was ready to be opened and the locals happily turned out in force for the ceremonies in January 1875. Local historian Susan Maxwell wrote: "The new Mangere Bridge began a busy life. Heavy cartloads of produce were soon crossing daily and pedestrians had to leap into the safety bays on the side to avoid the horns of cattle herded across the narrow bridge".[257]

The bridge quickly became the valuable commercial route first intended for the farmers of Mangere. But it was also used as a virtual racetrack by the high-spirited youth of the day on their horses – much to the concern of local authorities. A few years later, however, slow subsidence of the sea floor, combined with damage done by sea worms, resulted in an ongoing programme of repair and upgrade before, finally, a second bridge was built. But the original structure had done its job and lasted 40 years before being replaced. Today's bridge is the fourth such crossing.

Whether it was advising bridge builders on the best way to lay roadway planks, or dealing with the intricacies involved with opening an abdomen to remove tumours, cysts or complete organs, it all seemed to be in a day's work for Purchas.

---

257   Borchard, p 74.

Word of his success with Alice Jackson's surgery spread rapidly around medical circles in Auckland and the rest of New Zealand, and was immediately followed by other referrals. The most serious involved a young married woman who had endured a miscarriage on falling soon after her wedding – at age 17. She became pregnant again before long and after giving birth to a healthy baby boy, her nurse reported that she could feel a small tumour on the right side of the young woman's abdomen.

Over the next couple of years, she consulted five different doctors, including Dr Day, who had helped on the Tassell ovariotomy and Purchas's original Jackson operation. For whatever reason, the other doctors did not want to be involved any further in such a difficult case. Finally, Day and yet another doctor concluded that she did indeed have a growing ovarian tumour and recommended that she should talk to Arthur Purchas about an operation to have it removed.

Purchas first saw the young woman at the end of April 1874 and found a fluctuating tumour "occupying the whole of the front of the abdomen". He immediately arranged for her surgery, thinking she may actually be suffering from two or even three cysts or tumours. Purchas operated on June 8 to remove the cysts using the same technique, equipment, anaesthesia and scrupulous attention to hygiene, including the identical Lister antisepsis treatment with the carbolic putty dressing. After a day sleeping on June 9, the patient was "cosy, cheerful and feeling very comfortable," according to Purchas's post-operation notes. By June 12, she was eating and drinking a little beef tea, "looking quite well … the wound uniting rapidly". As before, no complications ensued and his patient was soon resuming a normal life.

While detailed notes on only seven of his 13 major abdominal surgeries remain, it would be safe to assume that, with each success, Purchas saw little reason to vary greatly any of his main procedures. When his patients awoke from the chloroform, they reported feeling very little pain. This changed slightly over the following days with the usual post-operative issues and discomfort associated with the human system re-engaging with small amounts of food and drink. The iron sutures were removed, two or three at a time over a period of 10 days or so – sometimes again with the help of a little chloroform – and the end results were little different from those of today except for larger scars.

To effect complete recoveries in all but the one case (which was complicated by a prior malignancy), after such major invasive surgery, was regarded then – and is still seen today – as a major triumph, not only in the New Zealand medical world, but in terms of worldwide surgical advancement. Professional medical opinion since – particularly that expressed by distinguished physicians and medical historians like Roche, Gluckman and Alley – has focused on a number of key factors that contributed to Purchas's success.

First, he was always consistently thorough when examining a patient and writing a carefully considered diagnosis – another legacy of his early Guy's training. Second, Purchas not only had great manual dexterity and touch – as evident from his flute playing and precise drawing skills – but also exhibited "great gentleness in the handling of living tissues". His profound faith was another major factor – in developing his confidence and skills in surgical work, and inspiring confidence in his patient as well. His beliefs assisted greatly by mobilising "the patient's own will to get well".

Finally, Purchas had an incredible ability to design surgical instruments that suited his purposes – complemented by his inbuilt passion for cleanliness and hygiene, and enhanced even further by his early adoption of Lister's antisepsis procedures. It might also be said that very few among the medical fraternity of those days would have had the courage and mental strength needed to attempt such advanced surgery. But Arthur Purchas, as we know, was no ordinary man.

CHAPTER 16

Final resignation

All this time, Purchas was still travelling to St Bride's at Mauku once a month—usually still on foot – to take services there, and was also officiating in Onehunga on the other Sundays. He was attending and conducting, or chairing, the regular meetings of the Auckland Institute and the medical society, the meetings and functions of the Society of Artists, and the various church assemblies and choral festivals in Auckland. Olivia was used to hardly ever seeing him at home, except for his regular consultations with the never-ending stream of medical patients in his room downstairs. During 1874, he also continued his work winding up the final Gundry estate matters, buying and selling a few more safe mortgages, and making good use of some of the money retained from the land sales, particularly on behalf of the Gundry's youngest son, Henry.

At the Auckland Institute that year, with Chief Justice Sir George Arney serving as president, Purchas remained on the council with others such as John Logan Campbell, J C Firth, John Kinder and Colonel Haultain. As in other forums in the same year, there was considerable debate being generated about forestry, the planting of trees and which species were best suited to New Zealand conditions. This was another subject which interested Purchas – always a keen and expert gardener and horticulturist. The Government, now under Julius Vogel, had put some emphasis on stimulating timber production as the economy grew rapidly and demand for building products increased accordingly.

The debate at the time was whether New Zealand native trees or 'exotic trees' (the imported species that European settlers knew so well) should be planted. The feeling was that native trees were too slow growing to be successful in production plantations. In fact, it was almost a 'given' in those days that imported species like oak, birch, elm and the like, would eventually displace the native timbers entirely – if not by man, then almost certainly by nature alone – according to the prevailing Darwinian theories of the day.

Purchas presented a well-reported paper on the subject.[258] His view was that some New Zealand trees might survive, but many would be unable to resist the advances of civilisation. He was probably referring to the huge swathes of kauri forest being cut down on the Coromandel and the native bush stands being burnt in other places for pasture. Purchas warned that "like the native birds, many would in time, almost entirely vanish". He urged his listeners and readers to make preparations to fill their places with trees that would accept ongoing cultivation.

That same year saw Purchas liaising frequently with Bishop Cowie. He and Olivia had formed a close relationship with Cowie – one which was to last until Olivia's death more than a quarter of a century later.

Meantime, Purchas's flax mill was back in operation, to his great satisfaction – although it was now in the hands of a new operator producing "upwards of 60 tons of flax fibre per year" according to the *Auckland Star*.

His only major disappointment was the betrayal of trust concerning the stone St James church at Mangere. As a result of the Waikato War, when Ngāpora had retired to the King Country, Purchas had to watch on as the church property was first confiscated – on the grounds of "native disloyalty" – and then the church itself was turned into a courtroom for the Government's compensation hearings.

These hearings were presided over by Purchas's old friend, and now senior judge, Frank Fenton. Once the Pākehā had taken the valued church for use as a courtroom, Ngāpora and his people lost interest, stating only that the adjacent cemetery and graveyard must remain untouched. Later, Fenton was responsible for drawing up a new trust deed – written almost certainly by him in a conscious effort at reconciliation – whereby the main church property was returned into the care of a joint Māori and Pākehā trusteeship, as it remains today. The Government also erected a stone memorial to the two Ngāti Mahuta chiefs buried there, the close family relatives of Tāmati Ngāpora.

Meanwhile, the indefatigable Purchas still managed to find time for yet another invention – this time an ingenious, independent spring system for four-wheel buggies. He had obviously been motivated – from personal experience travelling into Auckland and back so many times – to improve the comfort of the larger buggy, which bounced its occupants around alarmingly on the region's uneven roads, strewn with potholes. While a two-wheeler gig's body could be fairly easily suspended from the axle and made relatively comfortable as a result, the larger four-wheeler was a different matter.

---

258   Refer Proceedings of the New Zealand Institute 1874 (7), p 519.

Purchas's invention was the embodiment of simplicity – a hinged ringbolt system taking the place of a solid 'lock plate' used on the four-wheel vehicles. According to the *New Zealand Herald* report of the day, it promised "the motion of a two-wheeler with all the advantages and security of a four-wheel vehicle". The system did the job "admirably" and his influence on the Auckland gentry around the town's streets could be seen – and, perhaps more important, felt – through the very seats of their well-tailored trousers.

No doubt one of those four-wheel buggies was used a few months later at the first wedding in the family – that of fourth daughter Marian Elizabeth, known as Lizzie, to a young engineer called Charles Cooke. She was just 21, while Charles was a little older. The home which they moved into a few years later – on what was known as the Glen Orchard estate in the country area of St Heliers – would play a significant part in the future lives of not only Charles and Lizzie, but also Arthur and Olivia, and the entire Purchas family.

For Arthur and Olivia, the wedding was a signal that family life remained their constant priority. Christmas came and went, and there followed a renewed focus on the question of the children's higher education – particularly the sons, George (now 18), Arthur (15), Claude (14), Charles (12) and Frederic (9) – and the means with which to achieve it. For Purchas, this could only be realised by establishing a full-time medical practice.

He probably had a hint from Cowie about now that, finally, almost unbelievably and after so many years, a replacement for him might soon be found. A wink was as good as a nod this time it seemed, because at the AGM of the St Peter's trust board on January 20 1875, Purchas advised that he intended to "reactivate" his earlier resignation and would be presenting it again to the Bishop, but this time with full effect. He informed the meeting that he would now definitely be leaving the parish altogether. The time to get the ball rolling had well and truly arrived.

But before he could do anything else, he received the sad news two days later that his long-time and much-respected friend Te Paea – "Princess Sophia", niece of Te Wherowhero – had passed away at a comparatively young age, still only in her mid-fifties. She had not been in the best of health in recent years and died, having never married, at her home in the King Country. Her tangi was held at Waitomo.[259]

With this over, Purchas immediately made inquiries about a possible new home in the Newton-Ponsonby area, where he was keen to re-establish his medical practice. Leaving that job with an agent, he then booked a ticket for

---

259 A Ballara, Te Paea Tiaho, *Dictionary of New Zealand Biography*, 1993.

himself and his oldest daughter, Agnes (still unfortunately very ill), on a ship to Melbourne via Sydney, leaving in early March 1875. He regretted having to leave Olivia behind but she wanted to stay in Onehunga and help her daughter, Lizzie, now pregnant with her first child.

The purpose of the Melbourne trip, demonstrating the usual Purchas thoroughness and care, was to investigate other possible medical opportunities in that big city before making a final decision. He was also keen to visit his younger brother Albert (last seen just before Purchas left for New Zealand in 1846). Albert had been living with his family in Melbourne for the previous 25 years, having established himself as an engineer and surveyor.

Purchas inspected Melbourne carefully, writing home admiringly about its many fine buildings, gardens and parks, and its "tolerably good churches". He was particularly impressed with the city's transport system, both horse-drawn omnibus and light rail trams. This was an important observation and would assume far greater significance in his life just a few years later.

But after a thorough look around – and despite the many attractions of the city – he confided in a letter to daughter Emily that "he should have to put up with a good deal of underhand work on the part of some of the medical men" in Melbourne, were he to take up practice there. And after visiting Melbourne Hospital, he said he was very disappointed with what he saw – although admitting it was a fine building and very well supported. But, he added, "the mode of treating the patients is a long way behind the times".

He seemed to be leaning towards staying in Auckland and wrote again a few days later, this time to 19-year-old daughter Amy: "There is much to admire but it does not feel a bit like home to me." He added, a little sadly, that he could not see much improvement in Agnes after some hot-air-bath treatment. Indeed, Agnes would die just three years after returning home from the visit to Melbourne.

New home

Once safely across the Tasman and back home, and after consulting with Olivia, the decision was quickly made to stay in Auckland – and with it, the resumption of inquiries about a new home. Purchas soon found one, exactly where he wanted to be, in the new and fast-growing area of Karangahape Rd. It was the property of a George Holdship – a man who had started selling timber sashes, frames and doors about 15 years earlier, before establishing a thriving timber business and mill in Auckland, and entering local politics. He built a second mill at Grahamstown (Thames) on the Coromandel, which had also done well, sourcing timber from the Tapu area (kauri and kahikatea in particular). Now he was thinking of moving permanently to Thames to keep an eye on his expanding and profitable business.

The Auckland property comprised several lots, some of which housed small shops fronting Karangahape Rd, not far from today's Edinburgh St. The main 16-room house extended below them and behind a corner property on what was then Dublin St.[260] A deal was done and was announced by the newspapers in mid-July as a "sale" – but was more likely an initial lease with the intention to buy, while Purchas got some more money together. Everything was set and in early August 1875 the large Purchas family moved in. An actual sale was not officially transacted until exactly two years later with the conveyancing enacted and with Purchas funding it with some of his own money and a mortgage from the Auckland Savings Bank. This was probably secured to some extent with two small lots he still owned, namely those in Hillsborough and Mt Eden.

As for Purchas's clerical situation, Cowie had already called the parishioners of Onehunga together at a special meeting in the first week of June (1875), and advised them that he had accepted Purchas's resignation – which most already knew had been on the table for eight long years, since it was first handed to Selwyn. Cowie also wanted to discuss with the parishioners a successor – more than likely someone he and his team already had in mind. The meeting passed a resolution to the effect that the "disruption of the connection was not by the wish or desire of the parishioners" and that they were going to lose the services of an "upright, exemplary Christian gentleman and a devoted, sympathising minister and friend".

A couple of weeks later, the farewells began – kicking off with a special evening ceremony and presentation to Olivia by past and present pupils and teachers of the St Peter's Sunday school. She had been the superintendent there virtually since it was built. They presented her with an elegant pair of silver-mounted flower glasses or vases. She was also honoured by a large turnout, thanking her for her 20 or more years of service leading the Onehunga Ladies Benevolent Society – once again a pioneering New Zealand institution and forerunner of so many similar groups. A week later, the large Auckland Choral Hall was filled to capacity with men and women from all walks of life for the ceremonial farewell to Arthur and his wife.

The speakers referred in glowing terms to a gentleman "who had endeared himself to all classes and denominations by his uniform kindness and urbanity, and by the devotion of many years of his life to their interest and welfare". His

---

260   Renamed years later as Cobden St.

name, they said, would always be remembered and associated with every good work. The regard in which he was held was evident by the size of ceremonial purse presented to him – containing 137 gold sovereigns[261] – and the effusive wording of the testimonial accompanying it. The purse – especially made by a young woman in Onehunga – was an elegant affair of blue silk braid, ornamented with a silver bead fringe, and with Arthur's initials and motto 'semper paratus' ('always prepared') also in silver bead work.

In reply, Purchas spoke of their great regret in leaving Onehunga, having hoped he would end his days in the settlement. He had no personal desire to move, but it was only a short distance and not, as was once contemplated, to another colony. He thanked them for the handsome present and assured them it would be "of material assistance to him". Various citizens wrote warm letters to the press in the following days about his contributions to the community and, in particular, his work among the poor.

Purchas's replacement, a Mr Tomlinson[262], took his first service on August 3 and the Purchas family left Onehunga the same week. It must have been a satisfying moment for Arthur when he finally got to hang up his tile on the gate outside his new residence.

The final formality was completed at the next Anglican synod in October, when Cowie addressed the assembly, saying that Arthur Purchas "resigned on June 30 after 28 years' service". Mr Purchas had found it impossible to continue the thorough pastoral care of his parishioners, he said, with the continuance of his practice as a medical man. "And he was not in a position to relinquish the latter, however willing he might have been to do so."

John Kinder then rose to ask Cowie if he understood correctly the part about Purchas's 'resignation', because he (Kinder) clearly remembered being present in the synod many years earlier when Purchas had announced his resignation to Bishop Selwyn. He was "doubtful whether what had recently transpired could therefore be described as Dr Purchas' resignation".

Kinder was probably just testing his Bishop lightly and Purchas might even have broken into a wry smile on hearing his friend's question and attempt, on his behalf, to set the record straight. Cowie expertly tidied the matter up by answering that he had consulted with his best legal authority and the advice was that he should treat the matter as if he (Purchas) was still a minister in a parish, without reference to anything previously. Cowie then added, to everyone's

---

261 The nominal value in those days (£137) amounted to a substantial gift and equated to a very reasonable annual salary.

262 The Rev A R Tomlinson, MA, was formally instituted by Bishop Cowie on October 15, assisted by Purchas.

delight, that "Mr Purchas now holds a preacher's licence and he will, I hope, be able to assist us occasionally on Sundays in the churches of Auckland".[263]

To the casual observer of Purchas's life, it might easily be assumed at this point that, at the age of 54, he had already achieved enough milestones of significance and satisfaction. Far from it. Although the main purpose of the move to Karangahape Rd was to start a full-time medical vocation – it would also launch yet another chapter of civic involvement and service. The same fair share of success and high achievement, tragedy and bitter disappointment would feature in this period of his life, but it would also establish him fairly and squarely as one of Auckland's most well-known and respected citizens.

---

263   Papers Past, *New Zealand Herald*, Oct 20, 1875.

CHAPTER 17

Affluence

The timing of the move – even though a very long time coming – was also opportune in the wider context. The Vogel Government was forging ahead with new telegraph communications, road and rail development, and the abolition of the provincial governments. It was a time of rapid growth … of wheat and crop farms, the establishment of the large sheep stations in Marlborough and the Wairarapa, forestry and coastal trade. The new faster steamers began taking over from sail, assisting with the transportation of bulk goods and contributing to the growth around the country of many new coastal ports.

A new system of local boroughs was established in the place of provincial governments, followed by the introduction of free and compulsory primary education for all. The first university had been established in Otago (1869), and was followed by the launch of its medical school – just as Purchas opened his doors to new rooms fronting on to Karangahape Rd.

The personal profile of the kind and amiable doctor, and his reputation as a highly skilled and modern professional, of total trustworthiness and integrity,ensured a quality clientele from day one. He was still a chief surgeon at the Auckland Hospital and – having maintained his passionate interest in chemistry – an expert in the field of poisons and hazardous chemicals.

There are no financial records retained of his practice over this next decade, but it was clearly a very lucrative one from the start – despite much ongoing free medical care which he continued to dispense as before. A letter from daughter Emily to one of her sisters in 1876 told of her father having no fewer than 93 patients to see over six days in one particular week. Nearly a quarter of these he saw at home, and she added: "I forget how many visits he made also. I do wish he could refuse the non-paying ones but he would never agree to that."

Within two or three years, not only was Purchas able to gain title to his residence from virtually nothing, but he could also rest easy about the educational options for his children and the associated costs. He enrolled the three older sons at the Parnell Grammar in Ayr Street and began thinking about sending 16-year-old Arthur to medical school in London or Edinburgh. At the time, a student could obtain a medical degree from Otago, but the course still required a two-year stint at one or other of those "home" medical schools. So successful was Purchas's medical practice that he even began thinking about the possibility of acquiring other properties in due course.

Before too long, Purchas also found himself drawn into the new localised activity and administration resulting from the dissolution of the provincial government – in particular the Karangahape Highway Board and as chairman of the Newton East school committee.

On Sundays, he still donned his clergyman's dog collar and surplice, associating himself in particular with the nearby church of St Sepulchre, at the top of Khyber Pass. He made himself available either to preach or to lead services whenever called upon. And he was still the Auckland Anglican music leader and conductor of the large Diocesan Choral Society choir at their special festivals and events, attended by singers and people from all denominations. In fact, he conducted a special choir of 28 voices – drawn together from these various groups around Auckland – at a major festival in the Parnell Cathedral just days after shifting house to Karangahape Rd.

And there was also his beloved Auckland Institute, where he continued to chair its monthly meetings, often standing in for regular chairman J C Firth. One of his more detailed papers presented at this time (fully covered in the press) considered the best options for the proposed first telegraph link between Australia and New Zealand. The two governments had agreed to build the line but had yet to determine the best route for the undersea cable.

Purchas's paper covered three possible routes. The shortest, but more impractical line, was from Tasmania to a point on the South Island's west coast. The next option he considered was from Ahipara Bay in the north, to the New South Wales coast at Botany Bay – a distance of about 1170 miles he said, and with a very "favourable ocean floor". The other advantage of this route, Purchas added, was that the northern telegraph line had already been completed to within 40 miles of Ahipara, was well constructed and exposed to few possible hazards.

The third option would be to locate the New Zealand terminus on the beach south of the Manukau Harbour – but the extra 100 miles involved would probably negate this option. Purchas pointed out that Ahipara was also very suitable should the cable be extended to Kandavu in Fiji (only 1150 miles away), and to New Caledonia (about 850 miles). His meticulously prepared paper was put up for discussion and the meeting proposed that it be sent to the Government for consideration.

As Purchas settled in to his new routine in Newton, it also became clear that he would not be afraid – when the occasion demanded – to speak out in favour of the public interest. Public transport (road and rail) and in particular the state of the town's roads were always top of mind. It was a subject he was intimately acquainted with – from the very early days of surveying and helping to map roads in and around Onehunga, to larger projects like the bridge at Mangere … and even the design of suspension systems for carriages.

In 1876, he was quoted speaking out at a meeting of the Karangahape Rd Highway Board – exasperated with how the meeting was being conducted, and presumably unhappy with decisions being made on this new route and its maintenance. At the time, Karangahape Rd was gradually becoming the most important thoroughfare in Auckland.

His comments obviously did not go down well with someone, because next morning the schoolmaster at the Newton School – where the meeting had been held and where Purchas was committee chairman – advised him that someone had broken in overnight, breaking a window and some furniture, and causing other serious damage. Purchas told the reporter the next day, clearly making his stand, that he hoped "he should never witness another meeting like that on Monday".[264]

A few months later, a letter from Purchas was tabled at a regular meeting of the new Auckland City Council, highlighting his concerns about the state of the local roads. He had been driving quietly down the middle of Vincent St at night-time with both lamps lit, he said, when his horse fell in a hole. The hole was so deep that the horse could not extricate itself, was thrown onto its back and "considerably injured". The buggy's shafts and spring were broken, the harness damaged and "myself and servant narrowly escaped injury".

Since the accident was not caused by any carelessness on his part, Purchas asked the council to reimburse him for the damage, estimated at £25 – although he added "if £20 is paid at once, I shall be content to take that sum".[265] The council referred his claim to its streets committee with the comment that Vincent St was in bad condition because of all the extra traffic in Hobson St now being diverted into it. Presumably Purchas received his £20.

In between these events – and attending families all hours of the day and night during a large outbreak of scarlet fever – the final winding up of the bulk of the Gundry estate was notified, with Purchas and Pierce advertising that any final claims or issues had to be notified by September (1876). This may have been prompted by the unfortunate death a few months earlier, at the age

264 Papers Past, *New Zealand Herald, Auckland Star*, Aug 1, 1876.
265 Family papers, L Cocks.

of only 35, of the eldest Gundry son, William. He was the young man who had been involved in the Waikato War as an interpreter and surveyor – and who would later become a soldier and rise to the rank of captain while taking part in the pursuit of Te Kooti. At the time of his death, he was living in Patea, working again as an interpreter.[266] He left a widow and five small children who clearly would have needed the financial support.

By October, having organised the final legacies to William's family, Purchas stepped down from his role as guardian of the Gundry children, although he still remained the Gundry estate trustee. He had managed the large estate for the last 22 years or more for their direct benefit – with the help of another trustee and his family friend and solicitor, Frederic Brookfield. Of the seven Gundry children, only three were still alive.[267]

Highs and lows

Finished with his guardianship responsibilities, but having clearly derived immense satisfaction from them, Purchas was immediately called upon to take up the position of Honorary Medical Officer at the Howe St home for destitute and orphaned children in Mt Albert. It would be the start of yet another serious commitment, one which would last for the next quarter century, almost until he died.

The Howe St Industrial School, as it came to be called, had been re-established in 1869 as a home for destitute and neglected children, orphans and those with congenital disease or deformity. Originally the Parnell Orphan Home, it started at Point Britomart in 1860, before being relocated to a second building in Howe St, Ponsonby. This had originally been built as barracks-style quarters for the first immigrants. Now the home had been relocated once more, this time to Mt Albert – although it was still called the 'Howe St home'. When the original medical officer, Dr Kennedy, died suddenly, Cowie and other well-known city fathers on the board saw Purchas as the obvious replacement.

The Howe St Industrial School – together with other similar institutions in places like Wellington and Christchurch – came under the control of the new Education Department in 1882, and Purchas was formally appointed as its Medical Officer. The objective at the home was to make every effort to further educate the children and prepare them for life on the outside.

Within a few years, however, the number of children needing care in Auckland had grown to the extent that additional homes were needed and

---

266   D Brown, *Pioneer Surveyors of New Zealand*, 2005, Part IV, www.surveyors.org.nz
267   They were Helen (married to Francis Young), Olivia and 20-year-old youngest son, Henry.

eventually opened, in premises first established by Selwyn – namely the Kohimarama site of the first Kissling native school for boys, and St Stephen's in Parnell for girls. The extra homes virtually tripled Purchas's initial responsibility, not just in terms of the daily health care needed, but also the travel involved and the requirement of reporting quarterly to the Government. The true extent of the many and varied medical problems and crises involving the small children that Purchas attended to over those many years can only be imagined 140 years later.[268]

One of his reports (from May 1884), of which he wrote some 100 or so over his long period of service, illustrates the problems he was dealing with on any given day.[269] "I found 40 children present, of whom 10 were little boys … most were in excellent health. There were a few cases of congenital disease, one of which is very severe. It is that of a girl who has been suffering from infancy. She was for some time in the district hospital but was discharged as incurable and is now much to be pitied. Ulceration has destroyed her nose and will probably ultimately prove fatal … everything is as comfortable as can be expected with the exception of the cooking apparatus in the kitchen which is frequently out of order."

Of a visit to the home at Kohimarama, where another 93 boys were living, he reported that one boy was in bed suffering from a dislocation of the elbow, which Purchas had managed to relocate on his regular visit the day earlier. "All the rest were in fairly good health except one who had epilepsy and a few others with 'slight sores.'" He reported that the dormitories were too crowded for good health and the privies were "not as clean as they might be for want of a keeping up a proper supply of earth". But it was the lavatories themselves, he said, that were in great need of improvement and "the large wooden troughs in which a large number of boys have to wash together, is an arrangement which I can only characterise as filthy and loathsome".

To fix the problem, Purchas put on his engineer's cap and made a practical recommendation. He suggested a force pump be fixed in the well and a tank erected a few feet above the level of the lavatories, with pipes from the tank to the lavatories "so as to give a supply of water to a series of taps on the basins I have recommended". He wanted to install several smaller basins for the boys to use and added that there were plenty of iron pipes at the home to do the job and that "the pump would only cost a few pounds".

---

268   One of the orphans in his care was Albert Pomare, the five-year-old born in England when his Māori parents were on a visit (famous for their meeting with Queen Victoria, who became Albert's godmother). The child was later given up by his mother to be cared for at the Howe St home.

269   Appendix to the Journals of the House of Representatives, E3, p 10.

Purchas, shown here with one of his many grandchildren, was always known for his special affinity with children, especially those suffering from social or medical disadvantage.

PURCHAS FAMILY FILES

His many reports written over the years, of course, still do not tell the whole story of his contribution to children's health. Laurie Gluckman, in his book *Tangiwai – A Medical History of 19th Century New Zealand*, wrote that Purchas's work among the neglected and destitute children of Auckland in the last quarter of the 19th century was perhaps his most outstanding medical contribution of all … only seven deaths in his time in office was a remarkable achievement for the period.[270] When a couple of inquiries were launched into the management of the homes at different times, the chairmen made it their business to single out Arthur Purchas for his work. In 1880, he was publicly thanked "for his exertions and unwearied attention to the health of the children" – especially since he had apparently been suffering that year from some illness himself.

Others commented later on his kindness and amazing sense of duty: "When an inmate became seriously ill in Mt Albert, Arthur Purchas volunteered to visit her at any time day or night that his services were required" and "even the most timid child found courage in his kindly presence". His callouts to attend sick children were all part of the service he provided for some 30 years – even when ill himself – and always involved considerable travel.

The Howe St role of caretaker of Auckland's destitute orphans as a public health issue, added significantly to the already strong reputation he had acquired from the very early days as the chief 'watchdog or overseer' of the city's water supply system. By the 1880s Western Springs had become the main source of Auckland's water, while the borough of Onehunga continued to be entirely dependent on the Onehunga Springs. One of Auckland's main abattoirs or slaughterhouses, known as Young's (a large and unattractive meat

---

270 Gluckman, p 98. It is reasonably estimated that approximately 150 to 175 children in the three homes were in Purchas's care at any one time over the entire period of his service.

works), was sited in Newmarket and – as the population increased and spread – was increasingly being seen as a major environmental hazard. Moves were announced to relocate it to a site on the Panmure Rd, near the 55-acre St John's Lake, by today's Remuera golf course.

Purchas was outraged and immediately wrote to the Auckland and Onehunga mayors, his letter being reprinted in the press days later. "Sir, I have no hesitation in expressing my certain conviction, that all drainage from the slaughterhouse known as Young's must of necessity find its way into the Onehunga Springs. I believe it would be a public calamity if that site [Remuera] should be selected ... I cannot believe that the authorities would permit such a wholesale poisoning of the water supply and should imagine that the inhabitants of Onehunga would have a right to protection against such a scheme."

Purchas's objection was eventually heeded and years later St John's Lake was actually drained entirely. The Young's abattoir closed and was soon replaced by the Hellaby family's first abattoir in the west of Auckland, and the council's new Municipal Abattoirs at Western Springs. Ultimately, they would all move to locations at Westfield, in Penrose.

This was not the only battle he fought that year on behalf of 'his' Onehunga Springs water supply and the citizens of the borough. Just before Christmas, he attended a public meeting about a new cemetery planned in Ellerslie. Purchas expressed serious misgivings about the pollution likely to result from such a move. He enlightened the audience about a far more sensible proposition – that of a large new cemetery for Auckland in the Whau district (the origin of today's Waikumete Cemetery).

Meanwhile, solicitor Frederic Brookfield – who still lived in Onehunga with his wife Maria and several of his eight remaining children (three others having since died) – was by now a deputy judge in the Auckland District Court. He had also served two terms on the Auckland Provincial Council, the last up until its recent dissolution. His son, Frederic William Brookfield, was intent on following in his father's footsteps and had only recently graduated as a lawyer himself, initially living and practising in Tauranga. At 23, he was only four months older than one of the Purchas daughters, Edith.

The ensuing match must have been heaven-sent for the respective parents and the already strong family connection was further enhanced by Edith and Frederic's wedding in February 1878. It was a big event – the son of a prosperous family and legal man marrying the daughter of Arthur Purchas, the prominent surgeon, engineer, architect and churchman. Bishop Cowie performed the ceremony at St Matthew's in Hobson St and the couple went to live in Picton St, off Ponsonby Rd.[271]

A couple of weeks before the wedding, Purchas had learned of the death in Napier of his old friend and early St John's colleague, Bishop William Williams – the younger brother of Henry and the man to whom Arthur and Olivia had been indebted for his positive arbitration role at Onehunga.

Just four weeks later, Arthur and Olivia's eldest daughter, Agnes, finally passed away at home in Karangahape Rd aged just 29, after a long illness.[272] The two families once again came together for another funeral service at St Peter's in Onehunga, where Agnes was laid to rest alongside her two siblings, Arthur and Mary. Arthur and Olivia had hardly got over her passing, when they learned next of the death of George Selwyn, who passed away in England on April 11, 1878.

Interspersed with Purchas's growing involvement in civic affairs, his medical practice continued to thrive and another eight or nine of his groundbreaking abdominal surgeries were performed in the period 1873-1879. Throughout this time, Purchas continued to demonstrate great faith in the efficacy of Lister's antisepsis theories. Elsewhere in the medical world, suspicion still abounded about microbes and the contribution of Lister's theories towards any successful outcome. Treatment regimes such as the use of carbolic putty remained under intense scrutiny and were not even introduced to the London medical scene until the mid-1870s. In fact, Dr Philson, the long-standing superintendent of the Auckland Hospital and senior medical man in Auckland at the time, was known in the fraternity to harbour an "entire disbelief in microbes".[273]

Nevertheless, Purchas's work made a significant contribution to the advancement of such surgery. His outstanding success rate in such "formidable and precarious operations", as they were regarded in those early days – combined with his passionate support for and use of Lister's techniques – not only seriously challenged the local medical establishment, but also elevated his progressive and highly skilled status even further among the wider Auckland community.

Drainage problems

For the Purchas household of 11, life in their new Karangahape Rd home was

---

271   Frederic Jnr eventually joined his father's legal practice, to form Brookfield & Son. The law firm Brookfields still exists today. The opening page of the firm's website at the time of writing featured a picture of the magnificent Auckland Museum – fitting, perhaps, given Purchas's role as a founding father.

272   The actual cause is unknown but is likely to have been consumption/tuberculosis, pleurisy, scrofula or other similar pulmonary or respiratory diseases.

273   Refer Dr J Giles, *Early Auckland Doctors*, EMDML.

really looking up. The family had a spacious garden and grounds with access onto both Karangahape Rd and Dublin St, below a separate private property on the corner owned by someone else. And Purchas's income was growing steadily – enough for him to hire a reliable gardener and groom by the name of Richard Sedgman.

It was still seven years before the start of the first horse-drawn trams, but ever since his trip to Melbourne, Purchas had been thinking seriously about the possibilities of a public transport system for Auckland as the town's growth spread quickly in all directions. The first priority for a new tram route, he believed, should be from Queen St and the downtown area up to Karangahape Rd, then north-west to Newton and the wealthy dormitory suburbs of Ponsonby, St Mary's Bay, Grey Lynn and Surrey Hills.

At the Auckland Institute, where Purchas remained on the council after a second term as president, he continued to speak on a wide variety of current topics, including public transport. And there seemed to be nothing new in the world of discovery that escaped his attention. He presented papers on the "best methods of saving gold at Thames", microscopes, Bell's new telephone and microphone, railways, electricity, the fossils of ages past, horticulture and botany. One of his most widely reported talks at this time concerned the "photophone", another Bell invention which used light to transmit sound, so "people could hear a shadow" as Purchas put it. The photophone, he explained to his audience, was already effective over distances of 300 miles into the English countryside, and even across the English Channel.

But it was entomology – the study of insects – which next thrust him into the public spotlight. Three or four years earlier, in 1876, while pursuing this interest wandering through the Grafton Gully cemetery, he first observed what he thought was a very unusual bug crawling over an Australian kangaroo acacia tree. He knew enough by this stage to realise that he might have discovered something new – a small, soft-bodied, white-scale bug, finally proven a couple of years later to be a new species of insect. It attacked citrus trees in particular and was quickly identified as a serious threat. The insect was thought to have possibly arrived in New Zealand from Australia, although not a native of that country. Purchas's name re-entered the scientific world of entomology when, after the usual international formalities, he was advised that the new insect would be named after him – *Icerya purchasi*.[274]

From the lofty heights of entomological discovery, it was the humble subject of drainage which next brought Purchas into the public arena. The

---

274 Appendix to the Journals of the House of Representatives, H26, 1885. Prof T Kirk, *Fruit-Blights and Diseases of Fruit-Trees in New Zealand.*

problem was a fairly typical one of the day, but when it involved a well-known public figure such as the reverend doctor, people everywhere became very interested. It certainly brought him back to earth with a bump and had significant consequences.

In November 1879, following another drawn-out inquiry over the preceding six months, Purchas finally found himself charged with contravening the Public Works Act by "allowing a certain noisome matter to flow from land owned by him". The charge followed a series of complaints, by people in the Dublin St area, of overpowering smells said to be emanating from drains leading down from the Purchas home.

The court was told that, 12 months earlier, "the defendant Purchas had had a cesspit on his property into which the water closet emptied, before it found its way onto the road". But after a complaint, Purchas quickly disconnected this and had a new brick and cement cesspit built with a new drain at the rear of his property towards Dublin St.[275] Even though he did not believe the old cesspit had been the cause of any problem, he paid all costs to the complainant and rectified the matter at his own expense, which led to the withdrawal of the complaint and any case against him.

Now there was a new problem. Purchas's lawyer introduced a witness who said that, yes, he had been called in three years earlier (before Purchas had moved in) to repair a drain across Dublin St, into which the new cesspit emptied. Other residents living across the road in Dublin St said they had never seen any objectionable matter actually coming from the Purchas property. Purchas himself suggested that since all his drains were in order, the smells could only be coming from neighbouring residences into the Dublin St drain. The prosecutor told the magistrate, however, that it was "a flagrant breach and required being made an example of," especially since he had read so many comments quoting Dr Purchas on the necessity of efficient drainage and he was clearly well acquainted with the subject. And then he added that if Dr Purchas's drains were all in order, "he would have no reason to be leaving the district".

It seems from this remark that the preceding months of bickering over drains and "being made an example of" had been too much for Arthur and Olivia. They had already decided to move from Karangahape Rd, no matter which way the judgement went. The magistrate summed up the affair by saying there was insufficient evidence presented to show the problem had actually been caused by Dr Purchas. He then dismissed the case and awarded costs to Purchas. The drainage problem was left unresolved for the time being.

---

275 Very few homes in Auckland in those days had water closets. It was estimated that fewer than one in 10 had them even by the mid 1880s.

But the die had been cast and Purchas was already on the lookout for property on the other side of Karangahape Rd – closer to the centre of town if possible and maybe even with sea views.

Auckland was thriving and on the move. The demand for property was strong and prices were rising. Optimism and positive energy abounded. Purchas's medical practice had succeeded beyond his wildest expectations and the time appeared right to, hopefully, make one final move.

He was not to know, however, that in so doing, another severe test would be in store for him and his family. The new challenge would coincide with a sequence of dramatic events – not only for Purchas, but also for so many of his friends and colleagues, and even the town of Auckland itself.

CHAPTER 18

Boom ...

While Auckland was in a 'gung-ho mood' as a result of the booming economy, it wasn't the same story elsewhere in New Zealand. It has remained a minor mystery to various historians and social commentators why virtually none of the many intelligent and prosperous capitalists of late 1870s-early 1880s Auckland recognised the dangers ahead. The fact that the economic climate in every other province of New Zealand did not match that of Auckland should perhaps have been at least one very clear warning signal. Another was that the price of wool – the major contributor to New Zealand's income at the time – had begun to fall as early as 1877. Other obvious recessionary factors were starting to take hold in Britain and several other European economies. Although George Grey had confidently returned as Premier in the same year, his autocratic tendencies and failure to deal adequately with unemployment, productivity and all the issues of growth – or lack of it outside Auckland – had counted against him and he was quickly thrown out just two years later..

New Zealand's population by now was a little over half a million, with less than 50,000 calling themselves Māori. The Kīngitanga was virtually a spent military and political force, and its people's worst fears about land alienation were now being realised, with Pākehā finding new ways of acquiring it even quicker than before.

In Auckland, the pioneer business houses, distributors and retail merchants were all flourishing. Brown, Campbell and Company, Nathans, Henderson & Macfarlane, T & S Morrin the ironmongers – they were all doing business like there was no tomorrow. The town's capitalists and entrepreneurs – among them Firth, Daldy, Williamson, Buckland, Russell and Whitaker – were regarded as men of distinction ... purposefully leading the colony into a new era of wealth and purpose from their Queen St offices.

As R C J Stone wrote: "To be a capitalist in 1881 was no derogatory term but the badge of financial independence proudly to be worn."[276] The trading

---

276 R C J Stone, *Makers of Fortune*, p 42

banks were rich and generous. Loans, credit and highly competitive interest rates all tempted the northern entrepreneur and property seeker. The easy availability of credit, combined with this powerful feeling of prosperity and energy, led to an unchecked speculative boom and, in time, the inevitable bust. It would be a scenario repeated at least three times in the city's subsequent history.

In the streets of Victorian Auckland, however, where ordinary people lived mostly in rented houses, day-to-day life was not quite so easy. While most could find or change jobs relatively quickly as shopkeepers or assistants, builders or labourers, unbridled capitalism didn't necessarily bring prosperity to all.

It is one of the curiosities of those days that much of ordinary daily life consisted of ongoing disputes and altercations between neighbours. Social historians generally attribute a lot of these problems – such as Purchas's drainage issue – to the "understandable consequences of lives led, almost literally in each other's pockets".[277] Literally thousands of neighbourhood quarrels were aired daily in the courts or in the pubs – disputes over boundaries, water, debts owed, stray animals, gardens trampled and fences knocked down.

Access to water was at the heart of many an argument. And backyards, overrun by pigs, goats, fowls and sheep, were the source of many altercations over smells, unwanted noise and fences. Even those with more valuable properties found themselves drawn into disputes arising from inaccurate early surveying, boundary pegs replaced or falsely relocated, and council documents wrongly drawn up, unproven or sometimes unable to be found.

In this strained social environment, Purchas was now regarded "as a member of the Auckland upper set" – just like other senior clergymen, successful practitioners of a "learned profession as medicine", judges or magistrates, senior government officials or military men – although he would never have wanted to be identified as such.

The grandest resident of Auckland in 1880, says Stone, was James Williamson, president of the Bank of New Zealand and New Zealand Insurance, and "owner of the *Pah*, a suburban estate worthy of a British merchant prince". Williamson was also a fellow councillor at the prestigious Auckland Institute's table and undoubtedly someone from whom Purchas would have sought financial advice.

Whatever counsel may have come from such individuals that influenced his decision to move from Karangahape Rd – beyond the obvious impetus of the unwelcome drainage affair – Purchas soon acted. In January 1880, he saw a notice in the paper advertising some lots for sale by auction in Pitt St, closer

277 D Wilson, Community and Gender in Victorian Auckland, *New Zealand Journal of History*, Vol 30, No 1, 1996.

Challinor House in Pitt St, Auckland, soon after the new tramway system had been introduced in the mid 1880s. Note the original brick house facing onto Pitt St (adjoining the main dwelling), where the Purchas family lived while the main residence was being built.
AUCKLAND MUSEUM IMAGES PH PR-39

to town and in what he considered to be a very suitable location – with views down to the harbour and even across to the North Shore. On the property was a small brick house, facing the road, with a large backyard containing two smaller cottages.

His bid was successful. Using some of his own savings – and a significant amount of money from Olivia's earlier inheritance from her aunt – enough additional credit was easily available to also enable him to begin building a new residence on the Pitt St site. By March, the large Purchas family had moved in to the brick house at No 52, and presumably the two small cottages, while the new house went up alongside.

It was an impressive affair, built in timber of three floors and linked to the brick house via a separate locked door. There was a basement housing a large kitchen, wash house, and coal and wood storage rooms; a ground floor containing six dining, living and reception rooms, and a large pantry; and an upper floor on which were located eight bedrooms, two bathrooms and the water closet. The two upper floors opened onto full-width verandahs, while a winding staircase led visitors from the garden gate to the main front door on the first level.

While the original brick house faced east on to Pitt St, the new home and its verandahs faced north, with views across the harbour. It was called Challinor House, in recognition of Olivia's family and her aunt, whose legacy had largely helped to pay for it. Purchas soon reopened his medical practice, advertising his hours of consultation as being from 8am to 10am, between 1pm and 2pm, and after 6pm. The time in between was devoted to his work at the destitute children's home and Auckland Hospital, and to his many outpatients requiring house calls and all his other civic, church and family duties.

The property had been purchased from the estate of a William Gorrie, which also owned other lots next door in Pitt St, while another section backing on to the street at the rear of Challinor House was owned by a Robert Heighton. As soon as the main deal had been secured involving the primary lot (Lot 9), Purchas set about securing some of this adjoining land, involving a further six lots in total. The Gorrie family were happy to get involved in a little bit of buying and selling to accommodate Purchas's building plans, as was Heighton. He had the adjoining Lot 8 and ran a blacksmith's business there with a forge and small shop.

Over the next six months, while the home was completed, the lawyers organised all the paperwork and the final conveyancing, titles and settlements were carried out in three stages from November 12 to December 18, 1880. The property was bought in Olivia's name.

The final cost for the land and the original brick house and smaller buildings was £1940.[278] All appeared in order and everyone was happy – but not everything was quite as it seemed.

Trouble brews

Challinor House was an impressive Auckland landmark. Fruit trees were planted, paths laid, gardens established, fences built, and premises for horse, buggy and groom tidied up. Arthur and Olivia's sons, George (23), a surveyor trainee, Arthur (20), Claude (19), Charles (17) and Frederic (14) were all well advanced in their education. The first three boys had passed through the Parnell Grammar School in Ayr St during the last five or six years and the other two were still in attendance. Over those years, Arthur and Olivia had been loyal supporters of the school, but other families had quietly drifted away and the school roll was now falling.

Sometime in July 1880, about five months after they had all moved to

---

278   L Cocks, family papers, deeds.

Pitt St, one of the Parnell Grammar parents – no doubt aware of Purchas's connections with several of the school's board of governors – spoke to him in private about several matters of concern at the school. The matters, it was later disclosed, involved the quality of elements of the education, some of the discipline in the classroom and veiled hints, via some pupils, that perhaps one of the masters had been drinking liquor. Purchas's assessment of the parent's remarks was that, if true, they were not only detrimental to the pupils, but also an urgent call for reform.

He decided to go and talk to one of the board, Thomas Peacock, the Auckland mayor – a Scot whom he knew well and who was in the final process of bringing to fruition another public project first promoted by Purchas, the Auckland City Library. Peacock suggested the two of them talk to John Logan Campbell, the Parnell Grammar board chairman at the time.

The three men subsequently met and Purchas emphasised he was not standing up as a "public accuser". However, he thought the board should make some inquiries and get to the bottom of the matter.

From then on, things seemed to go wrong for Purchas. He received a note from Campbell asking him to set out the points on which he thought the board should try to get further information from parents and pupils. Purchas wrote a memo to Campbell with a few suggestions. Campbell then went overseas for some months.

After hearing that his memo to Campbell had been passed on to Colonel Haultain, his long-standing friend and board member, Purchas then inquired of him some months later if anything was being done. Haultain had to inform him, as per the formalities of the day, that because the memo had not been signed and therefore was not a specific request or formal complaint, the board would probably not proceed further. Still believing that the board should make some sort of inquiry, Purchas offered to sign his memo. He obviously did not realise the drastic implications of a simple signature.

A couple of months later he was advised that the board would investigate the situation. But then the secretary asked Purchas to be more specific about the origin of the concerns … i.e. some names of parents, masters and unhappy pupils. Purchas was now in a very sticky situation because, as he wrote later, this latest board request "seemed to put me into a different position from that which I had contemplated". His situation got even more difficult two weeks later when he received another note from the board secretary saying that if he did not reply immediately, they would take that to mean he did not intend to substantiate his statements!

By now, the press had been alerted. Suddenly they were reporting that

One of the few early photos of Parnell Grammar School, in Ayr St as it looked soon after its founding in 1856.

AUCKLAND LIBRARIES HERITAGE COLLECTIONS 4-1280

Purchas had laid serious complaints to the board about goings-on at the Parnell Grammar School. The school board set up a committee to recommend how the matter should be handled and it suggested an independent government inquiry. The board rejected this suggestion and decided such a high-level investigation wasn't warranted. Instead, members would look into the matter themselves, in private.

In the intervening months, Purchas's remaining sons had been removed from the school – which, of course, only added another angle for the local press and fuel to the fire. Why had he taken them out? Purchas's worst fears were now confirmed as he found himself, virtually by default, to be the "public accuser" – expected to bring in supporting witnesses, to lay down the evidence and to present the board with specific details about the staff and their alleged shortcomings.

The headmaster, a Mr McRae, and some of the staff were, of course, outraged at being named in public. Some of the parents, quite happy with their children's education, were sceptical at best. Others, who were themselves unhappy with the school and aware of various incidents, did not want to explain themselves in the full glare of the public arena. The board members, meanwhile, felt obliged to allow a reporter or two to at least be present at the start of their meetings – giving them enough background, unfortunately, to stir up controversy … for example: "Serious charges laid by prominent Auckland citizen against staff at prestigious Parnell Grammar School."

Purchas must have held his head in his hands and wondered, many times over, how on earth he had managed to get himself into such a predicament. He had been trying to uphold the reputation and best interests of the school – a school he had been intimately associated with since 1855 when he and others had set it up.

The press coverage went national as Purchas stepped up to address meetings of the board of governors – passing on only what he himself had been told and trying to explain that the information had not originated from him. Slowly, over a period of some months, the inquiry process ground on. By March the following year, some of the newspapers outside Auckland had even begun to sympathise with the unwitting Purchas and the way he had been portrayed by the local press as the "face of the campaign" – despite his strenuous efforts to remain impartial.

The end result of the affair was that classroom standards were finally deemed unsatisfactory, the headmaster resigned or was dismissed, protesting all the way, and the school went into even further decline. More and more parents withdrew their sons, many opting to send them to the newer Auckland Grammar School – by now well established in its own new premises. The Parnell school was finally closed in 1893, with the proceeds from the sale of the Ayr St property going to help a new church school for boys in Remuera – the eventual King's School and College. Purchas may well have reflected later in his life on the 'trials' he endured over the Parnell Grammar School in the early 1880s – and ultimately believed they were worth it considering the fine new school that resulted from its sale. But it had been another stressful business.

At the same time as all this was playing out, work on the Pitt St property was essentially completed – apart from a couple of niggling boundary issues and some discussions with the neighbour, Robert Heighton, about his proposal to rebuild on his land next door.

While dealing with these matters, Purchas had also entered into serious discussions with some senior Auckland businessmen and merchants – in particular Thomas Morrin, Thomas Macfarlane, William Aitken (an ASB trustee) and Henry (later Sir Henry) Brett – about big plans the group had for a public transport system in the city.

Purchas's interest was immediately stimulated given that ever since his visit to Melbourne, he had been wanting Auckland to develop a public transport system. He had even gone to the lengths of developing a scheme himself for a local railway system, believing that rail was the way of the future – using electric trams on rails, as he had seen in Melbourne. The virtues of his scheme had been lauded in a *New Zealand Herald* editorial and he had also prepared a detailed paper on the subject for an address at the institute. Loan capital and the technology and expertise were available, and with Auckland expanding so quickly, it was clearly time for someone to address the issue.

As people took advantage of the easy credit – fuelled even more by "lavish borrowing from the London capital markets" – the speculative boom in property and in the building of warehouses, shops, villas and cottages, continued to gather momentum in Auckland. It was led not just by already wealthy merchants and traders, but also by the city council – thus increasing the demand for timber, bricks, iron and building materials in general. Exports to markets in Australia were diverted to local purchasers. Owning or buying a share of a small sawmill, wireworks or brickworks became a licence to print money.

The men Purchas was talking to were all respected operators in their fields, several of them original shareholders in a small land investment company which had bought property in Northcote. This company then bought more land in St Heliers and by early 1880 was known as the St Helier's and Northcote Land & Building Investment Co.

When Purchas was introduced to the operation, its plans were to build a wharf at St Heliers (to make the company's land even more attractive to intending city purchasers, happy to commute by ferry) and to construct a city tramway system, using profits "guaranteed" from the anticipated sales of land, not only in St Heliers but also in Remuera. In times of such unrestricted economic activity, it did not seem unusual for what was basically a real estate company, to be building a wharf or even acquiring a paddle-steamer ferry boat, let alone developing a public transport system.

To better appreciate Purchas's interest in such an operation, it is necessary to understand how Auckland's residential situation was changing at this time. The influx of immigrants and the attraction (to rural folk) of new, better-paid jobs made a significant contribution to the city's spectacular growth. But with it, as we have seen, came dissatisfaction with much of the old cheek-by-jowl housing, ramshackle cottages and tenements that were a feature of Auckland's first 40 years of development. People now demanded nicer cottages and villas in better surroundings, more fresh air, green pastures, trees and reserves. Inevitably the suburban spread began westward, past Ponsonby and Newton, and along the Great North Rd. The areas southwards, heading to Eden Terrace, Kingsland, Mt Eden and Epsom, also proved highly attractive to the builders and speculators – as did several pockets on the North Shore, already well served in terms of transport by ferries.

So the St Heliers and Remuera possibilities – coupled with the opportunity to establish an inner-city tramway system and even a future branch line to St Heliers and other eastern suburbs – naturally piqued Purchas's interest. Furthermore, his daughter Lizzie was married to Charles Cooke, the engineer, who was also in the early throes of signing on with the same company to work on the horse tramway project.

Although well used to the ebb and flow of land speculation over previous years, Purchas had never seen demand like this. As with every other property and business scheme being bankrolled in Auckland at the time, it was obviously difficult for him to see how a relatively small investment in the St Heliers land and tramway project (promoted by such sound and shrewd men) could possibly be a risk.

He also knew, better than most, that the provision of affordable and reliable transport to these new outer suburbs was the key to the city's development. As R C J Stone said: "Nothing was more influential in bringing suburban blocks onto the market than the provision of transport facilities."[279] When presented with the opportunity to invest, and with his medical practice flourishing like never before, Purchas showed little hesitation. Years later, he wrote about this moment.[280]

"When things were very prosperous I was asked by a person in whom I had confidence, to join some others in the purchase of a valuable property at St Helier's Bay, the most beautiful and convenient site in the neighbourhood of Auckland. The sum required was £1000 and I was assured that I should be able to double that amount within six months and to get cash for it."

Inevitably, his banker quickly agreed to the £1000 on overdraft. Pleased to have a man of such integrity and standing as Purchas involved in the scheme, the directors then asked him to join them on the board of directors. It was an impressive group, which included the Auckland mayor, James McCosh Clark, ex-mayor Henry Brett, Graves Aickin, chair of the Chamber of Commerce, and Thomas Buddle, the prominent lawyer from the firm's solicitors, Whitaker & Russell. Surveys began on the land, before sections and roads were laid out, and engineers set to work immediately on designing and building the important St Heliers Bay wharf, and looking for a ferry to buy. One of those assisting in the original and distinctive street layout of St Heliers was none other than Arthur and Olivia's eldest son, George, now well settled into his new career as a surveyor.

---

279   R C J Stone, *Makers of Fortune*, p 119.
280   Family letters – A G Purchas to W Challinor, June 1888.

Life in the Purchas household continued to be a very prosperous one, with the happy family atmosphere around the evening dinner table only occasionally disturbed by the Parnell Grammar School business. The ongoing saga was relegated to an afterthought when Arthur and Olivia announced another engagement in the family – that of 25-year-old daughter Amy to Henry Roche – although it appears there may have been one small "qualification". Henry, an Irishman and engineer from Cork, was 18 months younger than his fiancée and had only recently arrived in the country. He might well have been asked to wait, at least until he had secured a position, because they would not marry for another 10 years.[281]

No sooner had the engagement been celebrated, however, than complications arose with Purchas's next door neighbour, the blacksmith Robert Heighton. During the toing and froing over the various lots in the original Pitt St sale, Purchas and Heighton had eventually agreed to buy and sell, respectively, a small strip between their two properties on which a hedge stood. The intention was that Purchas could thereby keep a small additional gap between his house and the noisy, smelly and smoky Heighton forge on the other side of the hedge.

Heighton had spent the previous couple of years in England and while he was away, the forge had recently burned down. Now back in Auckland, he wanted to rebuild. He thought he knew where the boundary was and laid out a foundation for the wall of the new forge accordingly. Purchas disagreed with where he was building, believing it was too close and on his new strip of land. Words were exchanged and Heighton stood his ground, unwilling to back down. An increasingly frustrated Purchas made his point by kicking out at the first row of freshly laid foundation bricks, scattering them all over the ground.

Over the next few weeks, and with tensions mounting, Heighton tried two or three times to build his wall in the same place and was challenged each time by Purchas. When he came back one day to find the wall up to about three feet high, he called in his sons who got to work with a battering ram and hammers to once again knock it down. Heighton saw red and since he believed the wall was on his land, pressed charges of trespass against Purchas, coupled with a claim for damages to his wall and interruption to his business.

In July 1881, Purchas and his lawyer found themselves once again in the civil court before a judge and a jury – Heighton the blacksmith versus Purchas the doctor and man of the cloth. It was another local "set-to", guaranteed to get the locals talking and sell more newspapers. In the complicated hearings

---

281 Henry Roche later achieved prominence by witnessing and then recording the first impressions of the Mt Tarawera eruption in 1886.

which followed over the next two days, it finally transpired that the cause of the dispute was simply slapdash survey work and documentation. "There was considerable overlapping" of various boundary lines and both parties had reasonable cause to believe that the wall was being built on their land.

The judge did his best to sum things up before handing it over to the jury who were asked to rule on the contradictory and complicated oral testimony. This they did, finding that, despite the earlier conveyance of the small strip of land in question from Heighton to Olivia Purchas, it appeared that earlier plans showed it was apparently Heighton's. The judge, likely frustrated with the proceedings, simply dismissed the case but still awarded Heighton his £125 claim for damages and loss of business.

However, Arthur and Olivia did not want a forge next to their gracious new home. Over the next few months, they found another way to skin this particular cat by obtaining Heighton's agreement to sell the entire section to Olivia – for another £400. And so the matter was finally resolved.

Auckland's new suburb

The land which the St Helier's and Northcote Land & Building Investment Company bought – immediately after it was registered and as Purchas joined its board – was acquired from the prominent Auckland Stud Company and the Glen Orchard Stud Company. Their St Heliers estate had been used to breed some very good horses, including the first New Zealand-bred horse to win the Melbourne Cup, Martini-Henry.

A few months later, once the land had been further subdivided, two of the first people to move there – onto a 10-acre parcel of Glen Orchard land including its lovely homestead – were Lizzie and Charles Cooke, Arthur and Olivia's daughter and engineer son-in-law. Land records of the time are unclear, but it seems Cooke may have had some assistance from his company to take up residence as "occupier and proprietor" with Arthur Purchas as his guarantor. It was certainly in the tramways company's best interests to have residents move onto the land quickly and such an arrangement would have suited all parties.

In town, the stock market was still buoyant, and new companies were being formed and registered at an alarming rate. Imports had risen by more than 50%, resulting in bulging warehouses and shortages of storage space. In some parts of Auckland, land which had fetched about £10 an acre 10 years earlier was now going for £450 with no shortage of buyers.

Purchas's £1000 investment seemed safe enough to him and even more solid when, in July 1882, the company announced it had secured an agreement with the city council to "provide a system of tramways for the city and suburbs". The agreement gave it the right to construct and run a tramways system for the next 21 years – and the terms of the concession, the directors added, "leave no room to doubt that the undertaking will be advantageous to the community and profitable to the proprietors".[282]

The company's plan was for horse-drawn trams on rails to run on two loops in the city and to share one depot at the Queen St wharf. Each loop was to run up Queen St, before turning either west or east at Wellesley St. The western line continued via Hobson St and Pitt St past the Purchas residence, along Karangahape Rd to Ponsonby and back down College Hill to the depot. The eastern loop went via Symonds St and Khyber Pass to Newmarket, before turning back to the city via Parnell. The rails were to be laid on sleepers made of puriri on top of a bed of concrete. The intention, at some stage, was to extend a branch line from Parnell, near today's Brighton Rd, over the Orakei Bridge to Kohimarama Rd and on to the St Heliers estate.

To finance the tramways project, the company decided it now needed to raise additional capital, up to £125,000, and to go to the public for the extra £1 shares. The plan was also to reconstitute the company slightly and eventually change its name to the City of Auckland Tramways and Suburban Land Company, to better reflect its public transport business.

Although he didn't realise it at the time, this was when things first started to go awry for Purchas. It is not known if he was present at the crucial board meetings when the new company proposals were discussed and voted on, but in those days of highly unregulated company practice, it might not have mattered anyway. The end result was that, as an original shareholder and investor, he suddenly found himself committed even further.

It was decided that each shareholder in the old St Helier's and Northcote Land & Building Investment Co, instead of being paid out in cash, would be paid by an extra allocation of shares in the reconstituted company, proportionate to their original investment – £1000 in Purchas's case. All he said later to his family was that, instead of getting his money back, "it was arranged" to pay out former shareholders in unpaid shares and debentures.

Purchas had entered this whole arrangement more as a visionary, keen to establish a public transport system for the city, and less as a land speculator. He hoped to have some input into its planning and construction, and to see his vision for a fully electric system realised, as in other large cities. Purchas left the ways and means of financing such a major project to others he supposedly trusted.

---

282 E T Jackson, *Delving into the Past of Auckland's Eastern Suburbs – Section 6, St Heliers Bay*, p 51.

In these times of such unrestrained optimism about the future of Auckland's business and property markets, Purchas saw no reason to be unduly concerned about financial matters and was still happy to be involved in the project. He may have been mildly disappointed at the time about not getting his promised money back. Instead, he found himself with some 4415 shares, although partly unpaid, plus some debentures. All appeared to be well, as he must have assured Olivia. The medical practice was generating substantial income, the Karangahape Rd rent was more than covering his low borrowing cost on the mortgage and the Heighton boundary dispute was now behind them.

So when the opportunity arose to become one of the very first in Auckland to have the amazing new invention, the telephone, installed in their new Pitt St home, Purchas jumped at it. He was allocated the telephone number 52, corresponding to the street number for Challinor House.[283] After speaking about the wonders of new technology for so long, he couldn't resist the temptation of actually putting a little money where his mouth was.

Purchas had also been occupied, as usual, with numerous other activities during this time, in between his morning and evening medical consultations. One of these involved leading a deputation, on behalf of Bishop Cowie and the church, in discussions with the Colonial Secretary about the difficult subject of prostitution and contagious diseases. Concomitant with Auckland's growth was the development of the same old social vices – and now they had reached alarming levels. The Government had even declared Auckland a "contagious diseases district" under a new act, but left the local council and police department to deal with the issue.

Purchas's representations emphasised there were two problems involved – one the physical diseases; the other, the evil of prostitution itself. But he was vociferous in pointing out that any act dealing with the problems would be useless without laws being made that applied equally to men and women. The "crime" he said was equally great on both sides and he criticised the police for being perfectly aware of the existence of houses of ill repute, but doing nothing about them. "The police just wink at the problem," he said. When it came to issues of public health, Purchas had never been afraid to speak out.

A few months later, one tangible result of his stance on the issue was the opening of what was probably New Zealand's first "women's refuge" for former prostitutes and unmarried threatened women, under a committee led by Bishop Cowie's wife, Eliza. It was only small, with a dozen or so beds, but

---

283   The first telephone exchange in New Zealand was opened in Christchurch in 1881, followed by the Auckland exchange with just 26 initial subscribers.

it was a start. Arthur and Olivia (who also lent her support) were pleased that the occupants could also earn a little income by providing a laundry, sewing and ironing service for the public.

And while this opened one chapter, a special event in another part of town closed another. This was the return to Auckland and Mangere – in January, 1882 as a result of a special invitation by the city's leaders – of Purchas's old Kīngitanga friends, King Tāwhiao and Tāmati Ngāpora, and about 45 other Ngāti Mahuta chiefs and supporters. While Purchas himself was unable to take any major part, other than being an invited guest to one of the formal dinners, the visit itself was a major celebration with thousands turning out to greet the Māori King and his retinue during their three-day stay. It seemed that the bitterness and savagery of the Waikato Wars 20 years earlier had finally been put aside as Tāwhiao was hosted and fêted at receptions, company visits, harbour tours and parades. It was the first time the King and Ngāpora had left the King Country and come to Auckland since going to live behind the border (aukati) in 1863.

Europeans and Māori responded warmly to each other. The former cheered and applauded as the official party went by, while the King and his chiefs admired the changes they saw and eagerly took part in the many festivities. With reconciliation the theme, the itinerary included a special visit to the old Ngāti Mahuta homes in Mangere and Purchas's historic St James Church. But when they crossed the Mangere Bridge and the church came into sight, Ngāpora, overcome with grief, told his hosts he could not enter the graveyard or church. Protocol would require him to tangi his family there. "I am too old and feeble to tangi my children," he said.[284] Ngāpora died just over three years later (August 1885) at his home on the banks of the Waipā River, not far from Pirongia. He was thought to be about 80.

By the end of August 1882, the 500-metre-long timber wharf at St Heliers was finished and the company had bought its first steamer, the *Tongariro*, to take prospective customers, sightseers and the new landowners back and forth between the downtown ferry terminal and the wharf. A newspaper report described the inaugural trip to St Heliers by a large group of ladies and gentlemen, including Purchas and his fellow directors, members of the Auckland Harbour Board and City Council, and various other VIPs. The correspondent gushingly concluded his report by advising "that with regular and frequent communication by means of tramway or steamer to the new wharf, it requires no stretch of the imagination to believe that this beautiful bay will

---

284   A E Tonson, *Old Manukau*, p 98.

become the *Brighton* of Auckland". In addition, the St Heliers company let it be known that the value of its land was increasing … and that it had received offers on several five-acre lots at prices up to £150 an acre.

A couple of months later Purchas was back on the *Tongariro* with another party heading to St Heliers. This time it was in yet another new role – that of first president of the Auckland Naturalists Field Club, established to encourage the study of natural history. He had also recently been sworn in for the first time as a Justice of the Peace, a role he retained for several years after.

Business remained buoyant and loan capital was still available to almost anyone who wanted to build or develop. About a fifth of the 64 new companies registered in Auckland since 1880 were involved in urban or harbour transport, or major suburban land projects. The shortage of bricks and timber became even more acute as the building boom continued unchecked. Elaborate ceremonies for the laying of foundation stones or for the opening of new buildings – like the Auckland Savings Bank in Queen St – were a regular occurrence.

In the South Island and in Wellington, however, it was quite a different matter. And still no one saw it coming.

... *to Bust*

Unfortunately, and in spite of the glowing initial publicity, there was an underwhelming public response to the take-up of the remaining £1 shares in the revamped St Helier's Land Company ... which was going to build a tramway ... after it had sold some land ... and construct a wharf ... and buy a ship. Perhaps that was the problem. The ordinary man in the street who had little money, even the longer-term investor and certainly the many speculators, did not want to wait until the tramway was built before getting their returns.

Whatever the reason, the company was disappointed to report early in the following year that, of the 730 acres they owned at St Heliers and Remuera, only 32 acres had been sold, and most of that in Remuera. It seemed Auckland's "Brighton", even with its impressively long pier, was still too far away from town for most. Additionally, share acceptances totalled only about 65,000 of the 125,000 on offer. On the other side of Auckland, however, in places like Avondale, it was a different story with a sold-out auction of 400 acres in parcels of various sizes – while many other auctions in Epsom, Mt Eden, Mt Roskill and Mt Albert had similar success. The demand for land in these places, however, only served to encourage the St Heliers Bay investors, including Purchas. Their time must surely come.

Around 1882-83, Purchas's public reputation probably reached a peak. As one of the colony's most skilled surgeons, his deeds were well known; his stamp was evident on so many of the city's institutions and organisations, and activities – from arts and culture to public health and the Auckland Hospital, and water and transport. He was one of the church's most senior and respected clerics, a close friend of the Bishop and a senior synod member, involved with education and charitable organisations like Howe St and the Freemasons. His *New Zealand Hymnal* was still in use every Sunday in churches all over New Zealand and was now being compared with, although eventually replaced by the Church of England's august *Hymns Ancient & Modern* no less. He owned sections in Onehunga and Mt Eden, and houses in Karangahape Rd and Pitt St.

Purchas was also serving a term that year as the new chairman of the Fruitgrowers' Association – largely as a result of his recent citrus bug discovery and his horticultural and botanical expertise. He also had a deserved reputation in these circles following the publication of his comprehensive list of New Zealand flowering trees and shrubs, with all their botanical classifications and arranged alphabetically in groups according to the months they flowered.

But if there were any figurative laurels on which to rest, the 61-year-old Purchas remained completely oblivious to them. The ceaseless rounds of routine work continued – and then there was the hosting of the new Governor, Sir William Jervois, at the Auckland Society of Arts' major exhibition in April … and a visit, as part of a city delegation, to the Onehunga Ironworks to see the first trials involving the conversion of Manukau iron sands into iron.

In between his Sunday services at St Sepulchre, Purchas also officiated at two personal funerals that year. One was for Harriet Austin, the widow whose husband's estate and financial affairs had been entrusted to him as a public trustee since 1858. She left him £50 for his services but he still had her large warehouse property in Shortland St and other minor assets to manage for a few more years.[285] The other funeral, mainly a family affair, was for Annie Grosse, the daughter of Olivia Gundry, who had been brought up in the Purchas home at Onehunga.

And when he wasn't delivering a paper at the institute, chairing a meeting of the Society of Arts, preaching on Sunday somewhere or conducting important funerals, he was still enjoying his music. A newspaper report in September 1882 commented on his performance at a concert in town, when he sang *The Village Blacksmith* accompanied by his daughter on the piano, before playing a solo on his flute and "exhibiting much skill on the mellow-toned instrument".[286]

Underlining his sense of confidence and optimism at this time, Purchas began looking for further investments in the Newton area. They were mainly on behalf of his adult sons at university, but also for his own retirement account, there being no superannuation or retirement funds available in those days. On October 24, 1883 he was in the crowd bidding at an auction of several vacant lots fronting on to Ponsonby Rd, not far from the corner of Great North Rd. The sale attracted one of the largest crowds in Auckland for many months, possibly because the terms were supposedly so generous – 20% cash and the balance over five years at 7%. Purchas came home with three lots, the main one with a frontage on to Ponsonby Rd, while the other two immediately behind

285   Purchas and his fellow trustee finally sold the warehouse in 1886, during the depression, for £3075 – and were fortunate to do so.
286   Papers Past, *Auckland Star*, Sept 30, 1882.

it fronted on to Maidstone St. The total price was £669.[287]

The land offered several advantages to Arthur and Olivia. It was close to their home in Pitt St and there was room for three homes for at least a couple of their sons if they wanted to build there. Alternatively, a shop, offices or professional rooms would be suitable on the Ponsonby Rd frontage with a couple of homes behind, each with separate entrances on to Maidstone St. The new tramway system would go right past the front door of the Ponsonby Rd lot.

And with that transaction resolved, Purchas finally turned his attention to the significantly larger project he had been thinking about for weeks ... his "grand design".

The "Purchas building"

One of Purchas's colleagues at the Auckland Choral Society, and also a member of the natural history committee, was an architect by the name of Edward Bartley. They had known each other for a while and Purchas was always impressed with the quality of Bartley's designs, the detail in his work, and his insistence on superior workmanship and the best materials. Bartley became a sought-after architect in Auckland. He designed – among many other buildings, including churches – the Auckland Savings Bank in Queen St, the Blind Institute building in Parnell, the Jewish Synagogue and the Mt Eden Library. All these buildings, including the large English red brick and Oamaru stone premises he was commissioned to design for Purchas, still stand today.

Since Karangahape Rd was fast becoming the retail centre of Auckland, Purchas's idea was to build a prestigious office and retail block on his property – an area described at the time as "the most thriving part of Auckland".[288] He planned to retain the 16-room house behind the frontage and continue renting it out, and fund the new building via a mortgage of £3700 from the New Zealand & River Plate Land Mortgage Company. This was a £2 million company, registered in London, with a head office in Auckland and a staff list of substantial local citizens. There were two separate mortgages secured on different blocks at Pitt St, both at a 10% interest rate.

Such was the demand for space that Purchas believed the rents would easily cover the interest payments. He was even offered £8175 just for the land, before deciding to reject the offer and to proceed with building – a decision he would later have great cause to regret. The brief he gave to Bartley was to design a substantial block of three storeys, comprising at least six shops at street

---

287   L Cocks, Gundry family documents.
288   Today's address of the Purchas building is 444-472 Karangahape Rd.

level, with site preparation work to begin as quickly as possible.

Back at St Heliers, land sales were still puzzlingly slow, again in marked contrast to other suburban land sales. In early December, the shareholders met and agreed to the name change from the St Helier's and Northcote Land & Building Investment Co to the City of Auckland Tramways and Suburban Land Co. The directors felt that not only would the new name better reflect the company's activities, but would also help in negotiating a loan. Such a loan, it was felt, would be the means by which the directors could avoid making a call on all the unpaid shares – their own included. And in Purchas's case that amounted to about £2500, at 10 shillings a share. A few months later, a £100,000 loan was indeed confirmed and the relieved shareholders were then able to safely redirect any of their spare capital elsewhere. That loan came from one of the tramways company's other directors, William Aitken, a man who would later play an important role in Purchas's financial affairs.

Not long after, Purchas had the misfortune to be involved in a nasty accident. He was travelling home along Karangahape Rd in his carriage with one of his sons, when some nails pulled from the carriage shaft. The severe twist then caused the horse to stumble and fall heavily. The carriage rolled forward, hitting an iron guard rail surrounding a tree before overturning and skidding to a halt. Purchas and his son were thrown out onto the roadway. It could have been a major blow as Purchas received a solid knock to the temple and serious bruising. Christmas that year, 1883, was spent recuperating at home and reviewing progress on his new Karangahape Rd building.

The economic storm clouds were still gathering on the horizon but few people were heeding the warning signs … including an inexorable downward trend in the number of new companies being registered.

Nevertheless, it was still a 'red-letter day' for the whole Purchas family when the magnificent Karangahape Rd block was finally opened in 1884, fully tenanted at top market rates. The return on such capital invested was still said to be 12-13% or more.

One of those new tenants was a very reputable chemist and apothecary, dispensing drugs and chemicals, and thus maintaining the link to medical services which had been there since the first Gundry chemist shop opened in the late 1840s.

By August, the first stage of the city's new tramway was also ready – up Queen St and Hobson St, then past Purchas's new building and his other property in Ponsonby Rd, and on to the reservoir. Each tram was pulled by two horses and could accommodate 49 passengers at 3d a fare. At last the tramways company had another income stream, even if it was initially only a trickle.

The Purchas building in Auckland's Karangahape Rd, built in 1883-84, one of the town's most impressive buildings in its day, as it looked 136 years later, in 2019.
TINA FRANTZEN

But this important event could not make up for the lack of land sales at St Heliers, which were now grinding to a halt. Still the penny did not drop, either for borrower or lender – even when only £80,000 of the £125,000 original share capital had been paid up, and the New Zealand & River Plate Land Mortgage Company came to the party on the balance, covered by substantial mortgages on six large allotments at St Heliers.

The land companies were not the only ones quietly drifting into trouble on the back of so much "risk" capital. A couple of gold companies reported increasingly poor results and even failed to pay a dividend. Although there were fewer companies being formed, their share issues suddenly became a hard sell and were poorly subscribed. Undersubscription added very quickly to a sudden change in mood around Auckland. When some other companies began reporting losses, like the blue-chip Northern Steamship Company, the sudden loss of confidence developed into wide-eyed amazement, doubt and then fright. Spending everywhere was curtailed, calls on unpaid shares began, retail sales slowed, wages fell, stock accumulated, discounting followed, and business confidence crumbled. Almost in the blink of an eye, the fight for survival had begun.

Like all the other landlords in Auckland, Purchas was soon under pressure from his Karangahape Rd tenants to reduce rents as their own sales and incomes fell away. Auckland's shopkeepers, goods stores and trading merchants were the first to feel the real heat. While Purchas had funded his building mostly by debt, at least he would have been reassured that he had other assets to cover part of that debt. And he still had a high income from his medical services, although his daughters continued to write of his "benevolence to everyone", meaning he probably was still not collecting all monies owed, or even charging the less well-off. But as the city's financial crisis developed, he was still in a better position than most, or so he thought, to ride out the initial strife.

Only 24 months earlier, businesses all over Auckland had thought nothing of borrowing heavily, at rates around 10-12%, to "take advantage of the rapidly growing trade opportunities" – opportunities which had simply failed to materialise. Literally within months, as Professor Stone recorded in his landmark book on the city's depression of the 1880s, "confidence was so seriously undermined not only in New Zealand but also in London.... that leading businessmen like J C Firth, Alfred Buckland, Thomas Morrin, James Williamson, Russell were struggling now too, under crushing interest burdens".[289]

Despair to hope

An occasion such as the one Purchas was invited to in February 1885 might, therefore, have come as a pleasant diversion. Together with Bishop Cowie, Purchas was asked to help officiate at the consecration of St Bride's Church on the hill in Mauku. When he and Selwyn had opened it a quarter of a century earlier, a full-time minister could not be provided. Selwyn then decided to make the church available to other denominations, thus delaying consecration until they could appoint a minister. Purchas's impact in the early days of settlement in the area (immediately before the outbreak of war) was recounted, including his influence on behalf of Governor Grey in negotiating the deal with local Māori for the road between Mauku-Patumahoe and Drury.

Further privilege was extended to Purchas that year (1885) when Cowie appointed him as a church "assessor", one of a few responsible for the final assessment (via examination and interview) of new ordinands for the ministry.

As the share market dipped, businesses collapsed and a mini avalanche of bankruptcies ensued (both private and corporate), the inevitable recriminations began. Banks started to press for overdraft reductions or total repayments. Mortgagee sales soon followed.

The City of Auckland Tramways and Suburban Land Co, itself in serious

---

289 R C J Stone, *Makers of Fortune*, p 66

Another Heritage NZ Grade I building, the Purchas church of St Bride's, photographed in 1887 by Josiah Martin. Still in active use today, the church was built in 1861 and remains one of Purchas's pleasing designs.
CRISPE FAMILY COLLECTION

difficulty, finally made the call on its thousands of unpaid shares. Its tramways business was doing well, except that all the cash proceeds were going to pay the company's enormous interest bills. Any thought of dividends for the shareholders was permanently shelved.

Then, when his own income dropped to half what it was a few months earlier, Purchas found himself "in great straits", as he described it. "I think I ought to have filed for bankruptcy," he wrote later.[290] He confessed his situation to his family and solicitor because he wanted to protect Olivia's large financial interest in the Pitt St home and land. But he was overruled and, instead, reluctantly conceded to taking out additional private mortgages on Challinor House and the Karangahape Rd building late in 1885 and again in 1886. The latter mortgage – arranged after the Auckland Savings Bank wanted its money back – was to none other than William Aitken, his fellow tramways director and trustee of the Auckland Savings Bank. Aitken had made a fortune in his own real estate dealings, still retained large investments in several areas and was apparently confident of riding things out himself.

Cutting back drastically at home, Arthur and Olivia managed to pay their mounting interest bills, and the final £1000 call on his tramways shares,

290 ATL, MS11116; A G Purchas letters.

before getting slightly behind. "We thought of giving up," he said. "But Arthur [his son][291] and wife asked to come and live with us and help pay the interest." Arthur Jnr had recently completed his medical training and had just married Evelyn Morse, so the arrangement suited them all. Arthur and Evelyn moved into one of the vacant homes on the Pitt St site and he took rooms in the Victoria Arcade in Queen St and began his own practice.

When the Bank of New Zealand could not pay a dividend in 1887, the rest of New Zealand finally sat up and took notice. The downturn experienced by Auckland businessmen was one thing – but the impact of their rash decisions on the rest of the country was another matter entirely.

As others began falling around him, Purchas's personal circumstances must have been a heavy burden – more so when, as a priest and spiritual advisor, he was called on to raise the spirits of so many of his business colleagues and friends, themselves now facing ruin and despair. Even Sir Frederick Whitaker was not immune. His eldest son took his own life in the Auckland Club one day in 1887, unable to face the humiliation of losing everything after joining the race for property.

These times were probably the most challenging of Purchas's entire life, even more than the desperate days of the war, his times of deprivation in Onehunga and the deaths of his children.

But in the midst of despair, with his own financial situation also crumbling before his eyes, it seems scarcely believable what Purchas was able to do next. In his letters at the time, there is no hint of recrimination or anger, given his precarious financial situation. Instead, his profound faith and ability to draw on an inner strength to "get on and sort things out for himself" came to the fore.

Next invention

His long-standing interest in technology had also encompassed the workings of engines and power plants, whether steam or electricity – or, in its latest form, from the internal combustion of explosive hydrocarbon fuels. The first primitive internal combustion engines had actually been designed much earlier in the century and the general principles of combining cylinder, fuel, controlled combustion, piston, crankshaft and driveshaft were well established before the 1870s. But the idea Purchas had been mulling over involved an ingenious design to improve the means of mixing the fuel more efficiently with the air in the combustion process. He rightly had grasped the idea that the efficiency

---

291   This son, Arthur Challinor Purchas, or A C Purchas, later specialised in ophthalmology.

and power of any internal combustion motor depended to a high degree on two things – the ratio of the air to fuel mixture and the means of automatically regulating this mixture at its optimum level, at varying speeds or as more fuel is introduced.

When Purchas had nutted out his idea, he called on well-qualified engineer John Friend to help him design and make the actual working parts, put together a working engine and conduct the necessary trials. It is not proven but Purchas probably funded the work himself when he first moved to Karangahape Rd and had the money available. But now, in 1887, desperately needing another source of income and far enough ahead with his design to be convinced of its potential, he decided to take the plunge.

Friend had connections in Australia and the pair decided that, if they wanted the engineering world to take notice, they should register a patent for the invention in that country first. Their tests and final calculations proved successful and amid concerns about his and New Zealand's financial situation, Purchas went to see his lawyer about applying for another patent.

After another six or seven months' work, Application for Patent No 5954 was finally lodged in the Australian patent offices in Melbourne on July 7, 1888. It read:

"Arthur Guyon Purchas, surgeon and John Edward Friend, engineer, both of Auckland, New Zealand, for improvements in hydrocarbon motors."

The description of their invention was given as follows:

"Our invention relates to that class of motor in which a mixture of hydrocarbon vapour or gas and air is admitted through suitable openings or ports into a cylinder where it is ignited ... and the objects of our invention are to produce a simple and efficient motor of this class and to provide improved means for mixing hydrocarbon vapour or gas with air and for supplying such mixture automatically to the said motor and for automatically regulating the supply of mixture to the cylinder of the motor."[292]

A slightly amended version was resubmitted a month later through their attorney in Melbourne, Edward Waters. The final document was a comprehensive six-page affair, with another 10 illustrations and detailed drawings of the individual engine parts. The application initially went into the system before Purchas and Friend were finally notified in June the following year that it would be heard that month, after any objections had been received.

What happened next remains something of a mystery ... but it seems likely there was some objection, perhaps from an engineer with a similar idea, and a

292 Original patent papers courtesy of the Victorian State Library – Patent Gazette, Aug 17, 1888.

final patent was never granted. An early family version of the story, however, was that someone, probably a disappointed John Friend, "absconded with the original plans", still convinced of their potential. Indeed, some 20 years later, a new patent application was lodged by John Friend, then described as an engineer of Annandale in Sydney, for a "rotary steam-fired engine", using the same principles as the Purchas/Friend design. Five years later, Friend surfaced again, this time in Auckland, with an application for another patent involving a "rotary engine operated by the firing of an explosive mixture".

In a letter written some time later to his brother-in-law in England, Purchas's description of his invention, in far less technical terms, underlines just how far advanced his understanding was of the internal combustion process. His concept might even loosely be described as a forerunner of a simple fuel injection or regulating system, which introduced the carburettor. He described it like this: "It is quite a new kind in which the power is developed by the ignition of a mixture of air and hydrocarbon. It is simple in the extreme and can be applied to a great variety of purposes. One is now being constructed for tramcar traction. It can also be used with perfect safety in coal mines troubled with fire because there is no external fire whatever."

Surgery continues

One minute Purchas was a mechanical engineer and inventor, and the next minute he was a surgeon again. At the same time as he had been putting the final touches to his patent application, Purchas was called on urgently at his rooms by Mr and Mrs Grindrod, the parents of a 14-year-old boy named Charles. They were referred by their local doctor, who was deeply concerned about what he thought was a large abscess in the boy's lower abdomen. When Purchas examined him, however, he quickly determined the real problem was that the "abscess" was in fact a tumour blocking the bowel. "I considered the case very dangerous," Purchas wrote, "and I informed the boy's mother that I believed the only chance of saving him was by an operation." He consulted with two other doctors, including his son Arthur Challinor, and at 5pm that same day, the boy was put under chloroform in an operation to remove the tumour.

On performing the laparotomy – the opening up of the abdominal cavity under the muscles – the tumour was located in its dangerous position and lanced. Purchas noted that "more than a pint of offensive material" was removed without any disturbance to surrounding organs. The accepted medical procedure for such an operation at the time was then to pack and close the wound and leave it to heal. Instead, again using his own technique, Purchas inserted a tube drain before closing the large incision with his fine iron-wire sutures. The unconventional procedure was not considered sound practice at the time. For Purchas and the boy's family, however, it proved 100% safe and effective. A smaller abscess, located where the initial incision had been made, was also treated and three weeks later – after continued attention to the draining process and hygiene – all was well again. To the Grindrod family, it was a miracle.

Elsewhere in the city, some of its wealthiest men were succumbing to the clutches of the depression. Josiah Firth, James Williamson, Thomas Morrin and J M Clark, the former mayor, were all engulfed by their debts. Morrin and Clark were, like Purchas, directors on the tramways board.

Morrin had been an enthusiastic promoter of the New Zealand Iron and Steel Company, which had invited Purchas and others out to Onehunga to see the Manukau iron sands being turned into iron ore. The scrip issued for this company would, like so many others, be worthless just three years later.

The effects on the general populace were also severe. As jobs were lost, families were torn apart when the menfolk opted to try their luck digging for gum, or scratching for grains of gold in the mounds of rubble left by the heavy machinery around Thames. The charitable institutions were only able to provide minimal shelter to deserted wives and children. Soup kitchens were the new norm.

As the bankruptcy hearings continued and the company meetings descended into verbal recriminations, the tramways company finally began its own slide into insolvency. Purchas's shares were now worthless. There was no hope of recovery. When Arthur and Olivia started to fall behind once again with their interest payments on Challinor House, the suggestion arose – possibly this time from Olivia herself – that they should write to her brother, William, in England and explain their plight. Things were desperate now. Perhaps he might be interested in loaning them the money to clear the Challinor House mortgage and take security himself over the property. In this way, Purchas reasoned, William might accept a lower interest rate than their current 10% – something they would be able to manage far more easily. And they would be able to stay in Pitt St, which the family considered absolutely vital to maintaining Purchas's medical practice and income.

Arthur's son wrote first to his Uncle William in May 1888. William had asked him to provide "some particulars," probably after an approach from Olivia a few months earlier. It must have been an excruciating and stressful wait for a reply, given that mail between England and New Zealand still took weeks by steamer via North America.

"We have passed through a very trying time," young Arthur wrote in something of an understatement. "I longed to ask for your advice but did not feel justified in troubling you." He explained the importance of retaining the Pitt St home, saying "that apart from the actual loss of the property, my father would lose the stand he has from which he works his practice, and that would mean a very serious loss … and there is no knowing what the result might be".

He went on to describe the property and the rents being received from the cottages on the site, and asked William if he would be interested in loaning them £3980 at 5%. Then, for good measure, he added that the trams passed the house every 10 minutes and a new wharf was nearing completion at the far end of the street.

Arthur Snr was apparently in Thames at this time, visiting his lawyer son Charles – and possibly also talking to George Holdship, at his Tapu mill, about whether he had any interest in buying back his original home on the Karangahape Rd property.

When Purchas returned, he also put pen to paper in another long letter to William, explaining their predicament and then briefing him on his new invention – saying that "he still hoped to get enough out of our new patented motor to redeem all" and that he was intending to apply for patents in America, France and Germany, as well as locally. Then, almost as an aside, and with a hint of embarrassment, Purchas suggested he could manage very well if William could "obtain the necessary sum at say 5%". He closed his letter by adding that "we live very carefully and pay for what we have as we get it, but are a very happy and united family, thank God … and have much joy".[293]

Just to add to Arthur and Olivia's worries at this time, came the news that their son-in-law Charles Cooke, the senior engineer at the tramways company, had lost his job and was about to lose his home. The "arrangement" concerning their Glen Orchard home had been under serious threat for the past year and Purchas had actually registered a caveat on the property in December 1886 to protect his own interest, probably as a result of a family guarantee. A year later as the tramways debacle continued to unfold, the Cookes were finally forced out. The Glen Orchard property was transferred, firstly out of its original tramways ownership to Cooke and then, on the same day, November 23, 1887, to Purchas, presumably at a bargain-basement price, albeit with another mortgage.

Whether a bargain or not, Purchas must have been very unhappy about having one more serious financial complication to deal with, let alone

---

293   ATL, MS 11116; also Purchas family letters.

the concern he and Olivia would have felt for Cooke and daughter Lizzie's situation. But one later report throws some doubt on the case, referring to Cooke "absconding to Australia" following some problem involving him and a terminated apprenticeship at the tramways company.[294] Whatever those circumstances, several months later it was one of the other sons-in-law who came to Purchas's rescue.

This time it was daughter Edith and her husband, Frederic Brookfield, who had recently joined his father's law firm to form Brookfield & Son. As soon as he could, Purchas was able to onsell the Glen Orchard property to them in 1890 – specifically to Edith – with the help of two new mortgages held by Henry Brett's son James, and auctioneer William Cochrane.

While all this was going on, and while he waited for a response from William, Purchas continued to deal with other important matters involving the city's health, on an individual and public level. The individual concerned this time was a Mrs Wymer, who was suffering from a serious ovarian tumour or cyst. Assisted by his son and Dr Hooper, the patient was sedated by chloroform at 3pm, the tumour was drained and severed, and everything was cleanly cauterised, stitched and put back in place with the help of the Purchas clamp. After the initial incision was stitched, it was covered with soft dry linen over the usual carbolic putty. Within an hour, Mrs Wymer was awake and reporting no pain at all. Purchas's notes say she enjoyed her breakfast of smoked fish two days later, and within the week she was sitting in her chair, "going well and in excellent spirits".

On the public health agenda, it was the danger of serious pollution to the town's water supply via the municipal abattoir near Western Springs which concerned Purchas. The abattoir's operators, he learned, had simply been ploughing all their slaughterhouse offal into the ground. Purchas wrote to the mayor and council, saying such nuisances had long been a threat to the city's health. He suggested that the whole area now needed to be trenched and that he also considered the disposal of the offal to be extremely wasteful. By proper application of heat, he said, and the use of dry earth, the whole refuse matter could be converted into valuable manure and sold. It took some time but eventually the problem was solved when the entire abattoir was moved.

Karangahape Rd sale

Unfortunately no record exists of William's response to the family's letters

---

294   See Ohinemuri Regional History Journal #6, 1966.

about a possible loan. Whether he declined to loan the money or whether he was simply unable to assist at that time is unknown. Times were not buoyant in England either. Whatever happened, no family loan was forthcoming. It must have been with great reluctance – and probably after long discussions with their sons and the Brookfield family lawyers – that Arthur and Olivia then decided to sell the Purchas building in Karangahape Rd and take whatever they could get for it.

By Christmas that year, 1889, Purchas had the bones of a deal sorted with his old colleague William Aitken, to whom he was already partially mortgaged. While the properties, including the home behind the shops, were fully tenanted and apparently paying their way, the risks associated with further interest rate rises, maintenance costs and even loss of the current tenants were too great for Purchas to bear. We don't know the sale price or whether he came out of the deal with any cash, but if he did, it would not have been much. By January 25, 1890, the mortgages had been squared off, conveyancing had been completed and it was time to move on once again.

The bankruptcies around Auckland continued apace. More and more previously wealthy men – who had been lured into the sticky web of fanciful dreams on borrowed money – fell by the wayside, impoverished or broken. The tramways company fiasco had also come to its inevitable end, as Purchas stepped down from its board. Almost completely insolvent, its only realisable assets – tramlines, horses and trams – were taken over by the Bank of New Zealand Estates Company, together with the valuable concession for an electric tramway in Auckland. Purchas had been pushing the case for electricity instead of horses up until the last moment (as late as the company's 1889 AGM) as a possible way out of insolvency, but to no avail. Ironically, the collapse of the tramways company would finally bring his vision to reality under its new owners. It was just unfortunate that it would no longer be his to realise.

With that worry off his plate, Purchas was now fast approaching his 70th birthday and the prospect of a well-earned retirement. Five of his adult children were married and grandchildren were appearing. His sons had not only survived the depression but were reasonably well established, one as a surveyor, two in medicine and another in law. He still had three daughters living at home, in their twenties, and Amy was in the process of finally setting her wedding date after a very long engagement.

Arthur and Olivia retained their property in Ponsonby Rd and the vacant plots in Hillsborough and Onehunga, which were either freehold or rented to cover a couple of small mortgages. If he stayed healthy and kept working in his medical practice, Purchas clearly figured he should still be able to keep up with the interest payments on the main Challinor House mortgage by renting out the other three cottages and homes on the same Pitt St property. They included the original brick house at number 52, still able to be divided from the main three-storey home by its two locked doors. These houses – occupied in earlier years by others in the family who were now in homes of their own – brought in almost £300 a year.

He and Olivia could survive by living extremely frugally, but still better than most around them. There were many things that still needed to be done in the church and community – and this was where he would focus his attention once more.

CHAPTER 20

Contributions continue

It was 1890 and the Auckland depression still had three or four more years to run before the city could shake itself loose and rejoin the national 'highway of progress'. There were several more trials and tribulations to be endured as it happened, including a frightening run on funds at the Auckland Savings Bank in 1893. Another disaster was only averted by a couple of trustees (with the support of local trading banks) who stumped up with the money to pay out the first worried clients and thereby assured the rest of the community that all was in order. The alarm bells switched off just as quickly as they had begun to ring.

The streets of Auckland, however, were still dotted with empty shops, warehouses to let and notices of property to rent at prices unheard of only a few years earlier. In some cases, weekly rentals were half what could have been obtained in 1884. But Purchas's decisions to buy his property in what he considered to be the most advantageous and affordable locations, now paid off. While the rents he collected on the Pitt St houses had halved, he at least had no apparent problem getting tenants – being close to town and on the main tramway route under its new owners.

Elsewhere in New Zealand, while the worldwide recession inevitably produced a stagnant economy with poorer working conditions and lower pay, the times also produced major breakthroughs ... notably the innovative refrigerated meat trade to Europe, which "radically changed the nature of farming in New Zealand".[295] The country was no longer so dependent on wool and timber.

But in Auckland at least, moderation and thrift were still to the fore. Women began entering the wider workforce, beyond domestic services, in many cases trying to make ends meet in the harsh economic climate. Unfortunately, they were followed by children, some as young as 10, after only the barest of education. While trying to deal with the effects of the depression, the new Liberal Party was also helping to change the face of New Zealand with its

---

295   M King, *The Penguin History of New Zealand*, p 237.

economic and social reforms under John Ballance and Dick Seddon. These were the days of party politics, women's rights, land and tax reform, and parliamentary representation for Māori.

The long period of depression did, however, produce much of value for the city of Auckland in particular. Many of the buildings and enterprises – despite ruining a fair number of the individuals and partners who established them – laid the foundation for a period of stunning growth and development a few years later. The tramway system linking city and suburbs, the waterfront reclamation, new businesses like the sugar refinery and the freezing works, and imposing bank buildings and mercantile premises all survived to leave a rich legacy. The human cost had been high, but it had not all been in vain.

With the hard times still not over, Purchas had little choice but to remain at work despite his advancing years. There would not be any relaxed, cosy twilight years for him. He was happy to continue working in his ideally located consultation rooms in Pitt St; and with his doctor son, Arthur, also establishing a strong reputation, the Purchas medical name carried a fair amount of clout.

Mixed in with his usual medical routines came continuing calls on his surgical expertise, such as a post-mortem in 1891 on a 70-year-old widow who had died unexpectedly in Howick. His notes on the examination make for fascinating reading: "There was a very firm almost ligamentous band from the right side of the liver stretching across to a fold of small intestine two or three inches from the pyloric end of the stomach and in the band were two small cysts containing two hard bodies which I have preserved ..."

Purchas continued his work as a prominent Justice of the Peace in Auckland, and as the Government medical officer for the destitute children's home. He remained a council member of the Auckland Institute and the Auckland Society of Arts, where he often served as chairman. And he was still a senior member of the Church of England synod and Bishop's assessor.

He also became heavily involved with Bishop Cowie, and one or two others, in discussing the possibility of establishing a permanent "institute" for blind people in Auckland and New Zealand. A few months earlier, in 1889, Cowie had called a meeting of those keen to help the many sightless citizens in the community. Out of that meeting came a group known as the Association of the Friends of the Blind, which included Purchas. They soon rented a small house in Parnell and appointed a teacher specifically to help teach blind children and young adults. The idea was to find ways of educating and integrating sightless people into mainstream society, something of a revolutionary but long-overdue concept in those days. Initially, the aim was to provide the blind with some elementary knowledge and to start teaching them a few simple handcrafts which they could use to earn a living or otherwise partially support themselves.

The association was influential enough to attract the attention and support of notable government ministers, local politicians, one or two philanthropists and, eventually, sections of the wider Auckland community. In July 1890, the association merged with the Jubilee Institute for the Blind – so named to mark the 50 years since the signing of the Treaty.[296] Once more, Purchas was a main founding member, beginning another lengthy commitment – of 16 years – to what became one of New Zealand's most enduring and important charitable and social institutions.

Within months, Purchas would be heavily involved in the institute's activities. He began singing classes, which were quickly found to be of great therapeutic value and enjoyment for the sightless children and adults. To help his pupils understand and read the music better, he developed a variation of his original singing book – this time using a kind of musical Braille "ladder" to help them find notes and learn the principles of harmony. His appeal to the public for a new harmonium was answered immediately and netted a piano as well. And Arthur Jnr was persuaded to provide unpaid medical services as the eye and ear doctor for the blind.

But Purchas's contribution to the Institute for the Blind, as it was known originally, did not end there. His inventive skills quickly came to the fore, as he devised various ways and means to make it easier for the blind to learn new skills and to enjoy leisure pursuits previously regarded as beyond their reach.

One of Auckland's prominent boatbuilders at the time – Charles (Chas) Bailey – was brought in especially by Purchas to build a full-size version of a model boat he had been working on. It incorporated a unique propulsion system devised just for the sightless, with a conventional propellor, shaft and gearing all operated by "two levers running the length of the boat, fore and aft". The system enabled a party of six or eight blind crew – assisted by a sighted helmsman – to work the levers and power the boat forward.

Such was the fun derived from the boat that the Parnell residents asked Purchas to invent a system to help them go fishing. The result was an attachment for the safe handling of the hooks, which they passed to the sighted skipper to bait and then returned to him to remove from their catch – all without being spiked by flapping snapper. Purchas's attachment was so successful that even sighted people wanted to use it. The *New Zealand Herald* reported that "the invention is now to be patented in another country".[297]

Possibly his most important invention at the institute during the 1890s

---

296 It also helped to mark the year that Bishop Cowie was appointed Primate of New Zealand.
297 Papers Past, *New Zealand Herald*, Jan 13, 1899.

was the "Purchas Braille Stereotype". It was a small but highly effective machine which enabled the residents to do their own embossing onto metal or stiff cardboard plates, using the familiar Braille system. Purchas came up with the idea initially as a way for the residents to print their own music – but it was quickly adapted to print reading material and books as well.

His design basically comprised a desk or table with a series of levers worked by the foot, linked to a rigid handle over the middle of the desk and above the blank plates to be embossed. The invention included a standard Braille writing frame, set up on a movable guide, so the transcriber could read continuously with his hands from the original and translate or copy simultaneously onto the new plates, via the feet.[298]

As a result of his work in helping to establish the institute, and his teaching, medical and all-round-support role, special tributes were paid after his passing. "Through all the intervening years, Dr Purchas took a very keen interest in the Institute's work, more particularly in the children. Week by week, until advancing age rendered it necessary for him regretfully to relinquish it, he conducted a singing class and his pupils of the present and past generations will never forget his kindly, sympathetic and successful efforts on their behalf." A special tablet remains on a wall in Parnell today in his memory.

Women's affairs

In March 1891, 10 years to the day since their engagement was announced, Amy Purchas and Henry Roche were finally wed in a crowded St Sepulchre with Purchas and Archdeacon Dudley officiating. The reception was held at Challinor House and the couple then sailed off to Sydney en route to London to meet the bridegroom's family. In the intervening years, Henry – known in the family as Harry – had established himself first as a surveyor and then as an engineer. He would return to New Zealand to become a senior and highly respected figure at the Waihi gold mine.[299]

The following two years were relatively uneventful for Arthur and Olivia as the pair worked to support their remaining daughters at home and put aside money for some form of retirement, should it ever happen. Now in his early seventies, he even muttered to his daughters that maybe he should step down from the institute council sometime soon and "let someone younger step up". This he finally did, in February 1892, although he remained an ordinary member.

---

298 An early sample from this Purchas machine is held in the Auckland Museum Library.
299 Henry Roche later became one of New Zealand's best known engineers, responsible for the design and construction of the first hydroelectric power generator on the Waikato River's Horahora Rapids.

In June, he chaired the Society of Arts AGM in the new art gallery building, reporting to the 176 honorary and working members that the society's annual exhibition had been a great success, their involvement in the schools had generated some meritorious work and, better still, the society had £102 in the bank. Purchas was re-elected a patron and committee member with Sir George Grey now the president, and Sir William Fox and Henry Brett the vice presidents.

The death in August of another of the Gundrys, Olivia Grosse, hit the Purchas family hard, especially since they had buried her daughter only a few months earlier. Purchas conducted the service at Purewa while the Purchas daughters, Edith, Lizzie and Gertrude, stood by silently. All would have been thinking about Olivia's children.

In recent years, Olivia had fallen on hard times. She died penniless, of consumption, in wretched circumstances and without any will. Once again Purchas was called in and, with daughter Edith Brookfield, arranged to take care of two of Olivia's three remaining children. Aged 13 and 11, they were homeless and had no other family to care for them. Edith and husband Frederic Brookfield became foster parents to the two girls, taking them in to their home at Glen Orchard.

With his medical work again building up into a reliable and reasonable source of income, Arthur and Olivia began to think about the possibility of a final return visit to England. They had been in New Zealand now for some 48 years, and were conscious of the physical demands of such a trip, given that Olivia was approaching her 70th birthday. They had many family and friends to see (perhaps for the last time), including Olivia's brother Will, who was not in good health, and Sarah Selwyn, still alive and in her late eighties.

Thoughts about the trip were put aside briefly, however, when Purchas was called on to perform what was probably his most serious – and most problematic – abdominal operation. He was 73 and his female patient had a history of ill health going back some 20 years. After his usual thorough examination and diagnosis of serious ovarian disease, Purchas wrote in his notes that he was "sorely perplexed" about performing an operation. He had grave doubts, not only about the extent of the disease, but also the patient's ability to cope with chloroform.

At this point, there must have been some serious discussion with the two doctors assisting him (Hooper and Dawson) about the usefulness or otherwise of proceeding. Purchas was perhaps persuaded by his colleagues, or possibly the woman's family, that they should go ahead, despite the patient's slim chances of survival. He noted simply that, after the discussion, "I then found it necessary to go on".

After making the incision and opening up the abdomen, he found extensive tumours on the left ovary, "the largest containing about 4 gallons of fluid" – an enormous sac which was nevertheless drained successfully. Other cysts "could scarcely be got at" and had to be left, although he did manage to drain another two "after more than an hour of incessant labour". Then, using the Purchas clamp, he removed as many of the other adhesions as he could, including a final small tumour or sac "the size of a pigeon's egg". It must have been a massive effort, and almost certainly a last-ditch attempt – one which Purchas felt compelled to make on his patient's behalf, despite the growing feeling of futility felt by all three doctors.

That evening, although his patient was cheerful and in little pain, Purchas was not confident about her recovery. He stayed with her all night "but the sinking increased and the question of transfusion occupied my serious consideration". His final notes reflected the grave dilemma. "In the face of the extensive adhesions or tumours, and the absence of any efficient help [for a transfusion], I did not think I was justified in re- opening the wound ... and without that, it was not likely that any permanent good result would follow. I was also entirely without the means of performing transfusion and should have required to go away in order to procure any." Although the end result was clearly inevitable – death from irreversible and serious ovarian cancer – it was the only unsuccessful conclusion in his 13 groundbreaking operations.

While Arthur and Olivia were thinking about their long-awaited trip to England, the opportunity of a shorter sea voyage came up suddenly that same year (1894) ,when Bishop Cowie asked them to join him and a small party he was leading to Norfolk Island on the Melanesian Mission's ship, *Southern Cross*. They enjoyed the chance to test their sea legs and to see some of the results achieved in the islands by "Johnnie" Selwyn, the former Bishop of Melanesia. This was the same Johnnie whose life, as a very small boy, Purchas had saved during the typhoid fever outbreak at Purewa in 1847.

Back in Auckland a few weeks later, Purchas had determined to make another stand at the upcoming Auckland synod on a subject which had long been important to him – the rights of women in the church and society. It was a topic on which he was well informed and it did not take much for him to make his mark.

Purchas had been one of the earliest 'promoters' of women deserving a greater say in church and public life, going back many years to the 1860s (long before female enfranchisement came to the Dominion). Back then, much to Purchas's chagrin, Selwyn's church had deferred any stand on the issue as far as church affairs were concerned. The wider debate over universal women's suffrage, which followed in the 1880s, had been a long and often bitter one. Now, following the triumphant women's suffrage petition and the 1893 Electoral Act, the hot topic of women's participation and recognition in church affairs was back on the agenda, particularly in Auckland, where Purchas's good friend Bishop Cowie presided.

Purchas's speech was typically direct. The question of women's rights to an equal say in all affairs – not just those of the church – was one he said "would have to be considered all over the world". It was not wise just to say: "Let women keep their places." He asked the synod to consider whether women had ever received justice in this matter, referring to the first time he had raised the subject nearly 30 years earlier on behalf of women who were doing much of the administrative work, but having no say on church boards and synods.

Purchas said he had no doubt that it was "both right and expedient" that this right should now be granted to women and he could see no reason to counter the granting of the privilege. "At present," he said, "they let the women do the work but give them no voice in the management." The following debate got somewhat heated when others attending the synod thought the matter should be decided by the whole Anglican Church at its international Lambeth Conference (not due until 1897) – not by the Auckland clergy.

When another local priest stood to say such a move would undermine the church and society, the Women's Franchise League, in full support of Purchas's stand, saw red. "This is one of the most mendacious libels ever uttered against women in the colony," they raged. The discussion which followed in the press created massive interest. While a delay in any decision was perhaps predictable inside a conservative local church, the fire was finally lit and the outcome was inevitable. Purchas had more than played his part in the significant changes that would follow a short time later.

UK visit

By 1895, day-to-day life within the Purchas household was at last assuming a sense of "normality". The language of recovery was now being used as the depression in Auckland finally began to lift. It seemed a good time to think seriously about that trip to England. The question may well be asked … how could Arthur and Olivia afford such a trip, probably of three or four months' duration, with no income coming in from the practice? There were a number of likely ways. Firstly, Purchas was probably able to save some money from his practice during the last three years by living a simple and thrifty life at home.

Secondly, he may have either sold, or been able to remortgage, his property on Ponsonby Rd. Thirdly, some assistance with accommodation and local travel while in England would have been offered by one or more of his children. Arthur Challinor was in Edinburgh at the time and their daughter Mil,[300] was on an extended visit staying in Liverpool with friends. Olivia also had relatives in Liverpool with whom she would have stayed.

The real answer, however, was that Purchas was able to obtain either a free or heavily discounted passage by working as the ship's surgeon on both voyages. Their travel was arranged on the New Zealand Shipping Company's ship, the SS *Tongariro*, a three-masted, iron steam ship which carried both passengers and freight. Arthur and Olivia sailed from Onehunga to Wellington in mid-March 1895 on the coastal steamer *Penguin* and boarded the SS *Tongariro* in the capital for the trip to London. The social pages of the *New Zealand Herald* noted their departure and wished them the usual "prosperous voyage and speedy return". Just two days out from Wellington, however, Purchas was already earning his fare. An elderly male passenger, out on deck in a heavy sea, was suddenly thrown to the deck by the ship's violent lurch. Among his injuries were two broken ribs. Despite Purchas's best endeavours – and reportedly having "received every attention from Dr Purchas" – the shock to the man's system proved too much and he passed away.

On arrival in England after an otherwise uneventful trip, Arthur and Olivia had an exciting and busy itinerary planned. It was sprinkled with family reunions and a couple of special invitations, particularly involving the Selwyn family and Cambridge University. Selwyn College, Cambridge, founded in 1882, just four years after George Selwyn's death (and obviously named after him), now had a new chapel, also funded by friends and admirers. William Gladstone, known as the GOM or "grand old man", had provided a new bell for the chapel and Purchas was hopeful of seeing both on his visit.

Their first stop was in Surrey at the family home of Silveracre, belonging to the Seth-Smiths. The priority was to meet the family of Hugh Seth-Smith, shortly to become the next of Purchas's sons-in-law via marriage to their 44-year-old eldest daughter, Emily. Seth-Smith, 47, was a very accomplished barrister and solicitor who had come to New Zealand in 1881, married and had risen to the senior rank of Auckland magistrate and Judge of the Native Land Court.[301] Purchas had multiple dealings with him over recent years concerning both land and church matters – when Seth-Smith was also serving on various Anglican Church bodies and trust boards. Seth-Smith had also served a term

---

300 Christened Ethel Mildred. Mil – or the Māori 'Miri' – was her family name.
301 He was also the first law lecturer at Auckland University and founding member of the University Council.

as president of the Auckland Institute in 1884. Sadly, his first wife had died earlier and for both families, the prospect of a possible union of the two was particularly pleasing.

From Surrey, Arthur and Olivia went north to meet up with daughter Mil, in Liverpool. This very large and bustling port city was also Olivia's home and where the pair had met when Arthur was surgeon at the Royal Liverpool Hospital. Here he was treated like royalty by the local university and hospital authorities, particularly by Rushton Parker – possibly, at this time, England's pre-eminent surgeon. He, like Purchas, was one of Joseph Lister's earliest disciples (a man whose work was now widely acknowledged). The two had a lot to discuss. Purchas was also invited to be an honoured guest at the ceremonial opening of the university's new Biological Hall. Olivia, meanwhile, spent precious time with her surviving brother and sister, William and Sarah – not having seen them since leaving Liverpool as a 21-year-old bride.[302]

In the meantime, their doctor son Arthur Challinor, who was completing more study at Edinburgh University, arranged another round of social activities, introductions and invitations. It might have proved almost too much for Olivia, however, because as they left Edinburgh, heading south to visit more relatives in Cumberland, she became unwell. Concerned for her welfare, Arthur decided to leave her with daughter Mil in Liverpool while he went on alone to attend two particularly special engagements. The first was to a meeting of the Melanesian Mission at Eton, Cambridge, where he was to provide a personal update on its activities following his own trip with Cowie to Norfolk Island.

But the main purpose of his visit to Cambridge was to see former bishop "Johnnie" Selwyn, now Sir John Selwyn (the second Master of Selwyn College), and his mother – the old lady herself, Sarah Selwyn.[303] The three enjoyed a weekend together at Sir John's residence in Cambridge where they reminisced about the early days at Purewa and the many experiences they had shared with George Augustus Selwyn, and discussed Purchas's more recent activities. Sir John, who was also honorary chaplain to Queen Victoria at the time, introduced Purchas to all the senior medical and theological men around Cambridge. And on the Sunday, Purchas (as an honoured VIP) was placed in a special seat for evensong in the beautiful King's College Chapel. It must have made for a memorable visit.

On leaving the Selwyns, Purchas had one more call to make. It was to see George and Sarah Selwyn's former nurse, Anna Stepley, the lady who had cared for their children at Purewa through thick and thin, half a century

---

302 William Challinor, a solicitor, died only eight months later, aged 75.
303 Sarah Selwyn was 86 at this time. She outlived Arthur Purchas, passing away, aged 98, in 1907.

ago. He spent two whole days trying to track her down. When he finally did so, he knocked on the door only to be advised by family members that she had unfortunately passed away just two days earlier. Nevertheless Purchas was later recorded as saying he had viewed the corpse and spent some time with the old lady's bereaved sister.

Inevitably, the more Purchas moved around, the more invitations he received to stay and meet people, and to relate his many experiences and stories from Britain's most far-flung colony. But his main objectives had been accomplished and with Olivia sufficiently recovered from her recent illness, the time had come to begin their long return voyage. They were back home in Pitt St at the end of September ready to resume their normal routines.

The E W Payton portrait of A G Purchas, painted for the Auckland Society of Arts Exhibition in 1895.
TINA FRANTZEN

Railway paper

Before they left for England, Purchas had been persuaded by the current president of the Society of Arts, E W Payton, to sit for a portrait. Payton was principal of the Elam School of Art and Purchas was happy for him to take it on – Payton's idea being that it would be shown at the society's main exhibition that year, alongside some new works by society members Charles Blomfield and L J Steele.[304] While undoubtedly Arthur and Olivia would have sought it out on their return, they had a more important personal milestone to think about. At Christmas, they would be marking 50 years of marriage with a major family celebration to organise.

Impending golden wedding anniversary or not, it was no surprise that on October 12, 1895 – having barely returned from overseas – Purchas was presenting another major paper at the Auckland Institute, this one entitled *The Railway and its Place in Social Economy*.[305] It was a very topical and somewhat

---

304 The Purchas portrait hangs today in St Peter's Church, Onehunga.
305 Refer to the Royal Society of New Zealand – Transactions & Proceedings, 1895: No 8.

contentious subject at the time and, having no doubt brought himself up to date while travelling around England only weeks before, Purchas was well qualified to express an opinion on the subject.

The paper was one of his best – well considered and expertly presented in clear and concise language. His aim was to focus on the place rail should occupy in what he called the "social economy" – and who should own what part of the entire network. While railways had started in most countries as new enterprises funded by private individuals, by this very process, he argued, they necessarily remained private property and the carrying or transport business became a very large private monopoly.

He said this was unavoidable because, quite properly, it had not been within the sphere of a government in those pioneering days to establish or fund a railway itself. And so, he explained, the idea of a railway as private property was "quite natural". But now, he said, railways, as the chief highways of traffic, ought to be the property of the people, just like the ordinary road. "The user must pay for the cost of transit of himself and his goods, but the road itself must be free."

He advocated a complete separation of cost between building and maintaining a railway line, and the traffic using it. The latter part he said – in a statement echoing many later problems involving New Zealand railway ownership and management – must be entirely independent of any political control, "a species of private ownership of the worst kind!" Instead, he said, the management of the transit of people and goods must be entrusted to the very best and most competent experts available. What he wanted to do now, he told the audience, was to get calm and reasonable consideration of the principle he had tried to set out.

If Purchas had not already been known for his many and varied dissertations on the subject of public transport, he might have been ignored. But he was not. Instead his presentation was reported as a useful and timely contribution to a key debate as New Zealand headed into the new century. It was a crucial time because the transport of goods by rail was becoming a vital part of the young nation's developing economy. And rail was also about to play an important role in the country's social fabric, connecting people and families who were previously reliant on horses or small coastal ships for transport.

Chapter 21

Final Years

The golden jubilee celebrations were a big family event, as was to be expected. Of the 14 Purchas children, 10 of the 11 surviving were there, together with no fewer than 23 grandchildren ranging in age from 20 down to tiny infants. Only Charles Cooke, Lizzie's husband, and Arthur and Olivia's son, Frederic, were absent. Frederic was completing his medical studies in Edinburgh[306] and Charles was still sadly elsewhere, probably in Australia.

Nine months later, in September 1896, Arthur Purchas turned 75. He still had a busy practice and was also travelling two or three times a week from Challinor House in Pitt St to the Institute for the Blind in Parnell or the Industrial Home in Mt Albert, where sick and destitute children needed his attention. In the evenings, he continued his consultations in the rooms at home and whenever clear of these, attended meetings of the Auckland Institute, the Society of Arts or the Fruitgrowers' Association, or engaged in his various choral and church activities.

Living at home in Challinor House with Arthur and Olivia were bachelor son Charles, a lawyer (presumably contributing to household costs), and daughters Gertrude and Emily. The entire Pitt St property of six acres, including a couple of smaller blocks formerly turned into lawn tennis courts, needed regular maintenance and upkeep. The original home connected to the main house was rented out, as were the smaller cottages behind Challinor House. And the family also had a vegetable garden, somewhat smaller now but still needing the usual daily care and attention. Pitt St itself had become a very busy thoroughfare, with its horse trams and general traffic adding to the noise, smells and atmosphere of a typical, late-19th-century Victorian city.

Clearly the burden of making the monthly mortgage payments for such a large property on time, and without penalty, began to tell about now, in spite of Purchas's reliable practice income. While he simply had no choice but to remain hard at work in the meantime, he also began to think about his options – in between the steady round of civic, cultural, medical, church and family duties and activities.

---

306   He was soon to graduate with a Bachelor of Medicine and Master of Surgery.

Arthur and Olivia on their 50th wedding anniversary, December 1895.
PURCHAS FAMILY FILES

He organised and led the music at the St John's College annual prize-giving the following year – in those days a significant ceremonial event attended by senior public or political dignitaries, mayors and even the Governor. He was re-elected a vice-president of the Society of Arts and remained constantly in demand for speaking engagements.

Then followed the marriage of daughter Emily to Hugh Seth-Smith at St Sepulchre, at the unusual time of 8am, with the reception held at Challinor House. The social pages of the day were full of the news, since not only were the groom and father of the bride well known, but the best man was Edmund Cowie, son of the Primate of New Zealand.

Whether it was the New Zealand & River Plate Land Mortgage Company which brought the matter of Challinor House to a head, or whether Arthur and Olivia initiated proceedings, is unknown and probably immaterial to the Purchas story. It is likely that the regular monthly mortgage payments finally became too much to bear. There had been a provision in the mortgage documents for a reduction in monthly interest of about 2% for "prompt and regular" payment. Perhaps Purchas had found it too difficult to fulfil that provision and was now paying the penalty. Perhaps the property itself had become too large to manage.

He first decided to sell three of the four vacant lots in Onehunga, which he had owned for the past 33 years. He did not need them anyway, now that his family were all mostly settled. The lots did not realise much but it all helped. Matters were then set in train during the winter of 1897 to finally make the big move and leave their Pitt St home of the last 17 years.

During the process he certainly had some of the best legal advice in Auckland freely available to him – early on from new son-in-law Hugh Seth-Smith (before he left with Emily for England), and from Frederic Brookfield and his son Charles.[307] By October, just three or four months later, Challinor House and its surrounding property was sold.[308] The family documents show the sale was settled over a few days – not all the various lots comprising the entire property having been under mortgage. Some of those smaller lots with separate titles were sold for sums of £132 and £268, still a far cry from their values of seven or eight years earlier. The original mortgage for the main property of Challinor House was for £3700 at interest rates of 10% and 9.5%. A deal was struck in which Olivia, as the title owner, agreed to allow the New Zealand & River Plate Land Mortgage Company to sell the property on her behalf, clear the mortgage and return £500 to her.

And while all this was going on in Auckland, on the other side of the world, son Frederic was getting married to Alice Cox in Gloucester. Olivia was happy that daughter Mil, still living in Liverpool, was able to represent them while they dealt with the Pitt St sale.

To Epsom

Arthur and Olivia's next move was to Epsom, on the corner of today's Manukau Rd and Clyde St. In those days, it was still a lightly populated area, comprising a combination of large and smaller homes, some with extensive gardens, many vacant lots and two dusty main roads – the Great South Rd leading to Ellerslie, Otahuhu and beyond, and the Onehunga Rd, as it was known then, being the main route to Onehunga. But it was relatively handy for Purchas's visits to Parnell. His main worry in moving out of Pitt St was whether he would be able to retain his medical clientele and deal with the

---

307 Charles formed a partnership in 1892 with Montagu Wynyard, the original partnership of today's Wynyard Wood law firm.

308 Challinor House remained a prominent Auckland property and a little later became the first maternity hospital in New Zealand, St Helens.

difficulty of getting to the city hospital, the orphans' home in Mt Albert and the areas of Newton, Ponsonby and St Mary's Bay, where so many of his long-standing family patients lived.

He did manage, however, to retain one advantage – his phone number 52. By good fortune, he was able to transfer it because the phone lines to the Onehunga Rd, and therefore the Clyde St area, had been connected about the same time as they were to his Pitt St residence.

The property itself, known as 'Flintoft', was a modest suburban house but with enough land for a small orchard and vegetable garden. Details of its purchase or lease are sketchy but it had been owned in the 1880s by a John Hancock who had the misfortune of seeing his original home, stuffed full of valuable English antique furniture, destroyed by fire. 'Flintoft' was the other smaller house on the property, a wooden bungalow with verandahs.

As soon as they were settled, Purchas immediately set about securing new rooms in the heart of the town, in Queen St, in a fellow doctor's surgery known as Haslett's. He placed advertisements in the Auckland papers publicising his "removal to the corner of Clyde St and Onehunga Rd" and with consultation times of 10-11am at Haslett's and 1-2pm at son Arthur's new rooms in Upper Symonds St. People would also be able to contact him by leaving messages at two chemist shops, in Karangahape Rd and Newmarket.

Letters from Olivia to Emily in England at the time give some indication of their new life in Epsom. "Your father had to go to town and Haslett's to keep two appointments this morning," she wrote, "otherwise he would have spent the holiday at home – over the books most likely." She spoke of bringing their fern house over from Pitt St and replanting the ferns in Epsom – and of Arthur planting the garden in between some rubbers of backgammon. Tellingly, in this same letter, Olivia gave the first hint that her own health may not have been quite so good ... "we are very grave and quiet. I am not merry enough to fight against it alone. I feel very much sobered down of late, what with influenza, the move here, and settling down ..."

A couple of weeks before Christmas, Frederic Purchas and wife Alice arrived back in Auckland on holiday, with his sister Mil, after their long stays in England and more recently in Australia, where Frederic had begun practising. A few days later, a group of nine senior Auckland doctors assembled in a private hospital in town to watch what was described as "an altogether unprecedented phenomenon". Three doctors from the same family were to perform an operation together. Arthur Challinor Purchas led the team, assisted by brother Frederic, while father Arthur was the anaesthetist, dispensing the chloroform. Having completed the operation successfully, Arthur Snr did the same for "a dear little girl while another surgeon re-fractured a badly set broken thigh bone and reset it," again with Arthur Challinor's help.

That Christmas, 1897, Purchas wrote to his daughter Emily Seth-Smith in England that "we have no money to spare and our move has very much reduced the opportunity of earning but has also in some measure, reduced our expenses, but I fear not in equal ratio". He said the casual consultations at the house in Pitt St – from which a good proportion of his income was derived – were at an end and those at Haslett's nowhere near made up for the loss. Clearly they were back to the hard times.

The following year, third son Claude was married[309] and it seems life in the Purchas home simply ran its course, thriftily but still happily. Gertrude stayed home at 'Flintoft' to manage the household while a continual stream of visitors, friends and family came up the path. Purchas managed to keep the wolf from the door by going to his two consultation rooms every day and by using his undoubted expertise in the garden – supported by Olivia who got used to hardly ever seeing him at home, except occasionally on the weekend. Her intimate and detailed diaries, of the days immediately before the turn of the century, throw some interesting light on their own lives and the wider Auckland society.[310]

Lucky escape

Purchas was also now (1898-99) regularly visiting and looking after several of his oldest and closest friends and acquaintances – people he had known since the very earliest days of the colony. Most were obviously of a similar age to himself, and increasingly infirm – people like the dying Colonel Haultain. Olivia noted on January 3 that Arthur went to see him, and returned to say "he was looking a little better". A day or so later, she reported that Charles's law partner, Montagu Wynyard, came to dinner to discuss something especially with Arthur, who did not arrive until dinner was half over. "He had been very busy," she wrote, "and there was a message for him to go to the North Shore as soon as he could."

Then in February, more excitement: "Arthur has had a narrow escape. He attempted to jump off the ferry steamer before the landing was fixed and fell between the pier and the ship. He held on to a rail by his hand and so kept himself from falling into the water. But he crushed his chest and back between

---

309   To Beatrice Eliott in October 1898.
310   AML, MS251.

the wharf and ship! Oh! I do wish he would not attempt such things," Olivia wrote.[311]

On Sundays, Purchas continued to participate in the early morning service at St Sepulchre with his friend Archdeacon Dudley, and also to help at St Mark's and St Matthew's. He would often take a service himself before calling in to see patients on his way home. And he would still attend any call-outs, many of which were emergencies that came via his phone – people knocked over by runaway horses, or children with broken bones or high fevers. In one well-publicised incident, a prominent businessman tripped and fell in Queen St, dislocating his shoulder among other injuries. Purchas happened to be nearby at the time and, using his own tried and proven methods, relocated the joint on the spot, to the astonishment of a gathering crowd of onlookers.

Finally, perhaps inevitably, sometime during the following year (1899) the 78-year-old's heavy schedule and physical efforts finally caught up with him. He contracted a serious bout of shingles combined with pleurisy. It laid him low for more than two months. Olivia's diary noted continually: "He had a very bad night"… and "very poorly today" … "Dr Gordon came and says the pain will go in time." It was the first time Purchas had suffered from any substantial illness (other than typhoid), and he did not enjoy it. On his birthday in September, Olivia wrote that Arthur had experienced a bad night but was feeling better by midday. Four days later, and still not right, he nevertheless told her he was getting up because "he had to go to the Costley Home tomorrow to see a lunatic there".

A few days after, she was still despairing, given her inability to make him rest. "He put on his cloak and Miri gave him his gloves and we opened the door for him to go out on the verandah – and lo! He was off like a shot, out on the path and through the gate. I hurried after him but could not overtake him until he turned back … he kindly allowed me to tuck him up for a rest … he slept until 5pm when he lay down again. Then afterwards he was busy writing patient notes in his diary." It was all typical Arthur Purchas.

When he did recover, the routine began all over again. Night after night, Olivia recorded: "Arthur away in town all day … Arthur came home 10pm … Arthur busy at Haslett's … Arthur called to Mt Albert to see children … Arthur in town all day …"

Gradually, through sheer hard work, Purchas was able to re-establish his medical practice at his new Epsom base – at least to the extent that he was able

---

311 It was not his only lucky escape on a ship. CMS missionary William Nihill claims to have saved
     Purchas's life many years earlier in some kind of accident when sailing on Selwyn's *Flying Fish*. Refer
     ATL, NZMS132.

to reach some relative equilibrium between expenses and income. He never for a second regarded the change in circumstances as unfortunate, bad luck or even bad management. It was what it was. Their lives were basically the same as they had always been – dedicated to making life easier and better for others.

He continued to derive great enjoyment from making himself available for family ceremonies, especially when they involved people he had known over his own lifetime. So in May 1901, at the age of 79, he travelled to Pukekohe on a cold and wet early winter's day to perform a wedding ceremony for a young woman. Purchas had officiated at her mother's marriage and her grandmother's as well. In the same month, his name was linked to another of the long-standing and significant family names of the Selwyn and missionary era, when youngest daughter Mil married John Kissling.

In the public arena, Purchas maintained a high profile. John Logan Campbell's gift of Cornwall Park and Maungakiekie to the people of Auckland had just been announced. The two men had worked together over many years, going back to the days when Campbell first acquired the One Tree Hill land, responding then to Purchas's request to help source a proper water supply for the town.

Purchas now led a deputation of his Scenic Preservation Society to meet with Campbell … to thank him for his gift, to "express the indebtedness of the community to Dr Campbell" and to pass on the society's willingness to help the new Cornwall Park trustees in any way possible. Campbell responded to Purchas's words by saying he was most "gratified at the deputation as it was composed of several old friends who had known him and the country for many years".[312] Purchas asked Campbell to become the next president of the society. How could the old man refuse? It all seemed to round off the entire matter very nicely indeed.

With Campbell in the chair the following year, and urged on by Purchas, the result was the planting of more than 80 pohutukawa, nikau and other native trees in the grounds of the other great public space in Auckland, the Domain. Many of those same trees still adorn the spaces below today's magnificent Auckland Museum – a structure whose construction was still 30 years away, but which might well have existed in Purchas's fertile mind.

The "protection" of the Auckland Domain was always a high priority for Purchas – in addition to his continual watch over it as a water source some 40 years earlier. When the early signs of a deadly flu epidemic began to appear in 1903 – and city authorities floated the idea of building a "suspects' hospital" in the grounds of the Domain in an attempt to isolate anyone with suspicious symptoms and keep them under observation – Purchas immediately wrote to the Town Clerk and the city's press:

"Sir, will you kindly inform the Mayor that I have no doubt whatsoever, that the placing of an observation or suspects' hospital on any portion of the Domain would be a source of danger, notwithstanding the erection of a fence of any height. The minute germs of disease cannot be fenced out by galvanised iron.

"I think it will be an evil day if any such buildings are allowed to occupy the site … I think I ought to add that in my opinion the double removal of patients to a suspects' hospital is likely to increase the danger to life of any patients so removed …"

The plan was stopped in its tracks. As one of the most influential guardians of Auckland's public health and its environment, Purchas (in his early eighties) was still well able to make his voice heard from a position of experience and authority.

A short time later, he was to be found sitting around the table with the same mayor, this time in connection with yet another new institution for the city. The Governor, Lord Ranfurly, had proposed that a home be established for war veterans, particularly those who had served in the recently concluded Boer Wars. The mayor called a meeting of about 20 leading citizens, including Purchas, Arthur Myers, the Roman Catholic Bishop and senior military figures. A committee was set up, which led to the foundation of the Ranfurly Home in Auckland.

Closure

One of the notable absentees from that meeting was William Cowie, now gravely ill at home in Parnell. He had resigned a short time earlier in 1902, worn out after a prominent and very successful church primacy. He passed away a few days later and Auckland prepared for what was described as one of the largest and most impressive funeral services yet seen in the colony. Vast crowds, walking quietly in from the suburbs in a huge procession clogged the footpaths and lined surrounding streets as the cortège moved from Parnell down St Stephens Avenue. Every organisation in the city was represented, from the military with its gun carriages, platoons and rifles, to classes of schoolchildren, troops of sea scouts, leaders of every institution and social organisation, banks and schools, libraries and churches. Businesses were closed and the entire town came to a standstill.

For Arthur and Olivia it was a time of sad reflection, since they had both enjoyed a very close and personal relationship with the Cowie family. Purchas assisted with the music for the funeral service in St Mary's Cathedral (led by a choir of 70 voices), before receiving the casket at St Stephen's and, apparently "deeply moved", voicing the committal "earth to earth, ashes to ashes".

The affection between the two had been genuine. Cowie was the man, after all, who had finally "released" Arthur and Olivia from Onehunga 27 years earlier. In his memoir Cowie had written: "Arthur Purchas and his family are among the oldest and most valued of our New Zealand friends. He is a man of much intellectual culture."[313]

Cowie's funeral service, in fact, was only one of many which Purchas was asked to lead in the early years of the new century – including the very large public affairs for Colonel Haultain and George Pierce.[314] But now at 82, and despite his natural vigour and faith, the strain of dealing with such personal losses, including those of his own family, was beginning to slow him down. At home, Purchas was also conscious of Olivia's apparent decline in health. She had experienced a few bouts of bronchitis, referred to in her diaries, coupled with the occasional shortness of breath and flu-like symptoms.

In June 1904, Olivia and Arthur were invited to the house-warming party at daughter Emily and son-in-law Hugh Seth-Smith's home in Remuera (they had just completed some additions and alterations after returning from England). After the party, Arthur and Olivia stayed the night and even though the weather was very bad, Arthur went into town the next morning as usual – leaving his wife with their daughter. The weather remained bad for the next couple of days, but eventually they got back home to 'Flintoft' with Olivia seemingly "not all the worse for the visit".[315]

But soon after, she was not feeling at all well. The following day, Arthur advised her not to get up. By the afternoon she was worse and he thought she was going to have another one of her bad attacks of bronchitis. By the next day, a Thursday, with Olivia now suffering from severe shortness of breath, Arthur summoned his doctor son, Arthur Challinor, who was "much alarmed" at his mother's condition.

By Sunday, Arthur was sending telegrams to members of the family in Wellington and elsewhere, and he arranged for Olivia's bed to be set up in the drawing room with a nurse alongside. By Monday morning, he had resigned himself to her imminent death and the family were all called in.

---

313 W G Cowie, *Our Last Year in New Zealand, 1887*; also AAA, Purchas papers.
314 Pierce was Purchas's fellow Gundry estate trustee and was widely known for his contributions to a very large number of charitable, church and Masonic institutions and causes in Auckland.
315 A G Purchas letter. Family documents.

Arthur Purchas and a rather frail-looking Olivia in their son's new Darracq car in 1903, possibly the first of its type in Auckland. The car was written off soon after, in a collision with a tramcar in Parnell – although Purchas was not the driver.
PURCHAS FAMILY FILES

"About 7am on Tuesday, June 21 she sat up in the bed and said goodbye to each by name and gave me messages for those that were absent," he wrote. "Then she lay down and gradually passed away, breathing her last just as the clock struck nine … it was lovely to see the gentle face with a sweet smile on it amidst beautiful flowers …"

Olivia's private funeral took place at Purewa near St John's College, in sight of the place where they had lived when they first arrived in 1846. Four of her sons carried the coffin to the grave, watched by her daughters, grandchildren, sons- and daughters-in-law. A brief report in the next day's newspapers said she died of influenza. Olivia was 79.

Arthur returned home to Epsom, supported by daughter Gertrude and lawyer son Charles. But Charles, a keen rider and hunter, was also unwell. Following a serious accident while out hunting some months earlier, he had sustained some kind of internal or head injury, which incapacitated him and severely disrupted his normal daily routines.

For the next 18 months or so, Purchas was finally forced to live life at a slightly less hurried pace. The death of his beloved Livy, together with Charles's ill health, seemed to take some, but not all, of the wind out of his sails. He still kept up his patient visits, took the phone calls, continued his work with the blind in Parnell and the orphans in Mt Albert, read lessons and sang at St Sepulchre, and tended his garden. He was even to be found on occasions assisting his son in surgery. Following in his father's footsteps, Arthur Challinor was now one of the city's leading medical figures ... and with his love of motor cars, president of the newly formed Automobile Association. Arthur Snr, at the age of 84, actually assisted as anaesthetist at one particularly prominent operation involving a boy who, unfortunately, later died, which resulted in a very public inquiry.

Arthur and Olivia in 1904, a photograph thought to have been taken in the drawing room of their Epsom home, 'Flintoft', very shortly before Olivia's death in June of that year.
PURCHAS FAMILY FILES

To the Auckland public, however, it was clear that Dr Purchas continued to be fully committed to looking after their best interests. A new letter appeared in the morning paper from their "champion", this time with a suggestion for defeating the highly injurious and very severe clouds of dust being whipped up by unusual summer winds and, in particular, the city's many tramway horses. The infragrant dust, wrote Dr Purchas, "is a positive menace to health". He had made several suggestions to the authorities, such as an electric watering car, or a light-oil sprinkling of the road surface, and glazed, closed-in cabs for the tramway drivers or "motormen". But this dust storm in the city's teacup would be the last time Purchas would participate in a public debate.

In April 1906, his son Charles suddenly deteriorated and passed away aged just 43, after a "long suffering, patiently borne." This may well have been the one last, savage blow for Purchas.

Possibly in an attempt to cheer the old man up – but also knowing of his passionate interest in ships and railways – his daughter Emily suggested they take a short holiday excursion to Wellington and back, via Napier and Hastings, mostly on the train but starting on a coastal steamer to Wellington. It was probably to see daughter Lizzie and family who were living there. Purchas seemed in excellent health and quickly regained his usual good spirits. It must have been something of a dream trip for him.

Somewhere on the journey – probably while at sea travelling down the east coast – he caught a severe chill following a typical 'walkabout' in the fresh air. They started out for Napier on the return train trip but very soon he was in trouble. Emily decided to break the trip immediately at Hastings and booked them into a local hotel. He rapidly became worse. Either that same night, or the night following, he was seized with a violent cough and acute bronchitis. With no family to call on, and in a strange hotel room in the middle of the night, Emily must have been frantic.

But there was nothing she could do. Two hours later Arthur Purchas was dead.

CHAPTER 22

Legacy

The death of "one of Auckland's oldest and most esteemed citizens" attracted widespread public interest. Over the next few days, as his body was returned from Napier on the *Tarawera*, the family prepared for a largely private funeral as per Arthur's wish and newspapers all over New Zealand began printing comprehensive and admiring obituaries and letters.

The funeral was held at St Mark's in Remuera on June 1, 1906, attended by family and friends, and preceded by a short procession from 'Flintoft'. Arthur's coffin, at his own request bedecked only in fern leaves and with no floral emblems, was taken to Purewa and interred alongside that of Olivia's.

Arthur Purchas as he looked at the turn of the century, as one of Auckland's most familiar father figures.
PURCHAS FAMILY FILES

The messages of condolence poured in from all parts of the colony. Tributes flowed from fellow doctors, the legal profession and the business community, members of the public and the government, and leaders of all the many organisations who had worked with Purchas or known of his exploits over so many years.

So how should he be summed up? A common theme of the various obituaries published at the time of his death was the difficulty editors had in covering a life full of countless significant and diverse contributions to so many areas of society. "Indeed," said one such editorial, "it is scarcely possible to assess adequately his influence on the development of Auckland and the Colony." Echoing that difficulty, Professor Cyril Knight, writing 50 years later in *An Encyclopaedia of New Zealand*, said: "Arthur Purchas' contribution to the growth of the Colony will probably never be fully evaluated … he came at the beginning of colonisation … and sought neither personal wealth nor fame …"[316]

In the *Christchurch Press*, Purchas was lauded as having been associated with the history of Auckland for over 60 years – "there being no more well-known citizen in Auckland than the worthy doctor". His soldierly figure and kindly face have been, during that time, a part of the city itself, the paper said. He was a man "of most estimable qualities, endearing himself to all with whom he came in contact, the friend of all – the enemy of none".

In Auckland, he was described as one of the city's "most highly esteemed residents … of striking personality … one who laid so faithfully all that is good and true in the social life of this colony". The lengthy *New Zealand Herald* obituary spoke of his many achievements and, in particular, his relationship with Māori: "His intimate knowledge of the Maori and their love for and faith in him, enabled him to do much to bring about a better understanding between the two races." It said that while Purchas never aspired to public office, "in his quiet unostentatious way, he did much for the benefit of early Auckland and its citizens," specifically mentioning his active interest in procuring a water supply for Auckland. The paper also referred to Purchas's exceptional far-sightedness, referencing remarks he made a quarter of a century earlier that "the time was not far distant when vehicles, propelled by internal combustion engines, would come into use".

There were, of course, many other prominent people who featured throughout those early colonial days of the 19th century and who set their own place around the high table of Auckland's history. Many cities or towns acknowledge their "founding father/s" (tellingly, there were few "mothers") – such as Campbell in Auckland, or Godley in Christchurch – whose contributions made a significant and lasting legacy.

There were also some in those days who achieved recognition in more than one discipline or profession. Several came from the ranks of the clergy – notably administrator-architect Frederick Thatcher, and clergymen-diplomats, linguists and negotiators like Hadfield, Williams and Hobbs. There were also high-ranking soldiers who became senior politicians like Haultain, senior lawyers who were also social engineers or reformers, landowners who were philanthropists, and so on.

In the main, though, the men and women who adorn our history books from the worlds of politics or business, education, arts, the military, law or Māoridom, are usually remembered for a singular talent or achievement

---

316   A H McLintock (ed), 'PURCHAS, Arthur Guyon', *An Encyclopaedia of New Zealand*, 1966. www.teara. govt.nz

in one particular field or activity. Very often, in the case of European men, public recognition came as a result of the accumulation, and sometimes loss, of property, initially, and then power. These figures were mostly brave, shrewd and entrepreneurial in nature. Few were timid, or frightened easily. They were positive, determined and daring individuals, and sometimes even bordered on the reckless. Arthur Purchas was all of these and more, wrapped up in a compassionate and generous nature with an extraordinary sense of social justice and goodwill.

Purchas the polymath

His great point of difference, however, was the expertise he possessed in so many fields, possibly unique in our history. There have been few, if any, men or women of such exceptional ability, across such a wide spectrum of activity, as Arthur Purchas. He had an array of natural talent and ability far above most of the other better known pioneer settlers who feature regularly in our history books. Consequently, he has been called a polymath and possibly "the most gifted man that ever came to New Zealand"[317] – and his multiple contributions to the country's development would seem to support such glowing praise.

He was, for example, an architect of outstanding merit. Five of his "Selwyn" churches are still in use today and stand among New Zealand's most important heritage buildings. He was an expert carpenter and builder, accomplishing serious building tasks such as the St Peter's spire relocation and enlargement, his Onehunga house and its two-storey alterations, the Onehunga stone school and Waiuku water mill. And Challinor House and the Purchas building in Karangahape Rd, although not specifically from his drawing board, certainly included some of his design concepts (the latter is still in use today as residences and shops).

Purchas was an engineer of note who designed the first Mangere Bridge, a vehicle suspension system, a Braille embossing machine for the blind and a water-powered flax machine. The machine contributed hugely to the New Zealand economy for many years after it was awarded the country's first patent.

He either founded or sat on foundation committees of many of Auckland's long-standing and important cultural or social institutions – notably the Auckland Institute (later to become the Auckland Museum), the Society of Arts, the Institute for the Blind, the Auckland Choral Society (and its equivalent in Sydney), the Ranfurly Home and the Scenic Preservation

---

317   Archbishop A W Averill, Primate of New Zealand.

Society – serving as president, councillor or chairman on numerous occasions. At the Auckland Institute he was a councillor for 39 years and three times its president.[318]

Purchas set up Auckland's first public library in Onehunga, served as a Justice of the Peace for many years, and championed the main Auckland Library and art gallery. He discovered two new species, which were named after him; was the first European to discover the Huntly and Drury coalfields; and was personally responsible for persuading Ferdinand von Hochstetter to complete his pioneering geological surveys of Auckland and other parts of New Zealand. He even had a volcano named after him when he pointed out to von Hochstetter a peculiarity in its cone formation.

Purchas designed an advanced air-fuel system for internal combustion engines and forecast the use of such engines to power vehicles. He was one of the first to recognise the potential of the black iron sand found on the west coast (knowing of the black sand used for so long by Japanese smiths), and continued to promote it despite the failure of early attempts to process it.

As a musician, he was not only an extremely competent singer and flute player, but also an expert piano tuner and repairer. He created a highly successful singing system to teach novice Māori and European students, and blind people to sing some of the most complex musical compositions of the day in four-part harmony – and published a book describing this system. He composed several hymns, both words and music, was the compiler and editor of the first New Zealand church hymnal, and was described later by church authorities as the "father of New Zealand church music".

Purchas was a highly accomplished artist, published a book on New Zealand flowering trees and shrubs, designed Auckland's first gravitational water supply system and, without doubt, was the first serious protector and caretaker of Auckland's public health. He was most likely the first promoter of healthy eating in Auckland, 100 years ahead of his time – advocating greater use of nuts, vegetables and plant oils in local diets. He was an expert horticulturist and an early chairman of the Fruitgrowers' Association.

Purchas was responsible for some of the early surveying and layout of Auckland and Onehunga roads, such as today's Mt Smart Rd and the Patumahoe to Drury Rd. And he lectured widely on new technologies like the telegraph, the telephone and electricity, and had one of the first private telephones in Auckland.

He had much to do with Auckland's first public passenger transport system

318   A Powell, *Centennial History of the Auckland Institute and Museum.*

and was a vociferous early promoter of the benefits of electric trams and rail. His brief foray into the city's boardrooms as a director of the ill-fated St Helier's and Northcote Land & Building Investment Company was an experience he probably regretted – a decision born out of his trust in others rather than his own commercial judgement. Harsh as this experience was, he never blamed or condemned anyone for its impact on the family's financial circumstances.

Purchas introduced his fellow colonial settlers and Māori to a veritable host of new things – from vegetable dyes and photography, to uses for flax products as diverse as brown-paper wrapping and new foods for cattle. As founder of the Auckland Naturalists Field Club, he was instrumental in educating people about natural history and the need to plant trees and preserve green spaces – as his legacy of pohutukawa in Auckland's Domain attests to today.

Then there was his work among Māori – his contributions to diplomacy, race relations, understanding and peace. That they were overwhelmed somewhat by the outbreak of the 1863 Waikato War must have been by far his greatest personal disappointment. He was a fluent Māori speaker and interpreter, quoted at one time as having such "delicate accuracy of pronunciation of Te Reo as had never known to be surpassed or equalled by any other Maori scholar".[319] His role as a communicator between Ngāti Mahuta and other Kīngitanga tribes, and between Ngāpora, the first two Māori Kings, Pōtatau and Tāwhiao, and Grey and Browne was significant – as was the part he played in trying to convince his fellow Pākehā that the Kīngitanga was a peace-seeking movement ... not a collection of rebels with no just cause.

And his work as a clergyman was acknowledged in numerous tributes. The July 1906 issue of the *Church Gazette*, a widely circulated and well-read paper in those days, contained the perfect summation of his zest for life.

"No man led a busier or a more active life in his day. With the responsibility of a large family, and with slender means derived from his cure, he ever had a brave heart in discharging the double duties of a clergyman and a doctor. It is a little short of marvellous that he should have found time to devote to other objects. But he took a practical interest in nearly every movement of public utility ... his familiar form and cheery voice will no longer be seen and heard in the synod which he delighted to attend with unflagging regularity ..."

Darwin's helper

His role as a parish priest has been extensively covered in earlier pages, and local

---

319   Dr J Giles – Purchas family notes.

histories of Onehunga and Auckland, written over the last 60 years or so, all devote time and space to Purchas's generosity of spirit, care for the afflicted and passionate concern for Māori and their equal inclusion in society. Throughout his church and public life, there are references to his "words of wisdom" and "weighty utterances". It is clear that from the time of his arrival at St John's as a young man, and throughout his 30 years as priest at Onehunga and afterwards, his opinions were always received with great respect. Even in the difficult times he experienced with Selwyn, and when settlers were urging their priests to stand beside them as they took up arms against the Māori, Purchas was able to command attention. While disagreeing with many of his colleagues over British actions in the build-up to the Waikato War, he managed to retain their trust and affection by the sheer force of his character.

In his presidential role at the Auckland Institute, Purchas's "weighty utterances" were perhaps at their peak in the course of the huge evolution-creation debate which ebbed and flowed for so many years after the publication of Darwin's *On the Origin of Species*. In fact, although Purchas did not speak officially on behalf of any bishop or church leader in the community, his standing always ensured his views were well publicised and had a broad impact. Because he was a highly regarded man of science, and a senior clergyman, his explanation of creation carried tremendous weight and credibility among many ordinary people struggling to bridge the gap between Biblical teachings and evolution.

That debate was at its peak in New Zealand in the 1870s and, as John Stenhouse wrote more than 100 years later[320], Purchas actually "prepared the way for Darwin" in New Zealand with his commentaries and speeches, particularly at the Auckland Institute. Throughout the 1870s, said Stenhouse, Purchas adopted the role of mediator, cautiously smoothing the way for the eventual acceptance of Darwin's theory of evolution.

Purchas's stance was essentially scientific and easily understood by the man in the street. He saw the entire evolution of species simply as a progressive act of creation, one which therefore should provide no contradictions or difficulties for the serious theologian or genuine believer. Purchas, said Stenhouse, was "decidedly liberal and open-minded about evolution". He gently and politely articulated what he believed was an obvious scientific fact and how it should be reconciled with religion. And he did so without ever generating any backlash or dissension among friends, clergy or laypeople struggling with Darwin's theory.

---

320 J Stenhouse, The 'battle' between science and religion over evolution in nineteenth century New Zealand.

Medical leader

Finally, there is Purchas's contribution to medicine and surgery to consider. What most impresses, again, is the sheer breadth of his specialist skills, which stood him apart from his medical contemporaries in New Zealand. He was a general practitioner, an expert obstetrician and gynaecologist, an inventive paramedic and trauma expert, and an extraordinarily skilful pioneer of abdominal surgery at a time when such operations were not only rare but dangerous. He was also an anaesthetist and qualified chemist or apothecary – and, unusually for the time, had an extensive knowledge of chemicals and poisons.

Most significantly, Purchas was perhaps one of the most creative and courageous medical innovators of his time. His inventiveness began with his pioneer treatment of typhoid in 1847. It was contrary to the worldwide medical practice of the day, but became so successful that it was soon adopted elsewhere New Zealand and beyond. It was this success and his subsequent surgical achievements, which later prompted the prestigious Cambridge University to offer him an honorary MD.

His innovations continued with the use of intelligent new techniques, such as those involving his fine-wire sutures, exterior drains from sealed wounds, and his early adoption of antisepsis measures. His methods of treatment at a far more basic level were just as effective – such as the unusual way he dealt with a patient's stubborn dislocated shoulder.

Purchas's medical practice developed further, into what we would call today a "holistic" approach to treatment and cure – using specific food and drink with care, paying careful attention to hygiene, including an entirely new approach to bandaging and dressings, and imparting a positive mental attitude (a reflection of his strong faith). Other doctors commented at various times how Purchas could uplift his patients' mental attitude and sense of hope by constant, kindly encouragement and a strong belief that they could play a major part in their own recovery.

As a family doctor, Purchas was always known for the great amount of unpaid work he undertook and his constant readiness to help anyone who needed it. A medical colleague said of him: "He treated large numbers of indigent persons without pecuniary consideration, frequently kept them at his own house for long periods for treatment and observation, even till late in convalescence and never mentioned anything that would suggest a fee."

But perhaps his general medical practice was best summed up in his work over so many years among the poor and destitute children of the Howe St home. As Dr Laurie Gluckman wrote[321], Purchas's outstanding record there spoke for itself and was quite possibly his single greatest accomplishment. In more than a quarter of a century of devoted work as the Government's medical officer in charge, only eight deaths occurred among the 700- 800 children who passed through the home – "a remarkable achievement for that period". Gluckman not only highlighted Purchas's skill as a practical surgeon, but also as an observer, a forensic scientist and a practical chemist – calling him "this really outstanding man".

Letters to newspapers after Purchas's death also spoke of his extraordinary kindness and patience, and how "his young patients welcomed his visits". A Sarah Jackson wrote that even at the age of 82, when he was living in Epsom, Purchas volunteered to go out to the Mt Albert home at any time, day or night, to attend to one particular child who was seriously ill. "It was characteristic of the Doctor," she said, "that no thought of his own health or comfort or of his age, caused him to hesitate at the call of duty" – and it was no easy journey from Epsom to Mt Albert in those days.[322]

In 1869, it was Purchas who first invited all the medical men of Auckland province to join the Auckland Institute and form a single and more cohesive medical association. This proved to be just another of his many highly effective and important initiatives, and was motivated in part by the inability of the earlier Auckland Medical and Surgical Society – which had no prior connection with the institute – to gain the confidence of the public and the full medical fraternity. Not only did Purchas's new group give local doctors the crucial professional standing and collegial support they had been looking for, but it also provided the first proper forum for the exchange of ideas and treatments at a time when medicine worldwide was making groundbreaking advances.[323]

Various attempts have been made over the last 50 years to assess Purchas's contribution to surgery and specifically that of abdominal surgery. It began in 1858 with his participation in the first Caesarean operation in New Zealand. And it continued through the 1860s with various minor surgeries dealing with fractures, broken limbs and even dental surgery. Between 1870 and 1894 he carried out 13 serious abdominal operations – mostly involving the removal of cysts and tumours – and with the loss of only one patient (already in a terminal state). His success derived from a combination of unusual manual dexterity, medical innovation and skill, and extreme attention to hygiene and Listerism

---

321 Dr Laurie Gluckman was one of New Zealand's most prominent physicians and psychiatrists, and a prolific writer of New Zealand medical history. He died in 1999.
322 *Church Gazette*, July 1906, p 138.
323 Out of this came the first Auckland Medical Society, formally established in 1883.

Purchas was always surrounded and supported strongly by his large family, although spending much time away and enduring the premature deaths of 3 of his 14 children.
PURCHAS FAMILY FILES

... to encourage faster healing and safer post-operative care.

His innovations included the early feeding of surgical patients, having obviously experimented and noticed the benefits, and extended to the careful management of steel sutures and the design of new surgical instruments. First among these was the Purchas clamp, made by a local blacksmith and used successfully in most of Purchas's ovarian operations.

Given the breadth of his achievements, it is not difficult to conclude that he may have been New Zealand's most eminent and skilful medical pioneer of the 19th century. Adding to Gluckman's assessment, Professor Pat Alley said: "His surgical notes are exemplary in their clarity and today's surgeons could do worse than follow his example. Not only was he a particularly shrewd clinician in respect of patient selection for surgery, but he was also a clever technical surgeon."

It is axiomatic that Purchas was a man of immense mental strength and determination. He faced many crises and tragedies in his life, several involving family and friends. The preventable death of his first son, Arthur, must have been a crushing blow to him and Olivia.

Purchas was also called on to attend some of the most appalling accidents, injuries and associated trauma among members of the wider public in his long working life, many involving children. He always seemed to be able to move on from any difficult circumstance and not allow himself to become discouraged or weighed down. His early clashes with Selwyn could well have derailed what would become a productive career (others were less fortunate in their dealings with the Bishop). He endured hard times, while still having to be a doctor, counsellor and cheerleader to the wider community.

That he was always a cheerful and positive person at home is also indisputable. But although he enjoyed his garden, he was not a 'homebody'. Olivia and the children clearly spent long periods at home without him, while he was attending or chairing meetings, preparing for public events, conducting musical activities or speaking to one audience or another.

Nevertheless, his personal family letters were always deeply affectionate and thoughtful, addressed to "my dearest wife" and ending with "best love, I remain dearest Livy, your own loving husband, Arthur". He clearly appreciated the enormous support she gave him, especially when it came to the family. Although not unusual for the times, for 22 years from 1846 to 1868, Olivia was pregnant for virtually half that time. Her prominent contribution to Arthur's public life, while mostly taken for granted in those days, would earn resounding acclamation today.

Daughter Gertrude said of her father: "We always thought he was a saint. He was so good to everybody. He could have died a wealthy man if he hadn't been so benevolent to everyone. Besides rearing 14 of us, he was also a guardian for seven others in need of a home" – referring specifically to the Gundry children.

Purchas's grandson, E H Roche, recalled him as follows: "I remember him chiefly by his happy smile, the lure of his soft brown eyes that twinkled and beckoned but never hardened, and his smooth untroubled brow. When old in years he still remained young in spirit, full of life and fun, quick of movement, a presence welcomed instinctively by children."

Yet sadly, few if any Aucklanders would recognise the name of Arthur Purchas today, let alone his physical likeness. This is illustrated only by the dusty Payton portrait hanging on a back wall of St Peter's Church in Onehunga, and a bronze bust, somewhat hidden away in a rear foyer of the John Kinder Theological Library. The Purchas bust was offered by the family to the Auckland Museum over 30 years ago as a way of marking his contributions there, but was strangely declined. It seems few working there at the time were aware of the part he played in the establishment of that magnificent edifice and its collections.

One final, succinct editorial was a fitting summation of his existence. "His was a truly noble life," it said. "His death will be regretted by the whole city."

The future children of Auckland should require no more appropriate epitaph for a founding father.

Appendices

An example of detailed operation notes by A G Purchas – Ovarian cyst surgery, 1874 (courtesy John and Ann Roche).

"The incision through the integument was made on the right side about four inches in length ... three small arteries were divided, two superficial which were seized with small Assalini forceps and left til the operation was over when they required nothing more. The other was deep-seated and was ligatured at once. Venous haemorrhage slight and soon ceased. After the division of the skin and subtegumental tissue, there was some vomiting and I waited til it was over and then proceeded to divide the muscles and inner fascia, then on opening the peritoneum the tumour was exposed, very firm and dense.

"The large trocar and cannula was plunged into the tumour but nothing flowed through the flexible tube until after great pressure, a very thick tenacious glue like fluid slowly passed into the bucket. Only one cyst being opened, the tumour was not much lessened and I found it necessary to enlarge the wound by cutting upwards on a director. After making pressure for several minutes on the punctured cyst, the rest of the tumour was with difficulty extracted and the pedicle found to be attached to the left side of the uterus. My screw clamp was fixed on the pedicle and the mass severed by a red hot cautery iron with a blunt edge.

"One of the arteries was rather difficult to stop but in a few minutes and by several applications of the cautery it was made safe and the pedicle was returned into the abdomen. A few very small clots were carefully removed and some fluid that had lodged between the bladder and the uterus was taken up by means of a very soft sponge and the wound was then closed by four, fine soft-wire sutures, through the peritoneum and adjacent fascia, which were brought straight up to the surface without any twisting. Three stout, soft-iron sutures were passed through the whole of the integuments except the inner fascia and peritoneum and eight needles were used to bring the edges of the skin into apposition. A figure of 8 was used, being wound over each of them and then the three stout wire sutures were loosely looped up. Very small strips of calico soaked in weak solution of carbolic acid were laid over the wound then a thin pledget of similarly soaked calico over the strips and a dry pledget over all and this was the only dressing used. On opening the abdomen a considerable quantity of ascetic fluid escaped and some of the glassy fluid from the cyst."

Purchas family members

Arthur Purchas	b 27/9/1821	d 28/5/1906
M Olivia Challinor 27/12/1845	b 7/12/1824	d 21/6/1904

Children

Arthur Guyon Purchas	1847-1855
Agnes Olivia Purchas	1849-1878
Mary Anne Purchas	1850-1850
Emily Mary Purchas M Hugh Seth-Smith	1851-1932
Marian Elizabeth "Lizzie" Purchas M Charles Cooke	1853-1938
Sarah Edith "Edie" Purchas M Frederic W Brookfield	1854-1927
Amy Charlotte Purchas M Henry Roche	1856-1940
George Henry Purchas M Annie Walker	1857-1933
Arthur Challinor Purchas M Evelyn Morse	1860-1941
Claude Phillip Guyon Purchas M Beatrice Eliott	1861-1938

Charles Edward Purchas   1863-1906

Gertrude Winifred Purchas   1864-1957
M William Stevenson

Frederic Maurice Purchas   1866-1948
M Alice Cox

Ethel Mildred "Mil" Purchas   1868-1951
M John Kissling

Glossary of Māori words

ariki	lord, chief
atua	god
haere mai	welcome greeting
haka	war dance
hākari	great feast
hāngī	native ground oven
hapū	subtribe, tribal grouping
hongi	nose rubbing salutation
hui	meeting for discussion
hunga whakapono	religious followers, believers
iwi	large family tribal grouping
kai	food
kāinga	village, settlement
kaitaka	finely woven cloak or mat
kānga	corn
karakia	call of worship, prayer
kaumātua	elders
kaupapa	agenda, theme, topic
kāwana	governor
kāwanatanga	government
kīnaki	small morsel of food
korowai	woven flax mat
kuia	female elder
kūmara	sweet potato
kūpapa	loyalist to the Crown
kuri	dog
kūware	a fool
mana	authority, status, prestige
mana moana	customary sea ownership

mana whenua	customary landownership
manuhiri	guest in land of others
marae	village centre, meeting place
mauri	life force, aura
mere	small hand-held weapon
mihinare	missionary
miri	black mat
mokai	slave
mokamokai	embalmed human heads
moko	tattoo
mokopuna	grandchild, descendant
muru	expunge by plunder, forgive or cancel out
nīkau	a native New Zealand palm tree
okewha	stone mere
patu	small flat club, see also mere
pounamu	greenstone, jade
pōwhiri	welcome, act of welcome
puke	hill
pūtōrino	native musical pipe, whistle
rāhui	notice of warning, prohibition
rangatira	tribal or iwi chief
rangatiratanga	chiefly authority or sovereignty
raupatu	seizure, confiscation
raupō	bulrush or sedge
rongoā	medicine
rongopai	good news, gospel
roopu	group, collection of people
rūnanga	council
taiaha	hand weapon, club
take	cause, justification, reason
tamariki	children
tangata whenua	people of the land, one's hosts
tangi	funeral, burial ceremony
taonga	treasures
tapu	sacred
taua	raiding or war party
taurekareka	slave
te	the
tino pai	very good

tītīmako	bellbird
tītoki	native New Zealand tree
toa	warrior
toetoe	large plant – 'cutty' grass
tohunga	priest, spiritual chief
tōpuni	dogskin mat
toroa	albatross
tūī	'parson' bird
utu	form of revenge
waahi tapu	sacred place
waiata	song
Waikato	group name for tribes in river catchment area
waipiro	foul smelling liquid, alcohol
wahine	woman
waka taua	war canoe
wero	ceremonial challenge
Whakatū	Nelson
whānau	family unit
whare	hut, house
whenua	land

Acknowledgements

It will be obvious that trying to make sense of such a diverse life as Arthur Purchas's some 112 years later, involves a lot of people. I was initially hesitant about tackling the job, knowing that at least two years' work would lie ahead, trawling through documents, records, notes, letters and the Internet. But the enthusiasm of three direct Purchas descendants, Tina Frantzen, John McMillan and Juliet McKinstry, and their early reassurance that this man was indeed "someone unbelievable", finally convinced me. Friend and fellow author Graeme Lay, first confirmed the story was an undoubtedly good one, so after a further 10 days checking it out – including a scouting mission to the excellent Auckland Museum Library – I was quickly convinced that it did, indeed, need telling.

I am therefore very grateful to them and also to Shona Caughey and Purchas's descendant Russell Williams, for initially putting me on the early information trail – to go with some detailed notes assembled many years ago by Purchas's grandson, E H Roche, and great-grandson, Melville Brookfield. Their documents were invaluable.

There followed numerous interviews with various family members who had stories, letters, clippings and references, including Alison Kissling, Judith Dexter, Rose Purchas, Sue Roche and members of the Gundry family, Linda Cocks and Jeanette Grant. I especially acknowledge Linda for the excellent work she contributed, which involved hours of research into the Purchas and Gundry land activities over a very long time. If I had medals to hand out, she would get one of the first.

I also thank Purchas's great-grandson John Roche and his wife Ann, with whom I enjoyed an entertaining lunch in their Titirangi home while perusing some rare and fascinating medical notes and stories. Cyril Skilton and Colin Freland of the Onehunga Fencible & Historical Society, whom I visited two or three times, also gave invaluable assistance with information and access to computer records and library while Auckland company Boyd Visuals greatly assisted by printing various manuscript editions for me prior to corrections.

On the medical side, distinguished and now-retired surgeon Professor

Pat Alley – who has also researched Purchas's medical work in recent times – was hugely instrumental in backgrounding and helping me to understand and assess the surgical details. We met several times over coffee near Purchas Hill Drive and I was able to get a far better understanding of some serious surgical matters with the help of Pat's expert drawings and explanations – including, at one stage, a quick sketch of the human abdominal anatomy explaining a couple of specific medical terms. Any medical anomalies or mistakes remain my own.

I am also greatly appreciative of the help given with family documents and photographs by Dr David Roche, Purchas's great-grandson. Similarly, Maria Collins and Juliet Hawkins of the Auckland Medical History Society willingly gave me open access to the Ernest & Marion Davis Memorial Library, while other members, including Dr Pat Clarkson, medical historian Dr Derek Dow and Professor Dr Bruce Hadden of the University of Auckland, were a wonderful source of information and direction with some early medical research and history.

It is also a pleasure to once again acknowledge the work done by the librarians in all the superb libraries we have in this country – Linda McGregor and other Alexander Turnbull Library staff who always impressed with their incredible efficiency in retrieving small documents and letters; the Auckland Museum Library's collections manager Martin Collett and Rebecca Loud who arranged for their staff to bring out trolley loads of material to me on numerous occasions and pointed me in the right direction; the Auckland Library and George Grey Collections area where Kate de Courcy and Keith Giles gave me every possible assistance; the Auckland Anglican Archives where Sarah Padey and Janet Marinkovich ushered me into a quiet room on two or three occasions before letting me loose on their valuable documents; Judith Bright and the team at the John Kinder Theological Library; and, of course, the superb National Library of New Zealand in Wellington with its amazing resources (Papers Past and Te Ara websites).

Final thanks go to readers Dr George Armstrong and Kelvin John for their comments and guidance on specialist areas and particularly to Michael Smith for his expert advice, direction and editing skill in many areas. He is the one who has corrected the errors of sequence, repetition, spelling or punctuation and help turn a somewhat scrappy, early manuscript into hopefully a readable and interesting story.

New Zealand book lovers will also know how much we depend on the judgment, expertise and professional commitment of a publisher like David Ling in a project like this. I am extremely grateful to him, not only for taking the gamble with an unknown, but for his advice, enthusiastic care and attention in doing such a fine job.

Bibliography

Abbreviations:

ATL	Alexander Turnbull Library
AML	Auckland Museum Library
JKTL	John Kinder Theological Library
AKL	Auckland Library
AAA	Auckland Anglican Archives
EMDML	Ernest & Marion Davis Library
NLNZ	National Library – Te Ara/Papers Past
NZETC	Electronic Text Centre – Victoria University
ENZB	Early NZ Books – Auckland University

Alington, M H, *An Excellent Recruit*, Polygraphia Ltd, 2007.

Belich, J, *The New Zealand Wars*, Penguin, 1985.

Binney, J (ed), *The Shaping of History – Essays from the New Zealand Journal of History*, Bridget Williams Books, 2001.

Boast, R, *Buying the Land, Selling the Land*, Victoria University Press, 2008.

Borchard, N, *Untold Stories of Onehunga*, 1993.

Brooks, P, *Henare Wiremu Taratoa – Noble Warrior*, Kale Print, 2014.

Brown, C, Peters, M, Teal, J (Eds), *Shaping a Colonial Church*, Canterbury University Press, 2006.

Buick, T L, *The Treaty of Waitangi*, Thomas Avery & Sons Ltd, 1936.

Burgess, L, *Historic Churches*, Penguin Random House, 2015.

Bush, G (ed), *The History of Epsom*, Epsom & Eden District Historical Society Inc, 2006.

Byrne, T, *Wing of the Manukau*, T B Byrne Publishing, 1991.

Caselberg, J (ed), *Maori is my Name*, John McIndoe, Dunedin, 1975.

Clarke, A, *Born to a Changing World*, Bridget Williams Books, 2012.

Cowan, J, *The New Zealand Wars Vol 2 (1845-1864)*, Government Printer, Wellington 1922.

Cowie, W G, *Our Last Year in New Zealand, 1887*, Kegan, Paul, Trench & Co, 1888.

Crosby, R D, *The Musket Wars*, Reed, 1999.

Crosby, R D, *Kupapa*, Penguin Books, 2015.

Dalton, B J, *War and Politics in New Zealand 1855-1870*, Sydney University Press, 1967.

Davidson, A K, *Selwyn's Legacy*, The College of St John the Evangelist, 1993.

Davidson, A K (ed), *Living Legacy*, Anglican Diocese of Auckland, 2011.

Davidson, A K (ed), *A Controversial Churchman*, Bridget Williams Books, 2011.

Davis, J K, *The History of St John's College*, Abel Dykes, 1911.

Drummond, A (ed), *The Auckland Journals of Vicesimus Lush*, Pegasus Press, 1971.

Drummond, A (ed), *The Waikato Journals of Vicesimus Lush*, Pegasus Press, 1982.

Fairburn, T, *The Orpheus Disaster*, Western Publishing, 1987.

Featon, J, *The Waikato War, 1863-4*, Auckland 1879

Garrett, H, *Te Manihera*, Reed, 1991.

Gibson, T, *The Maori Wars, The British Army in New Zealand 1840-1872*, Reed, 1974.

Gluckman, L K, *Tangiwai – A Medical History of 19th Century New Zealand*, Whitcoulls, 1976.

Gordon, M, *The Golden Age of Josiah Clifton Firth*, Pegasus, 1963.

Gorst, J, *The Maori King*, Victoria University, NZETC, 1864.

Grace, D, *A Driven Man*, Ngaio Press, 2004.

Jackson, E T, *Delving into the Past of Auckland's Eastern Suburbs – Section 6, St Heliers Bay*, 2005.

Jones, A and Jenkins, K, *Words Between Us – He Korero*, Huia, 2011.

Jones, Pei Te Hurinui, *King Pōtatau*, Huia, 2010.

Keenan, D, *Wars Without End*, Penguin, 2009.

Keene, F, *By This We Conquer- Letters of Richard Davis*, 1974.

King, M, *Te Puea – A Life*, Reed Publishing (4th edition), 2003.

King, M, *The Penguin History of New Zealand*, Penguin, 2003.

Knight, C R, *The Selwyn Churches of Auckland*, AH & AW Reed, 1972.

Limbrick, W (ed), *Bishop Selwyn in New Zealand*, Dunmore Press, 1983.

Main, W, *Auckland Through a Victorian Lens*, Millwood Press, 1977.

Martin, Lady M, *Our Maoris*, 1884, ENZB.

Maxwell, P, *Frontier – The Battle for the North Island of New Zealand, 1860-1872*, Celebrity Books, 2000.

McKay, W and Ussher, J, *Worship – A History of New Zealand Church Design*, Random House, 2015.

McLean, M, *Maori Music*, Auckland University Press, 1966.

Mogford, J, *The Onehunga Heritage*, Onehunga Borough Council, 1977.

Monin, P, *Hauraki Contested, 1769-1875*, Bridget Williams Books, 2001.

Moon, P, *A Savage Country*, Penguin, 2012.

Morgan, M, *A History of the Parochial District of Waiuku*, Ashford Kent, 1973.

Morrell, W P, *The Anglican Church in New Zealand*, John McIndoe Ltd, 1973.

Morris, N, *Early Days in Franklin*, Deed, 1965.

Nagy, S-F, *Brompton: The Smith Legacy*, Trafford, 2012.

Newman, K, *Bible & Treaty*, Penguin, 2010.

Newman, K, *Beyond Betrayal*, Penguin, 2013.

O'Malley, V, *Beyond the Imperial Frontier*, Bridget Williams Books, 2014.

O'Malley, V, *The Great War for New Zealand*, Bridget Williams Books, 2016.

Orange, C, *The Treaty of Waitangi*, Allen & Unwin, 1987.

Platts, U, *The Lively Capital*, Avon Fine Prints, 1971.

Porter, F (ed), *The Turanga Journals*, Price Milburn/Victoria University Press, 1974.

Purchas, H T, *The English Church in New Zealand*, Simpson & Williams, 1914.

Reeves, B, *Looking for Mrs Cowie*, B Reeves, 2005.

Selwyn, G A, *Journals & Letters 1842-1844*, Cambridge University Press, 2010.

Simpson, A, *Hallelujahs & History*, Auckland Choral, 2005.

Soar, E, *Old Onehunga – History of St Peters*, Centenary Souvenir, Church Army Press, 1948.

Sorrenson, M P K, *Studies of a Small Democracy* (Maori King Movement).

Stokes, E, *Wiremu Tamihana*, Huia Publishers, 2002.

Stone, R C J, *Makers of Fortune*, Auckland University Press, 1973.

Stone, R C J, *Young Logan Campbell*, Auckland University Press, 1982.

Stone R C J, *From Tamaki-Makau-Rau to Auckland*, Auckland University Press, 2001.

Sweetman, R, *Spire on the Hill*, St Andrew's, 1996.

Tonson, A E, *Old Manukau*, Tonson Publishing, 1966.

Travers, W T L, *The Stirring Times of Te Rauparaha*, 1872.

Vaggioli, D F, *History of New Zealand and its Inhabitants*, University of Otago Press, 2000.

Williams, D, *A Simple Nullity*, Auckland University Press, 2011.

Williams, F, *Through 90 Years – Life & Work Among the Maori*, Whitcombe & Tombs, 1940.

Wright, F A, *A Kindly Christian Gentleman*, Polygraphia, 2007.

Wright, M, *Two Peoples, One Land*, Reed, Auckland, 2006.

Other reference sources

Alexander Turnbull Library, Tiaki, Unpublished Collections, MS 4280, 3273, 3494, 3437, 4907, 5713, 11116, 5013, A G Purchas, MS273.

Auckland Anglican Archives, *Purchas Papers*; *G A Selwyn Journal, Part V, No XX*.

Auckland Library, George Grey Collection, Letters, Pictorial and Manuscripts, MS1415, 2043, 742.

Auckland Museum Library, Fairburn papers, MS1142, Nihill papers, MS132, G A Selwyn papers 1809-1878, MS283, MS1711/2, 88, 75, MS251, MS547/1.

Beattie, I D (ed), *Ever ready, the life of Arthur Guyon Purchas*, 1993.

Bradford, K, Cone But Not Forgotten, *Eastern Courier*, 2004.

Brett, H, *White Wings*, NZETC.

Brookfield, M, MB, ChB, FRACP, *Life of AGP*, 1991.

Cardy, G, *Life of A G P*, Purchas family papers.

Christ's College Archive, Lisa Trundley.

Clark, M, Early days in Huntly and the discovery of coal, *Auckland-Waikato Historical Journal*, 25, 1974.

Clark, W E, Background to Huntly, 1970, *Auckland-Waikato Historical Journal*, Sept 1988.

Cocks, L, *Gundry Family History and Deeds*.

Cotter Medical History Trust, *Medical Practitioners of New Zealand*, 2013.

Davis, J K, *New Zealand Illustrated Magazine, Vol VI*, 1902

Drummond, A, The Year of the Plague, *NZ Family Dr*, Dec 1967.

Dunedin Public Library, Heritage Collection Catalogue – *Guts, God and Gold, Dunedin in the 1860s*, 2011.

ENZB, www.enzb.auckland.ac.nz

Ernest & Marion Davis Library.

Hoare, M, The relationship between government and science in Australia and New Zealand, *Journal of the Royal Society of New Zealand*, 6:3, 1976.

John Kinder Theological Library, Judith Bright and staff.

Kear, D, Drury Coalfield, Auckland, *New Zealand Journal of Geology and Geophysics*, 2:5, 1959, pp 846-869.

Lowe, G J, The Remarkable Rev. Dr. Arthur Guyon Purchas, *New Zealand Memories, Issue 84*, June-July 2010.

Ernest & Marion Davis Memorial Library, *New Zealand Medical Journal*, 1954, 1970.

Masters, D, *Madmen, Militia and Missionaries, Auckland-Waikato Historical Journal*, Sept 1995.

Muir, B, Early Waiuku, *Auckland-Waikato Historical Journal*, 53, Sept 1988.

National Library of New Zealand, Papers Past, *Te Ara – The Encyclopedia of New Zealand*, www.teara.govt.nz

Ohinemuri Regional History, www.ohinemuri.org.nz

O'Malley, V, Choosing Peace or War, *New Zealand Journal of History*, Vol 47, No 1, 2013.

Paxton, C, *Church on the Corner*, 2016.

Powell, A, *Centennial History of the Auckland Institute and Museum*, 1967.

Ringer, B, Auckland Libraries – *Manukau Journey*.

Roche, E, presentations to the New Zealand Medical Association, *New Zealand Medical Journal*, Vol LIII, No 295, June 1954, pp 203-209.

Stenhouse, J, The 'battle' between science and religion over evolution in nineteenth century New Zealand,

www.mro.massey.ac.nz, Massey University, 1985.

Stumbles, J, Dr Purchas – What a Life, 1973.

Suter, H, *Manual of NZ Molluscs*, Wellington, 2013

Tawhiao – *King or Prophet, Turongo House, 2000*

Waterson, D, The Matamata Estate, *New Zealand Journal of History, Vol 3, No 1,* 1969.

Wilson, D, Community and Gender in Victorian Auckland, *New Zealand Journal of History, Vol 30, No 1,* 1996.

Wright-St Clair, R, *Historia Nunc Vivat,* Cotter Medical History Trust.

Interviews, family papers, websites

Auckland Medical History Society: Dr Pat Clarkson, Maria Collins, Dr Neil Anderson, Prof Bruce Hadden, Juliet Hawkins.

Averill, Archbishop, *Private Letters.*

Dr Derek Dow, University of Auckland, medical historian.

Edward Bennett, Karangahape Rd historian.

ENZB, *Memoir of Life & Episcopate of G A Selwyn.*

Google Books, Ballara, A, *Te Kingitanga,* p 62.

Gundry family members: Linda Cocks, Jeanette Grant.

John McAlpine, St Peter's Archivist.

John Stevenson, Auckland Choral Society.

New Zealand Anglican Church Gazette, 1906, *Sarah Jackson Letter,* p 138.

NZETC, *Maori Wars of the 19th century, The Old Frontier,* J Cowan; Cyclopaedia of NZ.

Onehunga Fencible & Historical Society, Cyril Skilton, Colin Freland.

Priscilla Williams, Williams Trust.

Professor Pat Alley, MBChB, FRCS.

Purchas family interviews: Russell Williams, Alison Kissling.

Purchas family, *Letters, Notes, Photographs,* Tina Frantzen, John McMillan, Judith Dexter, Rose Purchas, Juliet McKinstry, Melville Brookfield (dcd).

Rev Daniel Dries, Rector, Christ Church St Laurence, Sydney.

Rev Dr Noel Derbyshire.

Roche family: E H Roche (dcd), Sue Roche, John and Ann Roche, David Roche.

Ross Lawrenson, *Medical practice in New Zealand 1769-1860,* Vesalius, 2004.

St Arvans Council, Wales, Jonathan Richards.

Shona Caughey, Angela Caughey.

Von Hochstetter, F, *Nine Months in New Zealand,* 1867, ENZB.

Index